BARAKAMON

8

SATSUKI
YOSHINO

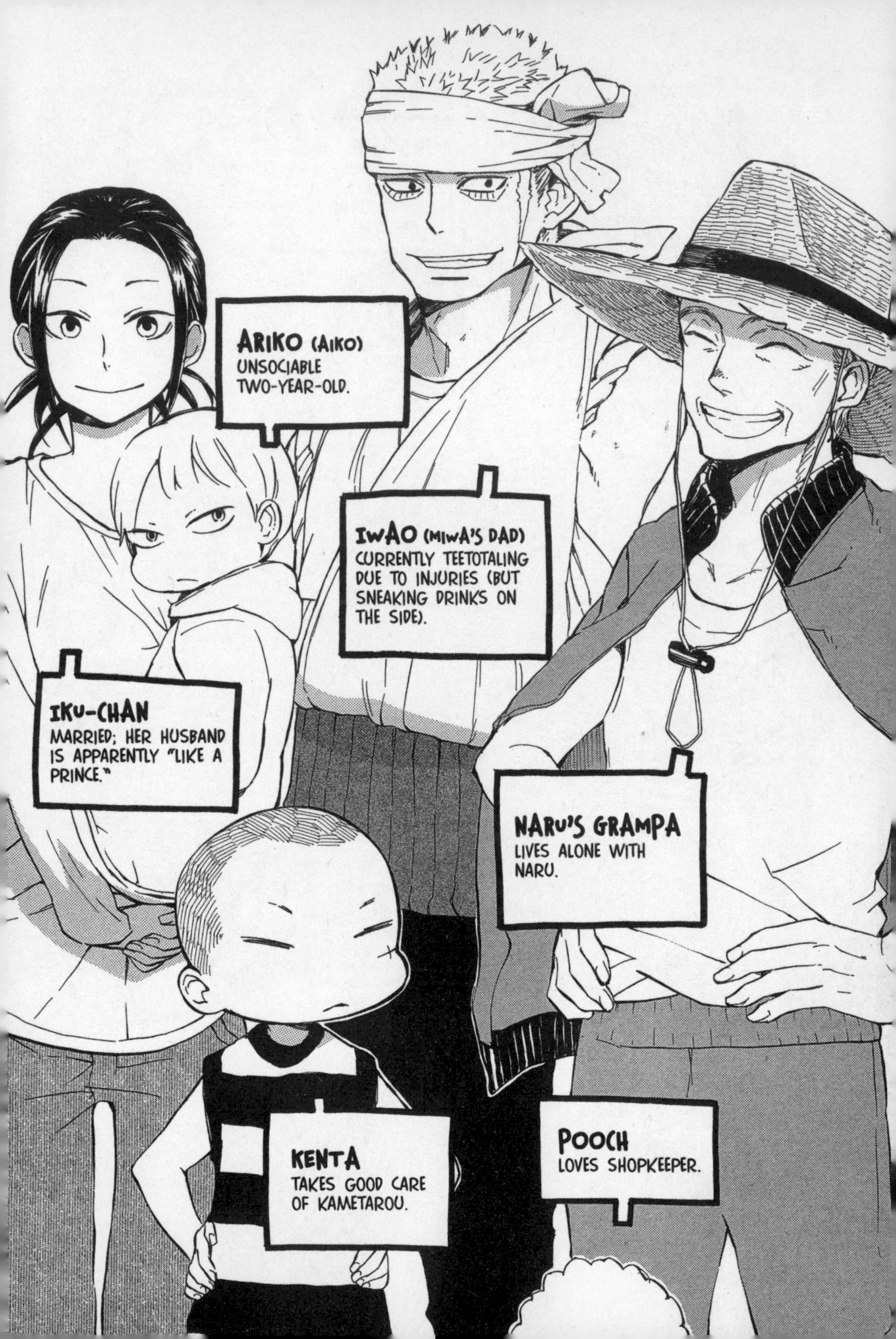
ARIKO (AIKO)
UNSOCIABLE TWO-YEAR-OLD.
IWAO (MIWA'S DAD)
CURRENTLY TEETOTALING DUE TO INJURIES (BUT SNEAKING DRINKS ON THE SIDE).
IKU-CHAN
MARRIED; HER HUSBAND IS APPARENTLY "LIKE A PRINCE."
NARU'S GRAMPA
LIVES ALONE WITH NARU.
POOCH
LOVES SHOPKEEPER.
KENTA
TAKES GOOD CARE OF KAMETAROU.

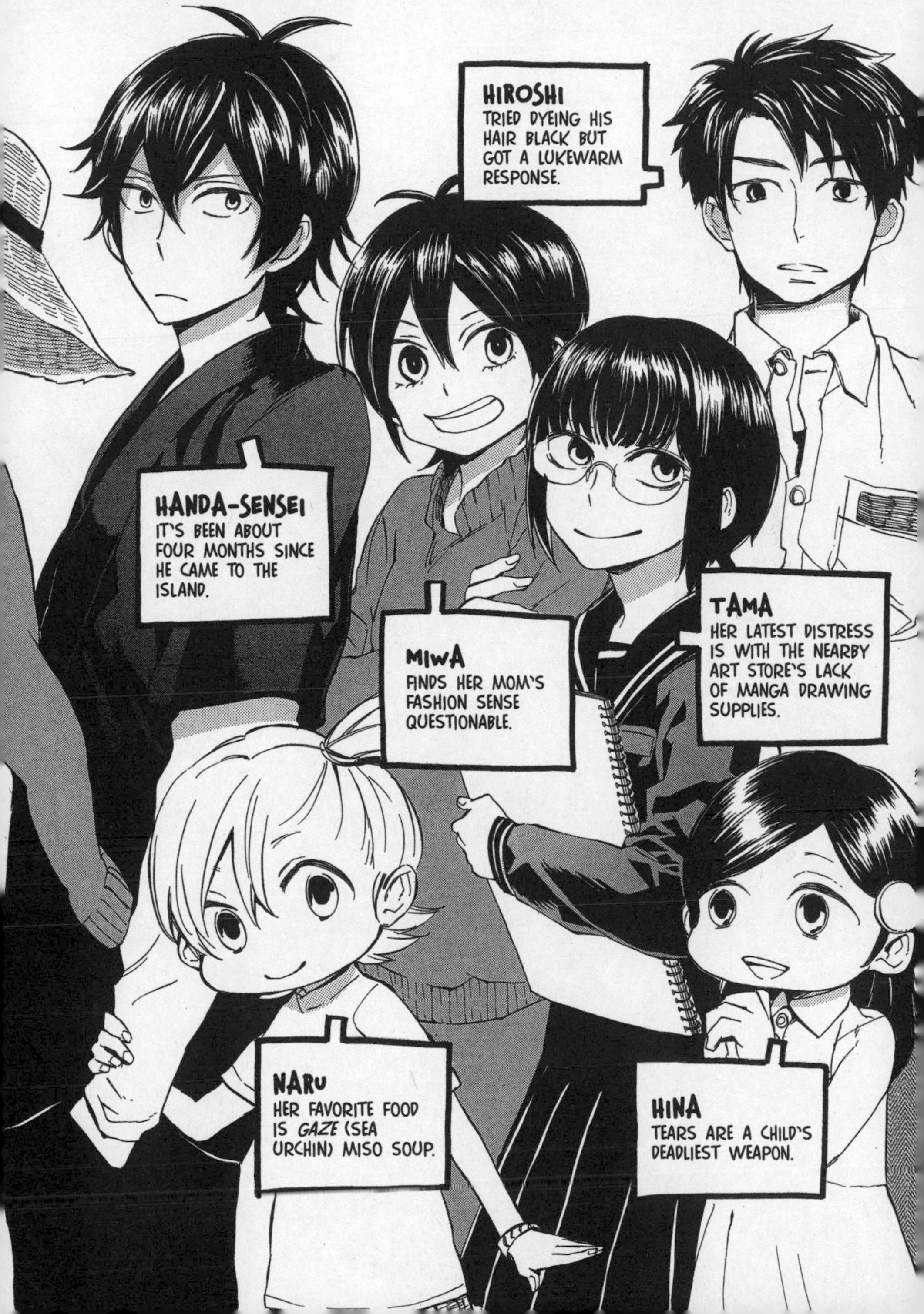
HIROSHI
TRIED DYEING HIS HAIR BLACK BUT GOT A LUKEWARM RESPONSE.
TAMA
HER LATEST DISTRESS IS WITH THE NEARBY ART STORE'S LACK OF MANGA DRAWING SUPPLIES.
MIWA
FINDS HER MOM'S FASHION SENSE QUESTIONABLE.
HANDA-SENSEI
IT'S BEEN ABOUT FOUR MONTHS SINCE HE CAME TO THE ISLAND.
HINA
TEARS ARE A CHILD'S DEADLIEST WEAPON.
NARU
HER FAVORITE FOOD IS *GAZE* (SEA URCHIN) MISO SOUP.

Contents

ACT.61

AMAKAMON BA KOJJAYU

(Translation: Make Sweets)

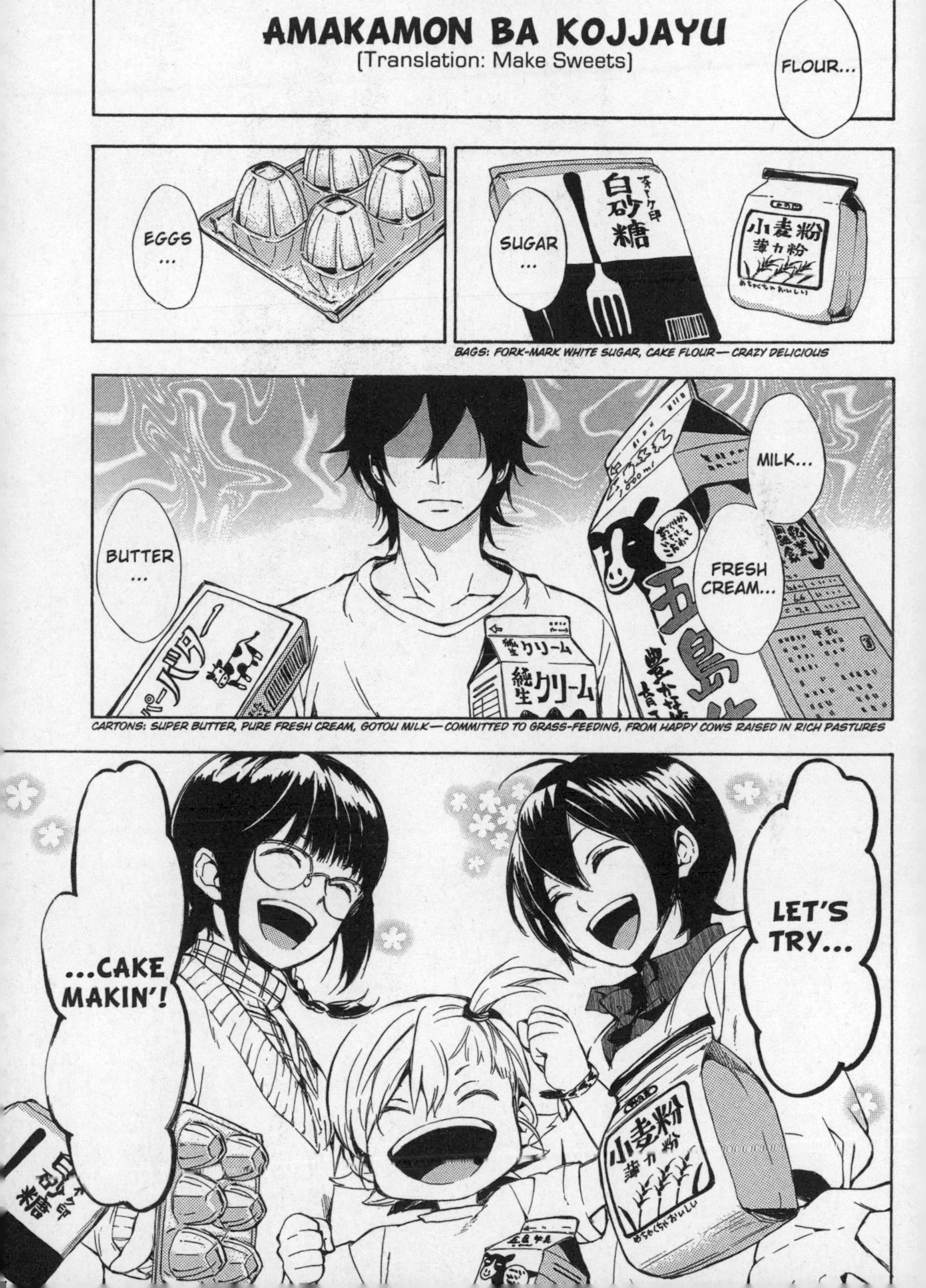
FLOUR...
SUGAR ...
EGGS ...
BAGS: FORK-MARK WHITE SUGAR, CAKE FLOUR—CRAZY DELICIOUS
MILK...
FRESH CREAM...
BUTTER ...
CARTONS: SUPER BUTTER, PURE FRESH CREAM, GOTOU MILK—COMMITTED TO GRASS-FEEDING, FROM HAPPY COWS RAISED IN RICH PASTURES
LET'S TRY...
...CAKE MAKIN'!

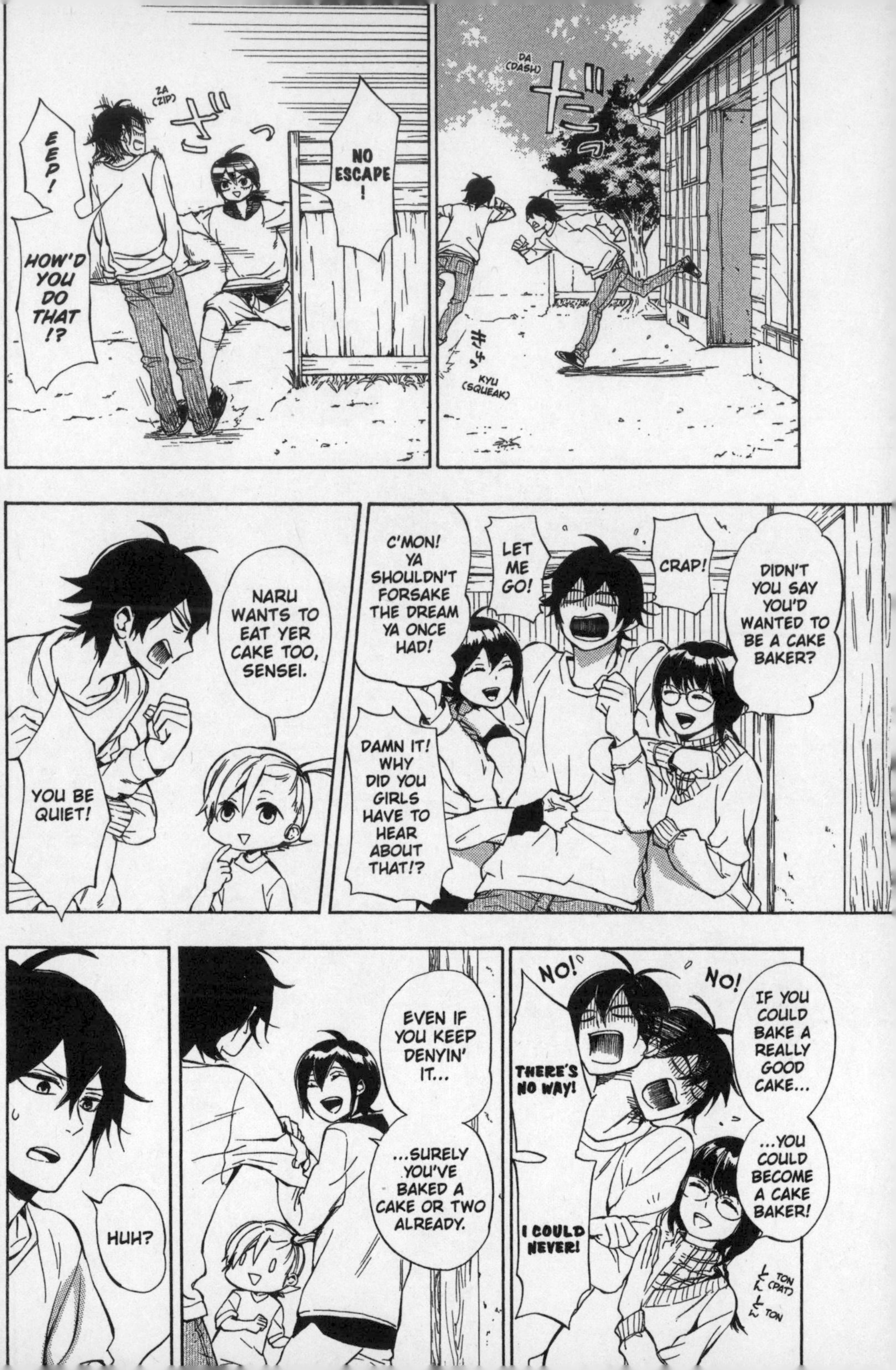
DA (DASH)
KYU (SQUEAK)
ZA (ZIP)
NO ESCAPE!
EEP!
HOW'D YOU DO THAT!?
DIDN'T YOU SAY YOU'D WANTED TO BE A CAKE BAKER?
CRAP!
LET ME GO!
C'MON! YA SHOULDN'T FORSAKE THE DREAM YA ONCE HAD!
DAMN IT! WHY DID YOU GIRLS HAVE TO HEAR ABOUT THAT!?
NARU WANTS TO EAT YER CAKE TOO, SENSEI.
YOU BE QUIET!
NO!
NO!
IF YOU COULD BAKE A REALLY GOOD CAKE...
...YOU COULD BECOME A CAKE BAKER!
THERE'S NO WAY!
I COULD NEVER!
TON (PAT)
TON
EVEN IF YOU KEEP DENYIN' IT...
...SURELY YOU'VE BAKED A CAKE OR TWO ALREADY.
HUH?

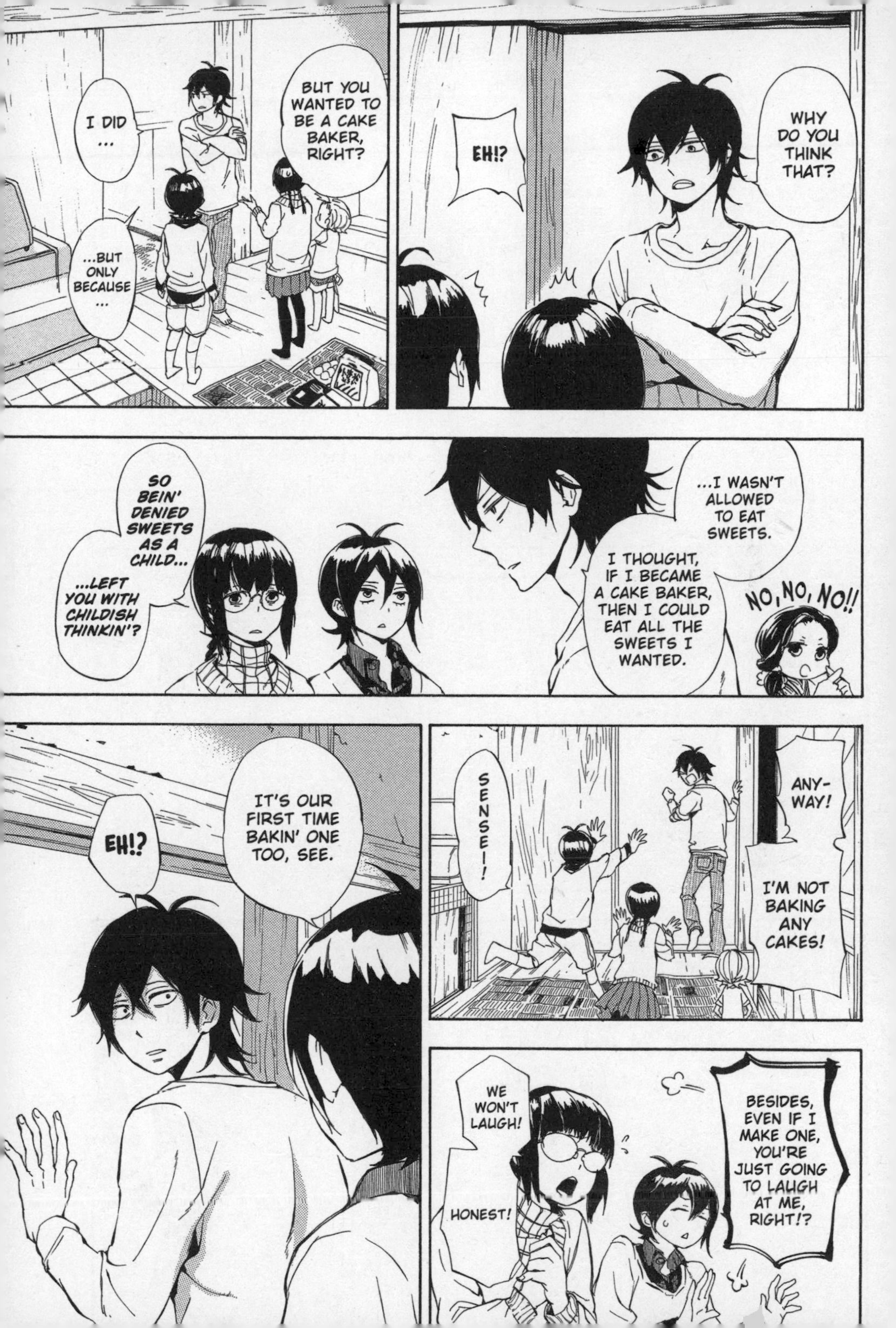
WHY DO YOU THINK THAT?
EH!?
BUT YOU WANTED TO BE A CAKE BAKER, RIGHT?
I DID ...
...BUT ONLY BECAUSE ...
...I WASN'T ALLOWED TO EAT SWEETS.
I THOUGHT, IF I BECAME A CAKE BAKER, THEN I COULD EAT ALL THE SWEETS I WANTED.
NO, NO, NO!!
SO BEIN' DENIED SWEETS AS A CHILD...
...LEFT YOU WITH CHILDISH THINKIN'?
ANY-WAY!
I'M NOT BAKING ANY CAKES!
SENSE-!
BESIDES, EVEN IF I MAKE ONE, YOU'RE JUST GOING TO LAUGH AT ME, RIGHT!?
WE WON'T LAUGH!
HONEST!
IT'S OUR FIRST TIME BAKIN' ONE TOO, SEE.
EH!?

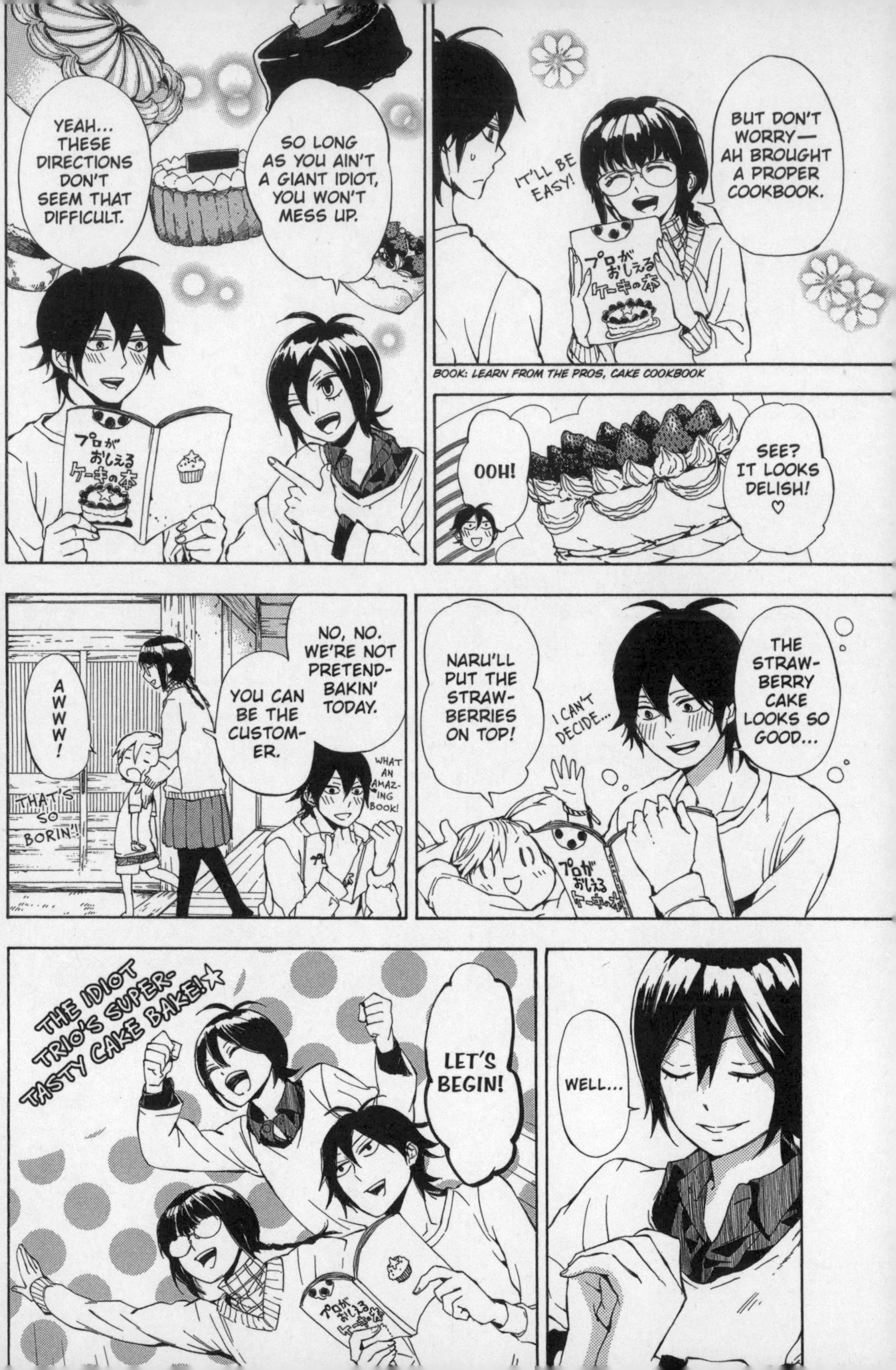
BUT DON'T WORRY—AH BROUGHT A PROPER COOKBOOK.
IT'LL BE EASY!
プロがおしえるケーキの本
BOOK: LEARN FROM THE PROS, CAKE COOKBOOK
SEE? IT LOOKS DELISH! ♡
OOH!
SO LONG AS YOU AIN'T A GIANT IDIOT, YOU WON'T MESS UP.
YEAH... THESE DIRECTIONS DON'T SEEM THAT DIFFICULT.
THE STRAW-BERRY CAKE LOOKS SO GOOD...
I CAN'T DECIDE...
NARU'LL PUT THE STRAW-BERRIES ON TOP!
NO, NO. WE'RE NOT PRETEND-BAKIN' TODAY.
YOU CAN BE THE CUSTOM-ER.
WHAT AN AMAZ-ING BOOK!
AWWW!
THAT'S SO BORIN'!
WELL...
LET'S BEGIN!
THE IDIOT TRIO'S SUPER-TASTY CAKE BAKE!☆

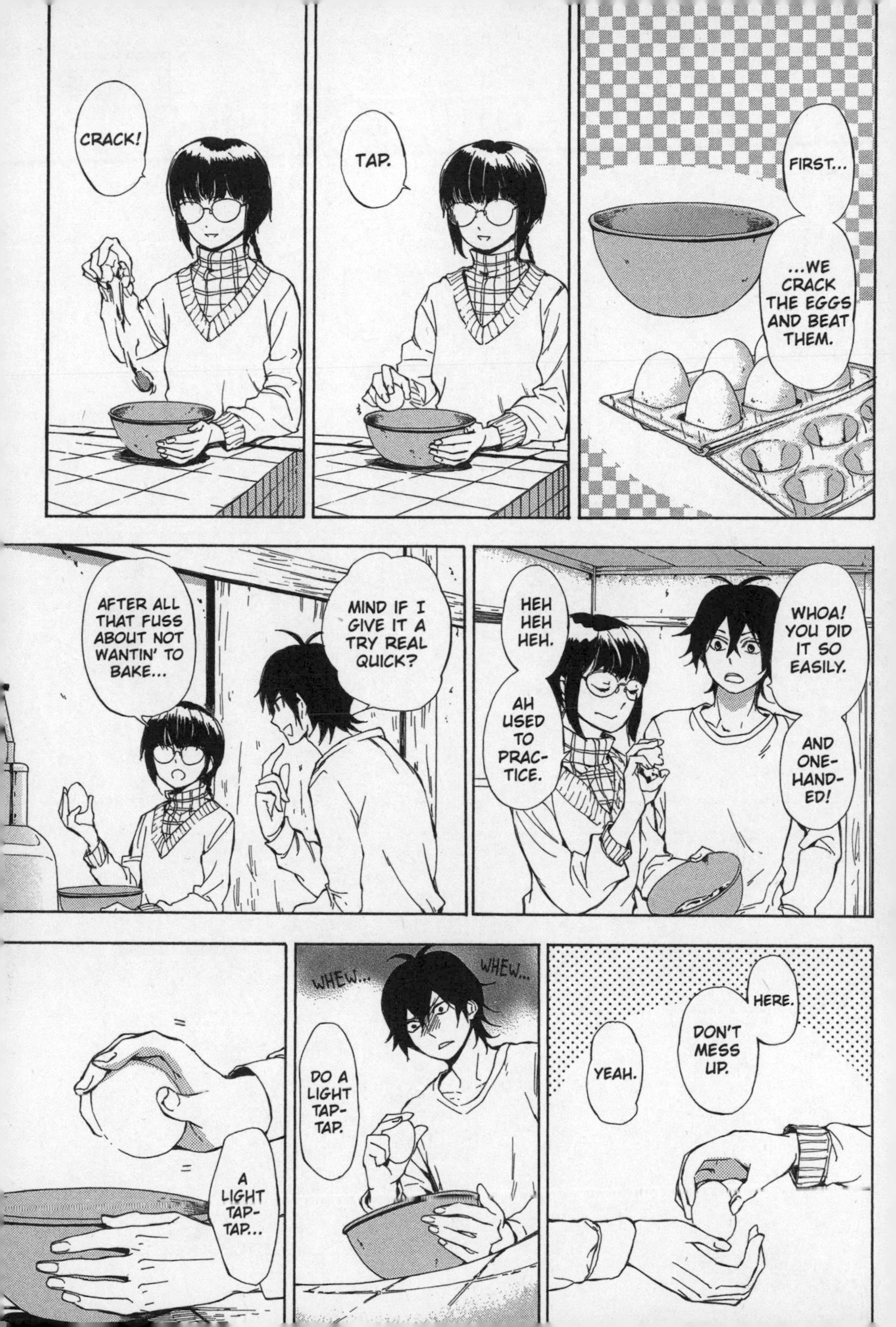
FIRST...
...WE CRACK THE EGGS AND BEAT THEM.
TAP.
CRACK!
WHOA! YOU DID IT SO EASILY.
AND ONE-HANDED!
HEH HEH HEH.
AH USED TO PRAC-TICE.
MIND IF I GIVE IT A TRY REAL QUICK?
AFTER ALL THAT FUSS ABOUT NOT WANTIN' TO BAKE...
HERE.
DON'T MESS UP.
YEAH.
WHEW...
WHEW...
DO A LIGHT TAP-TAP.
A LIGHT TAP-TAP...

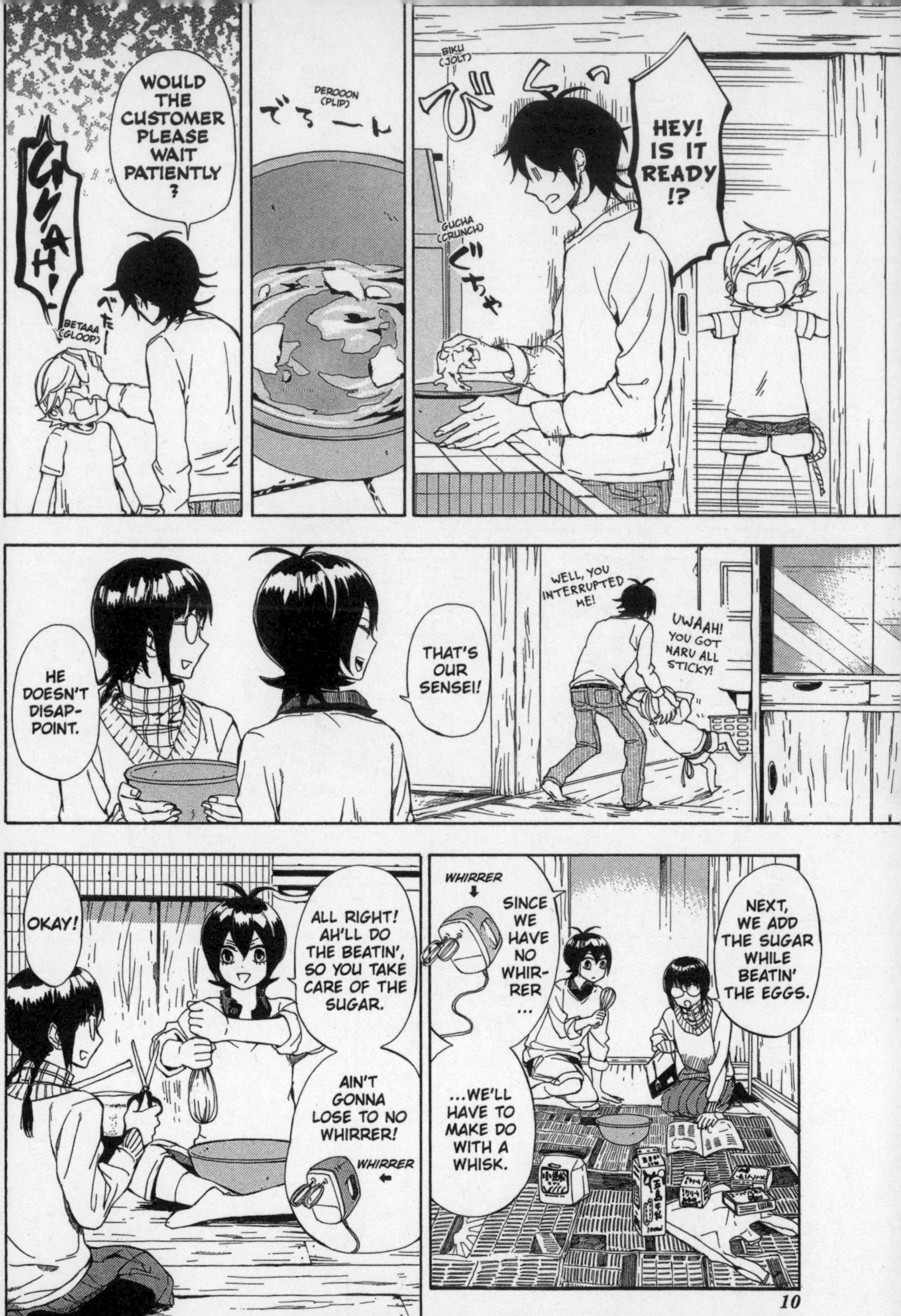
BIKU (JOLT)
びくっ
HEY! IS IT READY!?
GUCHA (CRUNCH)
ぐちゃ
DEROOON (PLIP)
でろーん
WOULD THE CUSTOMER PLEASE WAIT PATIENTLY?
UGYAH!
BETAAA (GLOOP)
べたー
UWAAH! YOU GOT NARU ALL STICKY!
WELL, YOU INTERRUPTED ME!
THAT'S OUR SENSEI!
HE DOESN'T DISAP-POINT.
NEXT, WE ADD THE SUGAR WHILE BEATIN' THE EGGS.
SINCE WE HAVE NO WHIR-RER...
...WE'LL HAVE TO MAKE DO WITH A WHISK.
WHIRRER
ALL RIGHT! AH'LL DO THE BEATIN', SO YOU TAKE CARE OF THE SUGAR.
OKAY!
AIN'T GONNA LOSE TO NO WHIRRER!
WHIRRER

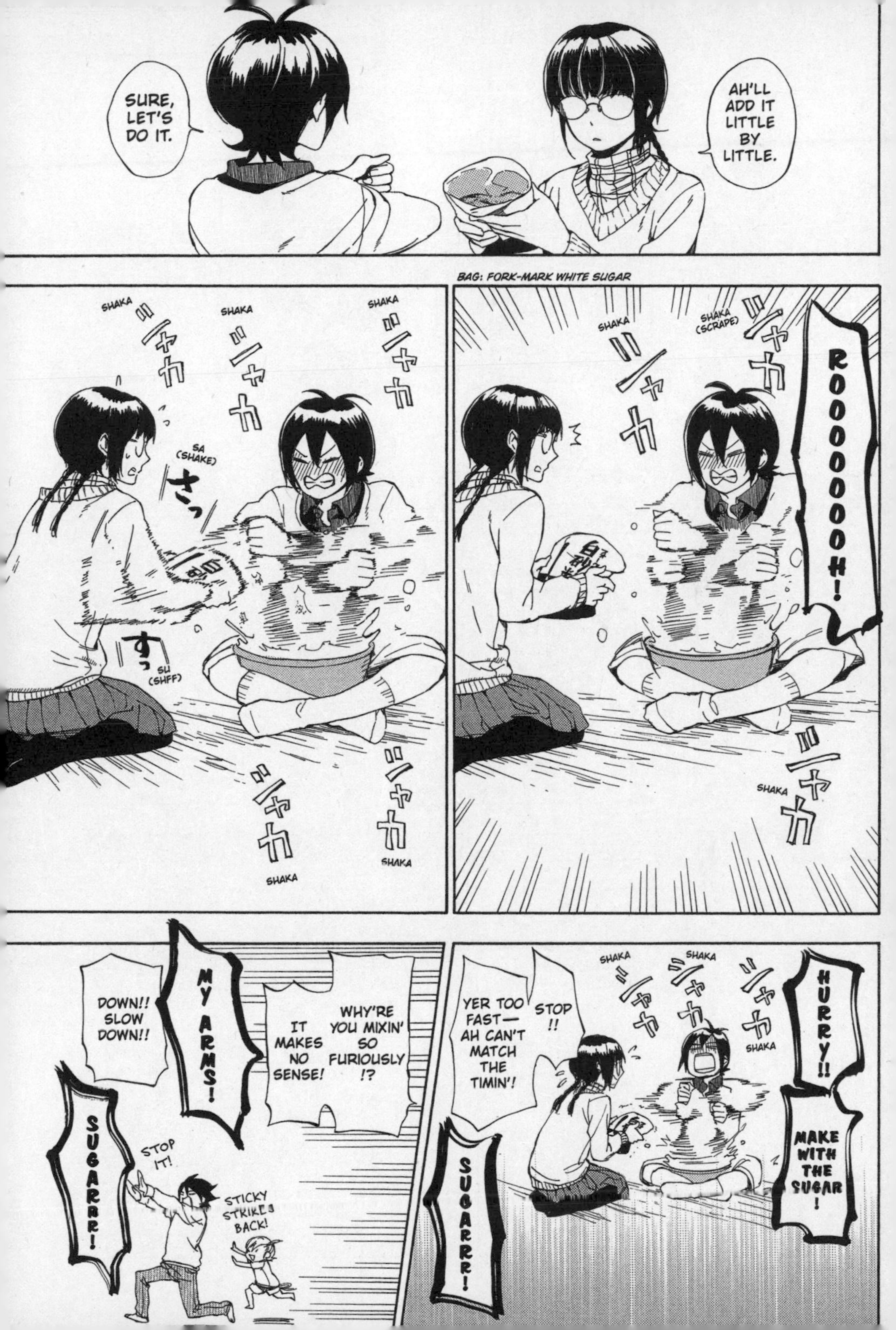
AH'LL ADD IT LITTLE BY LITTLE.
SURE, LET'S DO IT.
BAG: FORK-MARK WHITE SUGAR
ROOOOOOOOH!
シャカ
SHAKA (SCRAPE)
シャカ
SHAKA
シャカ
SHAKA
シャカ
SHAKA
シャカ
SHAKA
シャカ
SHAKA
さっ
SA (SHAKE)
すっ
SU (SHFF)
シャカ
SHAKA
シャカ
SHAKA
HURRY!!
MAKE WITH THE SUGAR!
シャカ
SHAKA
シャカ
SHAKA
シャカ
SHAKA
STOP!!
YER TOO FAST— AH CAN'T MATCH THE TIMIN'!
SUGARRR!
WHY'RE YOU MIXIN' SO FURIOUSLY!?
IT MAKES NO SENSE!
MY ARMS!
DOWN!! SLOW DOWN!!
SUGARRR!
STOP IT!
STICKY STRIKES BACK!

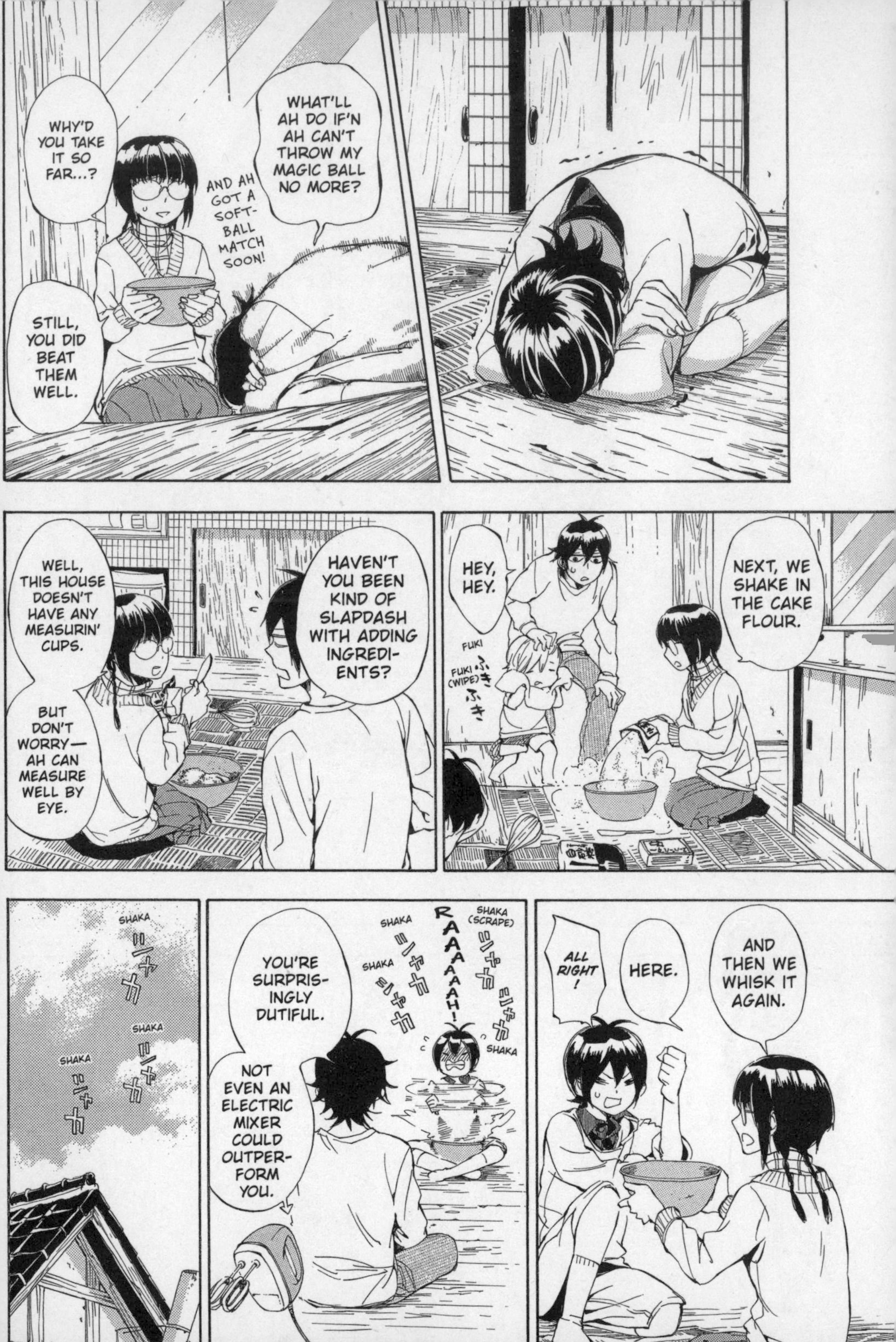
WHAT'LL AH DO IF'N AH CAN'T THROW MY MAGIC BALL NO MORE?
AND AH GOT A SOFT-BALL MATCH SOON!
WHY'D YOU TAKE IT SO FAR...?
STILL, YOU DID BEAT THEM WELL.
NEXT, WE SHAKE IN THE CAKE FLOUR.
HEY, HEY.
FUKI ふき
FUKI (WIPE) ふき
HAVEN'T YOU BEEN KIND OF SLAPDASH WITH ADDING INGREDI-ENTS?
WELL, THIS HOUSE DOESN'T HAVE ANY MEASURIN' CUPS.
BUT DON'T WORRY—AH CAN MEASURE WELL BY EYE.
AND THEN WE WHISK IT AGAIN.
HERE.
ALL RIGHT!
SHAKA (SCRAPE) シャカ
SHAKA シャカ
RAAAAAAAH!
SHAKA シャカ
SHAKA シャカ
YOU'RE SURPRIS-INGLY DUTIFUL.
NOT EVEN AN ELECTRIC MIXER COULD OUTPER-FORM YOU.
SHAKA シャカ
SHAKA シャカ
SHAKA シャカ

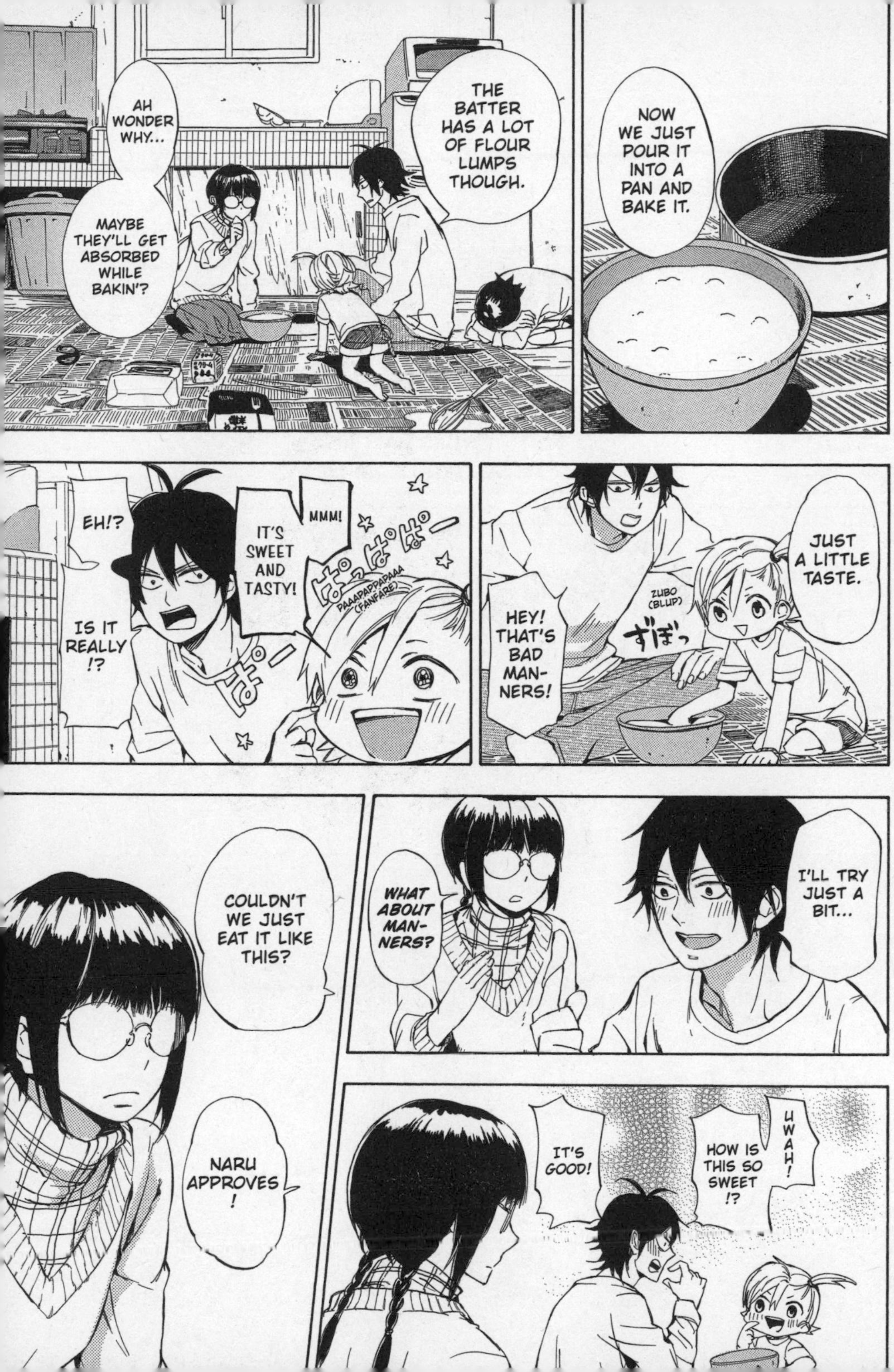
NOW WE JUST POUR IT INTO A PAN AND BAKE IT.
THE BATTER HAS A LOT OF FLOUR LUMPS THOUGH.
AH WONDER WHY...
MAYBE THEY'LL GET ABSORBED WHILE BAKIN'?
JUST A LITTLE TASTE.
ずぼっ
ZUBO (BLUP)
HEY! THAT'S BAD MANNERS!
MMM!
IT'S SWEET AND TASTY!
ぱっぱぱー
PAAAPAPPAPAAA (FANFARE)
EH!?
IS IT REALLY!?
ぱー
I'LL TRY JUST A BIT...
WHAT ABOUT MANNERS?
UWAH!
HOW IS THIS SO SWEET!?
IT'S GOOD!
COULDN'T WE JUST EAT IT LIKE THIS?
NARU APPROVES!

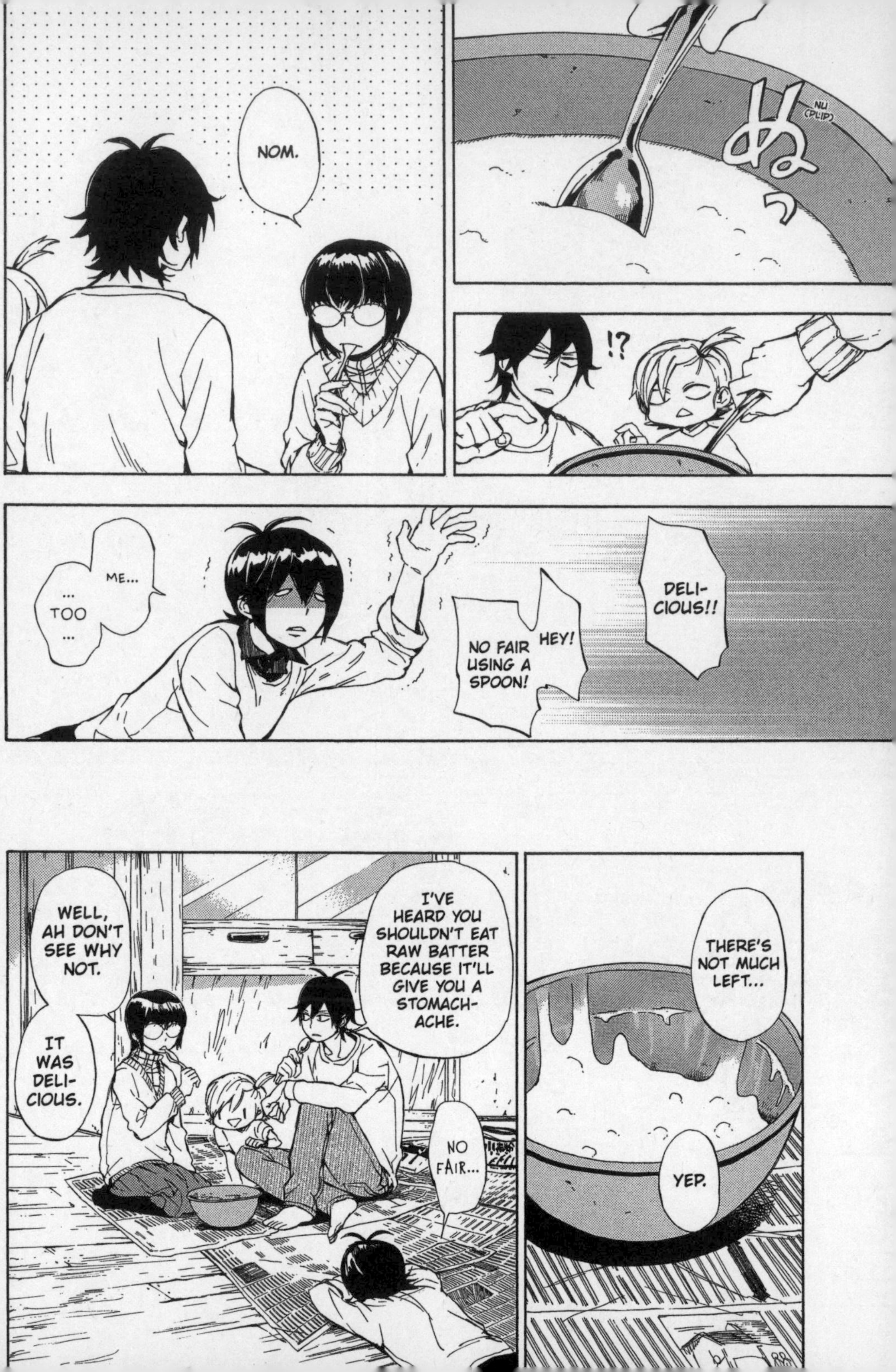
ぬっ
NU (PLIP)
!?
NOM.
DELI-CIOUS!!
HEY!
NO FAIR USING A SPOON!
ME...
...TOO...
THERE'S NOT MUCH LEFT...
YEP.
I'VE HEARD YOU SHOULDN'T EAT RAW BATTER BECAUSE IT'LL GIVE YOU A STOMACH-ACHE.
WELL, AH DON'T SEE WHY NOT.
IT WAS DELI-CIOUS.
NO FAIR...

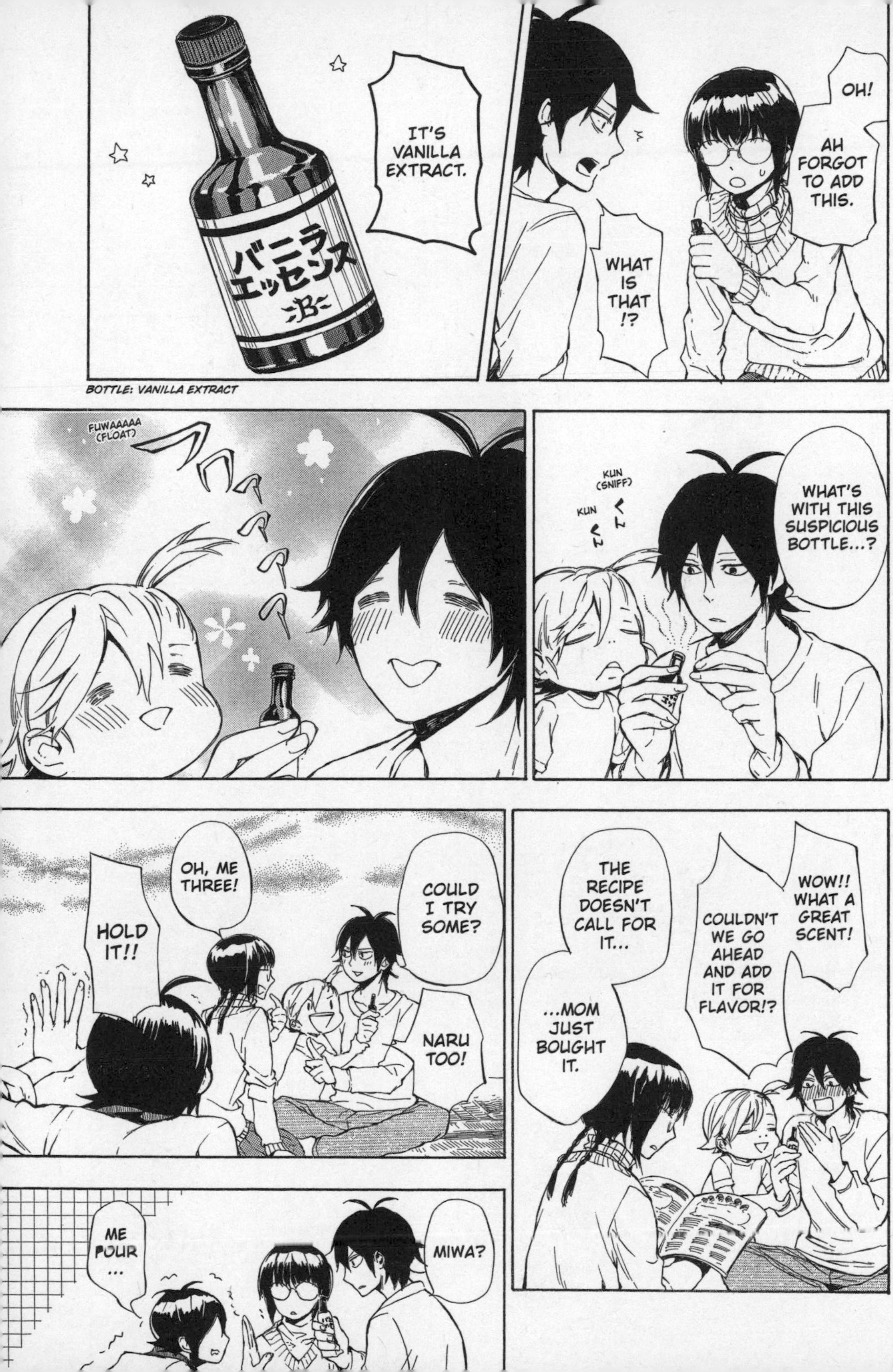
OH!
AH FORGOT TO ADD THIS.
WHAT IS THAT!?
IT'S VANILLA EXTRACT.
バニラエッセンス
BOTTLE: VANILLA EXTRACT
KUN KUN (SNIFF)
WHAT'S WITH THIS SUSPICIOUS BOTTLE...?
FUWAAAAA (FLOAT)
WOW!! WHAT A GREAT SCENT!
COULDN'T WE GO AHEAD AND ADD IT FOR FLAVOR!?
THE RECIPE DOESN'T CALL FOR IT...
...MOM JUST BOUGHT IT.
COULD I TRY SOME?
OH, ME THREE!
NARU TOO!
HOLD IT!!
MIWA?
ME FOUR ...

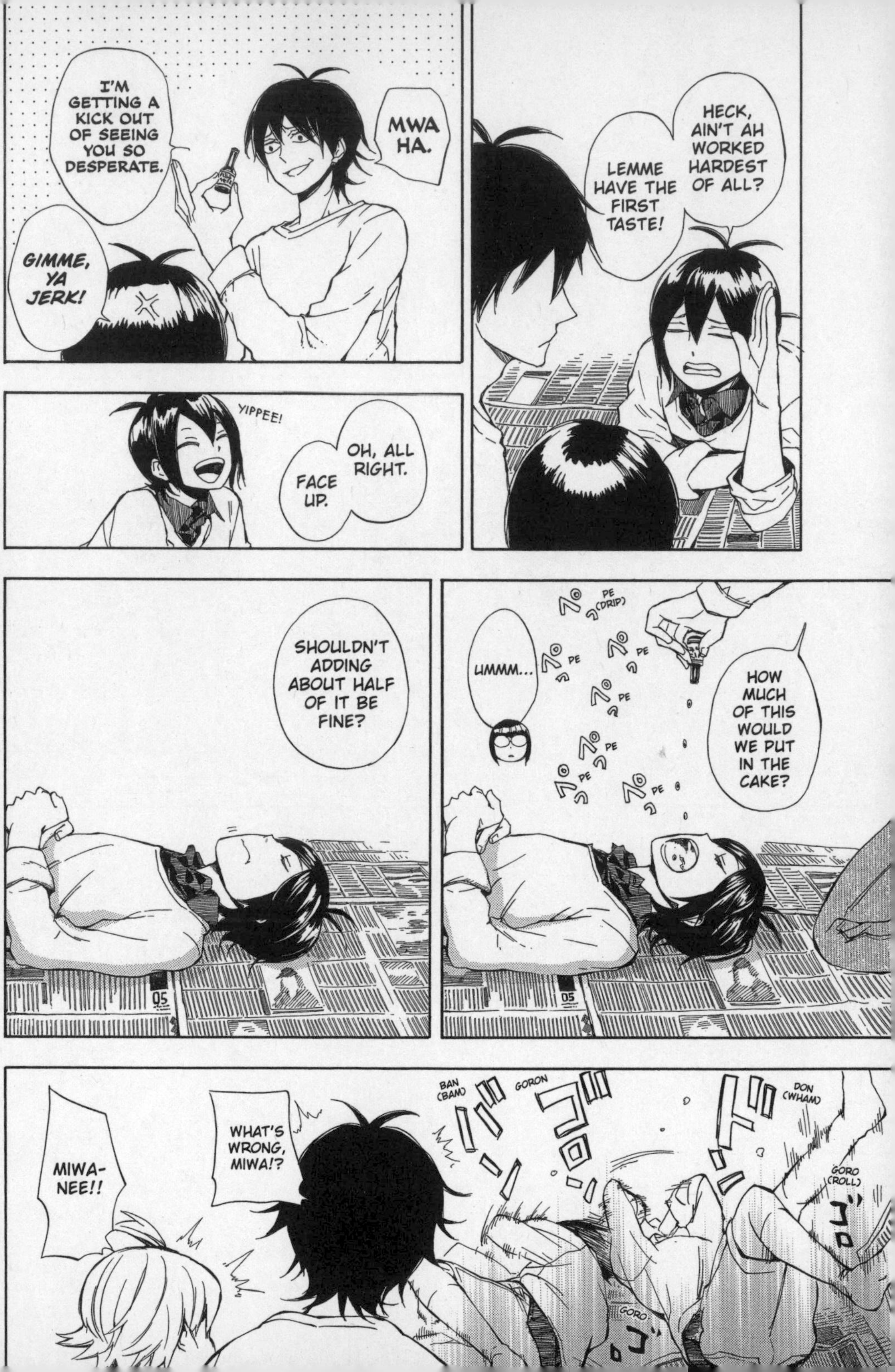

HECK, AIN'T AH WORKED HARDEST OF ALL?
LEMME HAVE THE FIRST TASTE!
MWA HA.
I'M GETTING A KICK OUT OF SEEING YOU SO DESPERATE.
GIMME, YA JERK!
OH, ALL RIGHT.
FACE UP.
YIPPEE!
PE (DRIP)
PE
PE
PE
PE
PE
PE
HOW MUCH OF THIS WOULD WE PUT IN THE CAKE?
UMMM...
SHOULDN'T ADDING ABOUT HALF OF IT BE FINE?
DON (WHAM)
GORO (ROLL)
GORON
BAN (BAM)
GORO
WHAT'S WRONG, MIWA!?
MIWA-NEE!!

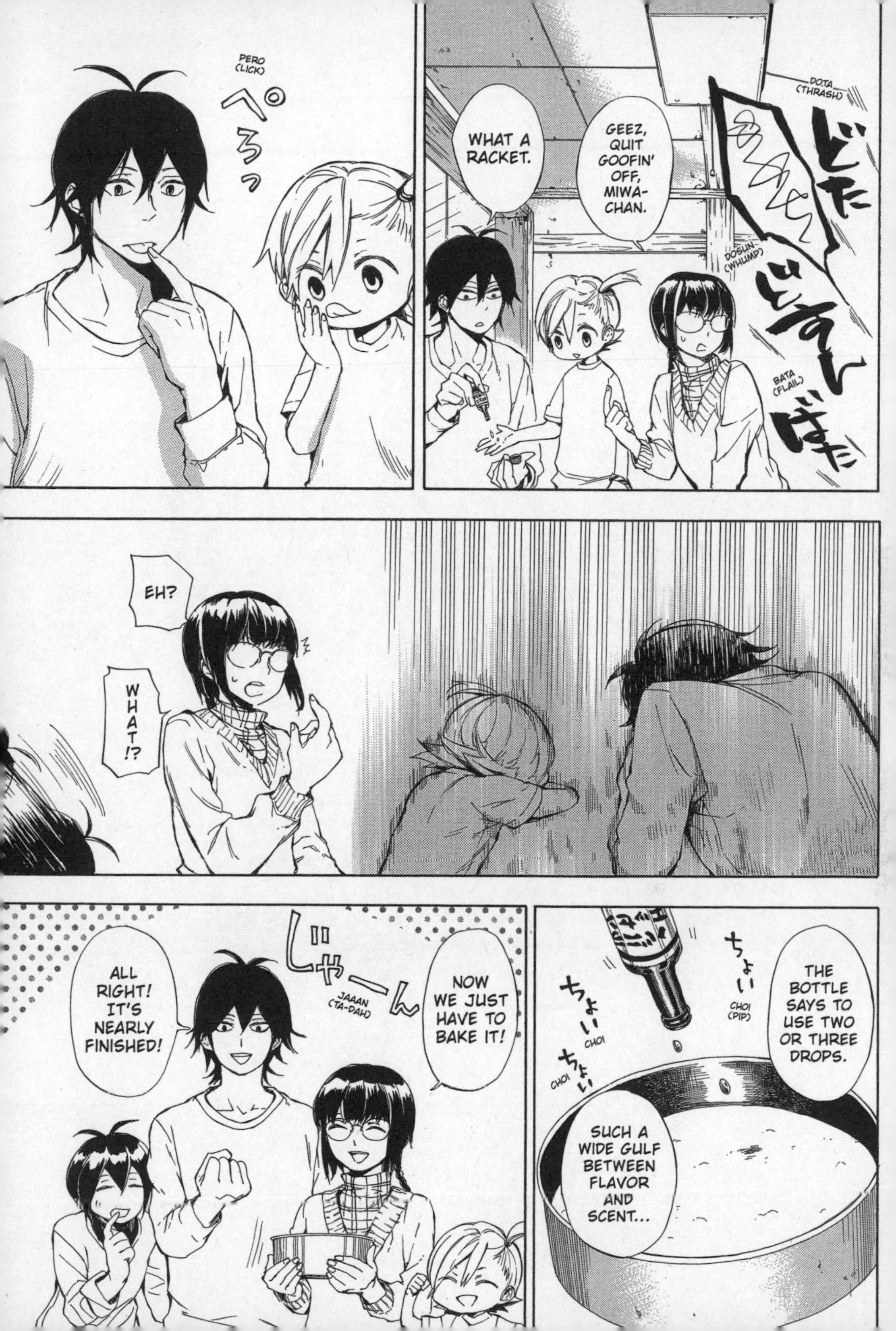
どた
DOTA (THRASH)
どすん
DOSUN (WHUMP)
ばた
BATA (FLAIL)
GEEZ, QUIT GOOFIN' OFF, MIWA-CHAN.
WHAT A RACKET.
ぺろっ
PERO (LICK)
EH?
WHAT!?
THE BOTTLE SAYS TO USE TWO OR THREE DROPS.
ちょい
CHOI (PIP)
ちょい
CHOI
ちょい
CHOI
SUCH A WIDE GULF BETWEEN FLAVOR AND SCENT...
NOW WE JUST HAVE TO BAKE IT!
じゃーん
JAAAN (TA-DAH)
ALL RIGHT! IT'S NEARLY FINISHED!

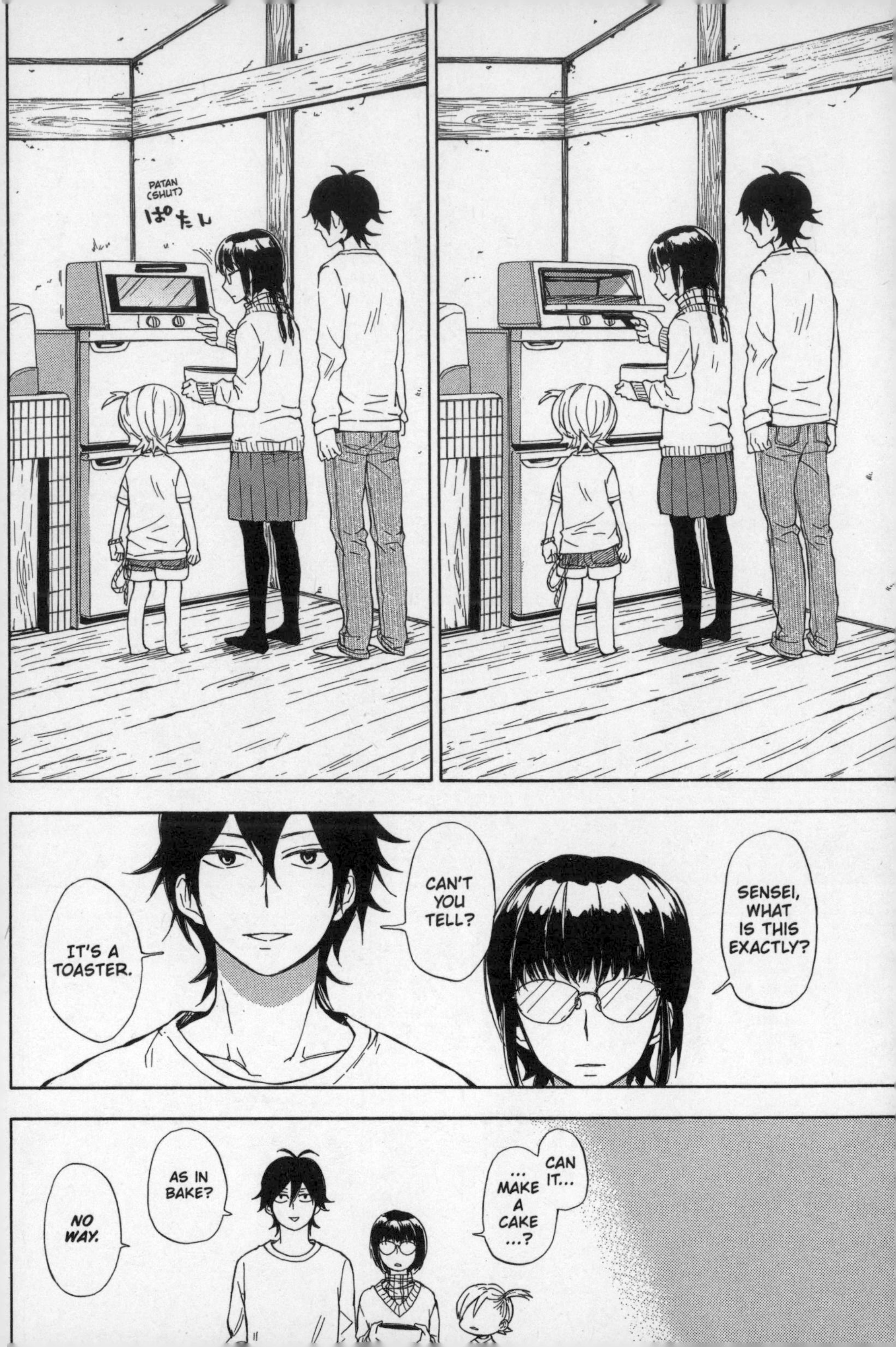
PATAN (SHUT)
ぱたん
SENSEI, WHAT IS THIS EXACTLY?
CAN'T YOU TELL?
IT'S A TOASTER.
CAN IT... ...MAKE A CAKE...?
AS IN BAKE?
NO WAY.

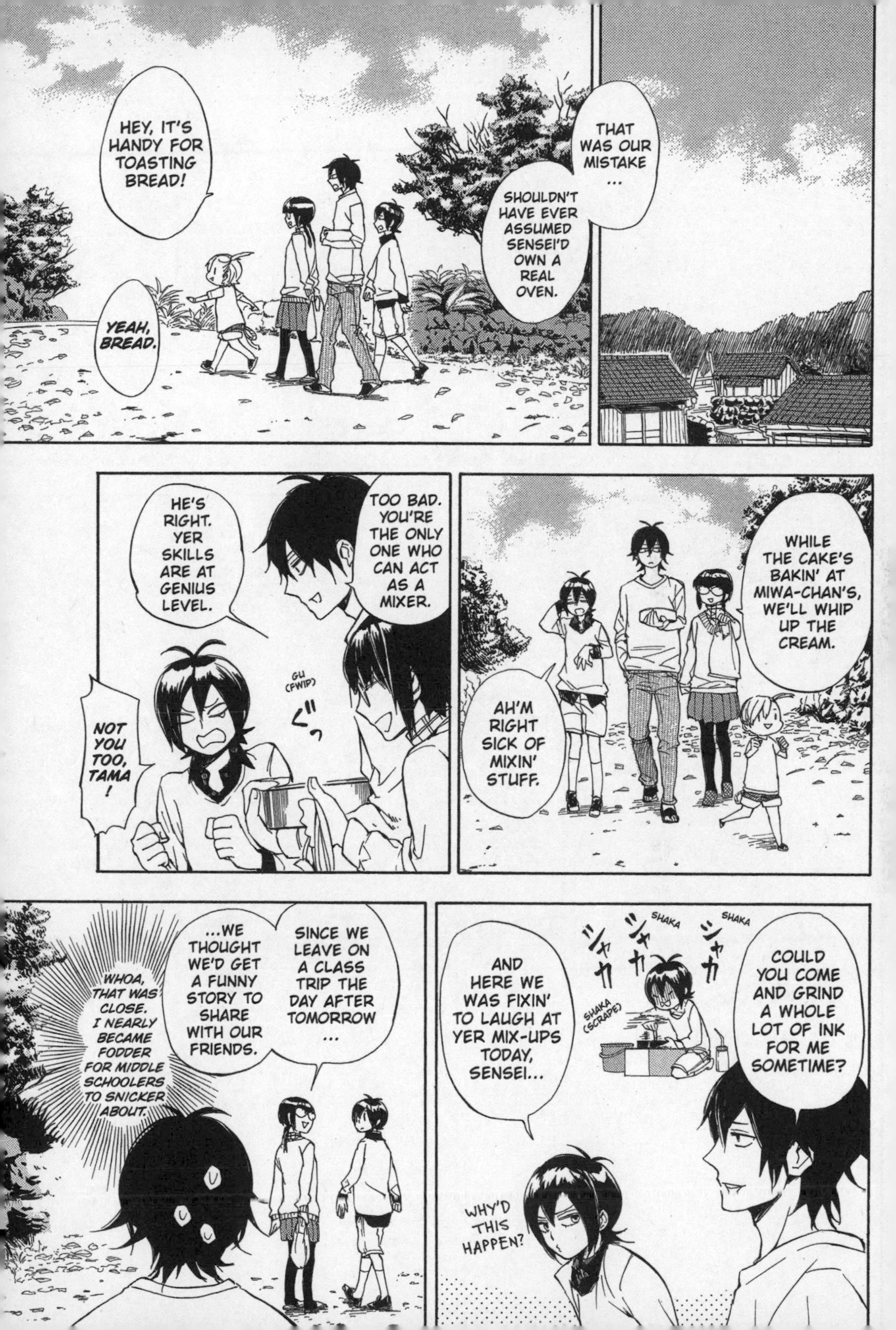
THAT WAS OUR MISTAKE ...
SHOULDN'T HAVE EVER ASSUMED SENSEI'D OWN A REAL OVEN.
HEY, IT'S HANDY FOR TOASTING BREAD!
YEAH, BREAD.
WHILE THE CAKE'S BAKIN' AT MIWA-CHAN'S, WE'LL WHIP UP THE CREAM.
AH'M RIGHT SICK OF MIXIN' STUFF.
TOO BAD. YOU'RE THE ONLY ONE WHO CAN ACT AS A MIXER.
HE'S RIGHT. YER SKILLS ARE AT GENIUS LEVEL.
GU (FWIP)
NOT YOU TOO, TAMA!
SHAKA
SHAKA
COULD YOU COME AND GRIND A WHOLE LOT OF INK FOR ME SOMETIME?
SHAKA (SCRAPE)
AND HERE WE WAS FIXIN' TO LAUGH AT YER MIX-UPS TODAY, SENSEI...
WHY'D THIS HAPPEN?
SINCE WE LEAVE ON A CLASS TRIP THE DAY AFTER TOMORROW ...
...WE THOUGHT WE'D GET A FUNNY STORY TO SHARE WITH OUR FRIENDS.
WHOA, THAT WAS CLOSE. I NEARLY BECAME FODDER FOR MIDDLE SCHOOLERS TO SNICKER ABOUT.

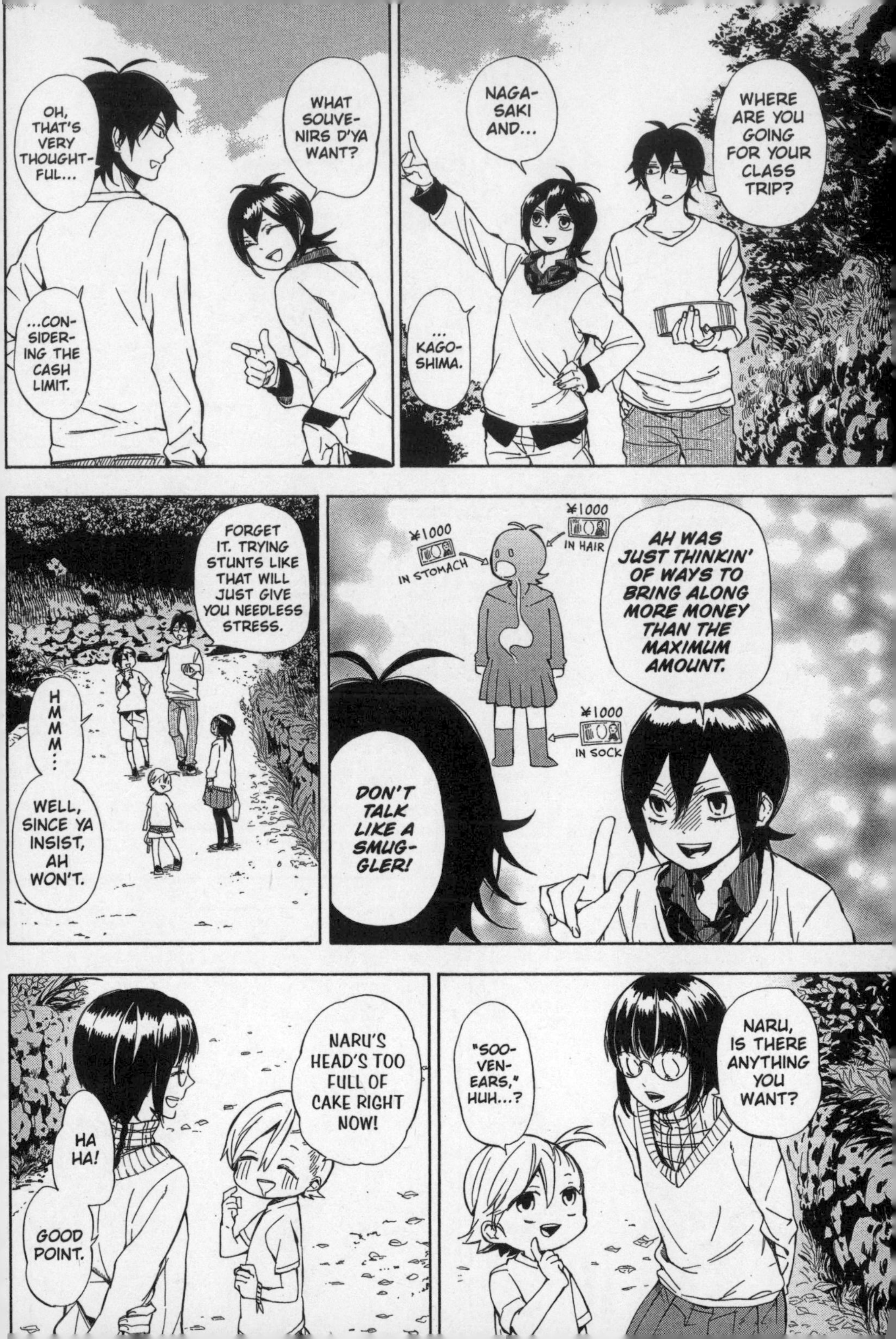
WHERE ARE YOU GOING FOR YOUR CLASS TRIP?
NAGASAKI AND...
...KAGOSHIMA.
WHAT SOUVENIRS D'YA WANT?
OH, THAT'S VERY THOUGHTFUL...
...CONSIDERING THE CASH LIMIT.
AH WAS JUST THINKIN' OF WAYS TO BRING ALONG MORE MONEY THAN THE MAXIMUM AMOUNT.
¥1000
IN HAIR
¥1000
IN STOMACH
¥1000
IN SOCK
DON'T TALK LIKE A SMUGGLER!
FORGET IT. TRYING STUNTS LIKE THAT WILL JUST GIVE YOU NEEDLESS STRESS.
HMMM...
WELL, SINCE YA INSIST, AH WON'T.
NARU, IS THERE ANYTHING YOU WANT?
"SOO-VEN-EARS," HUH...?
NARU'S HEAD'S TOO FULL OF CAKE RIGHT NOW!
HA HA!
GOOD POINT.

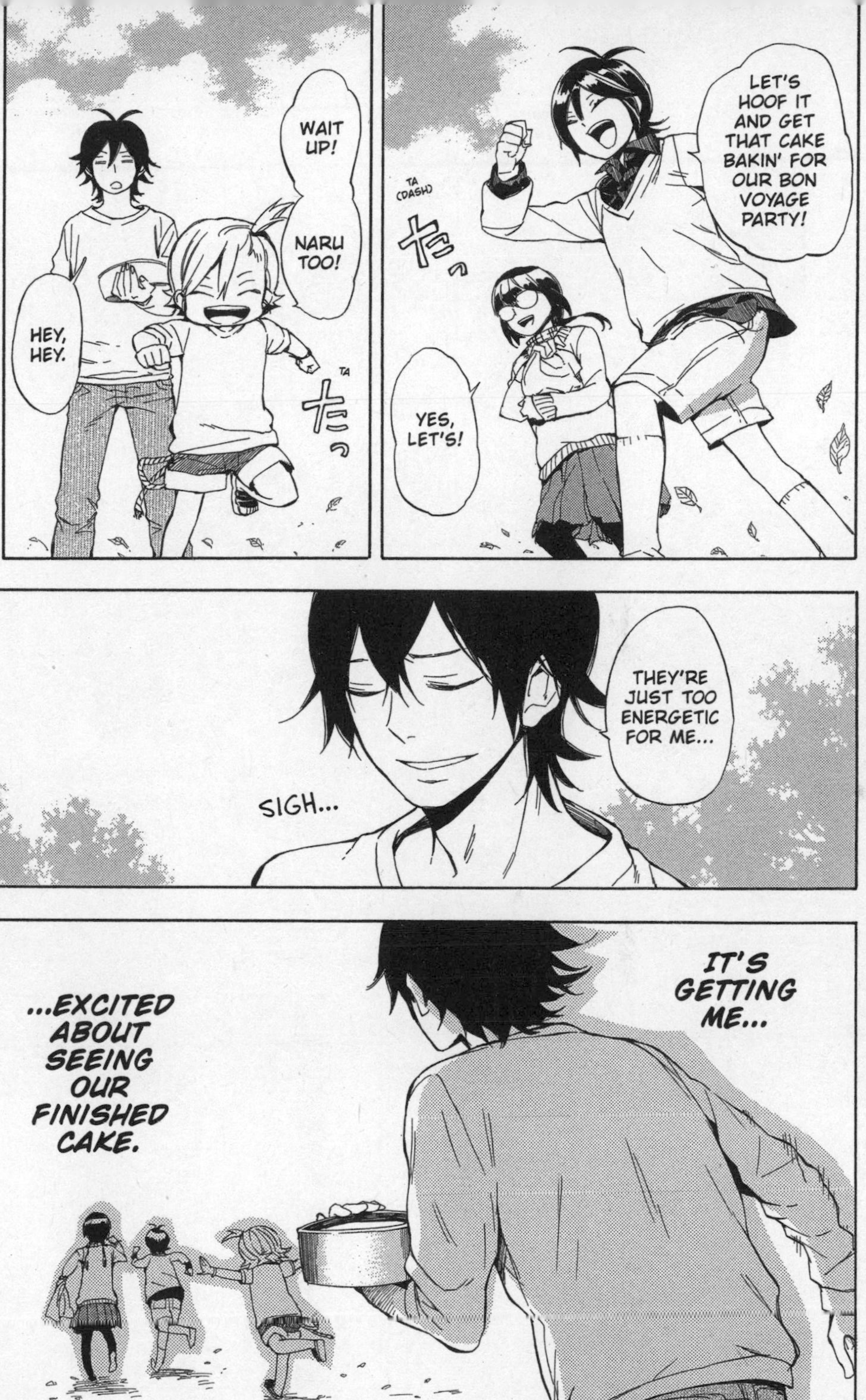

LET'S HOOF IT AND GET THAT CAKE BAKIN' FOR OUR BON VOYAGE PARTY!
TA (DASH)
たっ
YES, LET'S!
WAIT UP!
NARU TOO!
TA
たっ
HEY, HEY.
THEY'RE JUST TOO ENERGETIC FOR ME...
SIGH...
IT'S GETTING ME...
...EXCITED ABOUT SEEING OUR FINISHED CAKE.

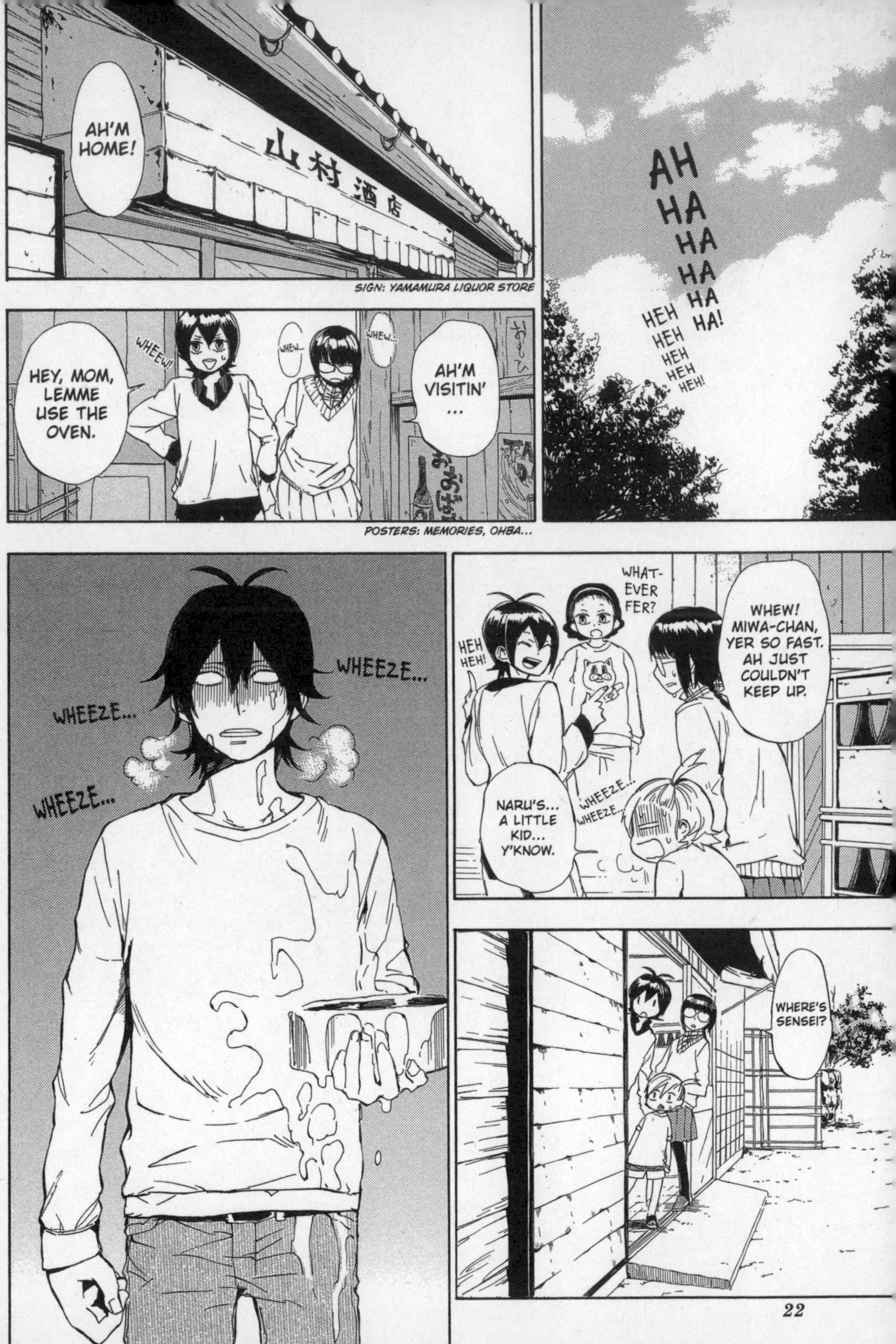
AH HA HA HA HA HA!
HEH HEH HEH HEH HEH!
AH'M HOME!
山村酒店
SIGN: YAMAMURA LIQUOR STORE
AH'M VISITIN' ...
WHEW...
WHEW...
WHEEW!
HEY, MOM, LEMME USE THE OVEN.
POSTERS: MEMORIES, OHBA...
WHEW! MIWA-CHAN, YER SO FAST. AH JUST COULDN'T KEEP UP.
WHAT-EVER FER?
HEH HEH!
WHEEZE... WHEEZE...
NARU'S... A LITTLE KID... Y'KNOW.
WHERE'S SENSEI?
WHEEZE...
WHEEZE...
WHEEZE...

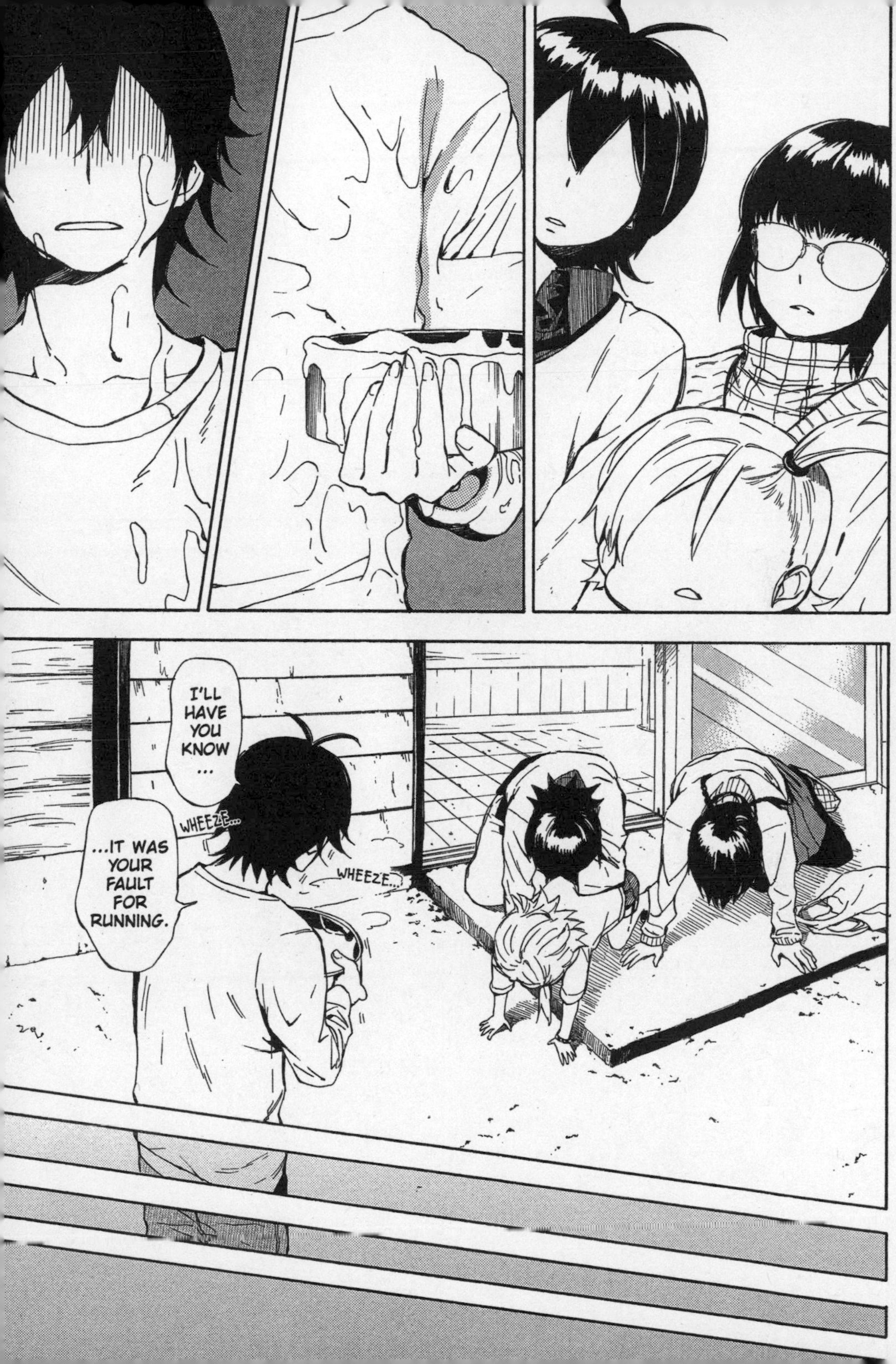
I'LL HAVE YOU KNOW...
WHEEZE...
...IT WAS YOUR FAULT FOR RUNNING.
WHEEZE...

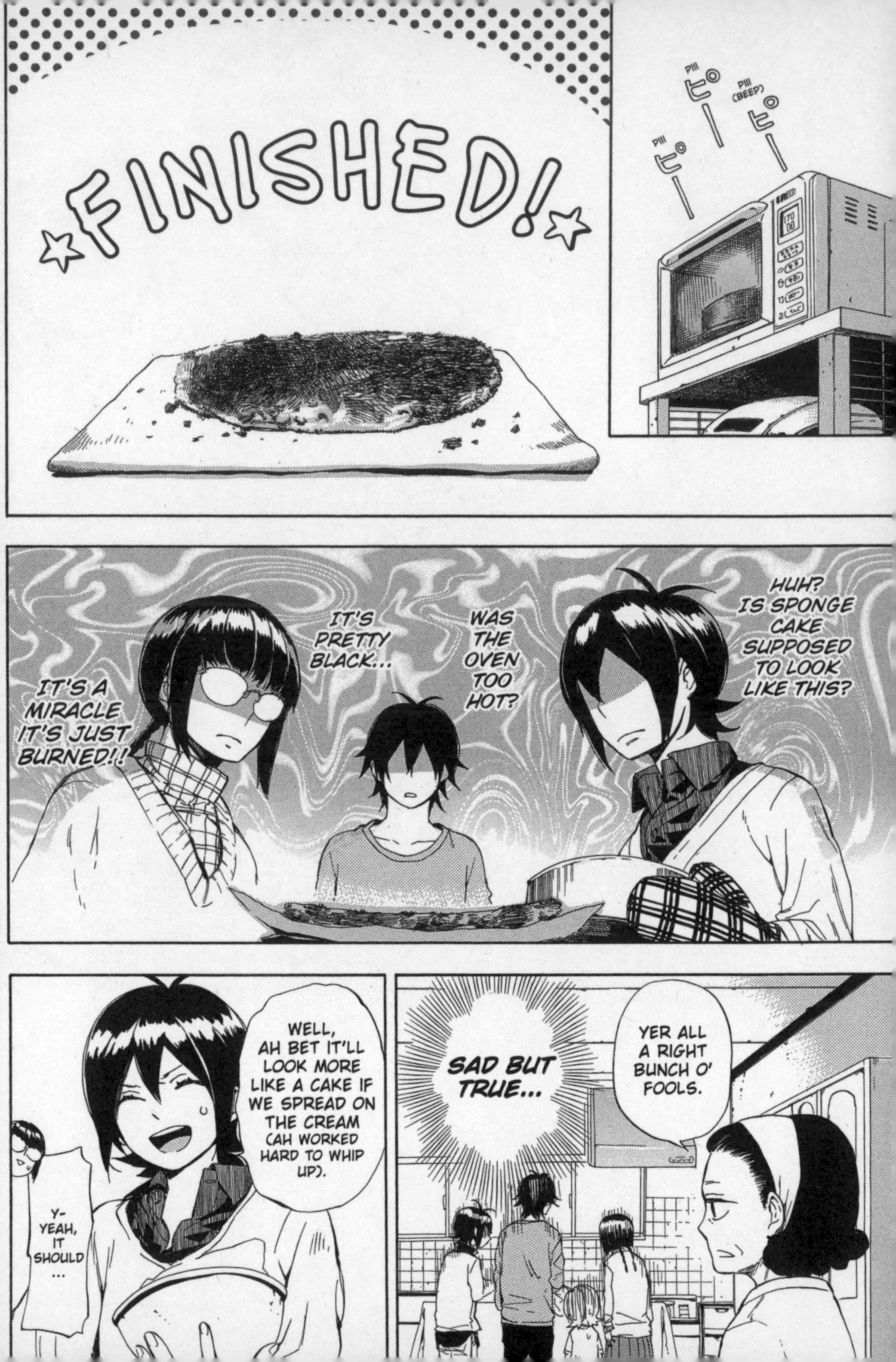
ピー PIII
ピー PIII
ピー PIII (BEEP)
FINISHED!
HUH? IS SPONGE CAKE SUPPOSED TO LOOK LIKE THIS?
WAS THE OVEN TOO HOT?
IT'S PRETTY BLACK...
IT'S A MIRACLE IT'S JUST BURNED!!
YER ALL A RIGHT BUNCH O' FOOLS.
SAD BUT TRUE...
WELL, AH BET IT'LL LOOK MORE LIKE A CAKE IF WE SPREAD ON THE CREAM (AH WORKED HARD TO WHIP UP).
Y-YEAH, IT SHOULD...

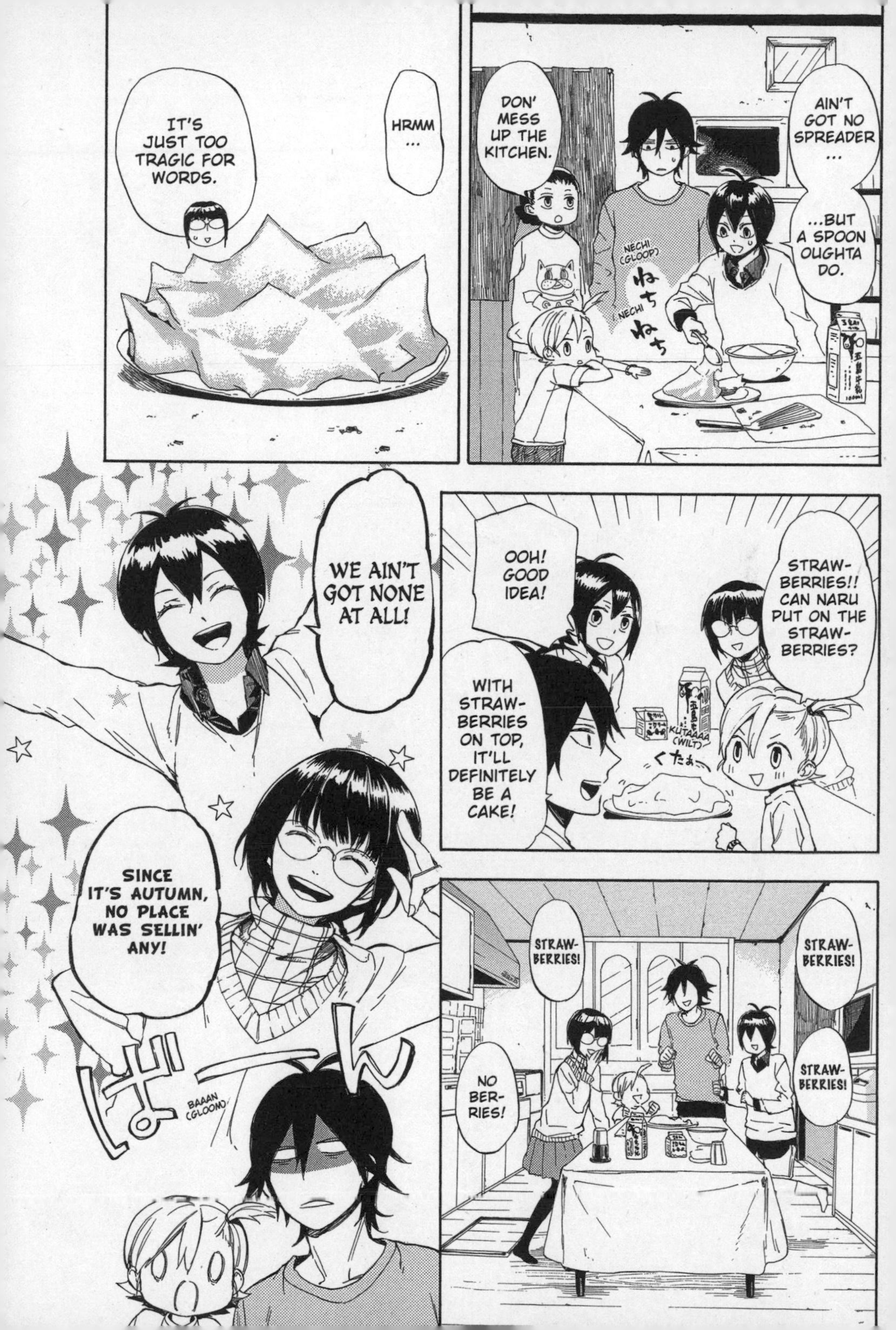
AIN'T GOT NO SPREADER ...
...BUT A SPOON OUGHTA DO.
DON' MESS UP THE KITCHEN.
NECHI (GLOOP)
ねち
NECHI
ねち
HRMM ...
IT'S JUST TOO TRAGIC FOR WORDS.
STRAW-BERRIES!! CAN NARU PUT ON THE STRAW-BERRIES?
OOH! GOOD IDEA!
WITH STRAW-BERRIES ON TOP, IT'LL DEFINITELY BE A CAKE!
KUTAAAA (WILT)
くたぁ
STRAW-BERRIES!
STRAW-BERRIES!
STRAW-BERRIES!
NO BER-RIES!
WE AIN'T GOT NONE AT ALL!
SINCE IT'S AUTUMN, NO PLACE WAS SELLIN' ANY!
BAAAN (GLOOM)
ばーん

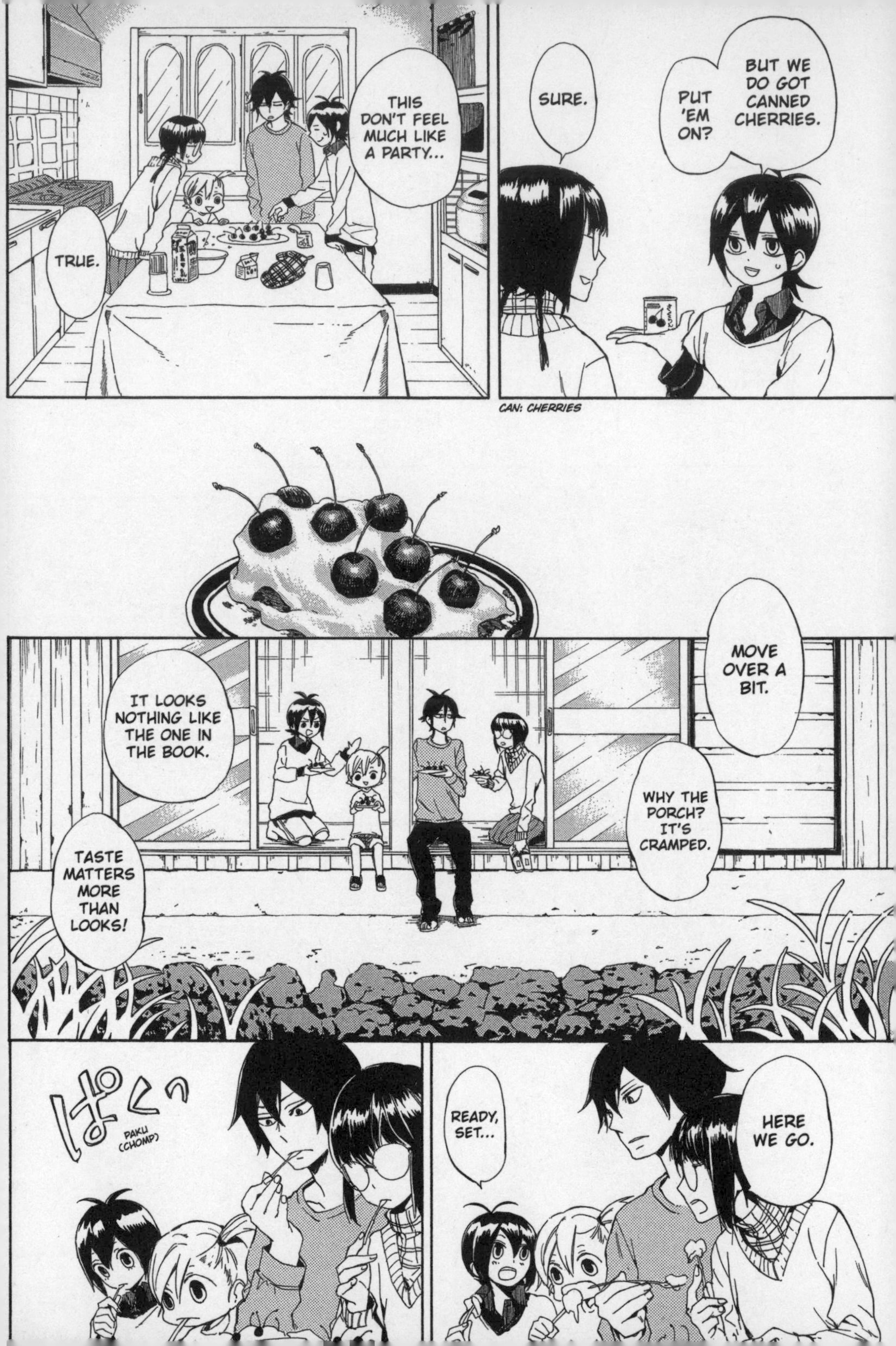
BUT WE DO GOT CANNED CHERRIES.
PUT 'EM ON?
SURE.
CAN: CHERRIES
THIS DON'T FEEL MUCH LIKE A PARTY...
TRUE.
MOVE OVER A BIT.
WHY THE PORCH? IT'S CRAMPED.
IT LOOKS NOTHING LIKE THE ONE IN THE BOOK.
TASTE MATTERS MORE THAN LOOKS!
HERE WE GO.
READY, SET...
ぱくっ
PAKU (CHOMP)

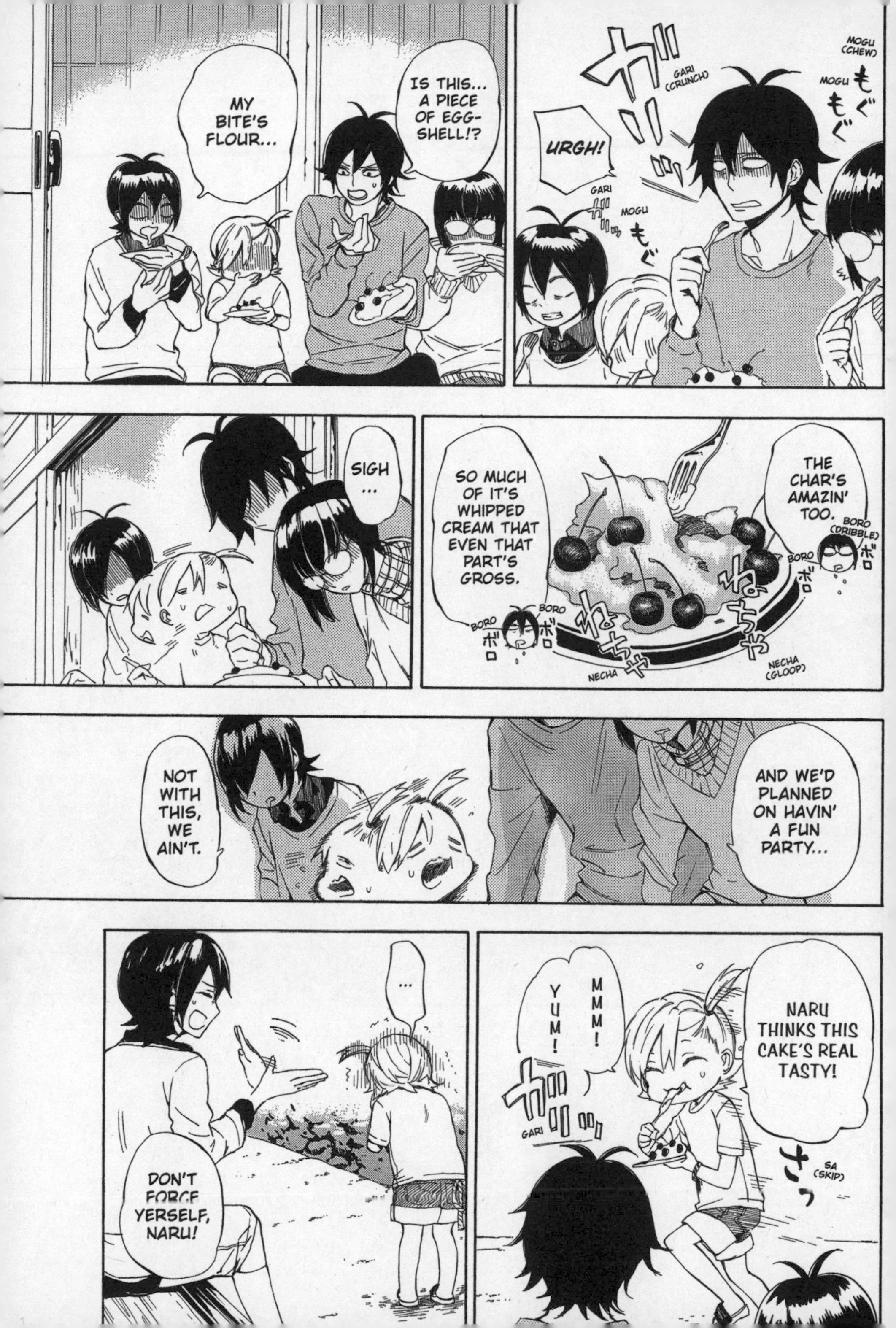
MOGU (CHEW)
MOGU
GARI (CRUNCH)
URGH!
GARI
MOGU
IS THIS... A PIECE OF EGG-SHELL!?
MY BITE'S FLOUR...
THE CHAR'S AMAZIN' TOO.
BORO (DRIBBLE)
BORO
SO MUCH OF IT'S WHIPPED CREAM THAT EVEN THAT PART'S GROSS.
BORO
BORO
NECHA (GLOOP)
NECHA
SIGH...
AND WE'D PLANNED ON HAVIN' A FUN PARTY...
NOT WITH THIS, WE AIN'T.
NARU THINKS THIS CAKE'S REAL TASTY!
MMM!
YUM!
GARI
SA (SKIP)
...
DON'T FORCE YERSELF, NARU!

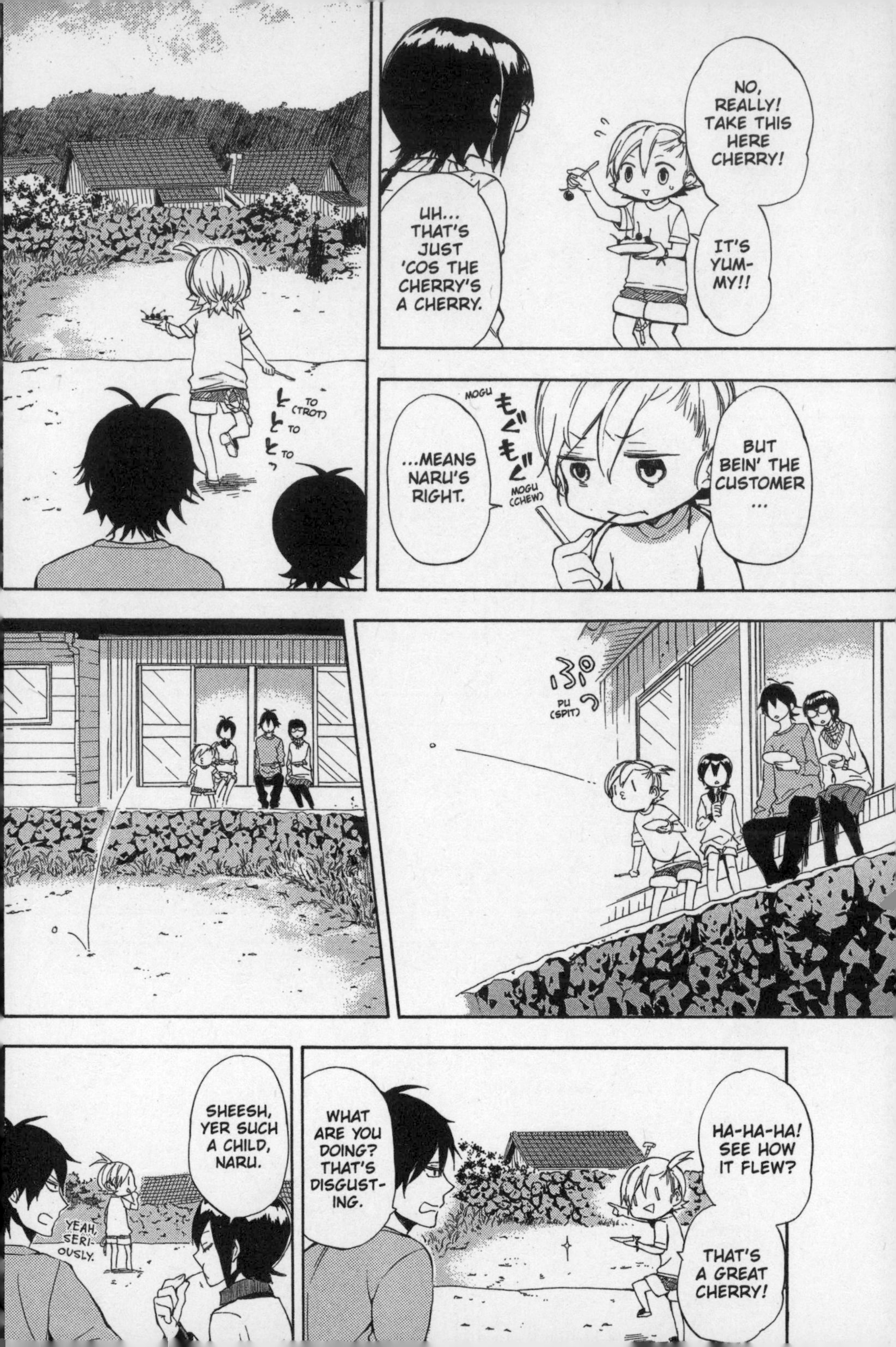
NO, REALLY! TAKE THIS HERE CHERRY!
IT'S YUM-MY!!
UH... THAT'S JUST 'COS THE CHERRY'S A CHERRY.
BUT BEIN' THE CUSTOMER ...
もぐ MOGU
もぐ MOGU (CHEW)
...MEANS NARU'S RIGHT.
と TO (TROT)
と TO
とっ TO
ぷっ PU (SPIT)
HA-HA-HA! SEE HOW IT FLEW?
THAT'S A GREAT CHERRY!
WHAT ARE YOU DOING? THAT'S DISGUST-ING.
SHEESH, YER SUCH A CHILD, NARU.
YEAH, SERI-OUSLY.

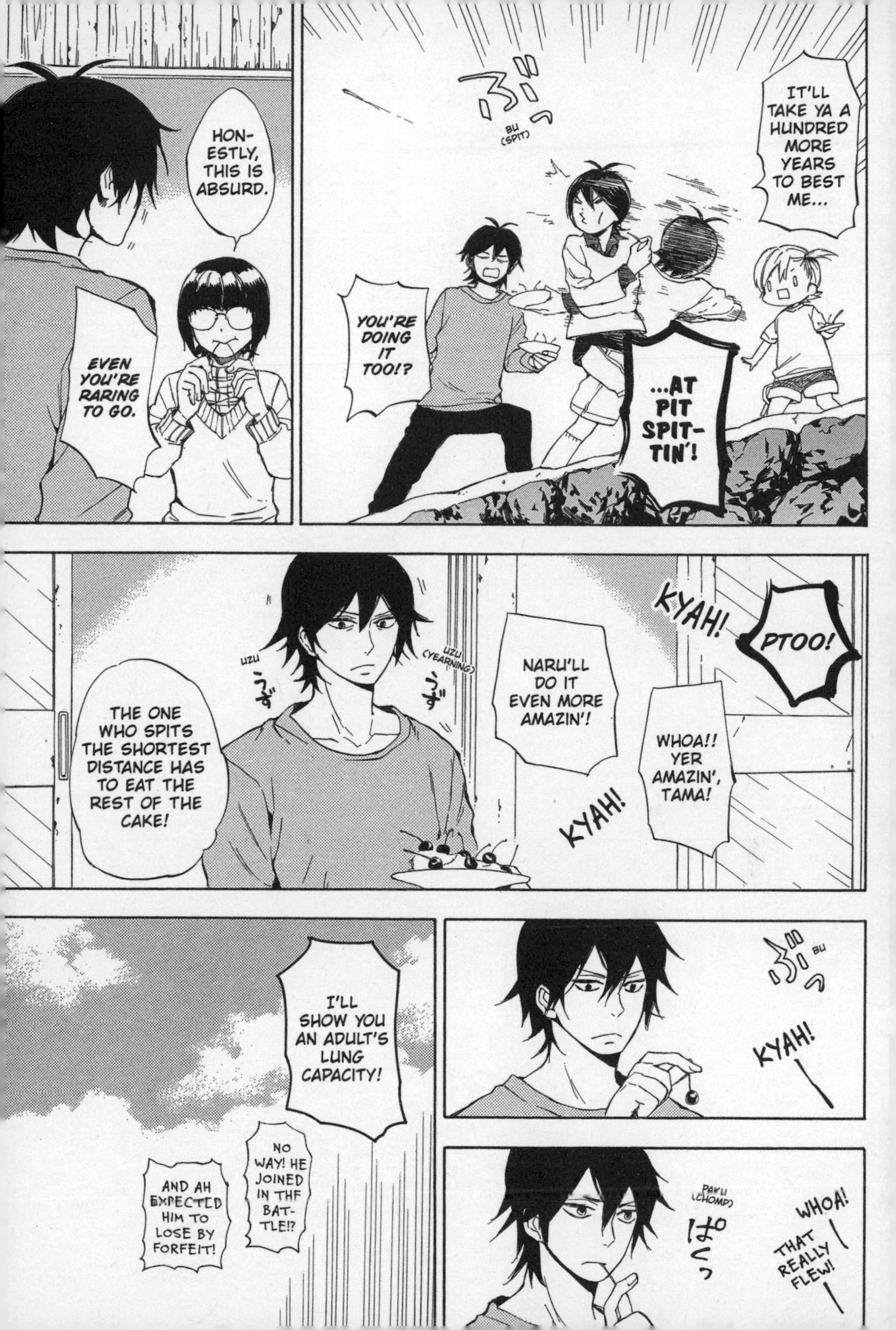
IT'LL TAKE YA A HUNDRED MORE YEARS TO BEST ME...
ぶっ
BU (SPIT)
...AT PIT SPITTIN'!
YOU'RE DOING IT TOO!?
HON-ESTLY, THIS IS ABSURD.
EVEN YOU'RE RARING TO GO.
PTOO!
KYAH!
NARU'LL DO IT EVEN MORE AMAZIN'!
WHOA!! YER AMAZIN', TAMA!
KYAH!
うず
UZU (YEARNING)
うず
UZU
THE ONE WHO SPITS THE SHORTEST DISTANCE HAS TO EAT THE REST OF THE CAKE!
ぶっ
BU
KYAH!
WHOA! THAT REALLY FLEW!
ぱくっ
PAKU (CHOMP)
I'LL SHOW YOU AN ADULT'S LUNG CAPACITY!
NO WAY! HE JOINED IN THF BAT-TLE!?
AND AH EXPECTED HIM TO LOSE BY FORFEIT!

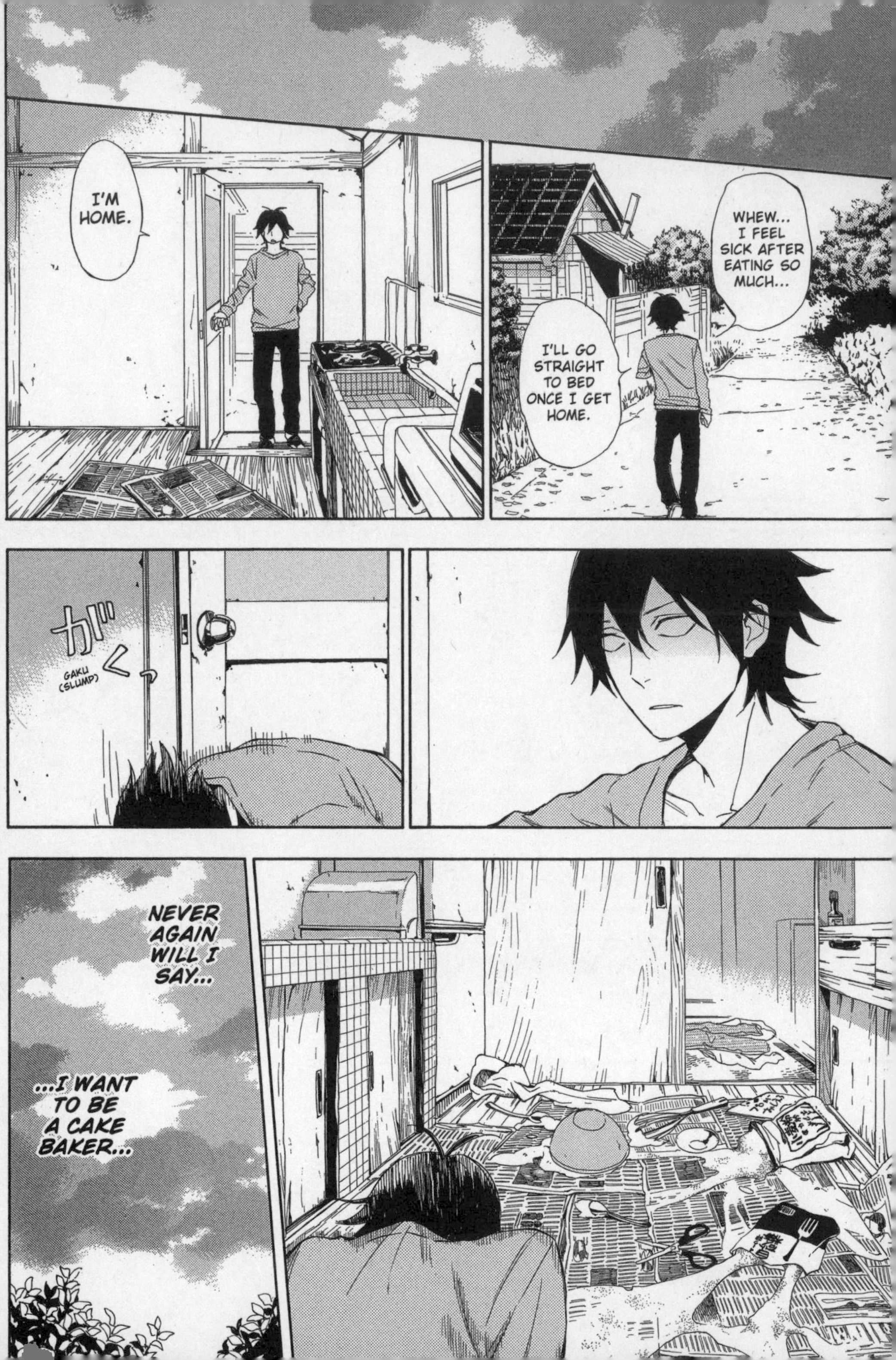
WHEW... I FEEL SICK AFTER EATING SO MUCH...
I'LL GO STRAIGHT TO BED ONCE I GET HOME.
I'M HOME.
がくっ
GAKU (SLUMP)
NEVER AGAIN WILL I SAY...
...I WANT TO BE A CAKE BAKER...

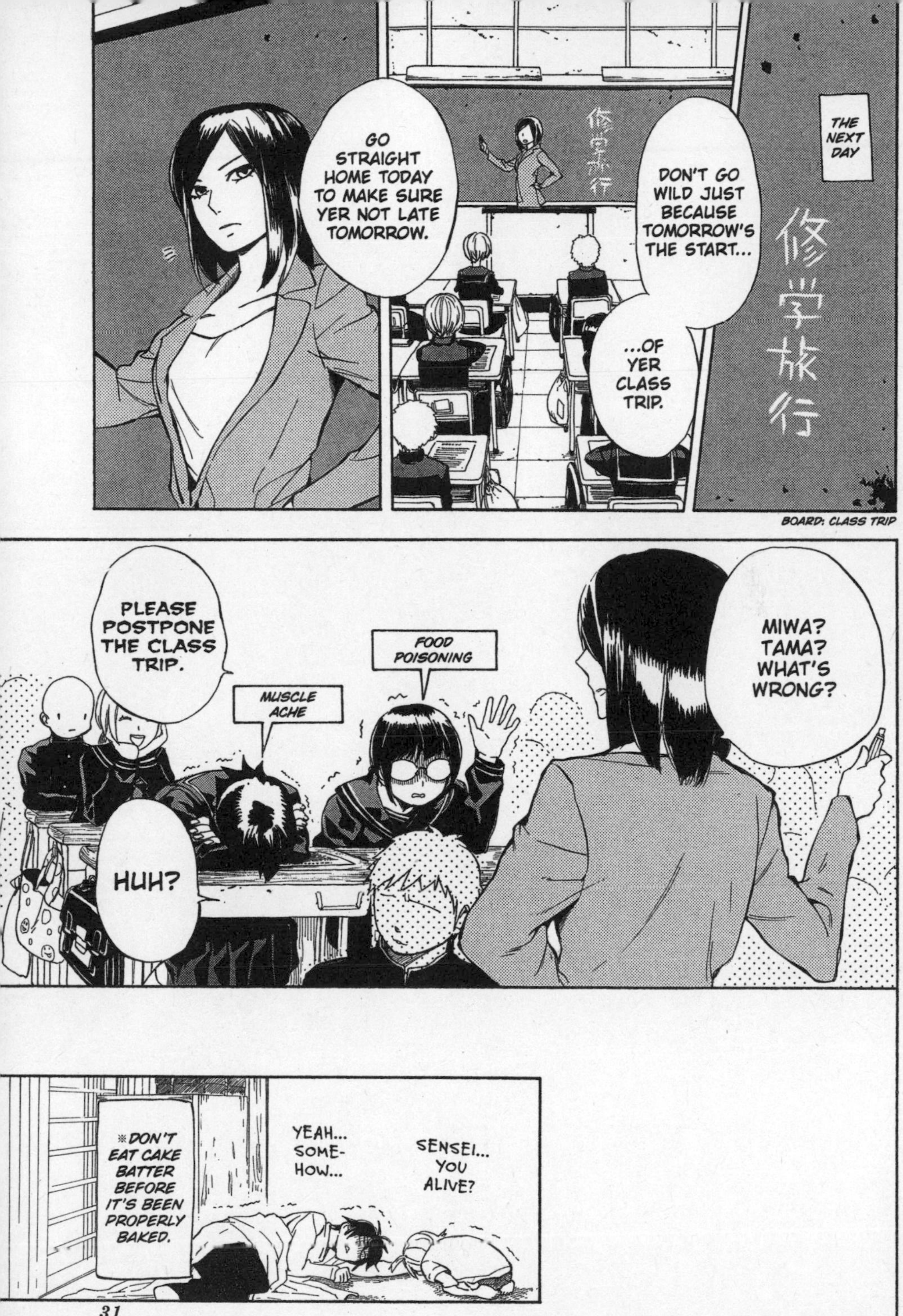
THE NEXT DAY
修学旅行
DON'T GO WILD JUST BECAUSE TOMORROW'S THE START...
...OF YER CLASS TRIP.
GO STRAIGHT HOME TODAY TO MAKE SURE YER NOT LATE TOMORROW.
BOARD: CLASS TRIP
MIWA? TAMA? WHAT'S WRONG?
FOOD POISONING
MUSCLE ACHE
PLEASE POSTPONE THE CLASS TRIP.
HUH?
SENSEI... YOU ALIVE?
YEAH... SOME-HOW...
※DON'T EAT CAKE BATTER BEFORE IT'S BEEN PROPERLY BAKED.

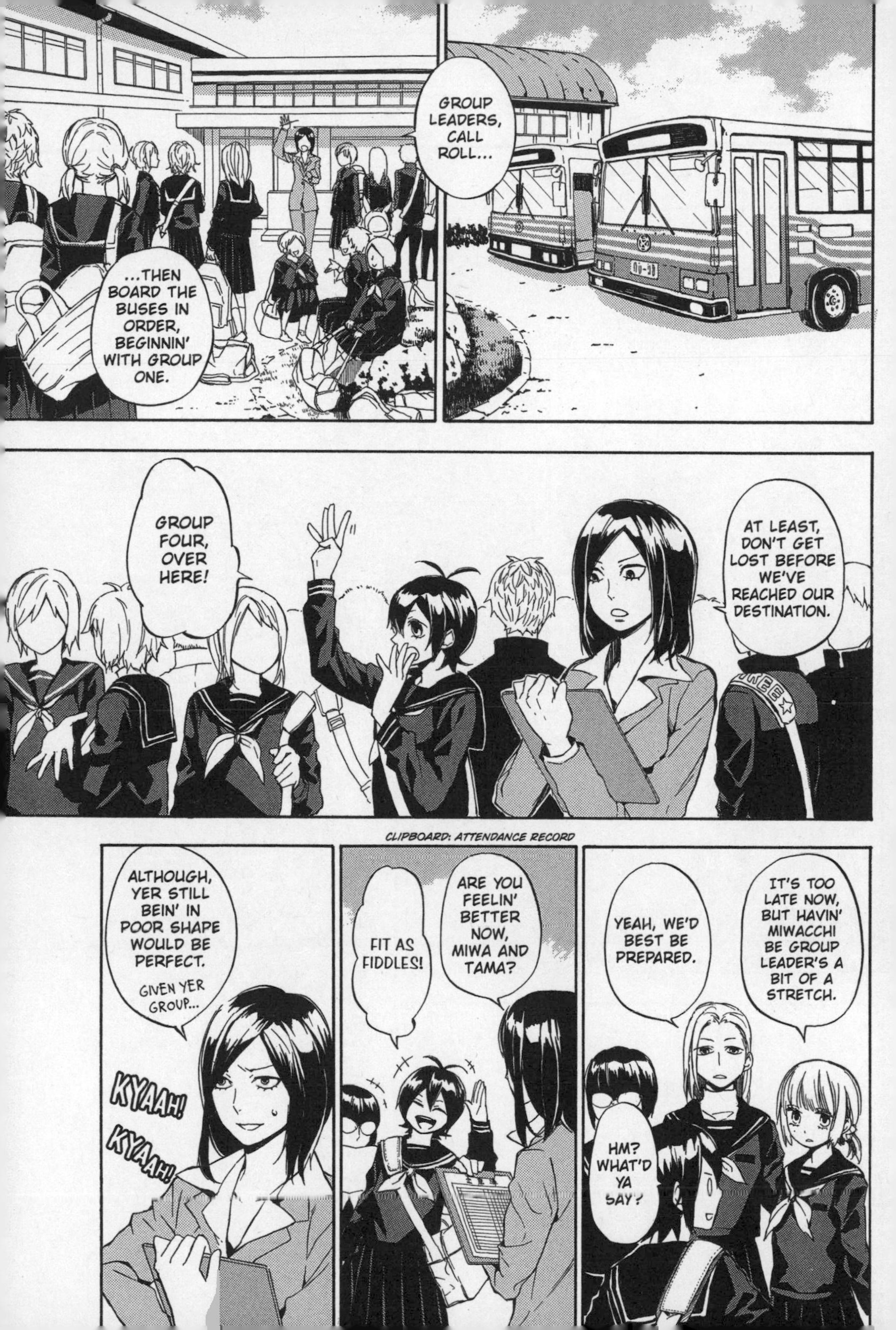
GROUP LEADERS, CALL ROLL...
...THEN BOARD THE BUSES IN ORDER, BEGINNIN' WITH GROUP ONE.
AT LEAST, DON'T GET LOST BEFORE WE'VE REACHED OUR DESTINATION.
GROUP FOUR, OVER HERE!
CLIPBOARD: ATTENDANCE RECORD
IT'S TOO LATE NOW, BUT HAVIN' MIWACCHI BE GROUP LEADER'S A BIT OF A STRETCH.
YEAH, WE'D BEST BE PREPARED.
HM? WHAT'D YA SAY?
ARE YOU FEELIN' BETTER NOW, MIWA AND TAMA?
FIT AS FIDDLES!
ALTHOUGH, YER STILL BEIN' IN POOR SHAPE WOULD BE PERFECT.
GIVEN YER GROUP...
KYAAH!
KYAAH!

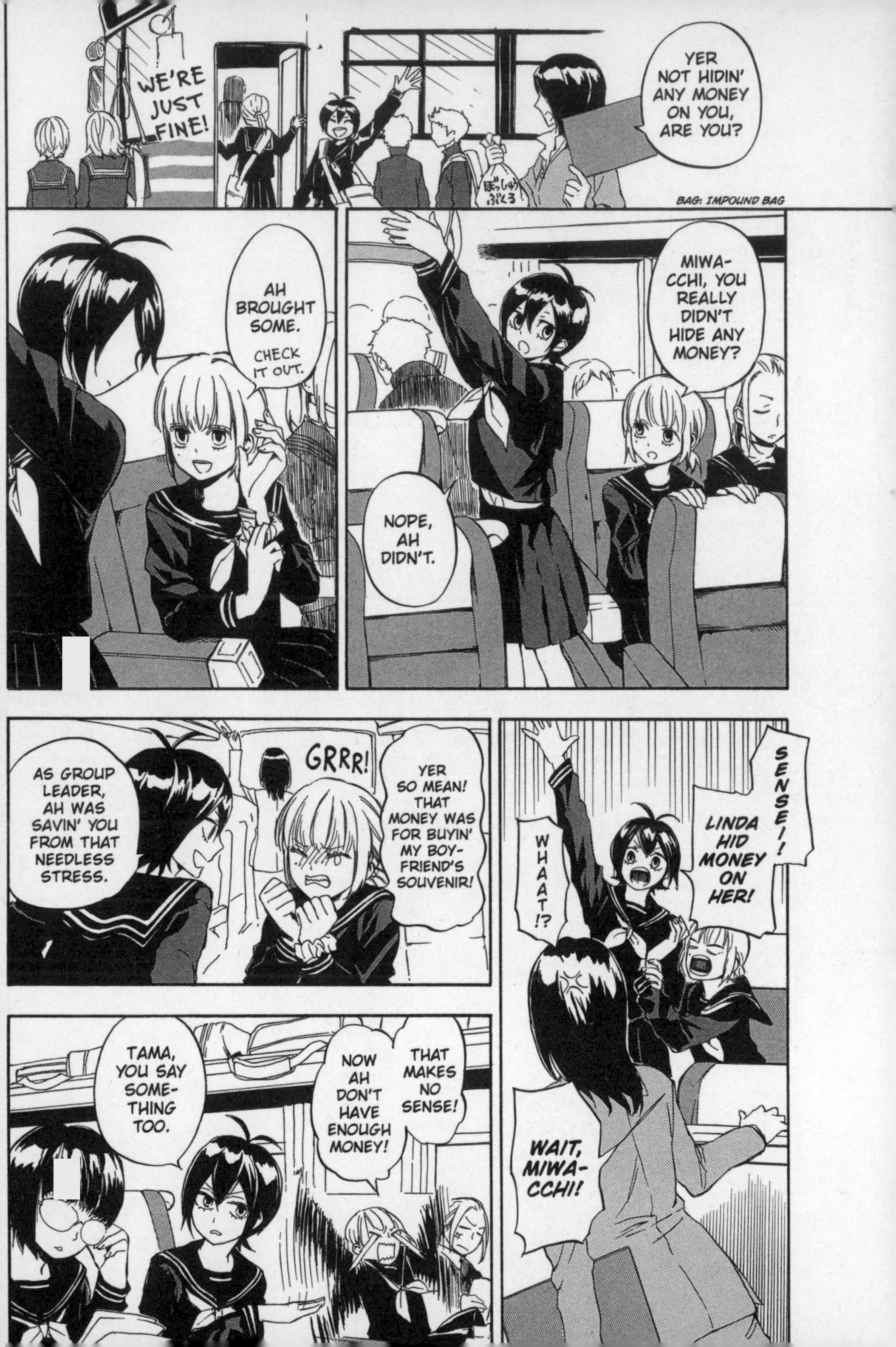
YER NOT HIDIN' ANY MONEY ON YOU, ARE YOU?
ぼっしゅう ぶくろ
WE'RE JUST FINE!
BAG: IMPOUND BAG
MIWA-CCHI, YOU REALLY DIDN'T HIDE ANY MONEY?
NOPE, AH DIDN'T.
AH BROUGHT SOME.
CHECK IT OUT.
SENSEI!
LINDA HID MONEY ON HER!
WHAAAT!?
WAIT, MIWA-CCHI!
YER SO MEAN! THAT MONEY WAS FOR BUYIN' MY BOY-FRIEND'S SOUVENIR!
GRRR!
AS GROUP LEADER, AH WAS SAVIN' YOU FROM THAT NEEDLESS STRESS.
THAT MAKES NO SENSE!
NOW AH DON'T HAVE ENOUGH MONEY!
TAMA, YOU SAY SOME-THING TOO.

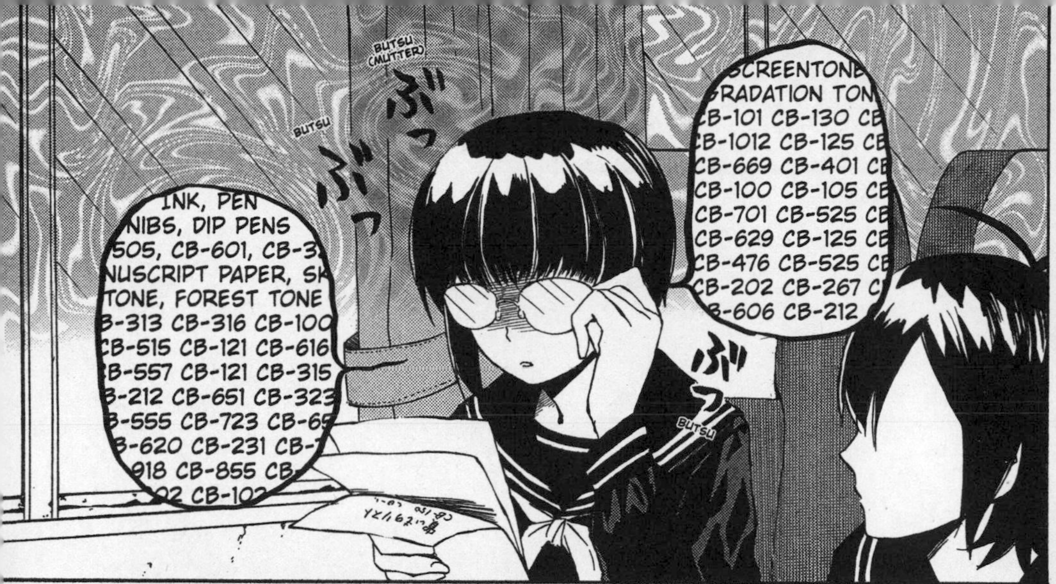

SCREENTONE GRADATION TON CB-101 CB-130 CB-1012 CB-125 CB-669 CB-401 CB-100 CB-105 CB-701 CB-525 CB-629 CB-125 CB-476 CB-525 CB-202 CB-267 CB-606 CB-212
BUTSU (MUTTER)
ぶつ
BUTSU
INK, PEN NIBS, DIP PENS 505, CB-601, CB-3 NUSCRIPT PAPER, SK TONE, FOREST TONE B-313 CB-316 CB-100 CB-515 CB-121 CB-616 B-557 CB-121 CB-315 B-212 CB-651 CB-323 B-555 CB-723 CB-65 B-620 CB-231 CB- 918 CB-855 CB- 02 CB-102
BUTSU

PAPER: SHOPPING LIST—CB-150, CB...

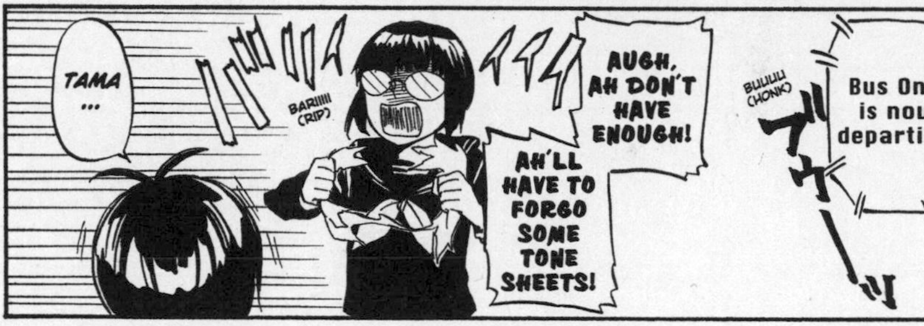

Bus One is now departin'.
BUUUU (HONK)
AUGH, AH DON'T HAVE ENOUGH!
AH'LL HAVE TO FORGO SOME TONE SHEETS!
BARIIIII (RIP)
TAMA ...

ACT.62
ORAU
(Translation: Yell)

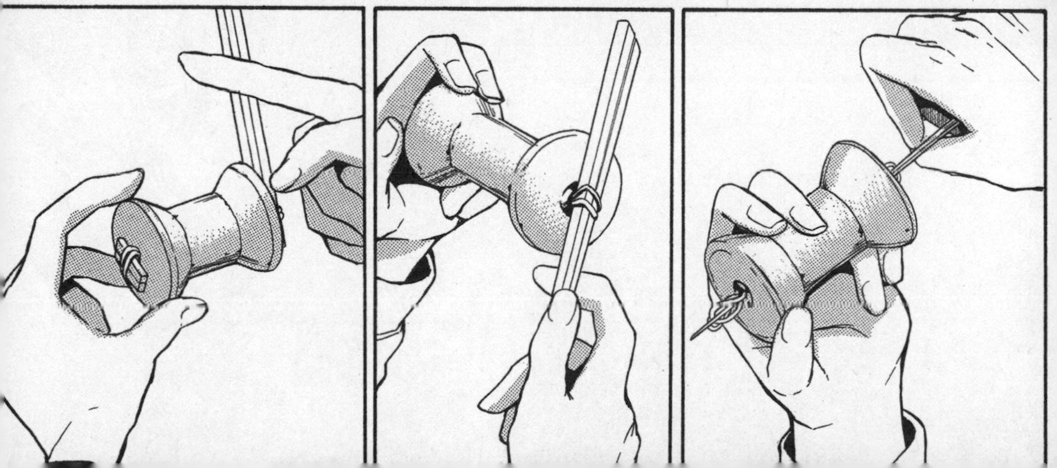

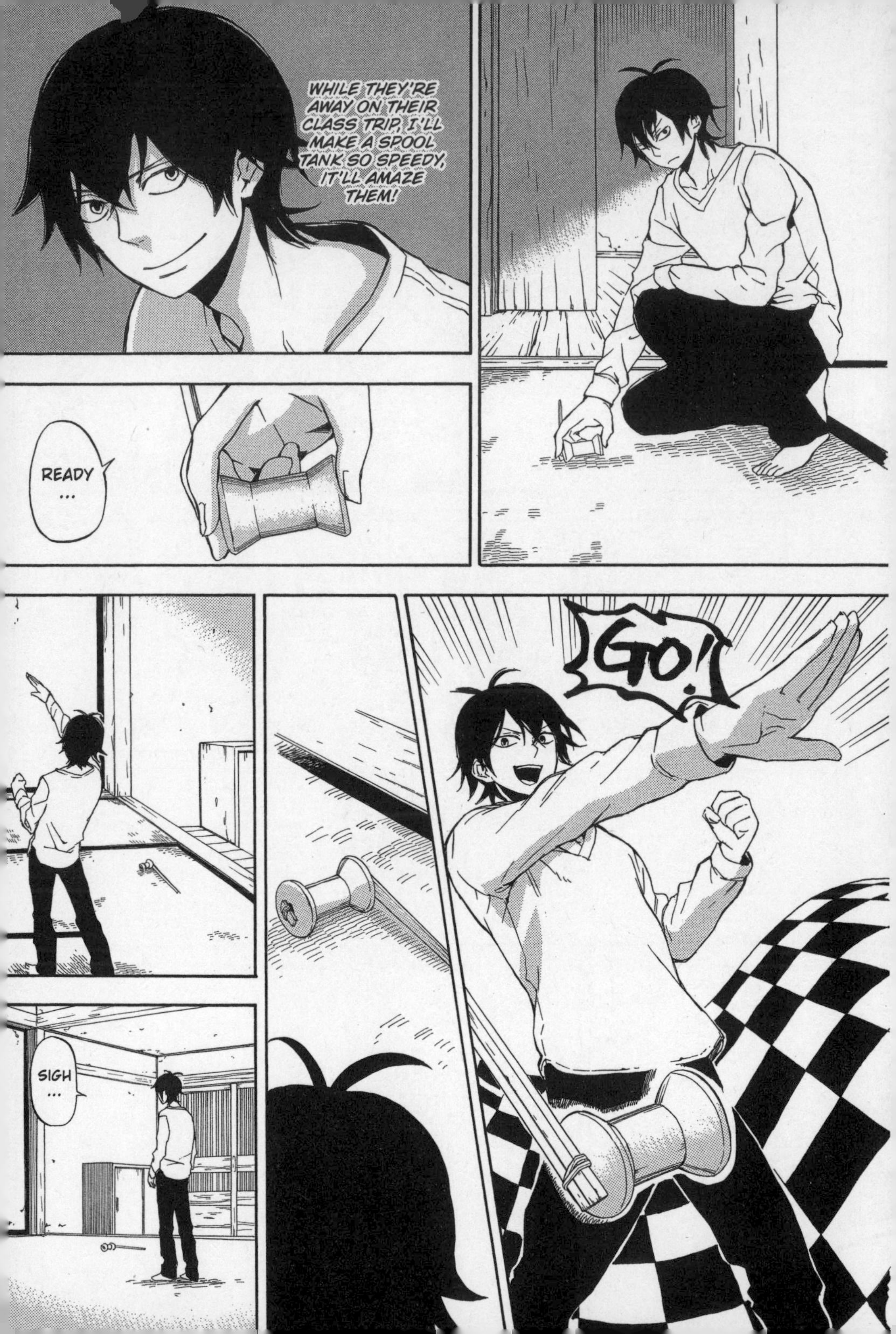
WHILE THEY'RE AWAY ON THEIR CLASS TRIP, I'LL MAKE A SPOOL TANK SO SPEEDY, IT'LL AMAZE THEM!
READY ...
GO!
SIGH ...

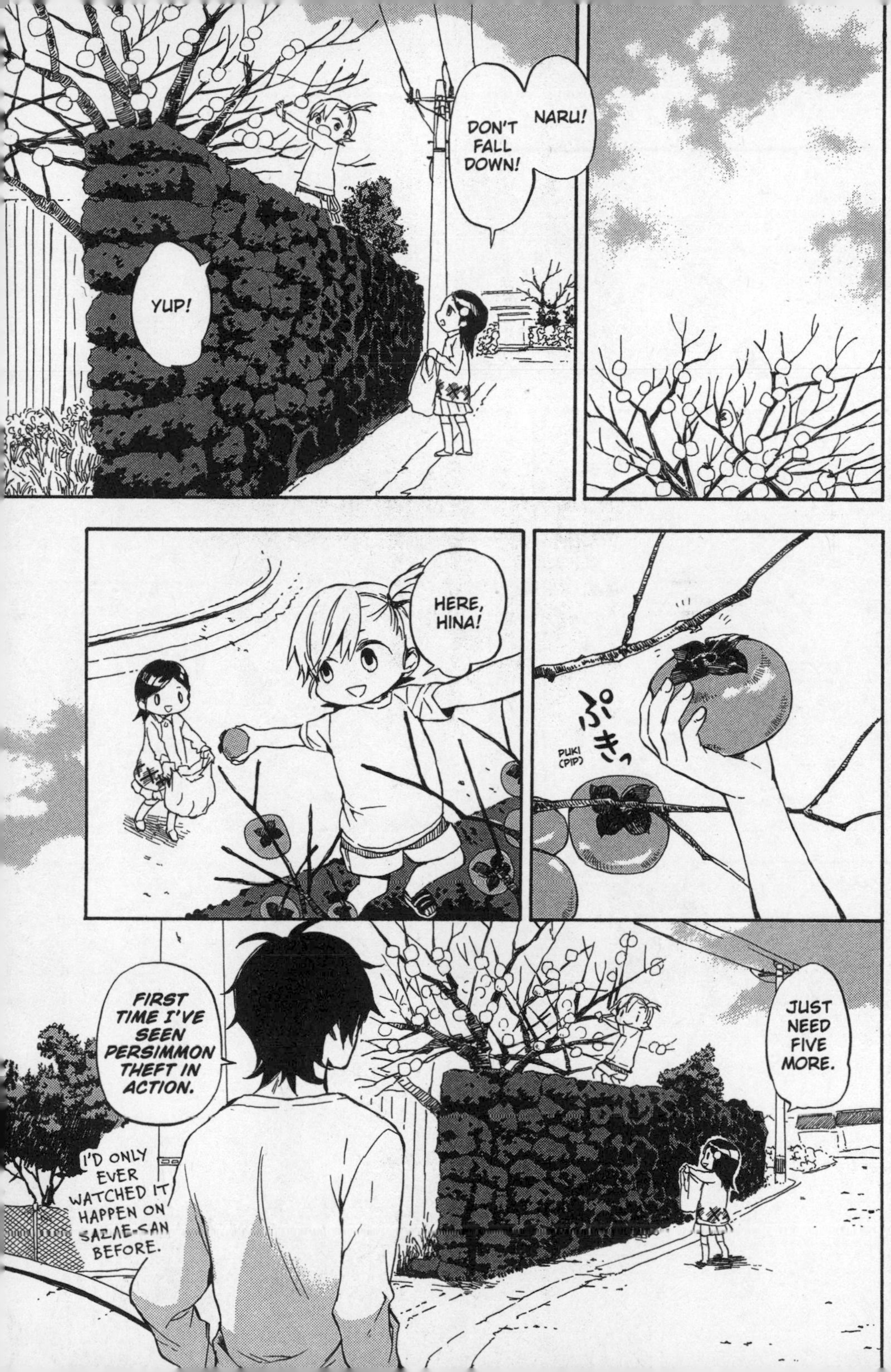
NARU!
DON'T FALL DOWN!
YUP!
ぷきっ
PUKI (PIP)
HERE, HINA!
JUST NEED FIVE MORE.
FIRST TIME I'VE SEEN PERSIMMON THEFT IN ACTION.
I'D ONLY EVER WATCHED IT HAPPEN ON SAZAE-SAN BEFORE.

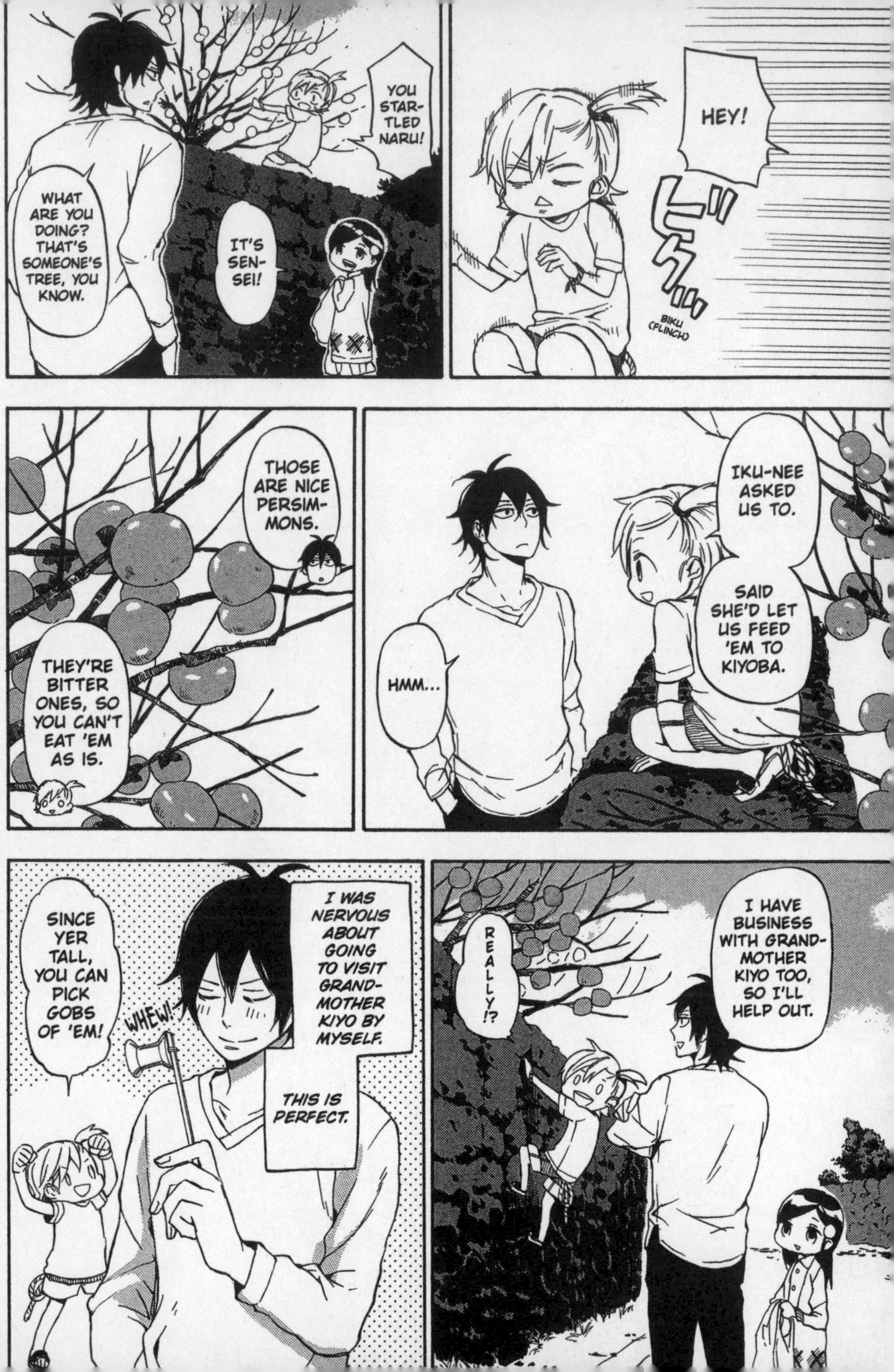
HEY!
ビクッ
BIKU (FLINCH)
YOU STARTLED NARU!
IT'S SEN-SEI!
WHAT ARE YOU DOING? THAT'S SOMEONE'S TREE, YOU KNOW.
IKU-NEE ASKED US TO.
SAID SHE'D LET US FEED 'EM TO KIYOBA.
HMM...
THOSE ARE NICE PERSIM-MONS.
THEY'RE BITTER ONES, SO YOU CAN'T EAT 'EM AS IS.
I HAVE BUSINESS WITH GRAND-MOTHER KIYO TOO, SO I'LL HELP OUT.
REALLY!?
I WAS NERVOUS ABOUT GOING TO VISIT GRAND-MOTHER KIYO BY MYSELF.
SINCE YER TALL, YOU CAN PICK GOBS OF 'EM!
WHEW!
THIS IS PERFECT.

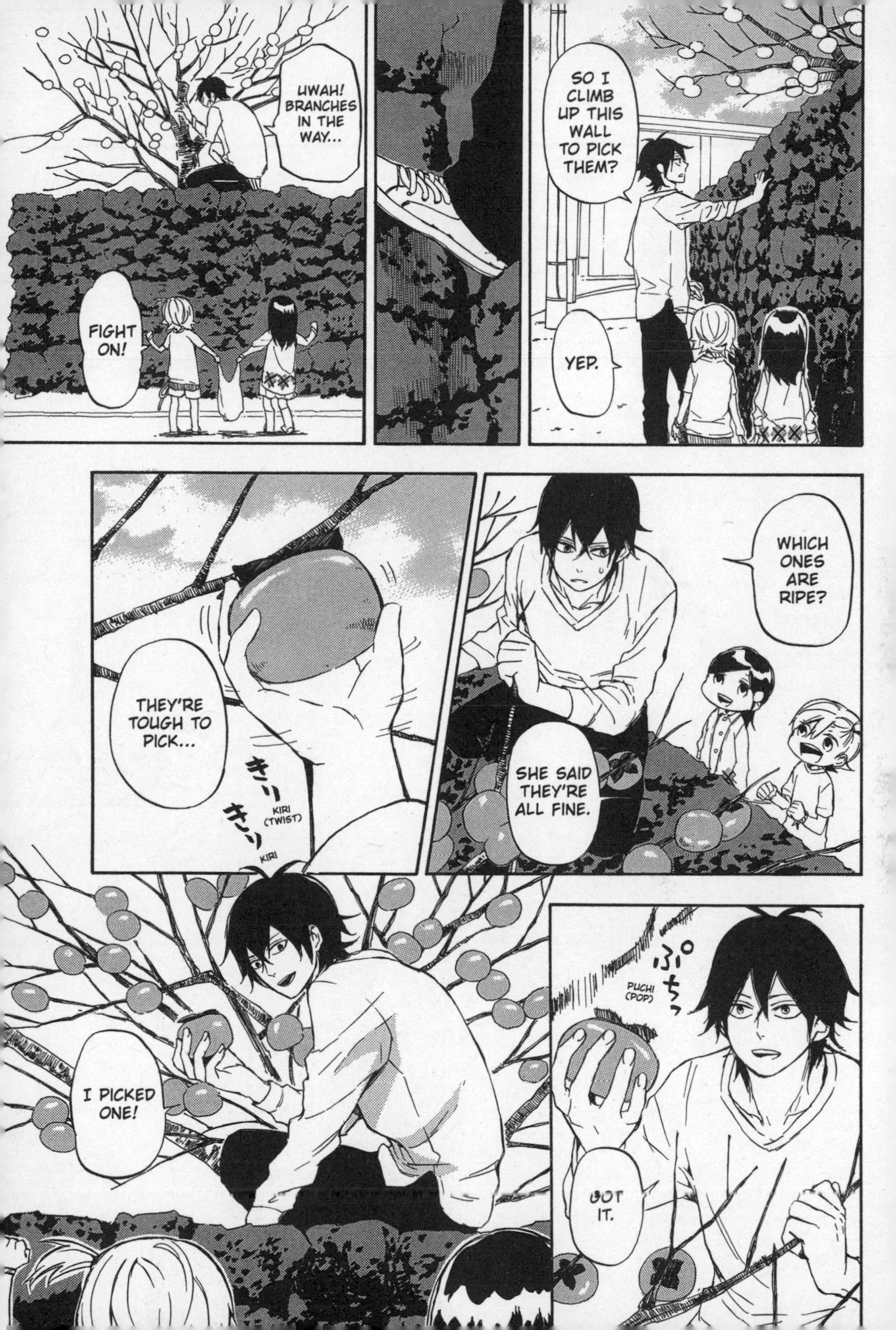
SO I CLIMB UP THIS WALL TO PICK THEM?
YEP.
UWAH! BRANCHES IN THE WAY...
FIGHT ON!
WHICH ONES ARE RIPE?
SHE SAID THEY'RE ALL FINE.
THEY'RE TOUGH TO PICK...
きり
KIRI (TWIST)
きり
KIRI
ぷちっ
PUCHI (POP)
GOT IT.
I PICKED ONE!

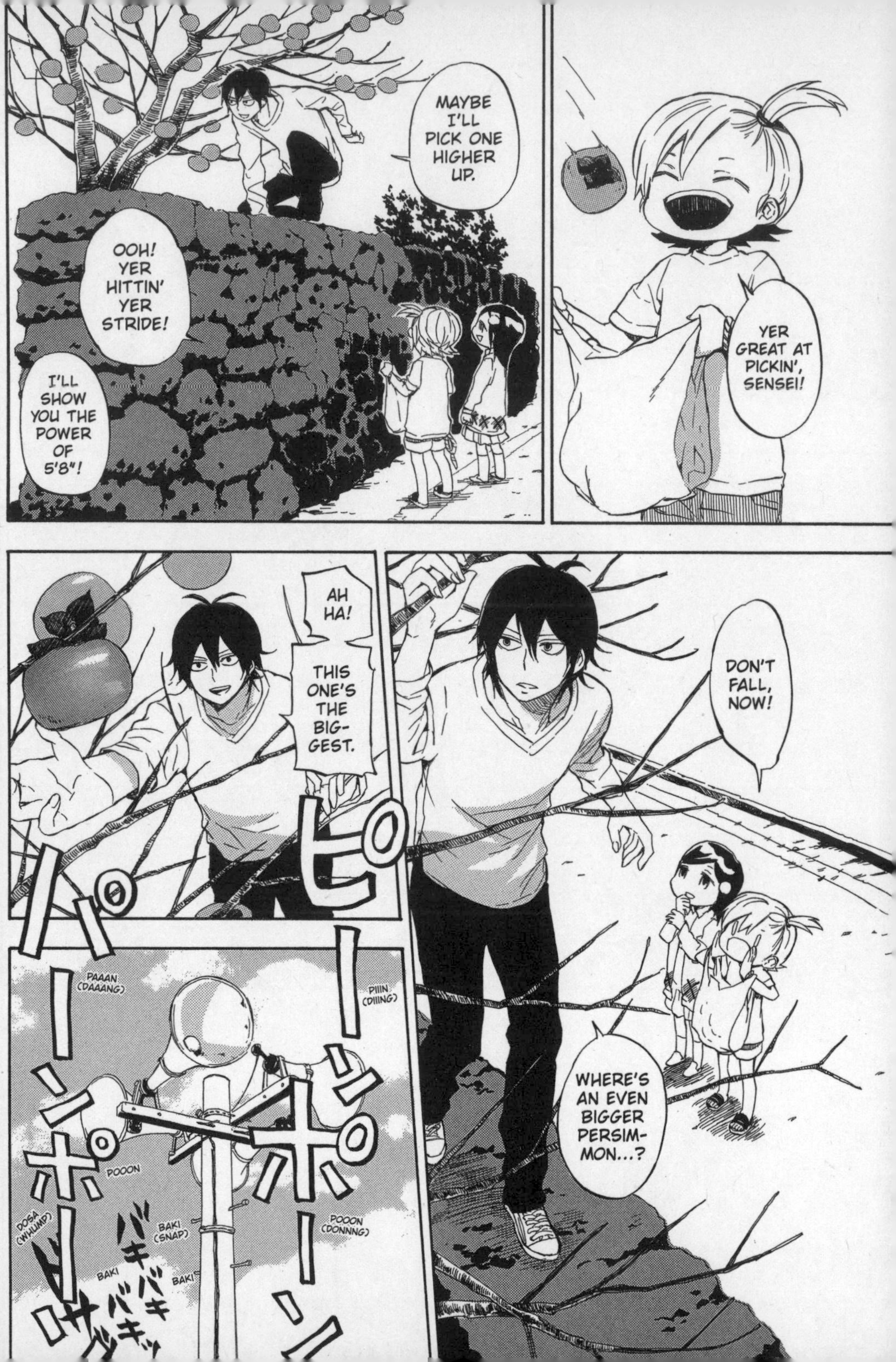
YER GREAT AT PICKIN', SENSEI!
MAYBE I'LL PICK ONE HIGHER UP.
OOH! YER HITTIN' YER STRIDE!
I'LL SHOW YOU THE POWER OF 5'8"!
DON'T FALL, NOW!
WHERE'S AN EVEN BIGGER PERSIMMON...?
AH HA!
THIS ONE'S THE BIGGEST.
PIIIN (DIIING)
PAAAN (DAAANG)
POOON
POOON (DONNNG)
BAKI (SNAP)
BAKI
BAKI
DOGA (WHUMP)

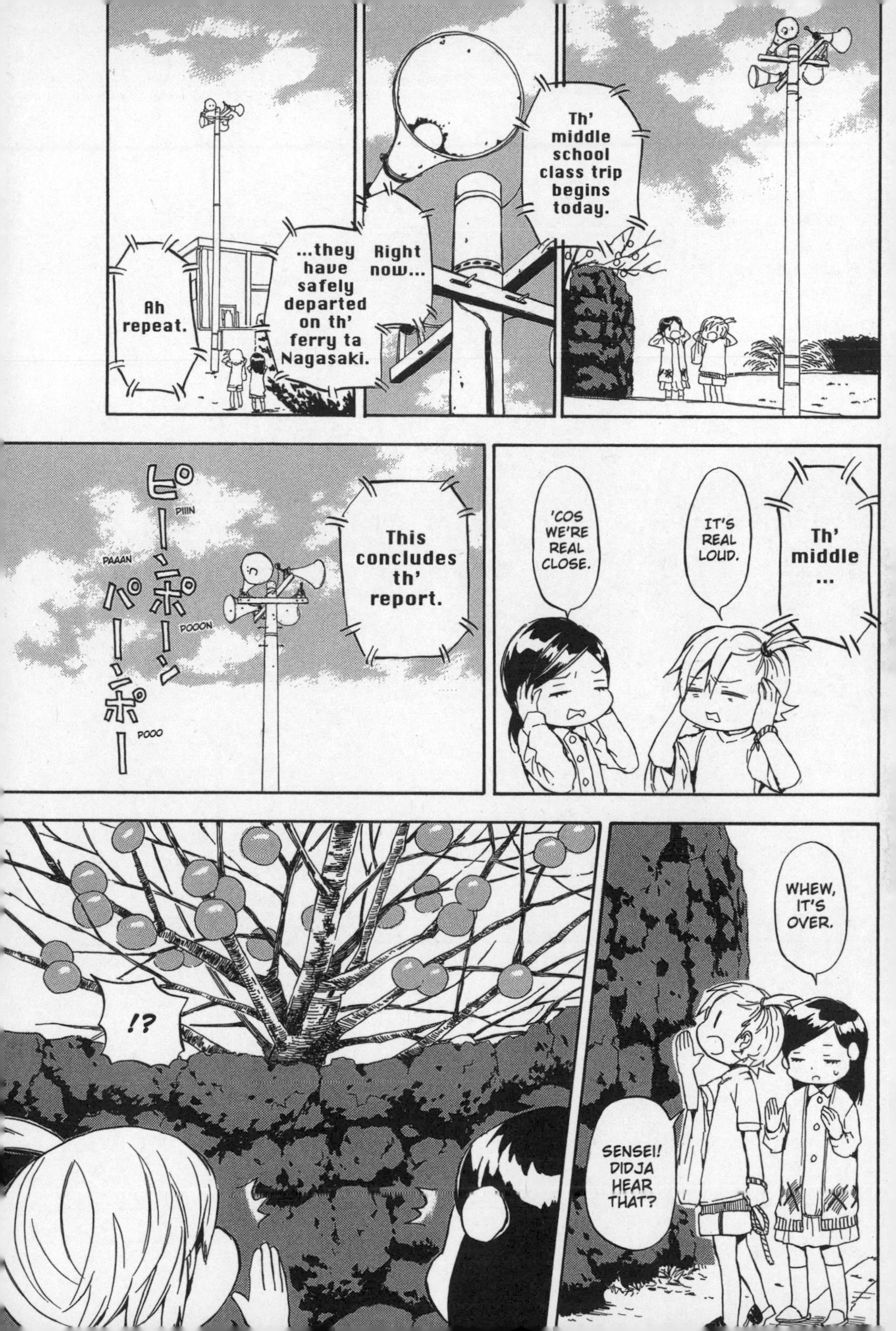
Th' middle school class trip begins today.
Right now...
...they have safely departed on th' ferry ta Nagasaki.
Ah repeat.
Th' middle...
IT'S REAL LOUD.
'COS WE'RE REAL CLOSE.
This concludes th' report.
ピーンポーン
PIIIN
POOON
パーンポー
PAAAN
POOO
WHEW, IT'S OVER.
SENSEI! DIDJA HEAR THAT?
!?

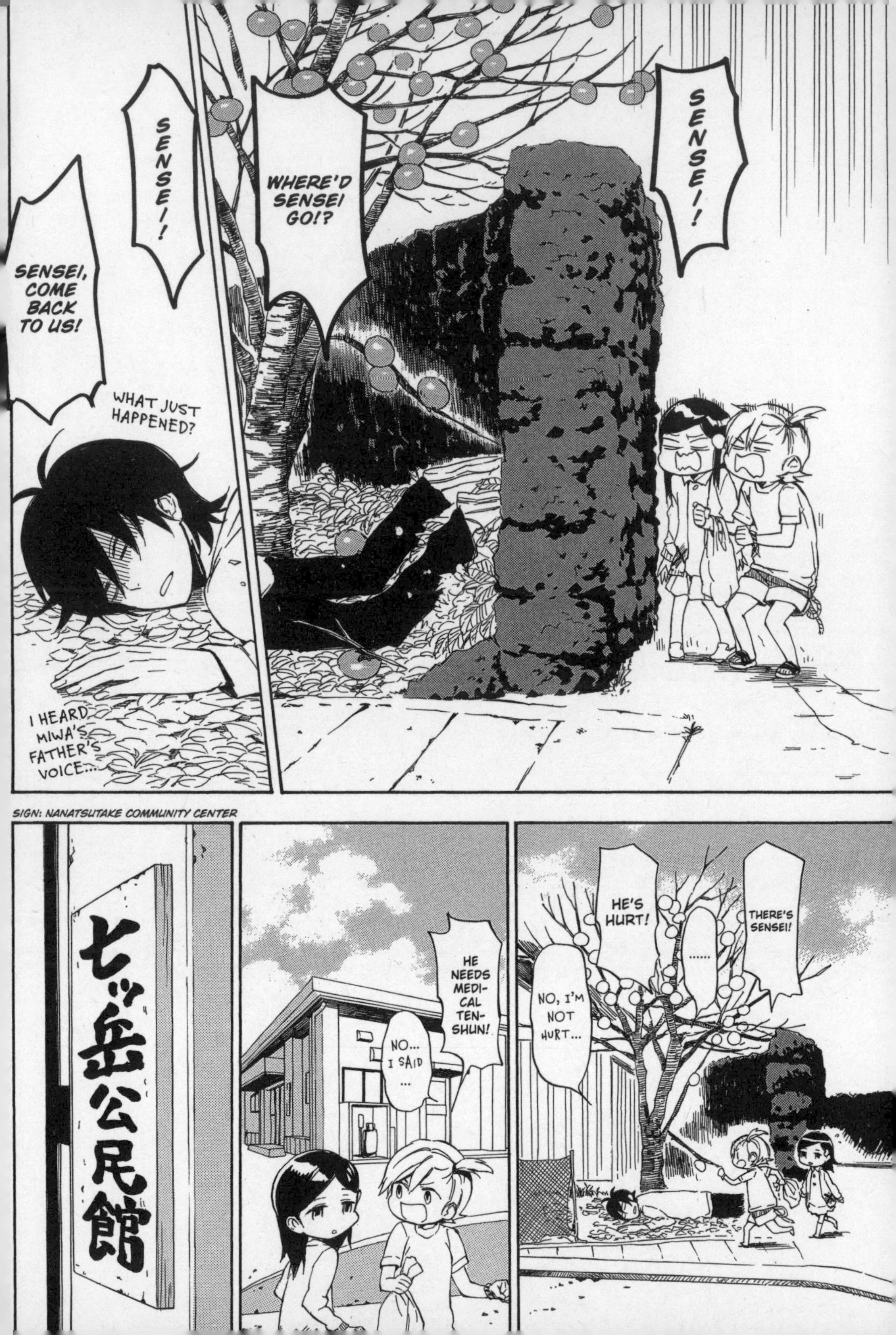
SENSEI!!
WHERE'D SENSEI GO!?
SENSEI!!
SENSEI, COME BACK TO US!
WHAT JUST HAPPENED?
I HEARD MIWA'S FATHER'S VOICE...
SIGN: NANATSUTAKE COMMUNITY CENTER
THERE'S SENSEI!
......
HE'S HURT!
NO, I'M NOT HURT...
HE NEEDS MEDI-CAL TEN-SHUN!
NO... I SAID ...
七ッ岳公民館

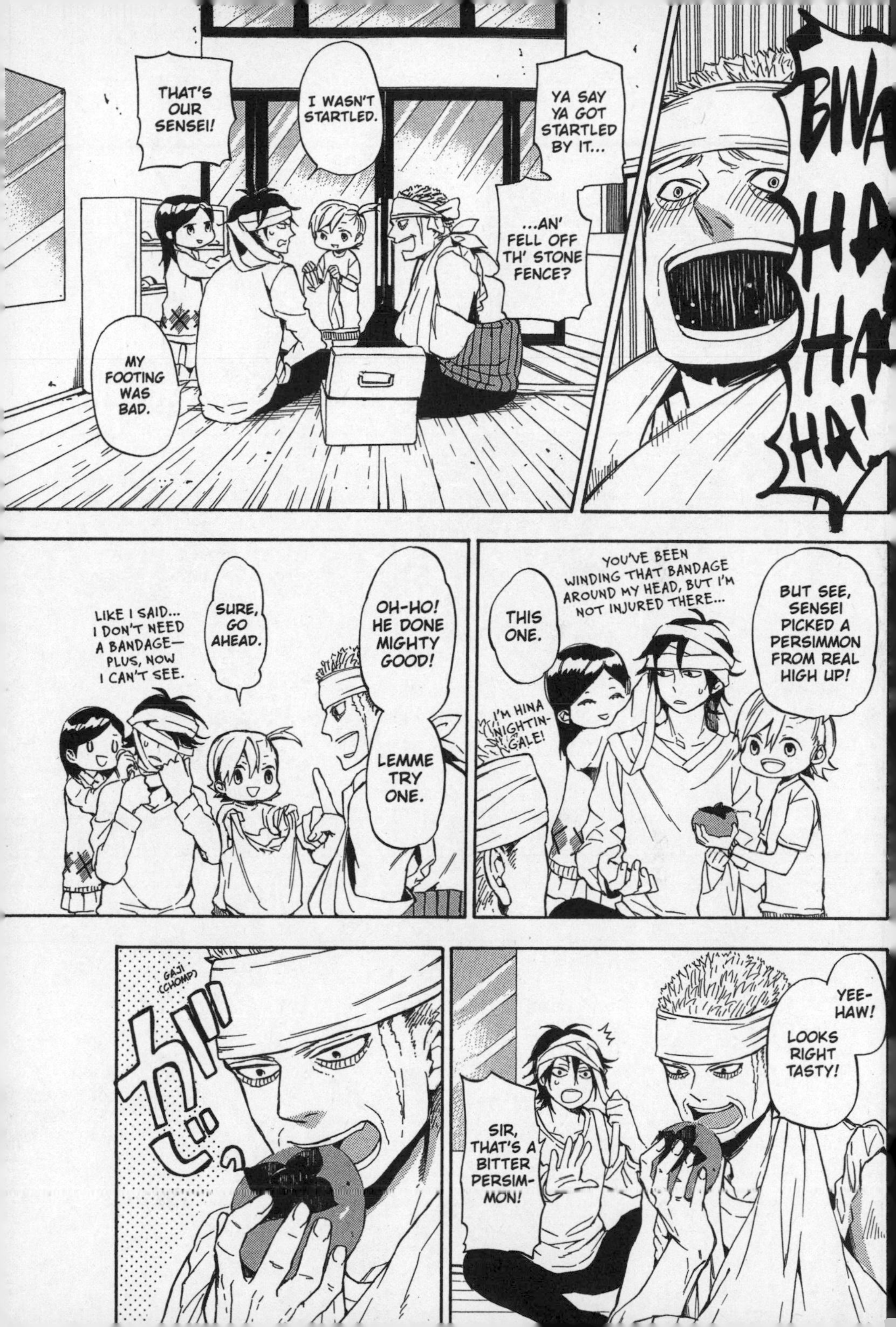
BWAHAHAHAHA!
YA SAY YA GOT STARTLED BY IT...
...AN' FELL OFF TH' STONE FENCE?
I WASN'T STARTLED.
THAT'S OUR SENSEI!
MY FOOTING WAS BAD.
BUT SEE, SENSEI PICKED A PERSIMMON FROM REAL HIGH UP!
YOU'VE BEEN WINDING THAT BANDAGE AROUND MY HEAD, BUT I'M NOT INJURED THERE...
THIS ONE.
I'M HINA NIGHTINGALE!
OH-HO! HE DONE MIGHTY GOOD!
LEMME TRY ONE.
SURE, GO AHEAD.
LIKE I SAID... I DON'T NEED A BANDAGE— PLUS, NOW I CAN'T SEE.
YEE-HAW!
LOOKS RIGHT TASTY!
SIR, THAT'S A BITTER PERSIMMON!
GAJI (CHOMP)

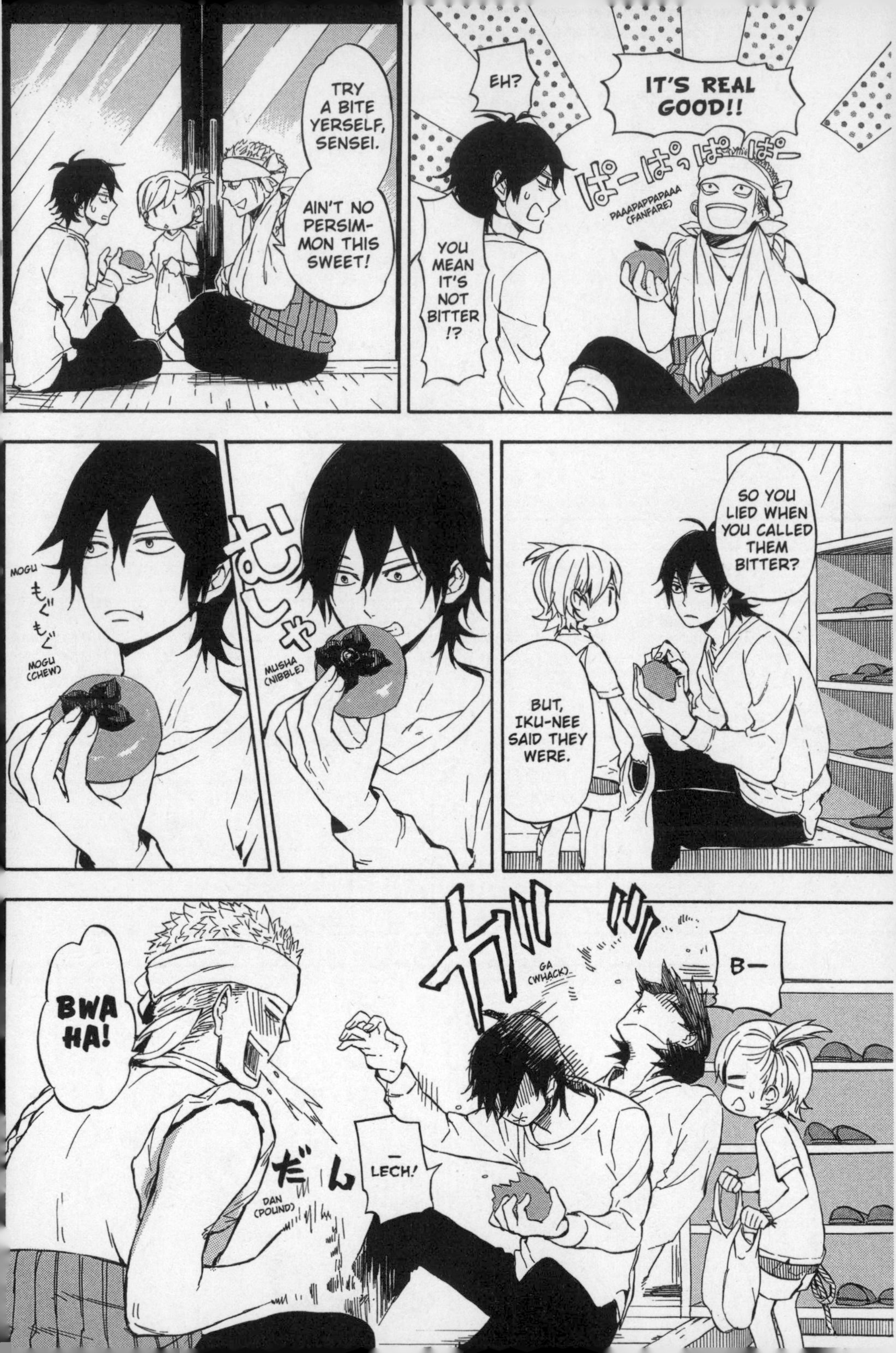
IT'S REAL GOOD!!
EH?
ぱーぱっぱっぱー
PAAAPAPPAPAAA (FANFARE)
YOU MEAN IT'S NOT BITTER!?
TRY A BITE YERSELF, SENSEI.
AIN'T NO PERSIMMON THIS SWEET!
SO YOU LIED WHEN YOU CALLED THEM BITTER?
BUT, IKU-NEE SAID THEY WERE.
むしゃ
MUSHA (NIBBLE)
MOGU
もぐもぐ
MOGU (CHEW)
B—
ガッ
GA (WHACK)
—LECH!
だん
DAN (POUND)
BWA HA!

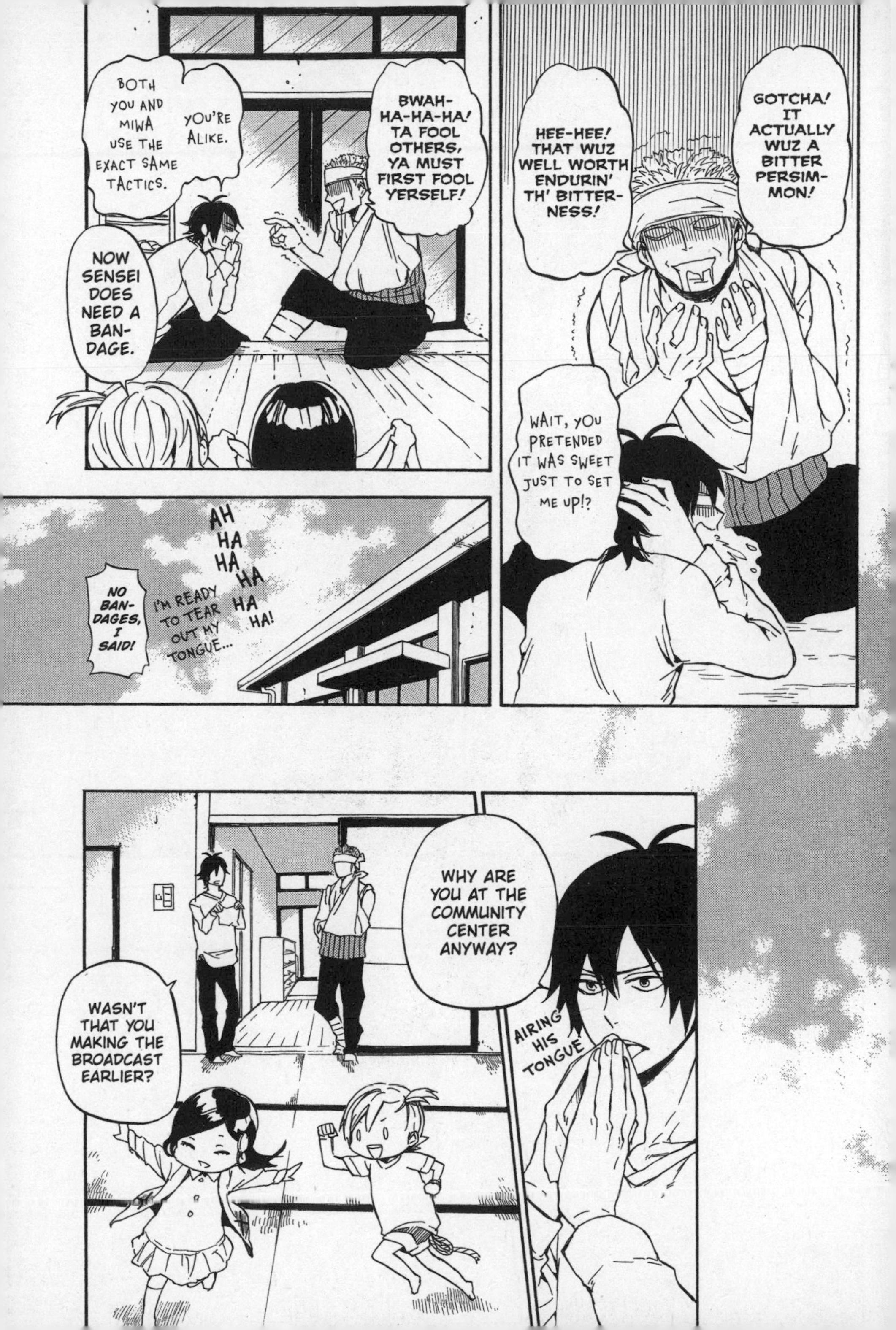
GOTCHA! IT ACTUALLY WUZ A BITTER PERSIMMON!
HEE-HEE! THAT WUZ WELL WORTH ENDURIN' TH' BITTER-NESS!
WAIT, YOU PRETENDED IT WAS SWEET JUST TO SET ME UP!?
BWAH-HA-HA-HA! TA FOOL OTHERS, YA MUST FIRST FOOL YERSELF!
BOTH YOU AND MIWA USE THE EXACT SAME TACTICS.
YOU'RE ALIKE.
NOW SENSEI DOES NEED A BAN-DAGE.
AH HA HA HA HA HA!
I'M READY TO TEAR OUT MY TONGUE...
NO BAN-DAGES, I SAID!
WHY ARE YOU AT THE COMMUNITY CENTER ANYWAY?
AIRING HIS TONGUE
WASN'T THAT YOU MAKING THE BROADCAST EARLIER?

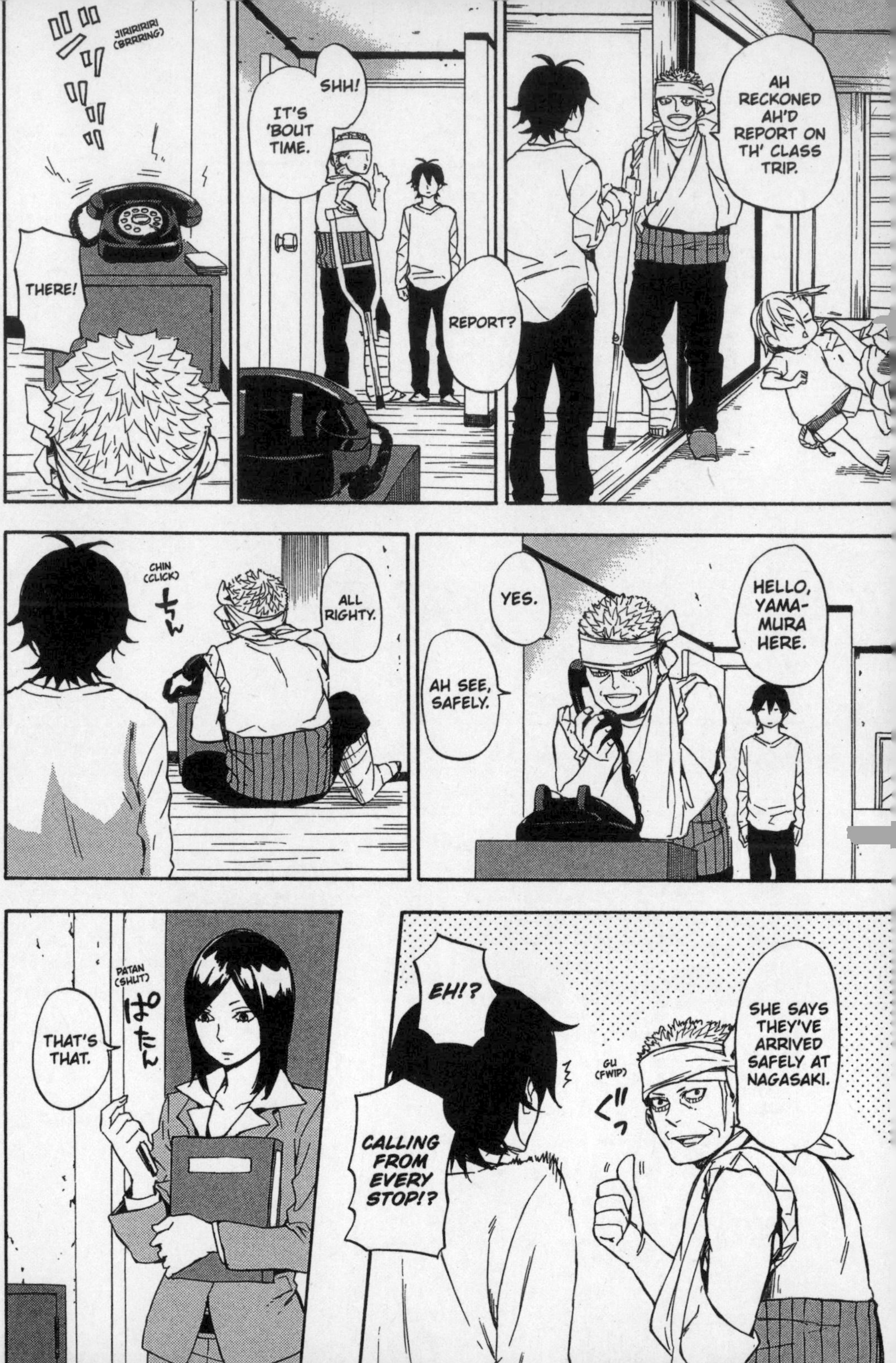
AH RECKONED AH'D REPORT ON TH' CLASS TRIP.
REPORT?
SHH!
IT'S 'BOUT TIME.
JIRIRIRIRI (BRRRING)
THERE!
HELLO, YAMA-MURA HERE.
YES.
AH SEE, SAFELY.
ALL RIGHTY.
CHIN (CLICK)
ちん
SHE SAYS THEY'VE ARRIVED SAFELY AT NAGASAKI.
GU (FWIP)
ぐっ
EH!?
CALLING FROM EVERY STOP!?
PATAN (SHUT)
ぱたん
THAT'S THAT.

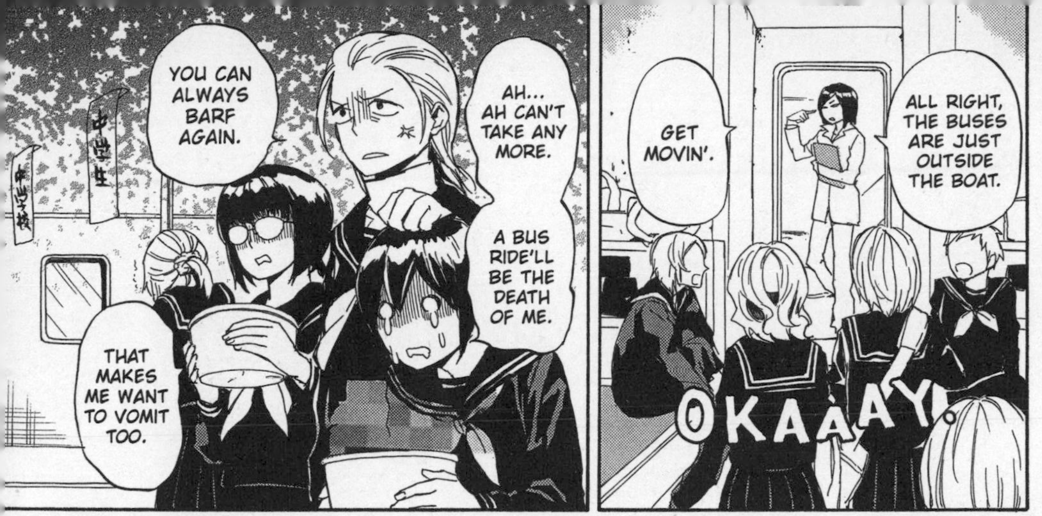
ALL RIGHT, THE BUSES ARE JUST OUTSIDE THE BOAT.
GET MOVIN'.
OKAAAY!
AH... AH CAN'T TAKE ANY MORE.
YOU CAN ALWAYS BARF AGAIN.
中学生
中学校
A BUS RIDE'LL BE THE DEATH OF ME.
THAT MAKES ME WANT TO VOMIT TOO.

BANNERS: MIDDLE SCHOOLERS

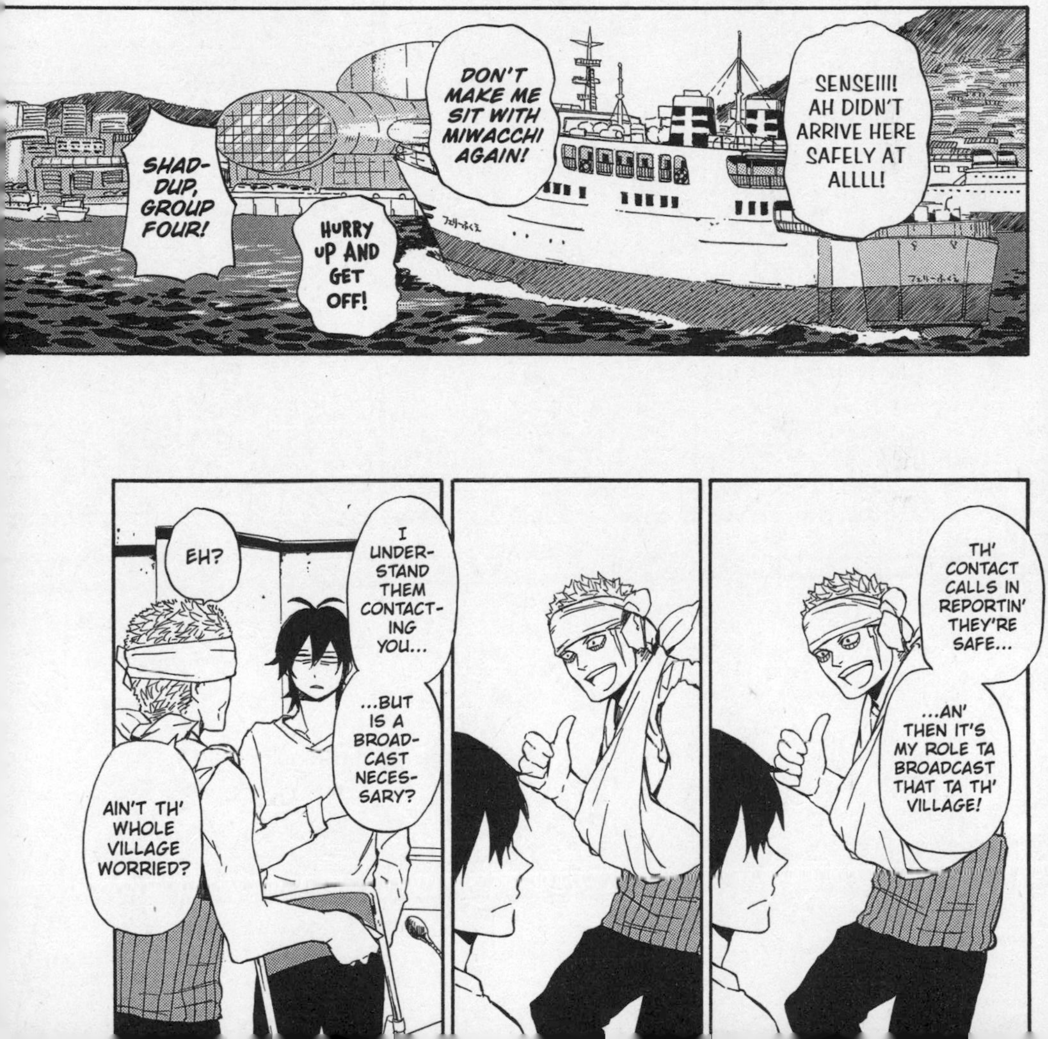
SENSEIII! AH DIDN'T ARRIVE HERE SAFELY AT ALLLL!
DON'T MAKE ME SIT WITH MIWACCHI AGAIN!
SHAD-DUP, GROUP FOUR!
HURRY UP AND GET OFF!
フェリーふくえ
TH' CONTACT CALLS IN REPORTIN' THEY'RE SAFE...
...AN' THEN IT'S MY ROLE TA BROADCAST THAT TA TH' VILLAGE!
I UNDER-STAND THEM CONTACT-ING YOU...
EH?
...BUT IS A BROAD-CAST NECES-SARY?
AIN'T TH' WHOLE VILLAGE WORRIED?

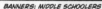

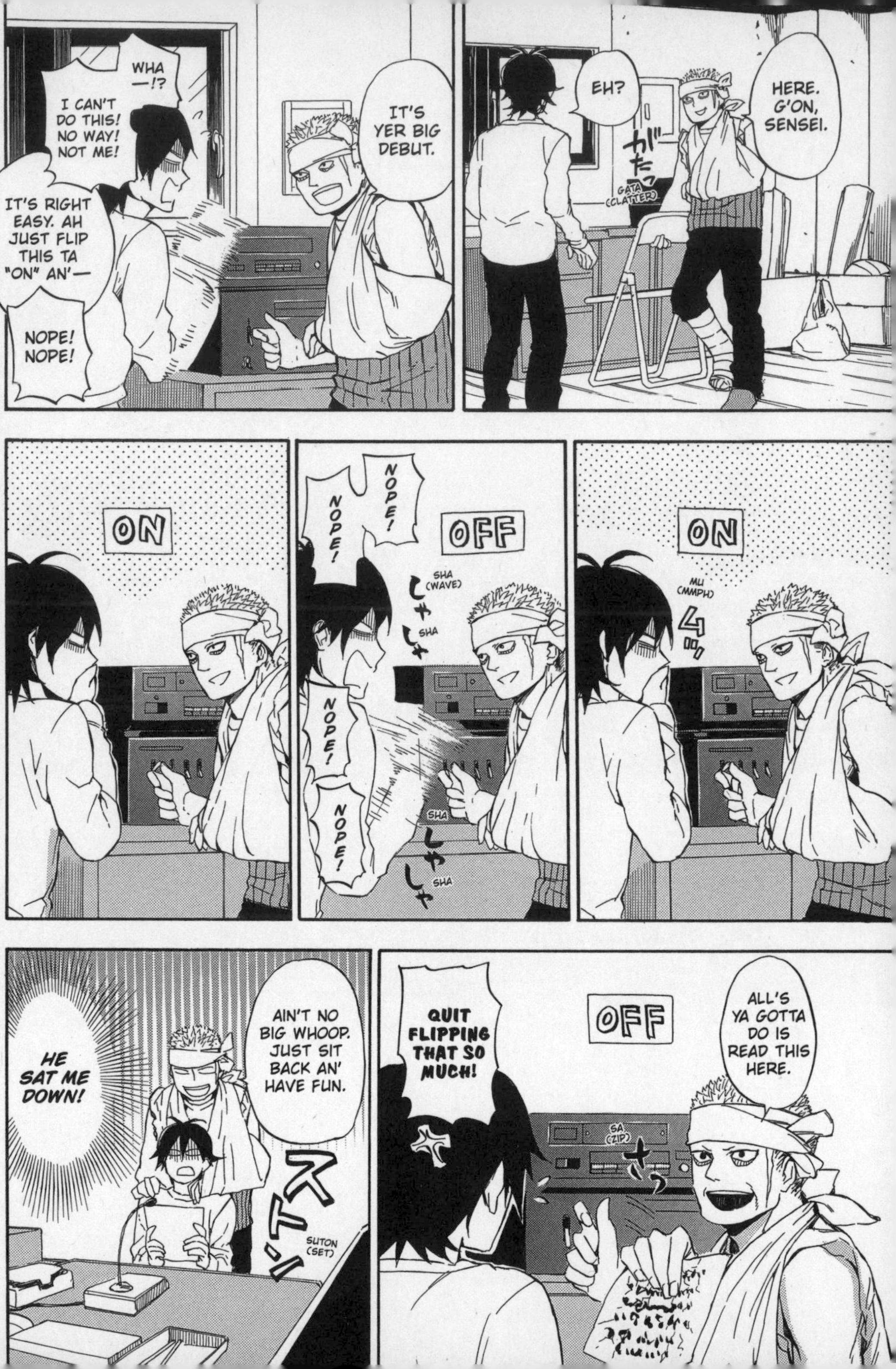
HERE. G'ON, SENSEI.
EH?
GATA (CLATTER)
IT'S YER BIG DEBUT.
WHA—!?
I CAN'T DO THIS! NO WAY! NOT ME!
IT'S RIGHT EASY. AH JUST FLIP THIS TA "ON" AN'—
NOPE! NOPE!
ON
MU (MMPH)
OFF
NOPE! NOPE!
SHA (WAVE)
SHA
NOPE! NOPE!
SHA
SHA
ON
OFF
ALL'S YA GOTTA DO IS READ THIS HERE.
QUIT FLIPPING THAT SO MUCH!
SA (ZIP)
AIN'T NO BIG WHOOP. JUST SIT BACK AN' HAVE FUN.
HE SAT ME DOWN!
SUTON (SET)

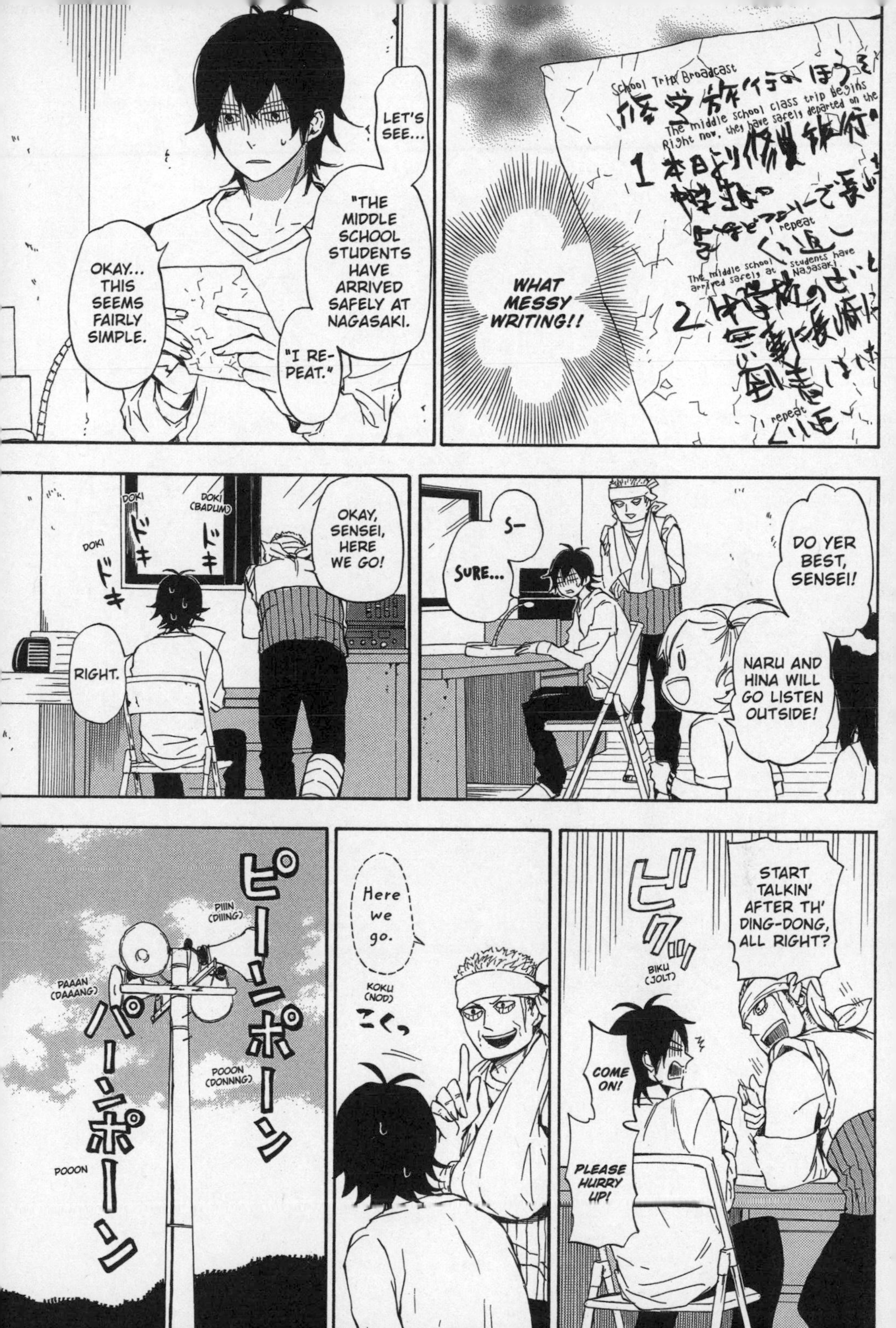
School Trip Broadcast
The middle school class trip begins
Right now, they have safely departed on the
I repeat
The middle school students have arrived safely at Nagasaki.
I repeat
WHAT MESSY WRITING!!
LET'S SEE...
"THE MIDDLE SCHOOL STUDENTS HAVE ARRIVED SAFELY AT NAGASAKI.
OKAY... THIS SEEMS FAIRLY SIMPLE.
"I RE-PEAT."
DO YER BEST, SENSEI!
S- SURE...
NARU AND HINA WILL GO LISTEN OUTSIDE!
OKAY, SENSEI, HERE WE GO!
DOKI (BADUM) ドキ
DOKI ドキ
DOKI ドキ
RIGHT.
START TALKIN' AFTER TH' DING-DONG, ALL RIGHT?
ビクッ
BIKU (JOLT)
COME ON!
PLEASE HURRY UP!
Here we go.
KOKU (NOD)
こくっ
ピーンポーン
PIIIN (DIIING)
PAAAN (DAAANG)
パーンポーン
POOON (DONNNG)
POOON

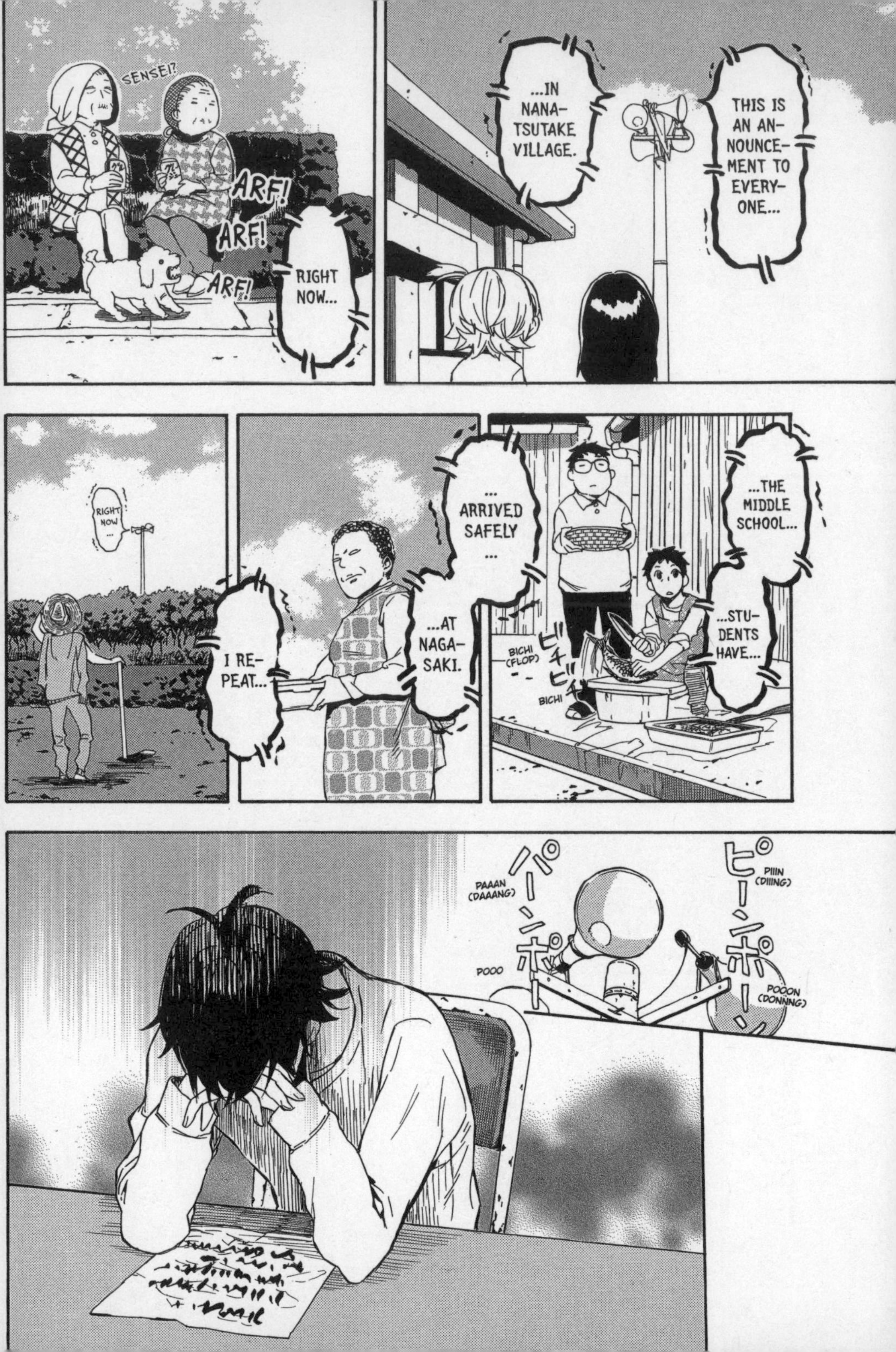
THIS IS AN ANNOUNCE-MENT TO EVERY-ONE...
...IN NANA-TSUTAKE VILLAGE.
RIGHT NOW...
SENSEI!?
ARF!
ARF!
ARF!
...THE MIDDLE SCHOOL...
...STU-DENTS HAVE...
ビチビチ
BICHI (FLOP)
BICHI
... ARRIVED SAFELY ...
...AT NAGA-SAKI.
I RE-PEAT...
RIGHT NOW ...
ピーンポーン
PIIIN (DIIING)
POOON (DONNNG)
パーンポ
PAAAN (DAAANG)
POOO

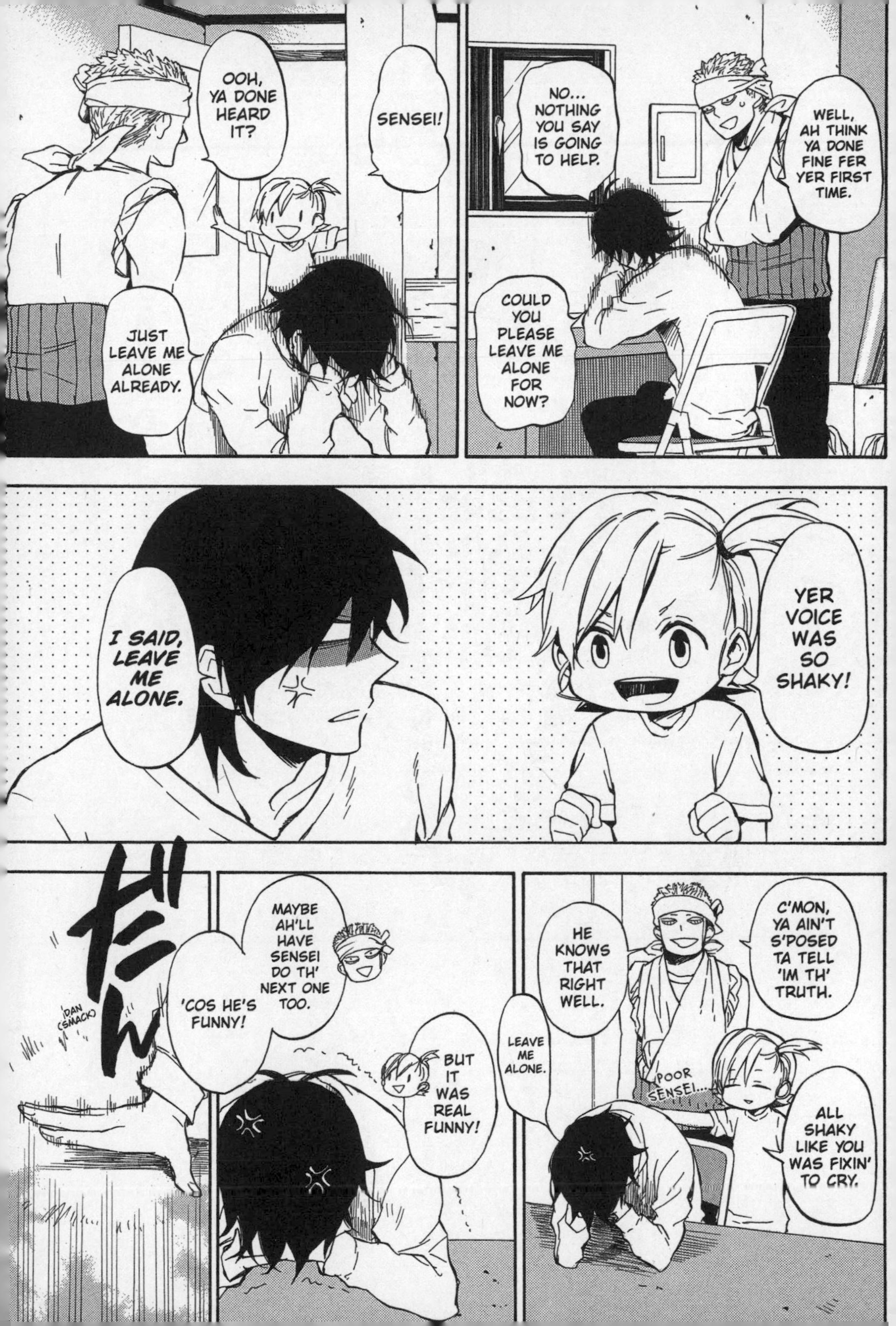

WELL, AH THINK YA DONE FINE FER YER FIRST TIME.
NO... NOTHING YOU SAY IS GOING TO HELP.
COULD YOU PLEASE LEAVE ME ALONE FOR NOW?
SENSEI!
OOH, YA DONE HEARD IT?
JUST LEAVE ME ALONE ALREADY.
YER VOICE WAS SO SHAKY!
I SAID, LEAVE ME ALONE.
C'MON, YA AIN'T S'POSED TA TELL 'IM TH' TRUTH.
HE KNOWS THAT RIGHT WELL.
POOR SENSEI...
ALL SHAKY LIKE YOU WAS FIXIN' TO CRY.
LEAVE ME ALONE.
MAYBE AH'LL HAVE SENSEI DO TH' NEXT ONE TOO.
'COS HE'S FUNNY!
BUT IT WAS REAL FUNNY!
DAN (SMACK)

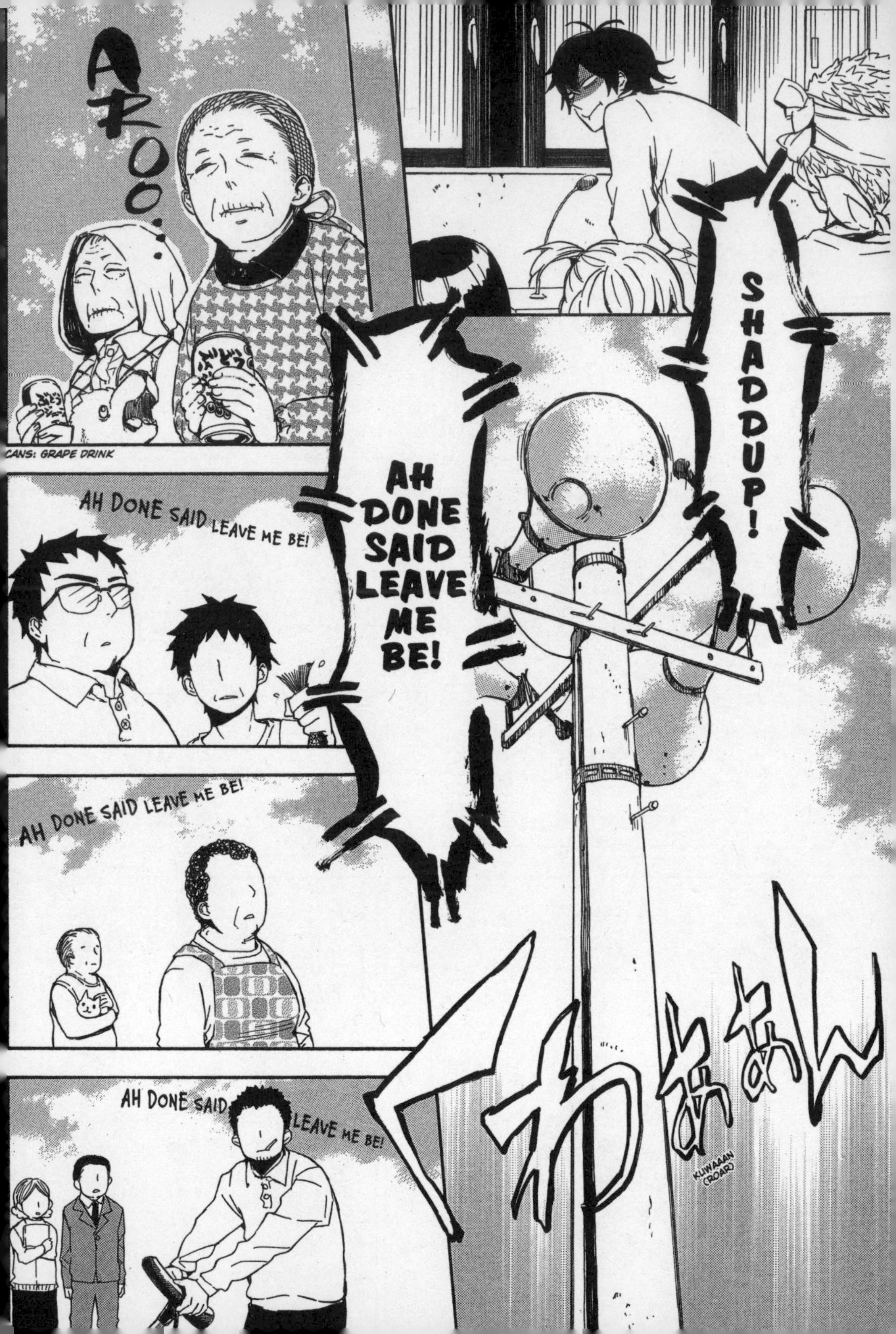

SHADDUP!
AROO...
CANS: GRAPE DRINK
AH DONE SAID LEAVE ME BE!
KUWAAAN (ROAR)
AH DONE SAID LEAVE ME BE!
AH DONE SAID LEAVE ME BE!
AH DONE SAID LEAVE ME BE!

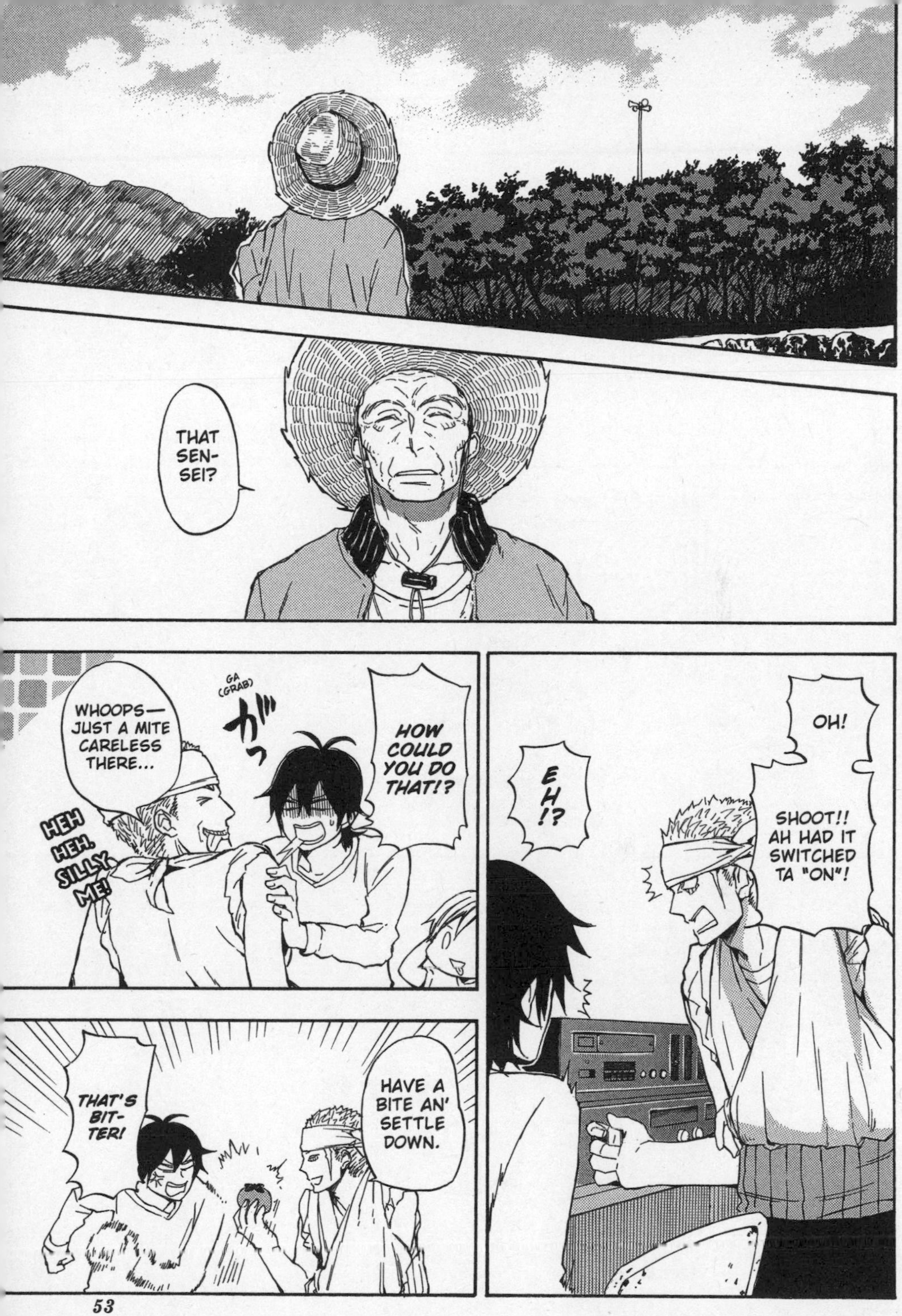
THAT SEN-SEI?
OH!
SHOOT!! AH HAD IT SWITCHED TA "ON"!
EH!?
HOW COULD YOU DO THAT!?
GA (GRAB)
WHOOPS— JUST A MITE CARELESS THERE...
HEH HEH. SILLY ME!
HAVE A BITE AN' SETTLE DOWN.
THAT'S BIT-TER!

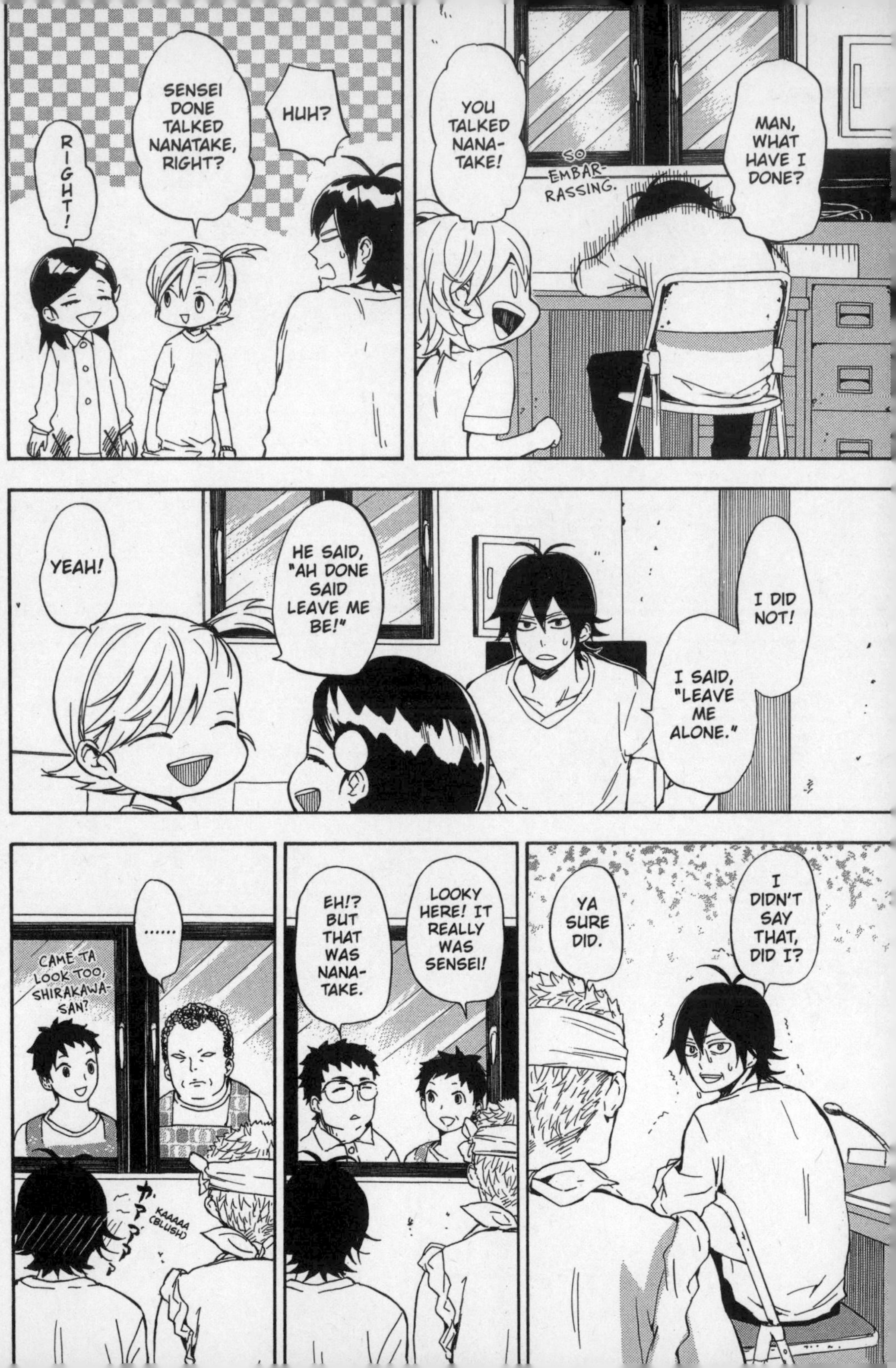
MAN, WHAT HAVE I DONE?
SO EMBARRASSING.
YOU TALKED NANATAKE!
HUH?
SENSEI DONE TALKED NANATAKE, RIGHT?
RIGHT!
I DID NOT!
I SAID, "LEAVE ME ALONE."
HE SAID, "AH DONE SAID LEAVE ME BE!"
YEAH!
I DIDN'T SAY THAT, DID I?
YA SURE DID.
LOOKY HERE! IT REALLY WAS SENSEI!
EH!? BUT THAT WAS NANA-TAKE.
......
CAME TA LOOK TOO, SHIRAKAWA-SAN?
KAAAAA (BLUSH)

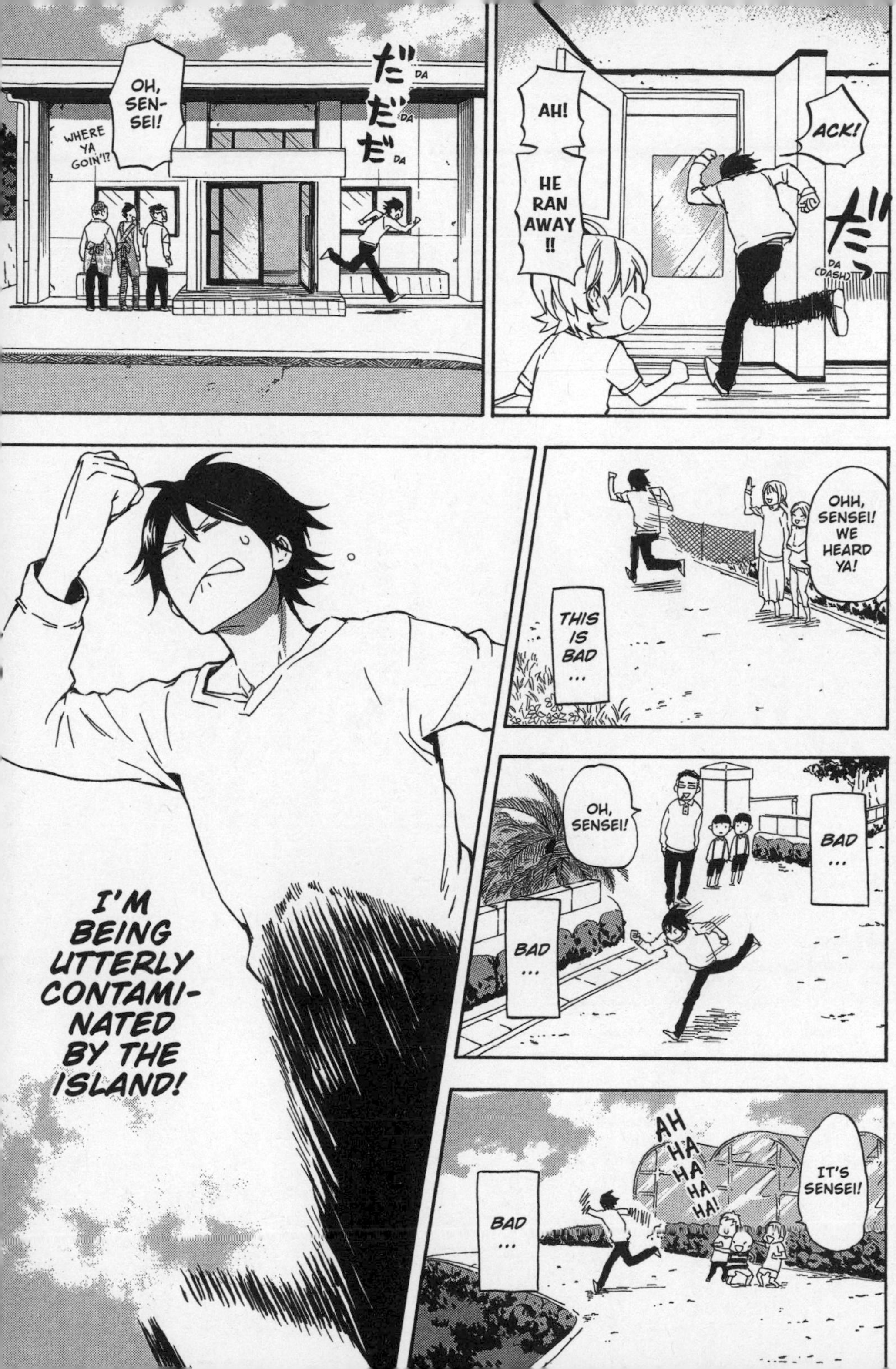
ACK!
AH!
HE RAN AWAY!!
だっ
DA (DASH)
OH, SEN-SEI!
WHERE YA GOIN'!?
だ DA
だ DA
だ DA
OHH, SENSEI! WE HEARD YA!
THIS IS BAD...
BAD...
OH, SENSEI!
BAD...
IT'S SENSEI!
AH HA HA HA HA!
BAD...
I'M BEING UTTERLY CONTAMI-NATED BY THE ISLAND!

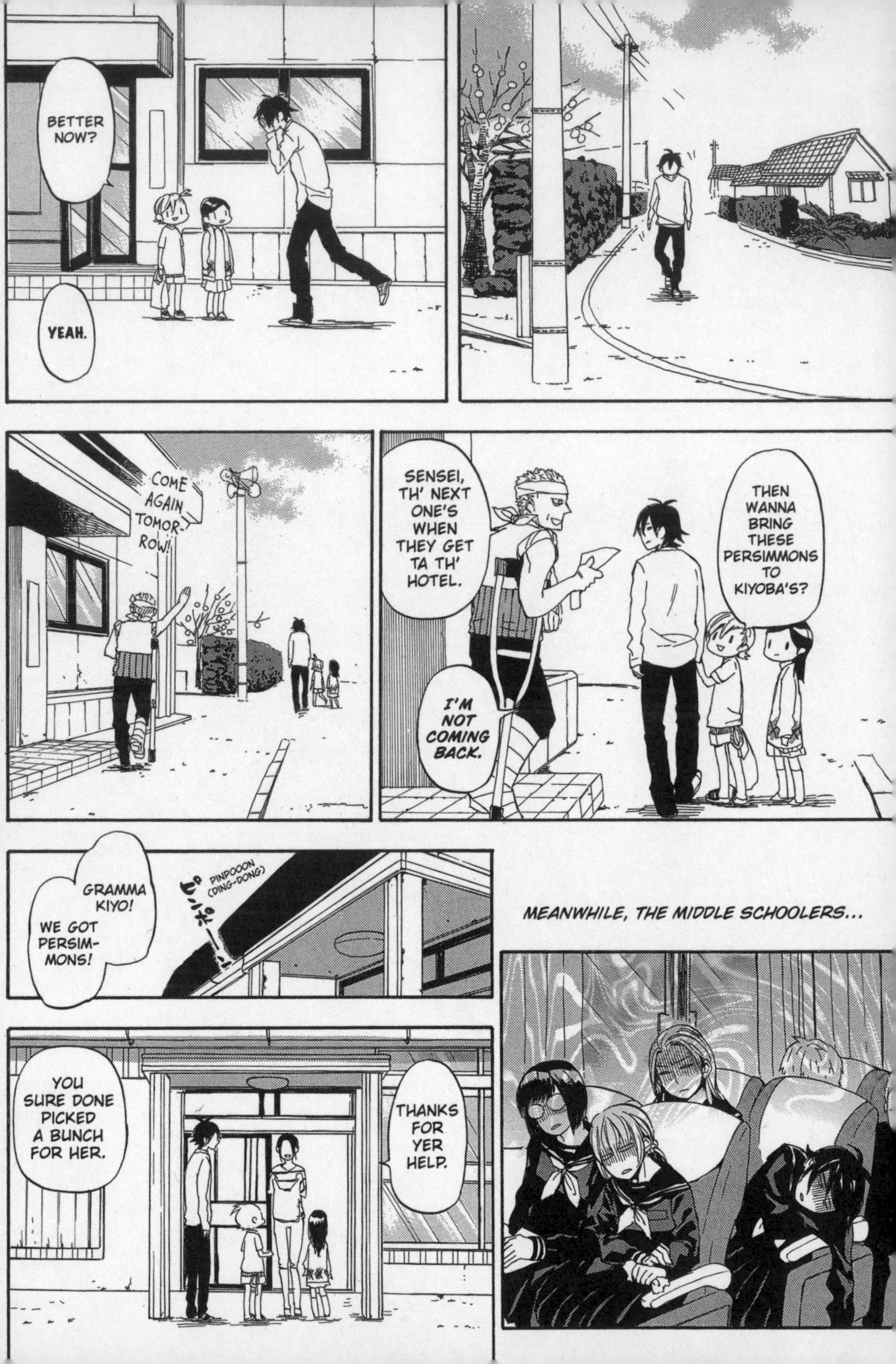
BETTER NOW?
YEAH.
THEN WANNA BRING THESE PERSIMMONS TO KIYOBA'S?
SENSEI, TH' NEXT ONE'S WHEN THEY GET TA TH' HOTEL.
I'M NOT COMING BACK.
COME AGAIN TOMOR-ROW!
MEANWHILE, THE MIDDLE SCHOOLERS...
PINPOOON (DING-DONG)
GRAMMA KIYO! WE GOT PERSIM-MONS!
THANKS FOR YER HELP.
YOU SURE DONE PICKED A BUNCH FOR HER.

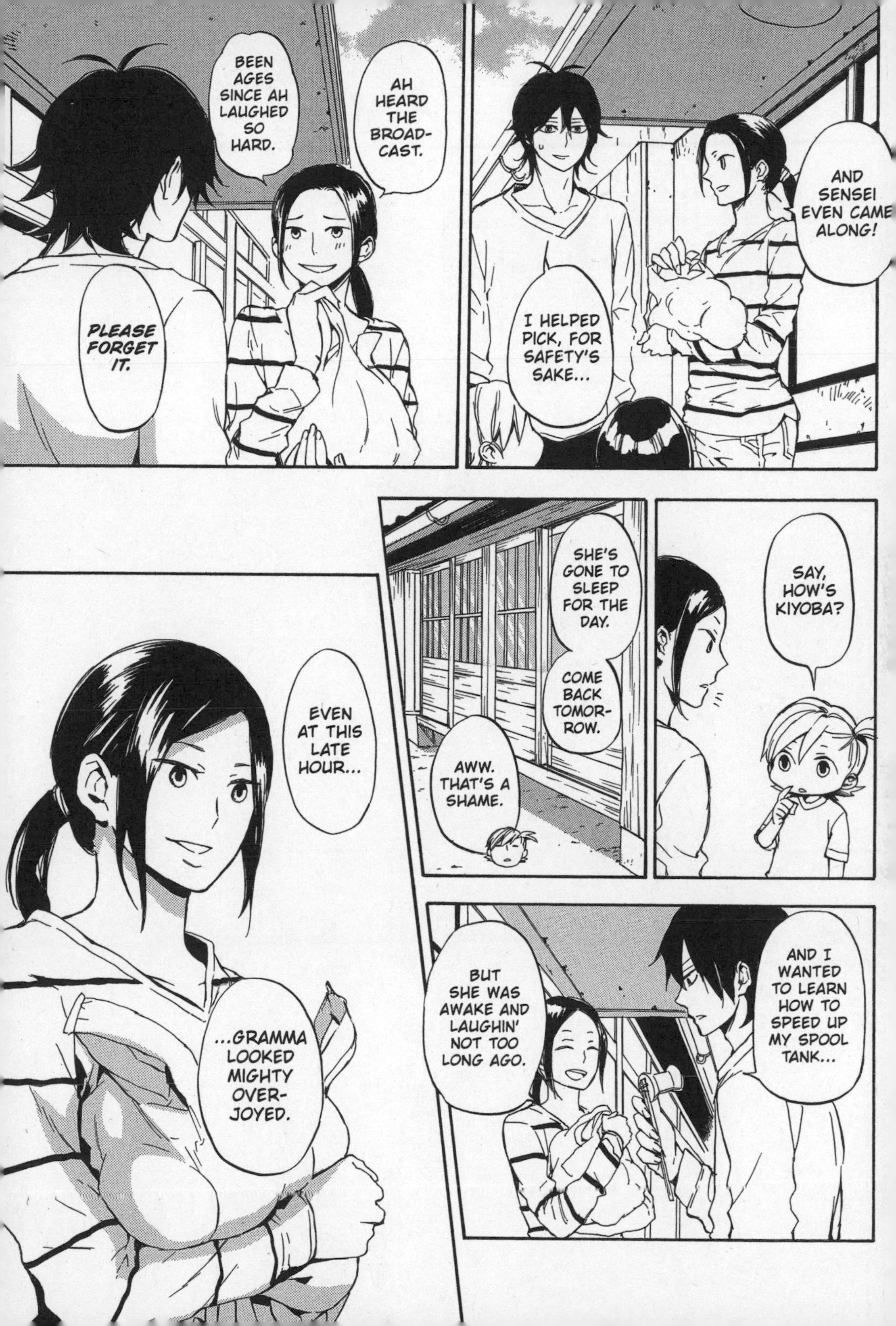
AND SENSEI EVEN CAME ALONG!
I HELPED PICK, FOR SAFETY'S SAKE...
AH HEARD THE BROAD-CAST.
BEEN AGES SINCE AH LAUGHED SO HARD.
PLEASE FORGET IT.
SAY, HOW'S KIYOBA?
SHE'S GONE TO SLEEP FOR THE DAY.
COME BACK TOMOR-ROW.
AWW. THAT'S A SHAME.
AND I WANTED TO LEARN HOW TO SPEED UP MY SPOOL TANK...
BUT SHE WAS AWAKE AND LAUGHIN' NOT TOO LONG AGO.
EVEN AT THIS LATE HOUR...
...GRAMMA LOOKED MIGHTY OVER-JOYED.

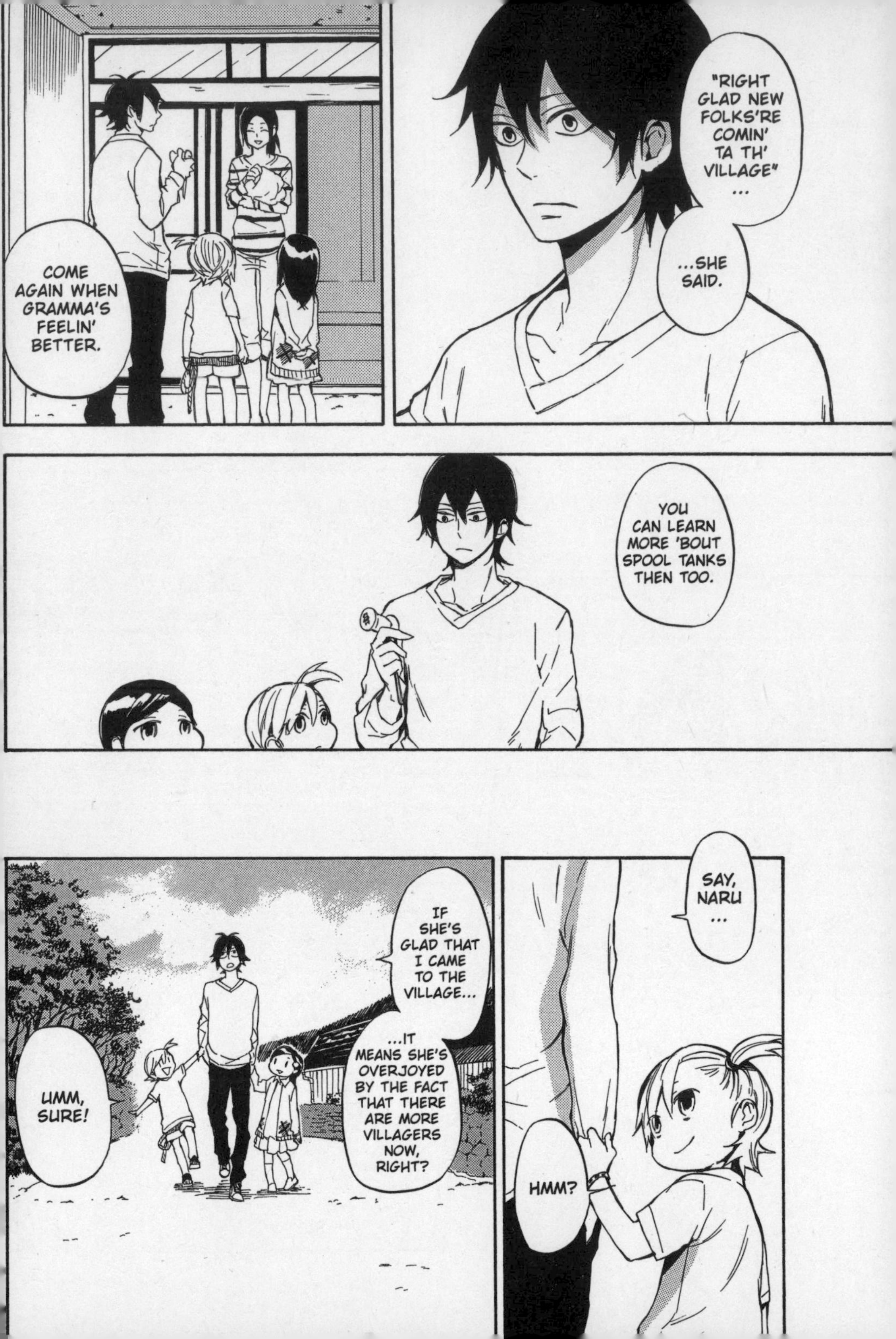
"RIGHT GLAD NEW FOLKS'RE COMIN' TA TH' VILLAGE" ...
...SHE SAID.
COME AGAIN WHEN GRAMMA'S FEELIN' BETTER.
YOU CAN LEARN MORE 'BOUT SPOOL TANKS THEN TOO.
SAY, NARU ...
HMM?
IF SHE'S GLAD THAT I CAME TO THE VILLAGE...
...IT MEANS SHE'S OVERJOYED BY THE FACT THAT THERE ARE MORE VILLAGERS NOW, RIGHT?
UMM, SURE!

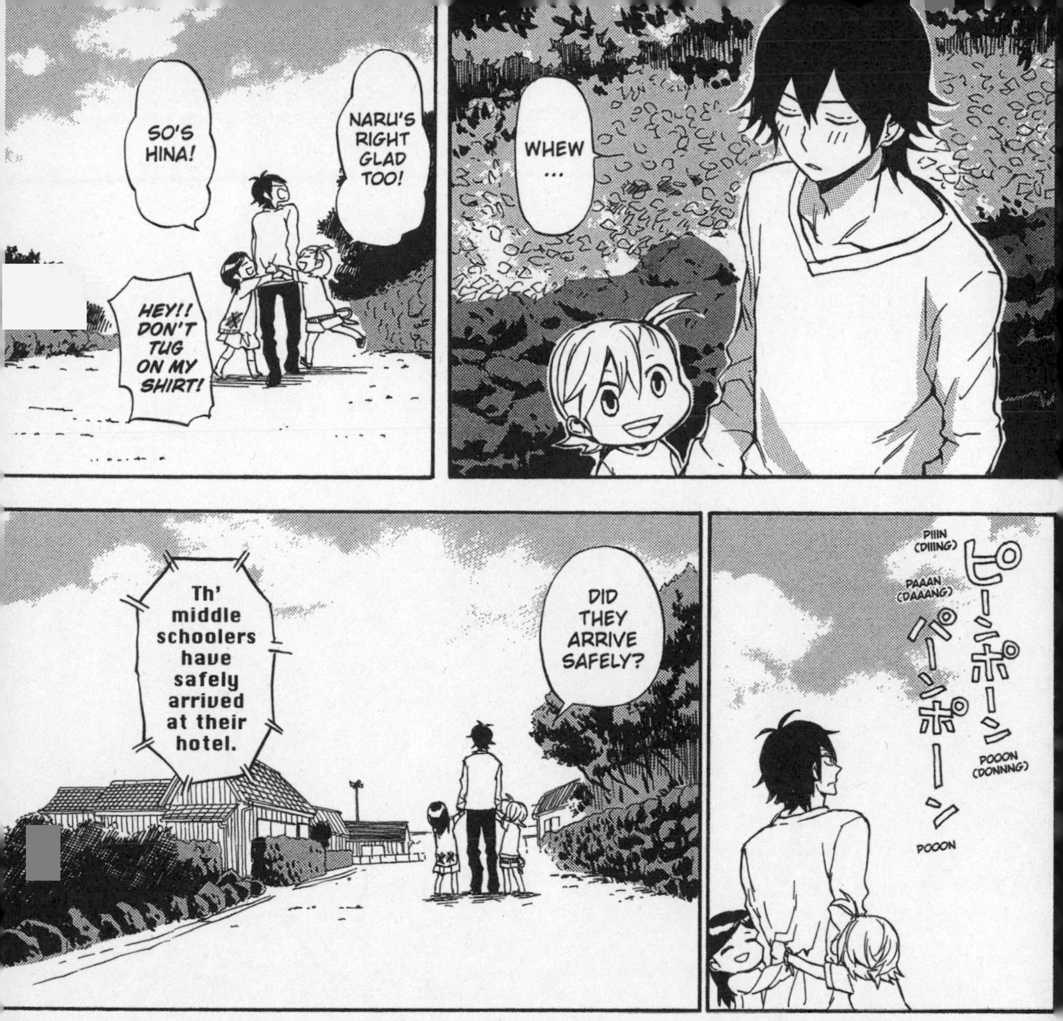
WHEW ...
NARU'S RIGHT GLAD TOO!
SO'S HINA!
HEY!! DON'T TUG ON MY SHIRT!
PIIIN (DIIING)
PAAAN (DAAANG)
POOON (DONNNG)
POOON
DID THEY ARRIVE SAFELY?
Th' middle schoolers have safely arrived at their hotel.

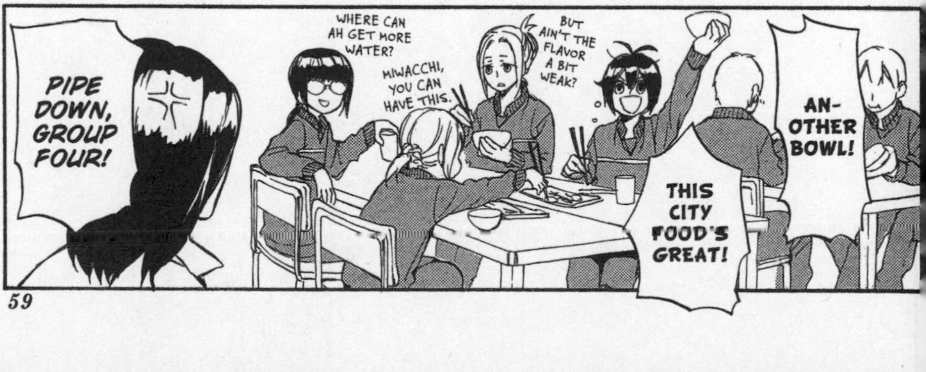
AN-OTHER BOWL!
THIS CITY FOOD'S GREAT!
BUT AIN'T THE FLAVOR A BIT WEAK?
MIWACCHI, YOU CAN HAVE THIS.
WHERE CAN AH GET MORE WATER?
PIPE DOWN, GROUP FOUR!

NAMU...

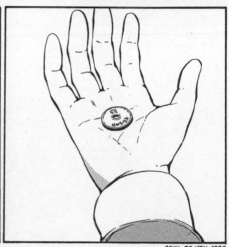

COIN: 50 YEN, 1980

THERE!

KA
CTINK!

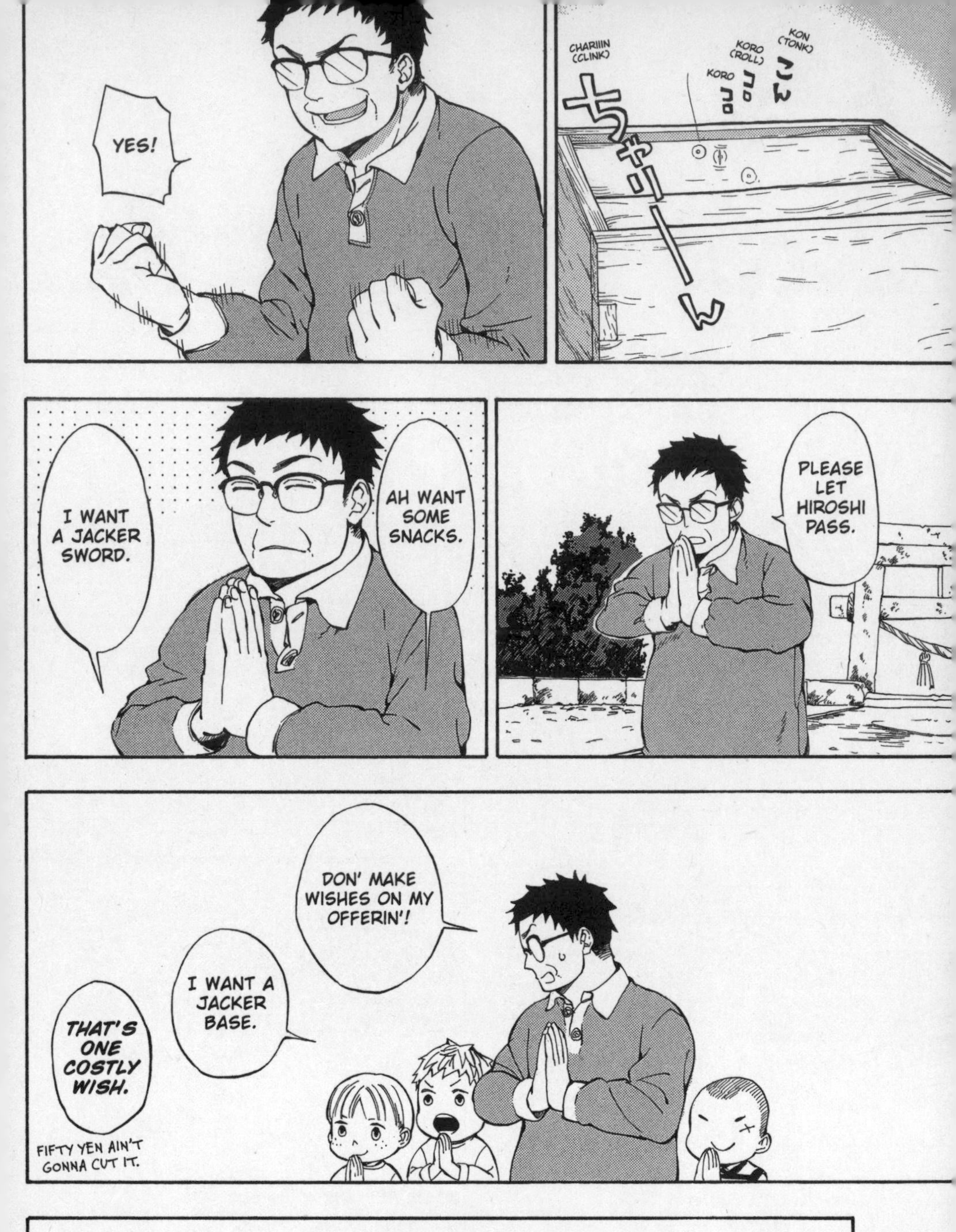
KON (TONK)
こん
KORO (ROLL)
KORO
ころころ
CHARIIIN (CLINK)
ちゃりーーん
YES!
PLEASE LET HIROSHI PASS.
AH WANT SOME SNACKS.
I WANT A JACKER SWORD.
DON' MAKE WISHES ON MY OFFERIN'!
I WANT A JACKER BASE.
THAT'S ONE COSTLY WISH.
FIFTY YEN AIN'T GONNA CUT IT.

ACT.63
UKARUGOTE
(Translation: So That He'll Pass)

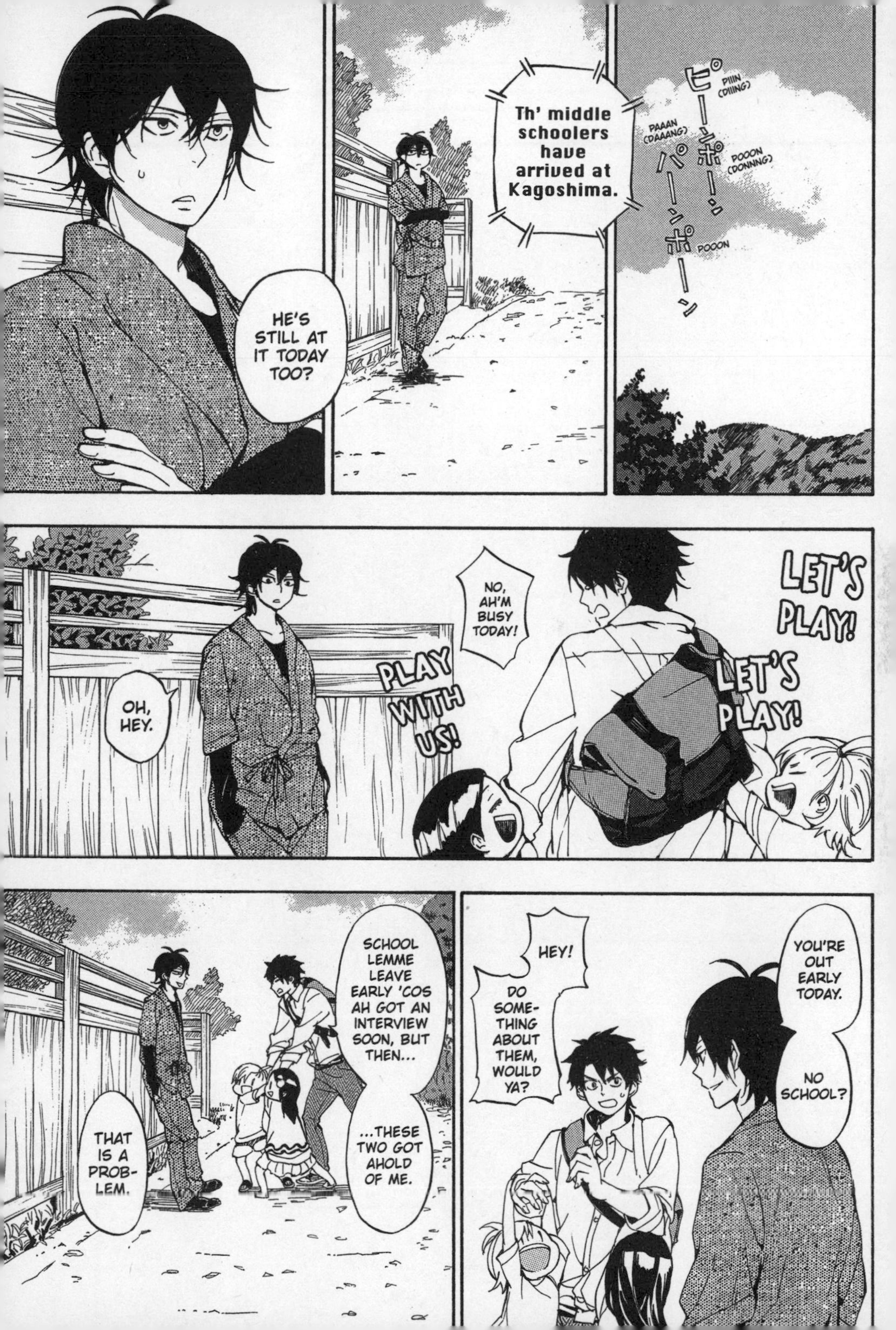
ピーンポーン
PIIIN (DIIING)
POOON (DONNNG)
パーンポーン
PAAAN (DAAANG)
POOON
Th' middle schoolers have arrived at Kagoshima.
HE'S STILL AT IT TODAY TOO?
LET'S PLAY!
LET'S PLAY!
NO, AH'M BUSY TODAY!
PLAY WITH US!
OH, HEY.
YOU'RE OUT EARLY TODAY.
NO SCHOOL?
HEY!
DO SOMETHING ABOUT THEM, WOULD YA?
SCHOOL LEMME LEAVE EARLY 'COS AH GOT AN INTERVIEW SOON, BUT THEN...
...THESE TWO GOT AHOLD OF ME.
THAT IS A PROBLEM.

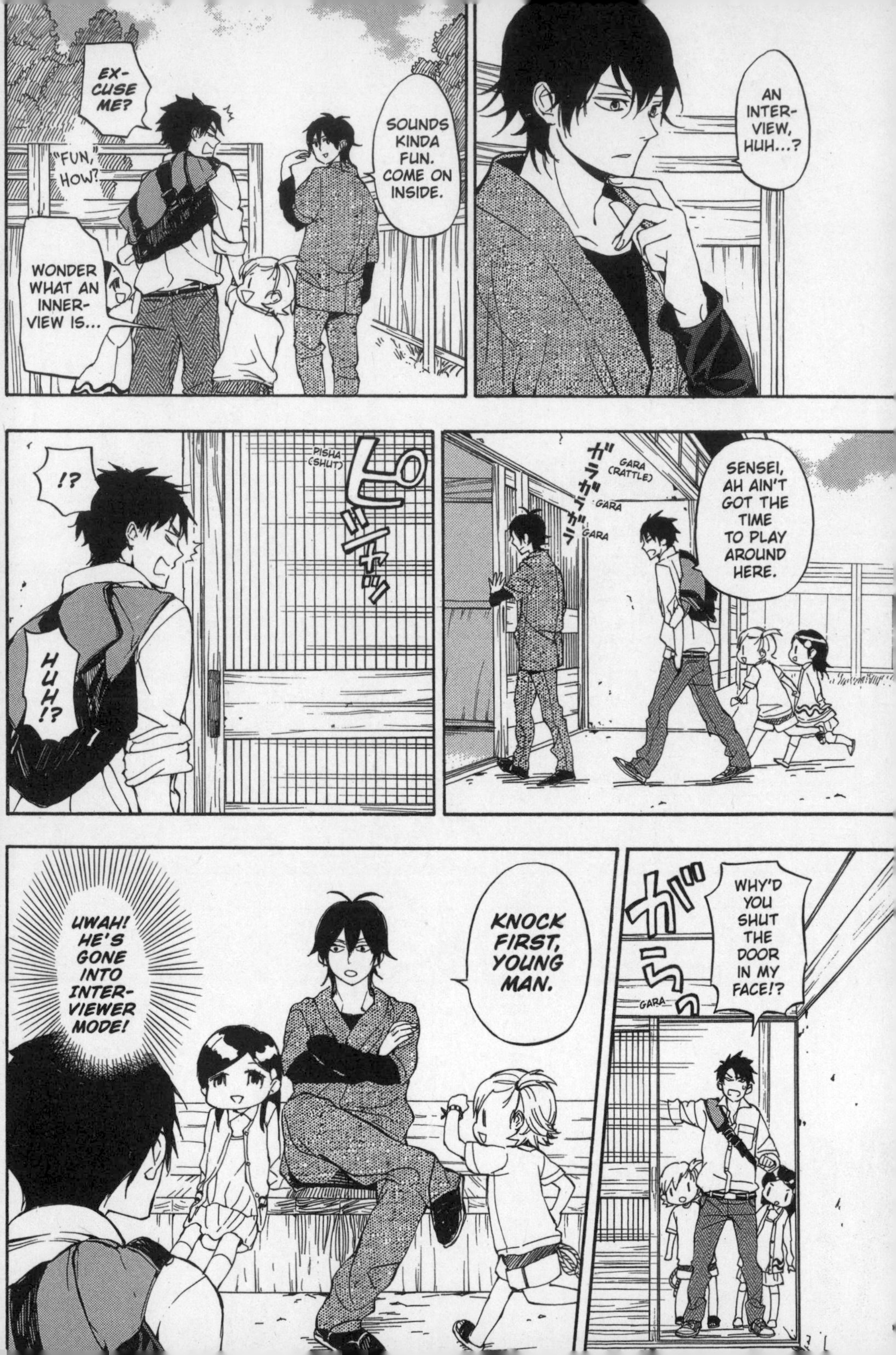
AN INTERVIEW, HUH...?
SOUNDS KINDA FUN. COME ON INSIDE.
EX-CUSE ME?
"FUN," HOW?
WONDER WHAT AN INNER-VIEW IS...
SENSEI, AH AIN'T GOT THE TIME TO PLAY AROUND HERE.
GARA (RATTLE)
GARA
GARA
PISHA (SHUT)
!?
HUH!?
WHY'D YOU SHUT THE DOOR IN MY FACE!?
GARA
KNOCK FIRST, YOUNG MAN.
UWAH! HE'S GONE INTO INTER-VIEWER MODE!

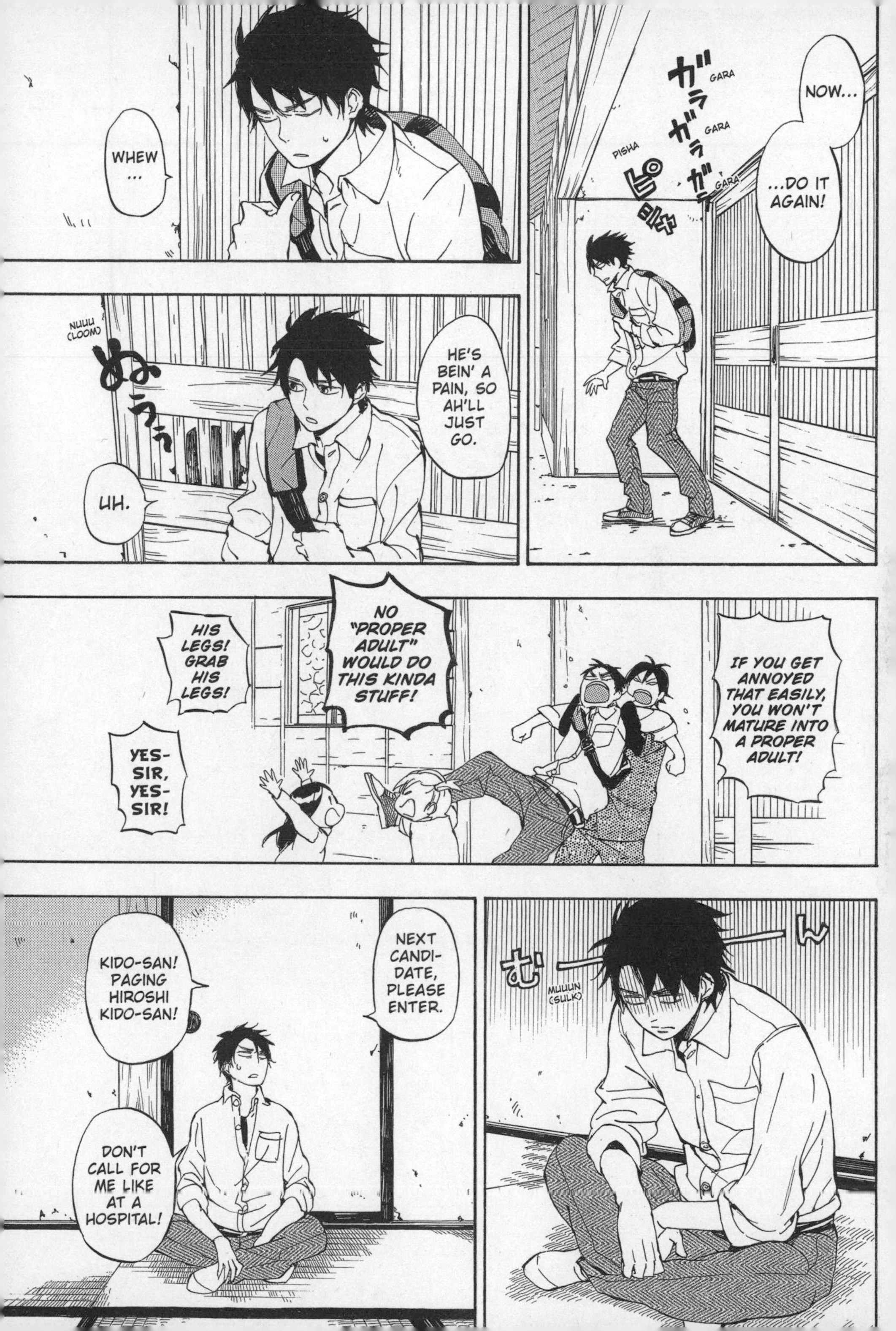
NOW...
...DO IT AGAIN!
GARA
GARA
GARA
PISHA
WHEW...
NUUU (LOOM)
HE'S BEIN' A PAIN, SO AH'LL JUST GO.
UH.
IF YOU GET ANNOYED THAT EASILY, YOU WON'T MATURE INTO A PROPER ADULT!
NO "PROPER ADULT" WOULD DO THIS KINDA STUFF!
HIS LEGS! GRAB HIS LEGS!
YES-SIR, YES-SIR!
MUUUN (SULK)
NEXT CANDI-DATE, PLEASE ENTER.
KIDO-SAN! PAGING HIROSHI KIDO-SAN!
DON'T CALL FOR ME LIKE AT A HOSPITAL!

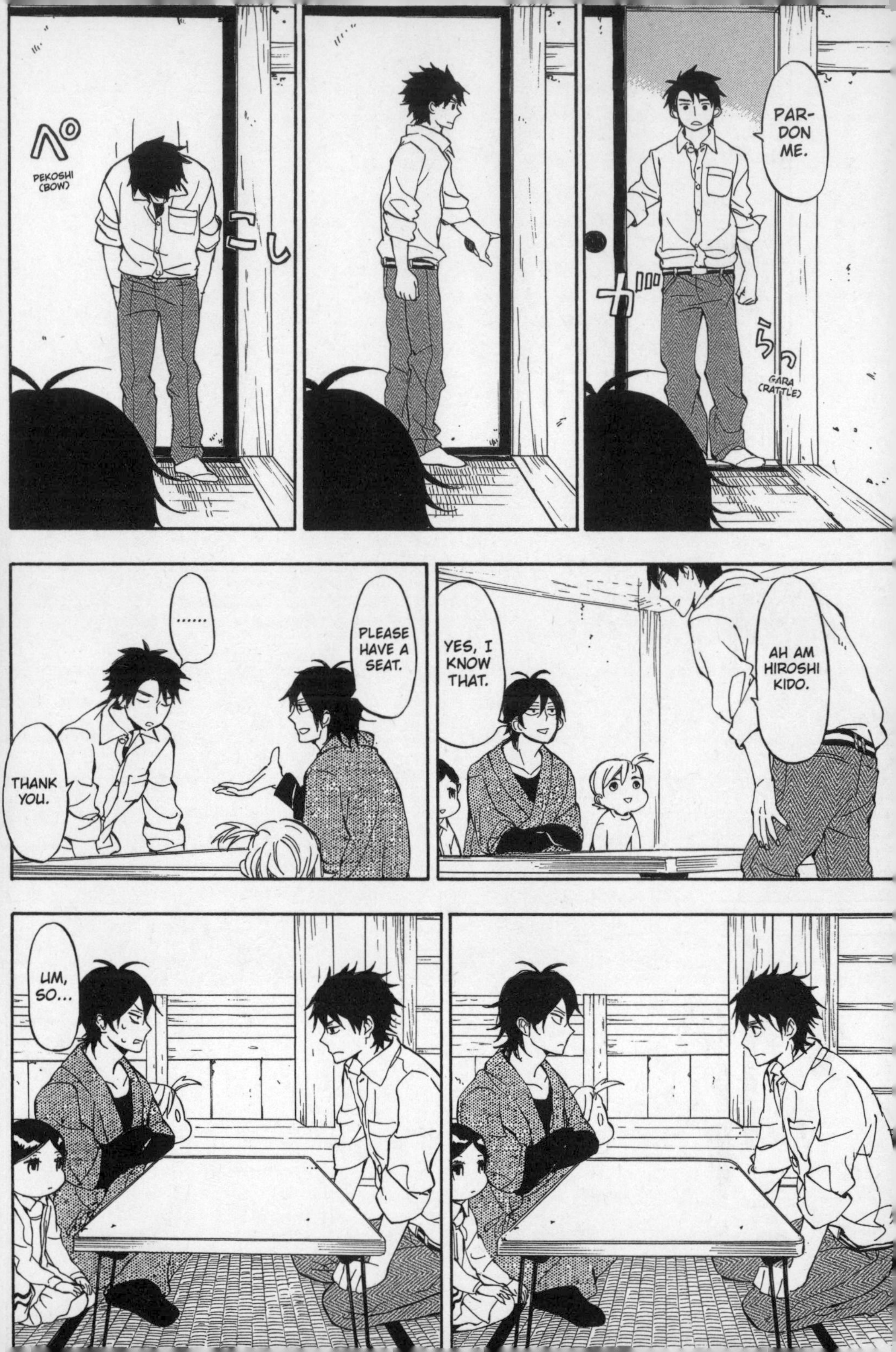
PAR-DON ME.
GARA (RATTLE)
PEKOSHI (BOW)
AH AM HIROSHI KIDO.
YES, I KNOW THAT.
PLEASE HAVE A SEAT.
......
THANK YOU.
UM, SO...

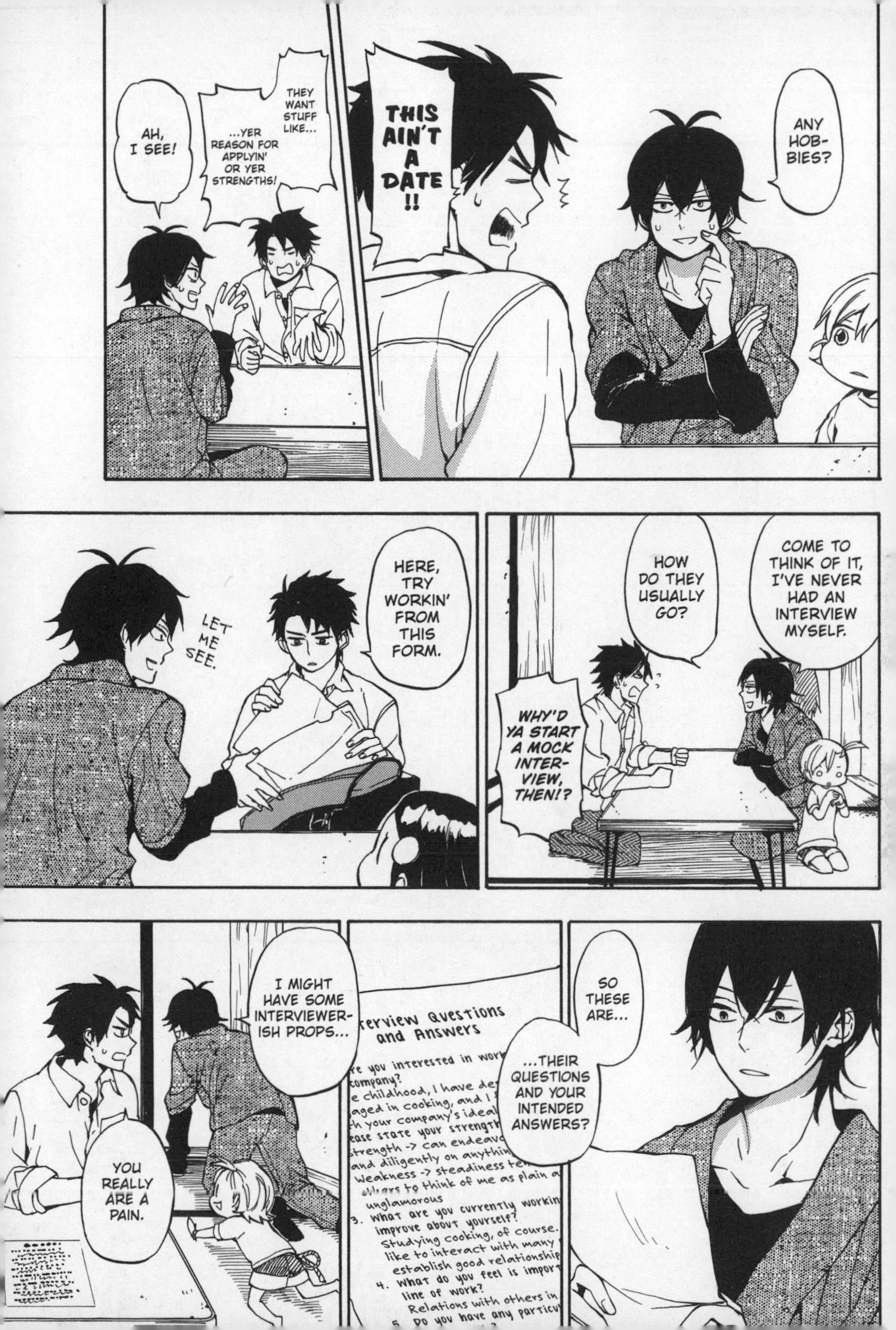
ANY HOB-BIES?
THIS AIN'T A DATE!!
THEY WANT STUFF LIKE...
...YER REASON FOR APPLYIN' OR YER STRENGTHS!
AH, I SEE!
COME TO THINK OF IT, I'VE NEVER HAD AN INTERVIEW MYSELF.
HOW DO THEY USUALLY GO?
WHY'D YA START A MOCK INTERVIEW, THEN!?
HERE, TRY WORKIN' FROM THIS FORM.
LET ME SEE.
SO THESE ARE...
...THEIR QUESTIONS AND YOUR INTENDED ANSWERS?
terview Questions and Answers
re you interested in work
company?
e childhood, I have de
aged in cooking, and I
h your company's ideal
ease state your strength
strength -> can endeav
and diligently on anythin
Weakness -> steadiness te
others to think of me as plain a
unglamorous
3. What are you currently workin
improve about yourself?
Studying cooking, of course.
like to interact with many
establish good relationship
4. What do you feel is impor
line of work?
Relations with others in
5. Do you have any particu
I MIGHT HAVE SOME INTERVIEWER-ISH PROPS...
YOU REALLY ARE A PAIN.

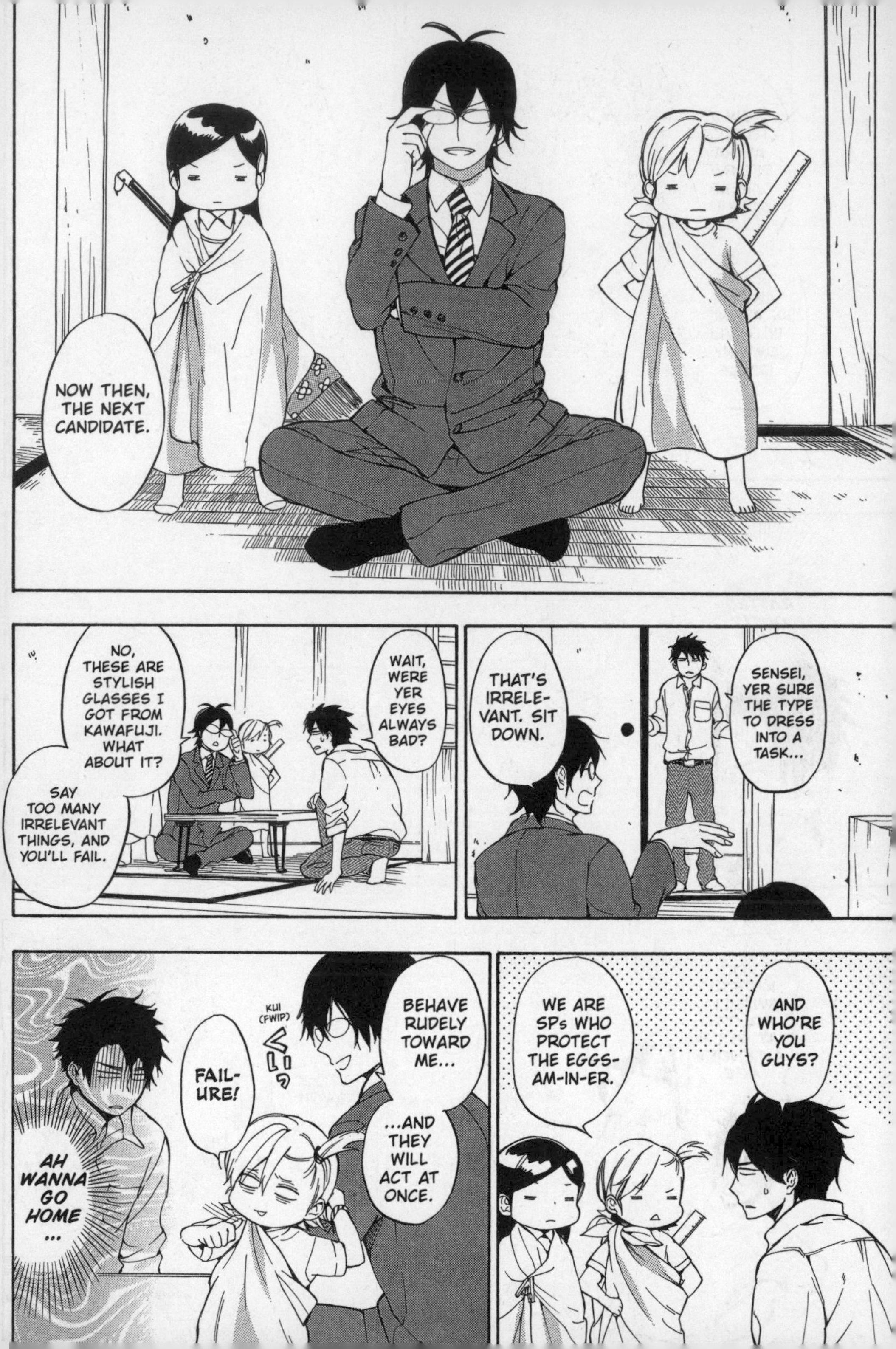
NOW THEN, THE NEXT CANDIDATE.
SENSEI, YER SURE THE TYPE TO DRESS INTO A TASK...
THAT'S IRRELEVANT. SIT DOWN.
WAIT, WERE YER EYES ALWAYS BAD?
NO, THESE ARE STYLISH GLASSES I GOT FROM KAWAFUJI. WHAT ABOUT IT?
SAY TOO MANY IRRELEVANT THINGS, AND YOU'LL FAIL.
AND WHO'RE YOU GUYS?
WE ARE SPs WHO PROTECT THE EGGS-AM-IN-ER.
BEHAVE RUDELY TOWARD ME...
...AND THEY WILL ACT AT ONCE.
KUI (FWIP)
FAIL-URE!
AH WANNA GO HOME ...

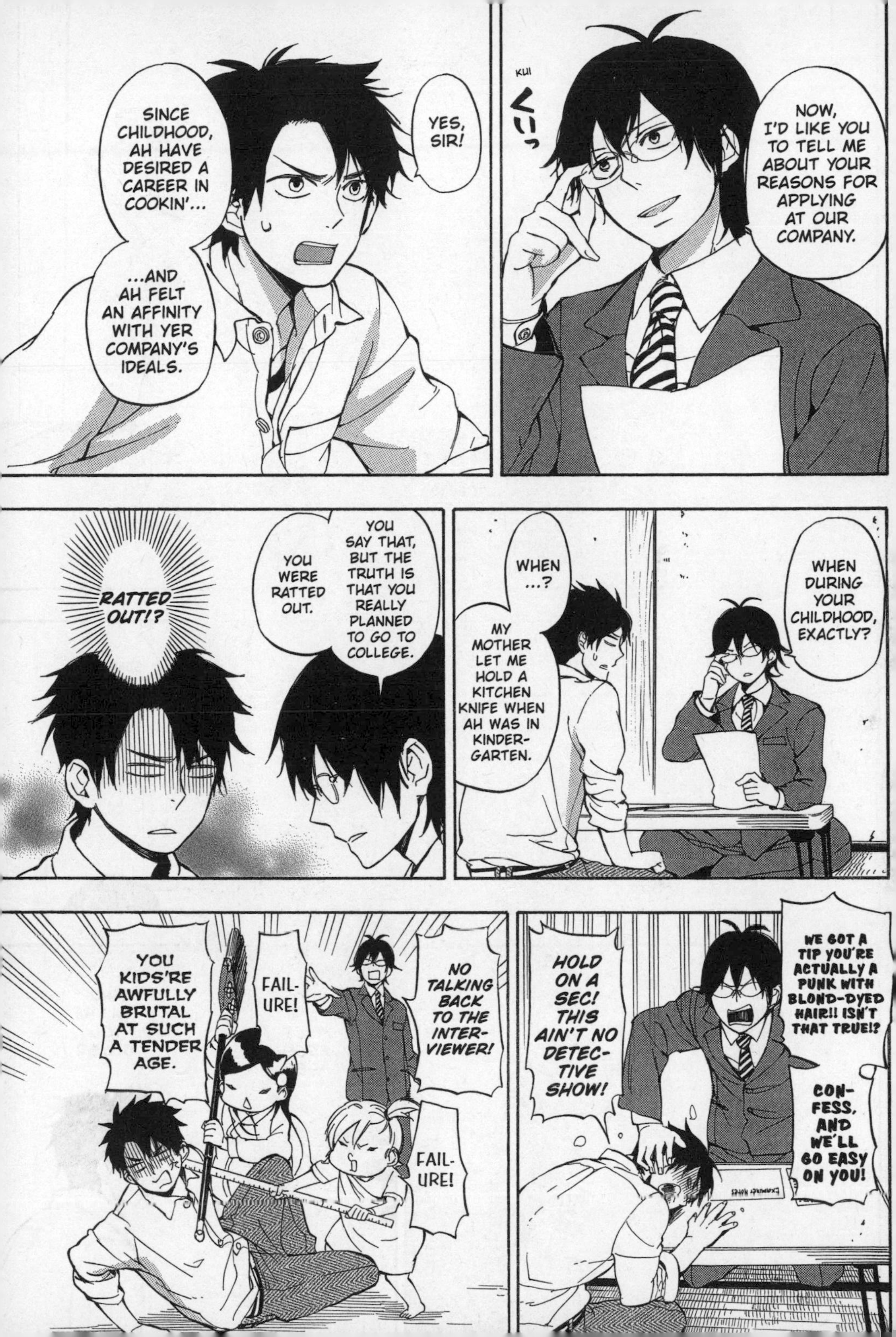
KUI
くいっ
NOW, I'D LIKE YOU TO TELL ME ABOUT YOUR REASONS FOR APPLYING AT OUR COMPANY.
YES, SIR!
SINCE CHILDHOOD, AH HAVE DESIRED A CAREER IN COOKIN'...
...AND AH FELT AN AFFINITY WITH YER COMPANY'S IDEALS.
WHEN DURING YOUR CHILDHOOD, EXACTLY?
WHEN ...?
MY MOTHER LET ME HOLD A KITCHEN KNIFE WHEN AH WAS IN KINDER-GARTEN.
YOU SAY THAT, BUT THE TRUTH IS THAT YOU REALLY PLANNED TO GO TO COLLEGE.
YOU WERE RATTED OUT.
RATTED OUT!?
WE GOT A TIP YOU'RE ACTUALLY A PUNK WITH BLOND-DYED HAIR!! ISN'T THAT TRUE!?
CON-FESS, AND WE'LL GO EASY ON YOU!
HOLD ON A SEC! THIS AIN'T NO DETEC-TIVE SHOW!
NO TALKING BACK TO THE INTER-VIEWER!
FAIL-URE!
FAIL-URE!
YOU KIDS'RE AWFULLY BRUTAL AT SUCH A TENDER AGE.

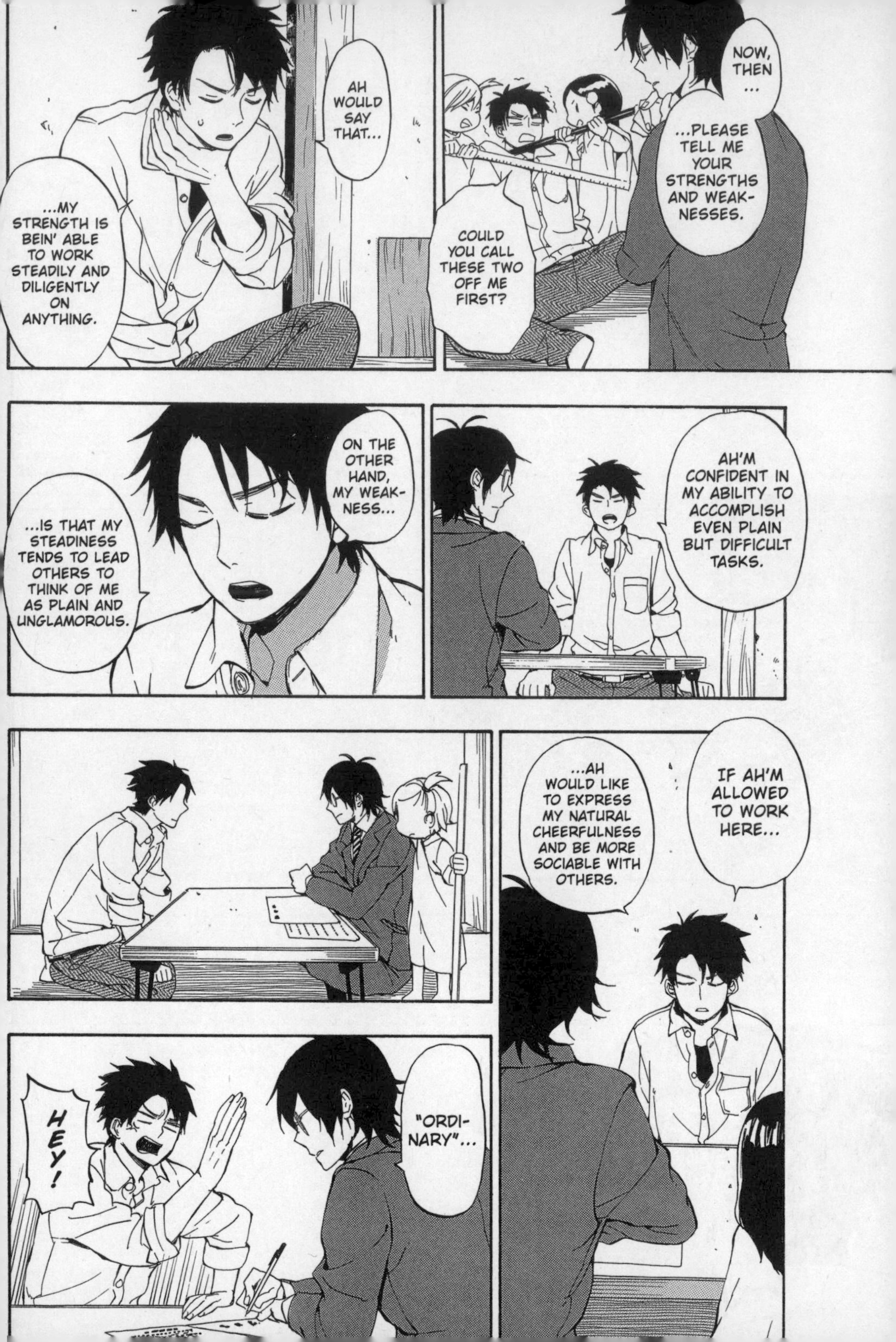
NOW, THEN...
...PLEASE TELL ME YOUR STRENGTHS AND WEAK-NESSES.
COULD YOU CALL THESE TWO OFF ME FIRST?
AH WOULD SAY THAT...
...MY STRENGTH IS BEIN' ABLE TO WORK STEADILY AND DILIGENTLY ON ANYTHING.
AH'M CONFIDENT IN MY ABILITY TO ACCOMPLISH EVEN PLAIN BUT DIFFICULT TASKS.
ON THE OTHER HAND, MY WEAK-NESS...
...IS THAT MY STEADINESS TENDS TO LEAD OTHERS TO THINK OF ME AS PLAIN AND UNGLAMOROUS.
IF AH'M ALLOWED TO WORK HERE...
...AH WOULD LIKE TO EXPRESS MY NATURAL CHEERFULNESS AND BE MORE SOCIABLE WITH OTHERS.
"ORDI-NARY"...
HEY!

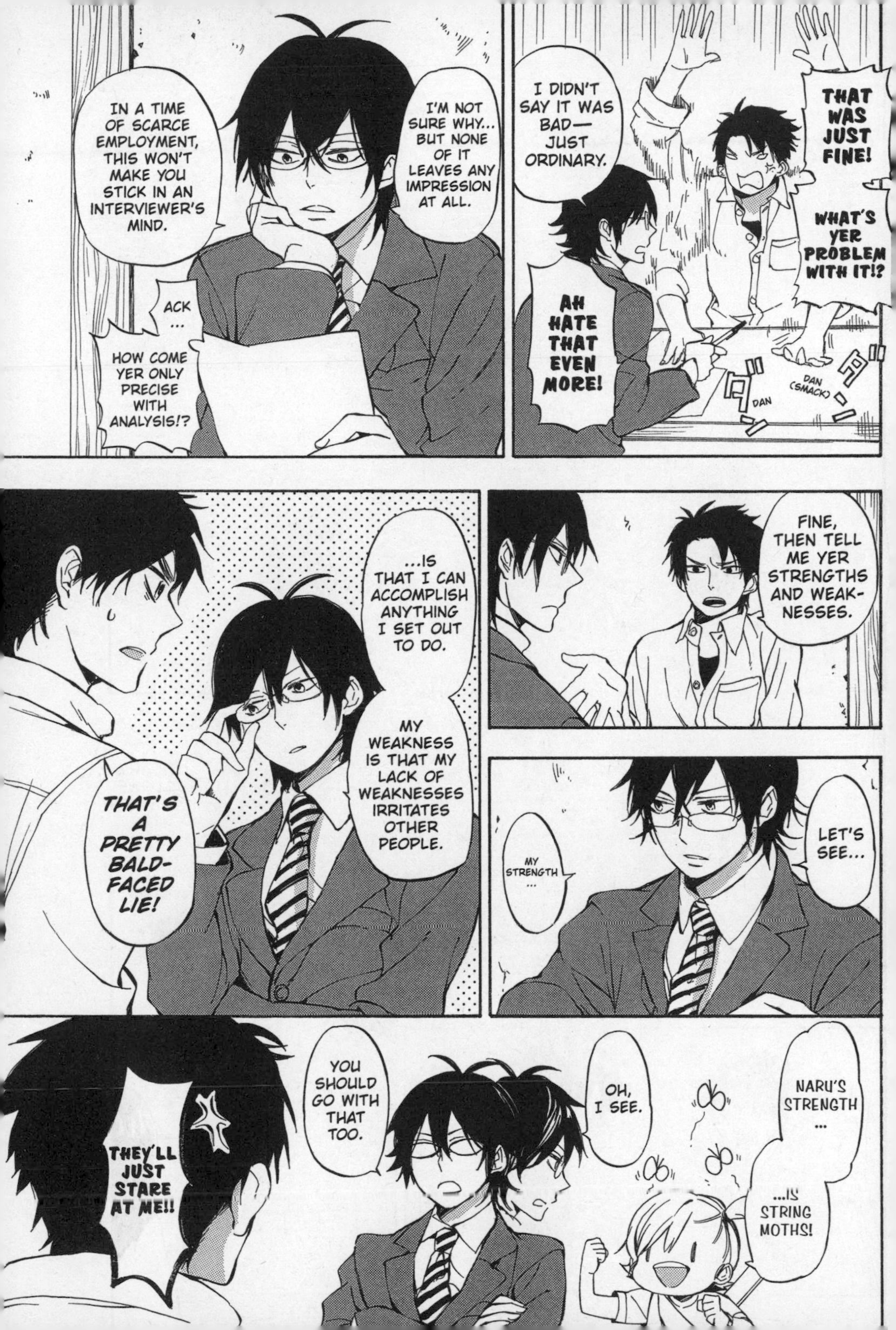
THAT WAS JUST FINE!
WHAT'S YER PROBLEM WITH IT!?
I DIDN'T SAY IT WAS BAD—JUST ORDINARY.
AH HATE THAT EVEN MORE!
DAN (SMACK)
DAN
I'M NOT SURE WHY... BUT NONE OF IT LEAVES ANY IMPRESSION AT ALL.
IN A TIME OF SCARCE EMPLOYMENT, THIS WON'T MAKE YOU STICK IN AN INTERVIEWER'S MIND.
ACK...
HOW COME YER ONLY PRECISE WITH ANALYSIS!?
FINE, THEN TELL ME YER STRENGTHS AND WEAKNESSES.
LET'S SEE...
MY STRENGTH...
...IS THAT I CAN ACCOMPLISH ANYTHING I SET OUT TO DO.
MY WEAKNESS IS THAT MY LACK OF WEAKNESSES IRRITATES OTHER PEOPLE.
THAT'S A PRETTY BALD-FACED LIE!
NARU'S STRENGTH...
...IS STRING MOTHS!
OH, I SEE.
YOU SHOULD GO WITH THAT TOO.
THEY'LL JUST STARE AT ME!!

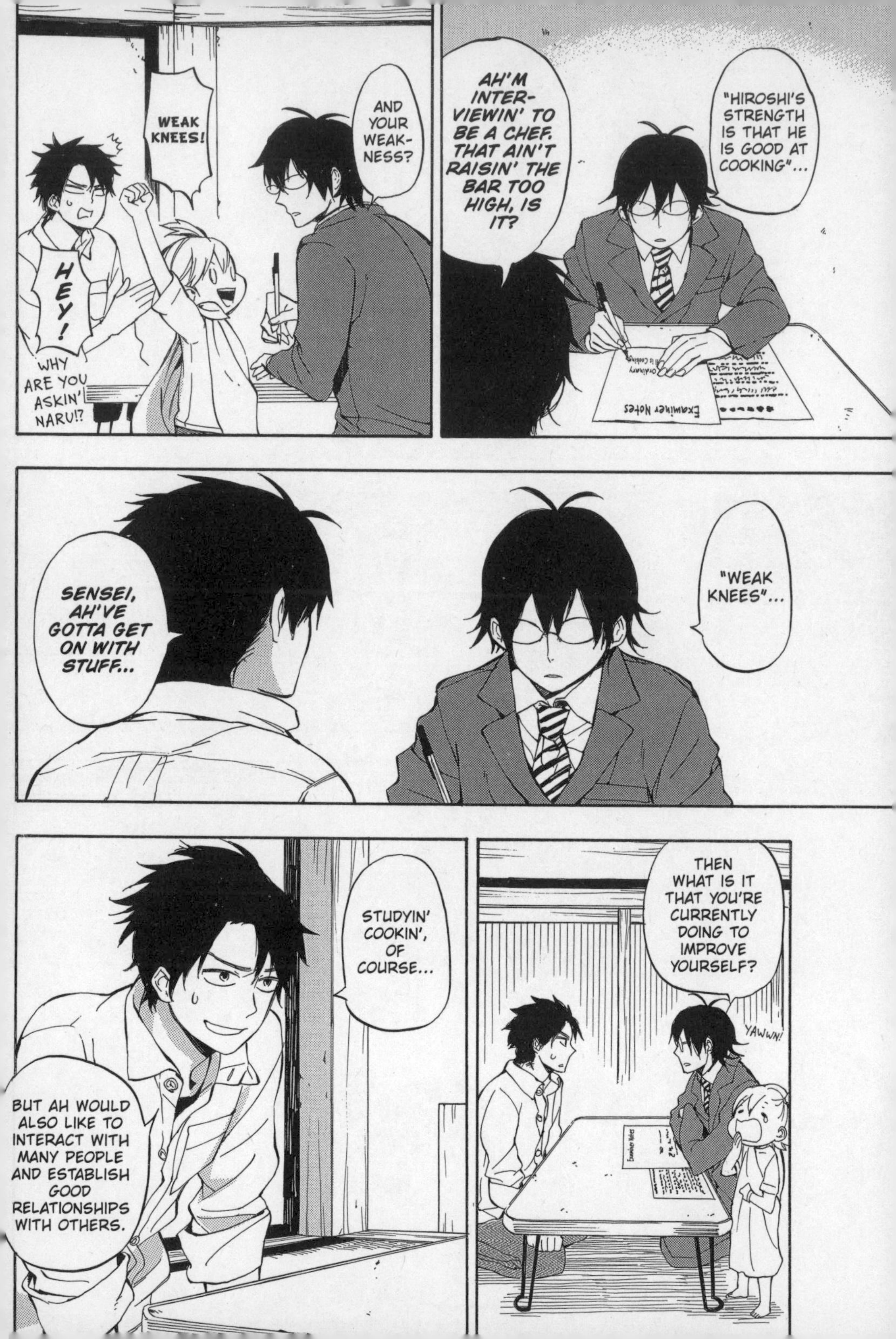
"HIROSHI'S STRENGTH IS THAT HE IS GOOD AT COOKING"...
AH'M INTER-VIEWIN' TO BE A CHEF. THAT AIN'T RAISIN' THE BAR TOO HIGH, IS IT?
Examiner Notes
AND YOUR WEAK-NESS?
WEAK KNEES!
HEY!
WHY ARE YOU ASKIN' NARU!?
"WEAK KNEES"...
SENSEI, AH'VE GOTTA GET ON WITH STUFF...
THEN WHAT IS IT THAT YOU'RE CURRENTLY DOING TO IMPROVE YOURSELF?
YAWWN!
STUDYIN' COOKIN', OF COURSE...
BUT AH WOULD ALSO LIKE TO INTERACT WITH MANY PEOPLE AND ESTABLISH GOOD RELATIONSHIPS WITH OTHERS.

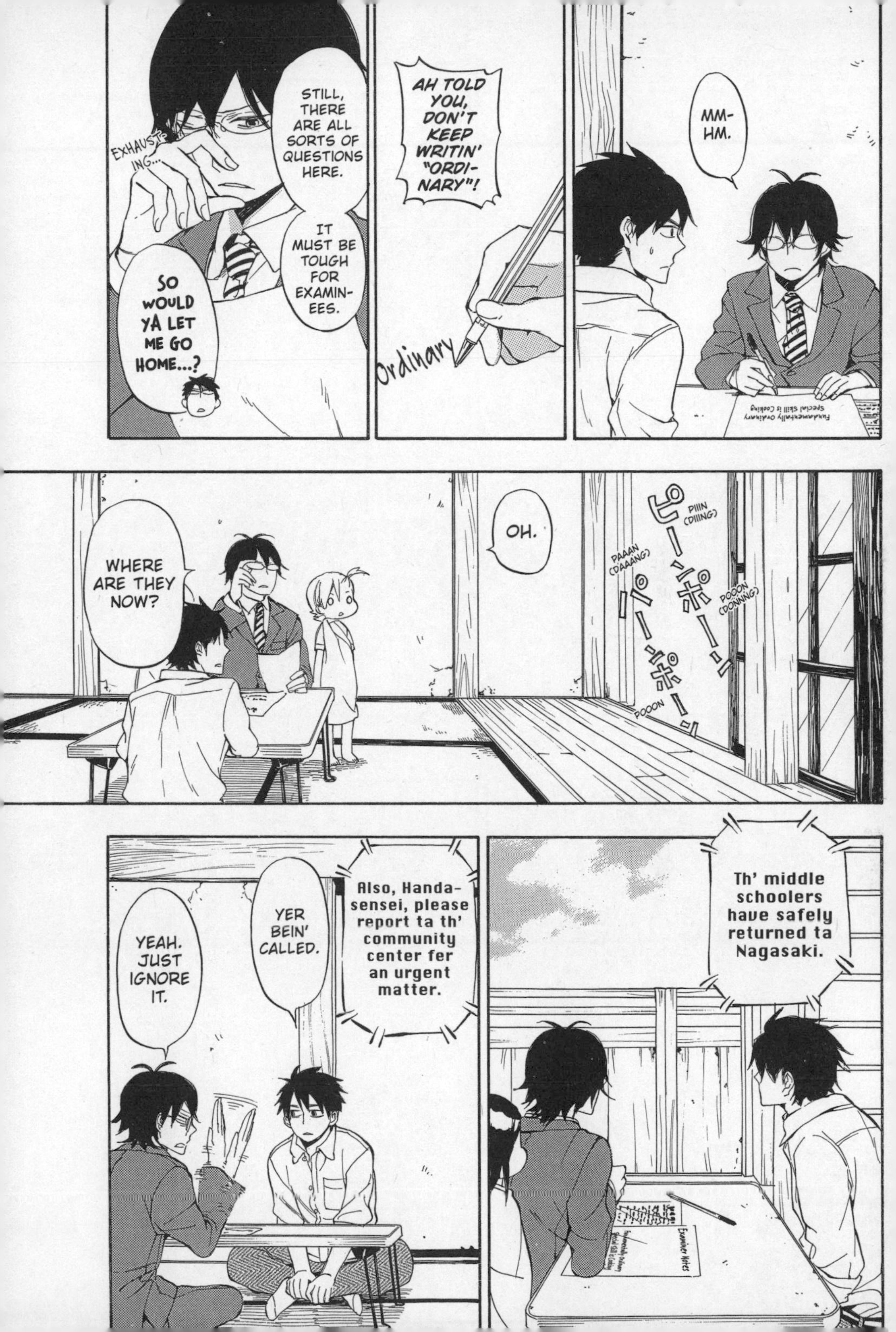
MM-HM.
Fundamentally ordinary
Special skill is Cooking
AH TOLD YOU, DON'T KEEP WRITIN' "ORDINARY"!
Ordinary
STILL, THERE ARE ALL SORTS OF QUESTIONS HERE.
IT MUST BE TOUGH FOR EXAMINEES.
EXHAUSTING...
SO WOULD YA LET ME GO HOME...?
ピーンポーン
PIIIN (DIIING)
POOON (DONNNG)
パーンポーン
PAAAN (DAAANG)
POOON
OH.
WHERE ARE THEY NOW?
Th' middle schoolers have safely returned ta Nagasaki.
Also, Handa-sensei, please report ta th' community center fer an urgent matter.
YER BEIN' CALLED.
YEAH. JUST IGNORE IT.
Examiner Notes

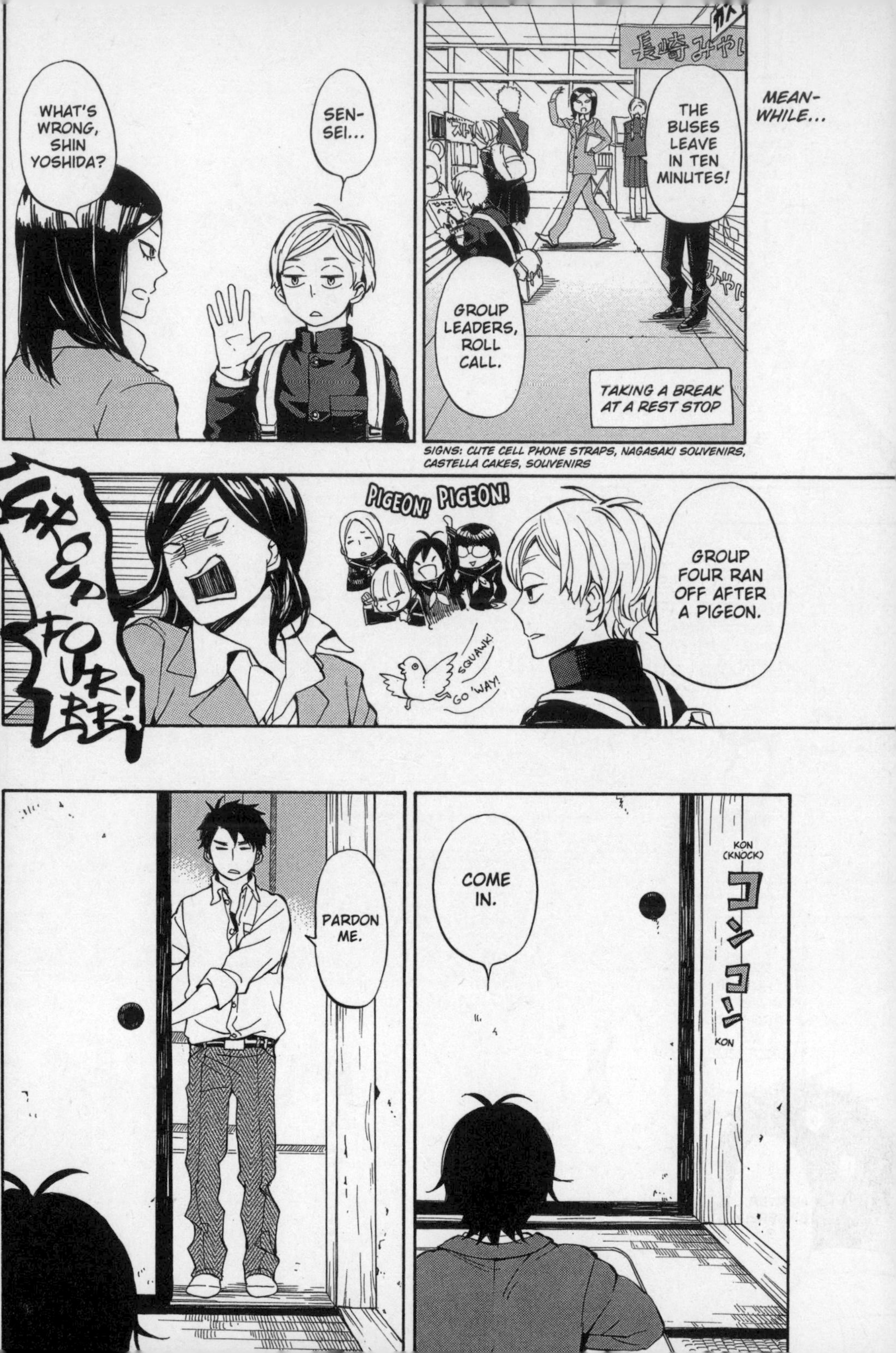
MEAN-WHILE...
THE BUSES LEAVE IN TEN MINUTES!
GROUP LEADERS, ROLL CALL.
TAKING A BREAK AT A REST STOP
SIGNS: CUTE CELL PHONE STRAPS, NAGASAKI SOUVENIRS, CASTELLA CAKES, SOUVENIRS
SEN-SEI...
WHAT'S WRONG, SHIN YOSHIDA?
GROUP FOUR RAN OFF AFTER A PIGEON.
PIGEON! PIGEON!
SQUAWK!
GO 'WAY!
KON (KNOCK)
KON
COME IN.
PARDON ME.

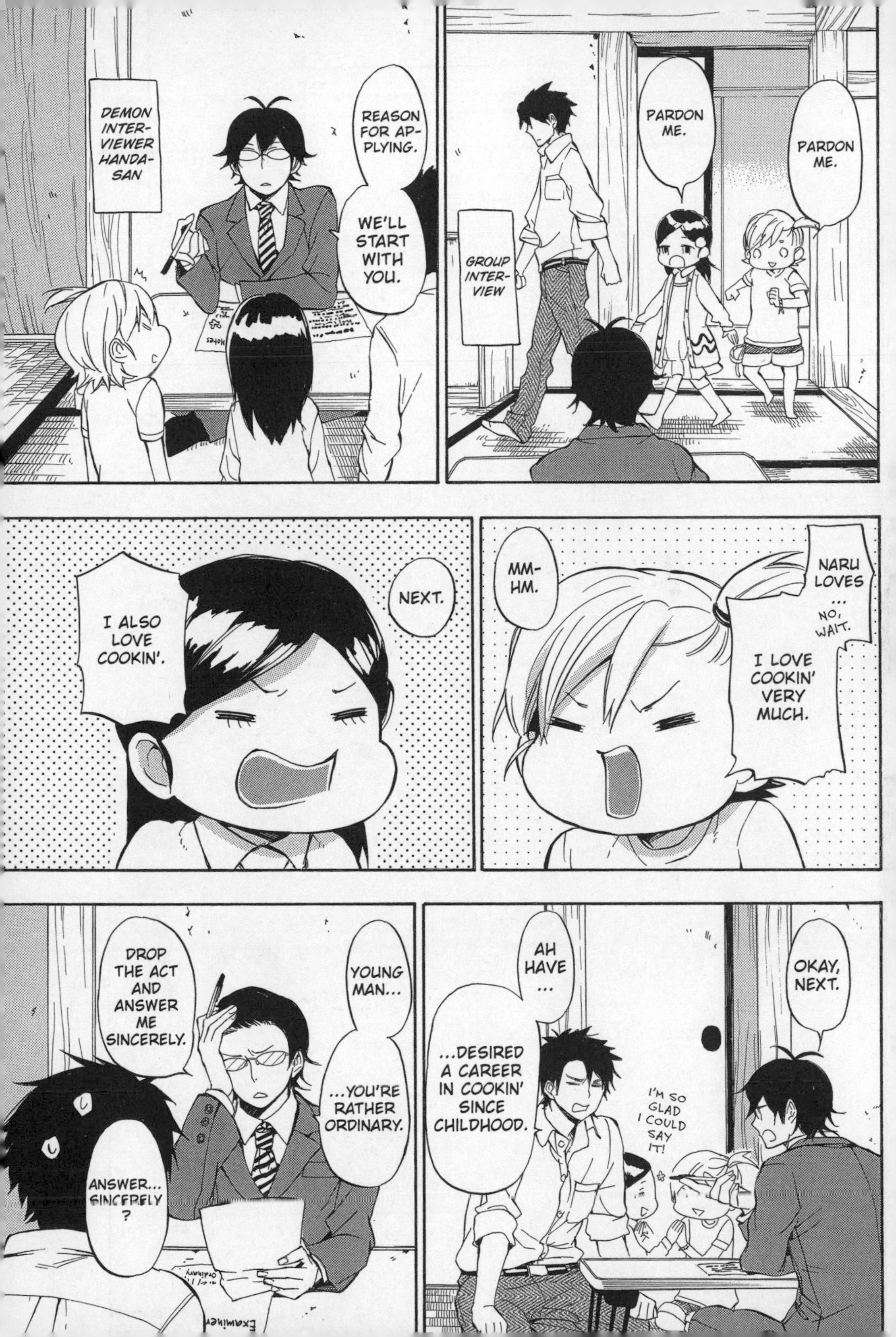
PARDON ME.
PARDON ME.
GROUP INTER-VIEW
DEMON INTER-VIEWER HANDA-SAN
REASON FOR AP-PLYING.
WE'LL START WITH YOU.
NARU LOVES ... NO, WAIT.
I LOVE COOKIN' VERY MUCH.
MM-HM.
NEXT.
I ALSO LOVE COOKIN'.
OKAY, NEXT.
AH HAVE ...
...DESIRED A CAREER IN COOKIN' SINCE CHILDHOOD.
I'M SO GLAD I COULD SAY IT!
YOUNG MAN...
...YOU'RE RATHER ORDINARY.
DROP THE ACT AND ANSWER ME SINCERELY.
ANSWER... SINCERELY?

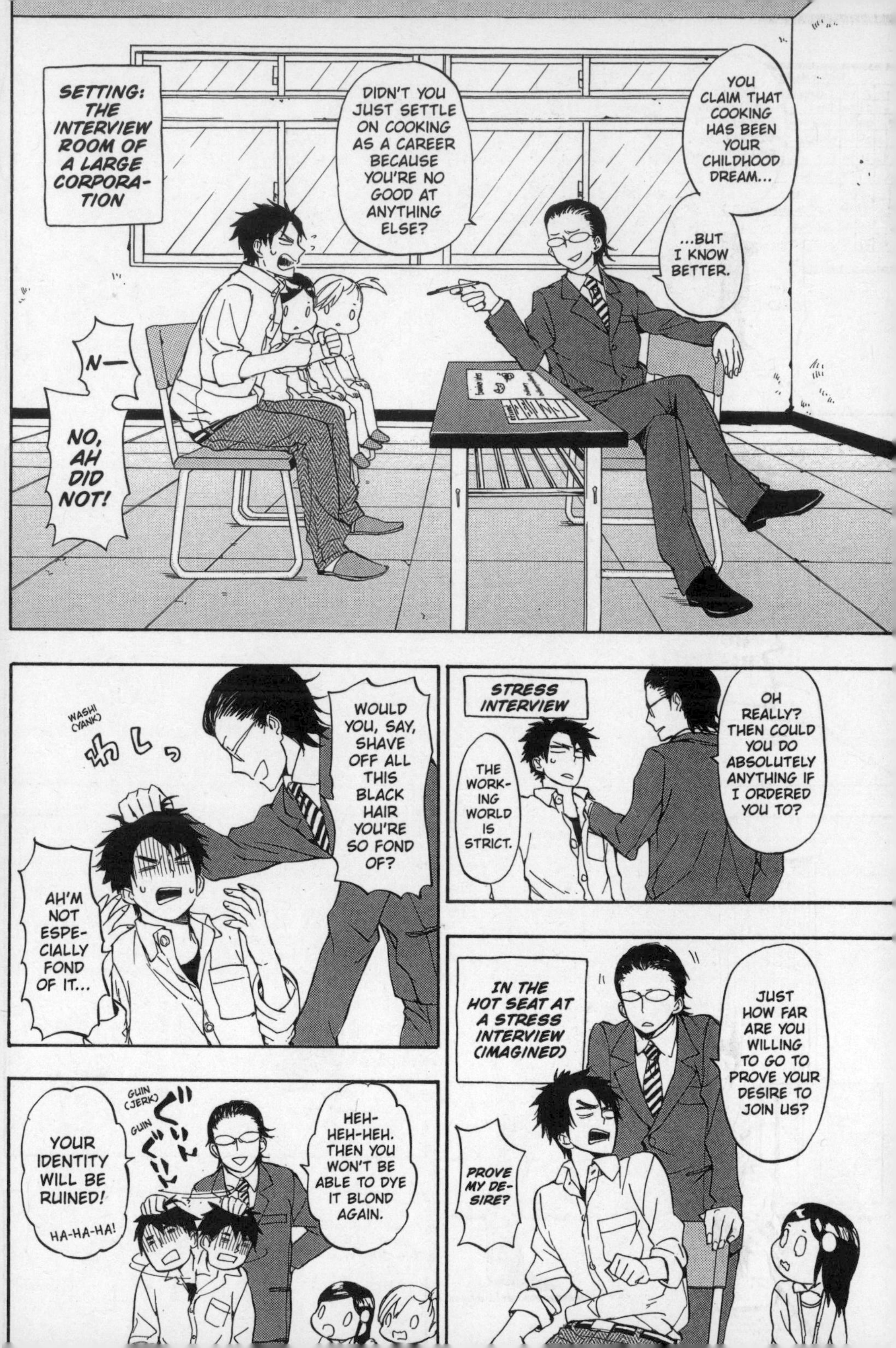
YOU CLAIM THAT COOKING HAS BEEN YOUR CHILDHOOD DREAM...
...BUT I KNOW BETTER.
DIDN'T YOU JUST SETTLE ON COOKING AS A CAREER BECAUSE YOU'RE NO GOOD AT ANYTHING ELSE?
SETTING: THE INTERVIEW ROOM OF A LARGE CORPORA-TION
N—
NO, AH DID NOT!
OH REALLY? THEN COULD YOU DO ABSOLUTELY ANYTHING IF I ORDERED YOU TO?
STRESS INTERVIEW
THE WORKING WORLD IS STRICT.
WOULD YOU, SAY, SHAVE OFF ALL THIS BLACK HAIR YOU'RE SO FOND OF?
わしっ
WASHI (YANK)
AH'M NOT ESPE-CIALLY FOND OF IT...
JUST HOW FAR ARE YOU WILLING TO GO TO PROVE YOUR DESIRE TO JOIN US?
IN THE HOT SEAT AT A STRESS INTERVIEW (IMAGINED)
PROVE MY DE-SIRE?
HEH-HEH-HEH. THEN YOU WON'T BE ABLE TO DYE IT BLOND AGAIN.
ぐいん ぐいん
GUIN (JERK)
GUIN
YOUR IDENTITY WILL BE RUINED!
HA-HA-HA!

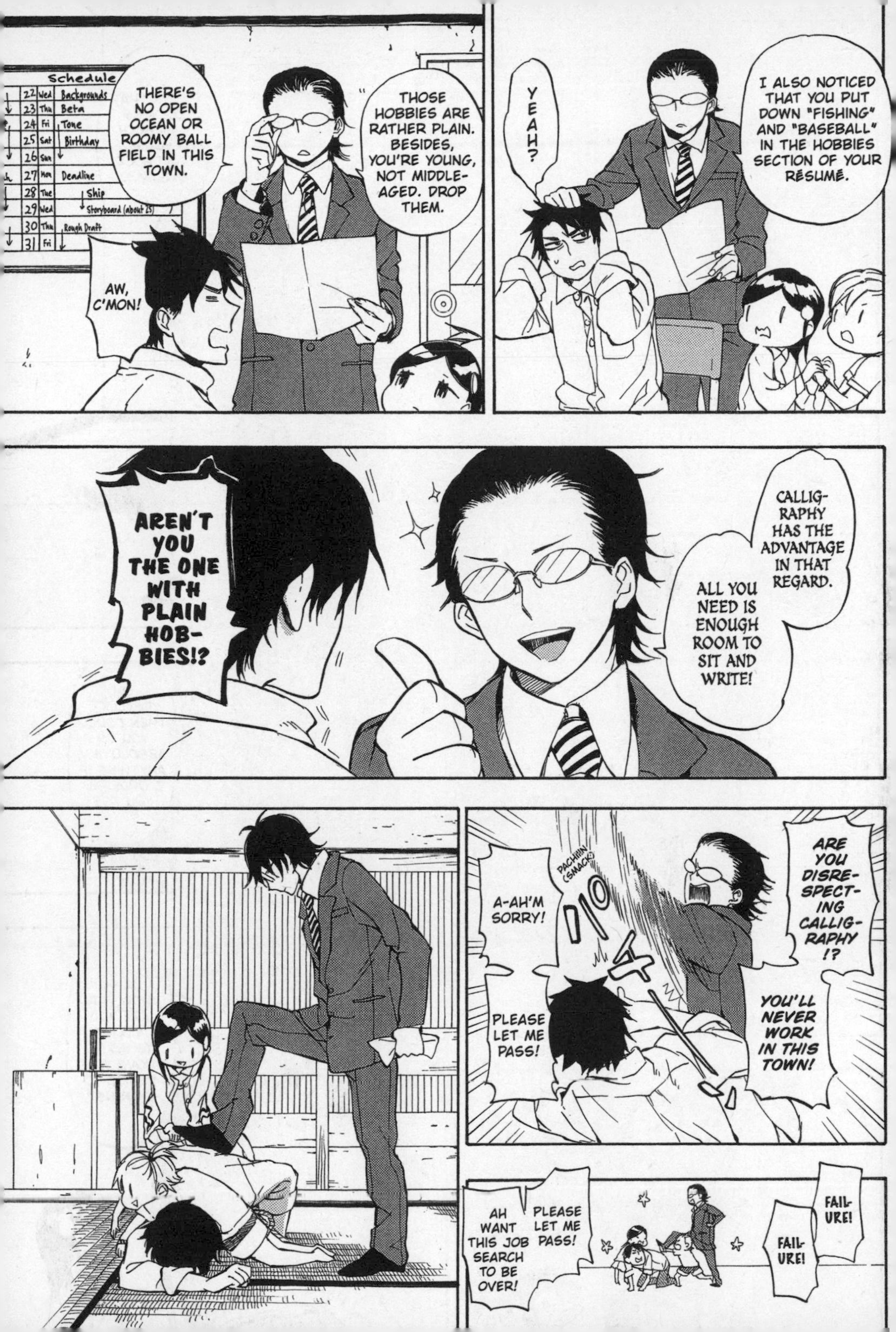
I ALSO NOTICED THAT YOU PUT DOWN "FISHING" AND "BASEBALL" IN THE HOBBIES SECTION OF YOUR RÉSUMÉ.
YEAH?
THOSE HOBBIES ARE RATHER PLAIN. BESIDES, YOU'RE YOUNG, NOT MIDDLE-AGED. DROP THEM.
THERE'S NO OPEN OCEAN OR ROOMY BALL FIELD IN THIS TOWN.
Schedule
22 Wed Backgrounds
23 Thu Beta
24 Fri Tone
25 Sat Birthday
26 Sun
27 Mon Deadline
28 Tue Ship
29 Wed Storyboard (about 25)
30 Thu Rough Draft
31 Fri
AW, C'MON!
CALLIGRAPHY HAS THE ADVANTAGE IN THAT REGARD.
ALL YOU NEED IS ENOUGH ROOM TO SIT AND WRITE!
AREN'T YOU THE ONE WITH PLAIN HOBBIES!?
ARE YOU DISRESPECTING CALLIGRAPHY!?
PACHIRIN (SMACK)
YOU'LL NEVER WORK IN THIS TOWN!
A-AH'M SORRY!
PLEASE LET ME PASS!
FAILURE!
FAILURE!
PLEASE LET ME PASS!
AH WANT THIS JOB SEARCH TO BE OVER!

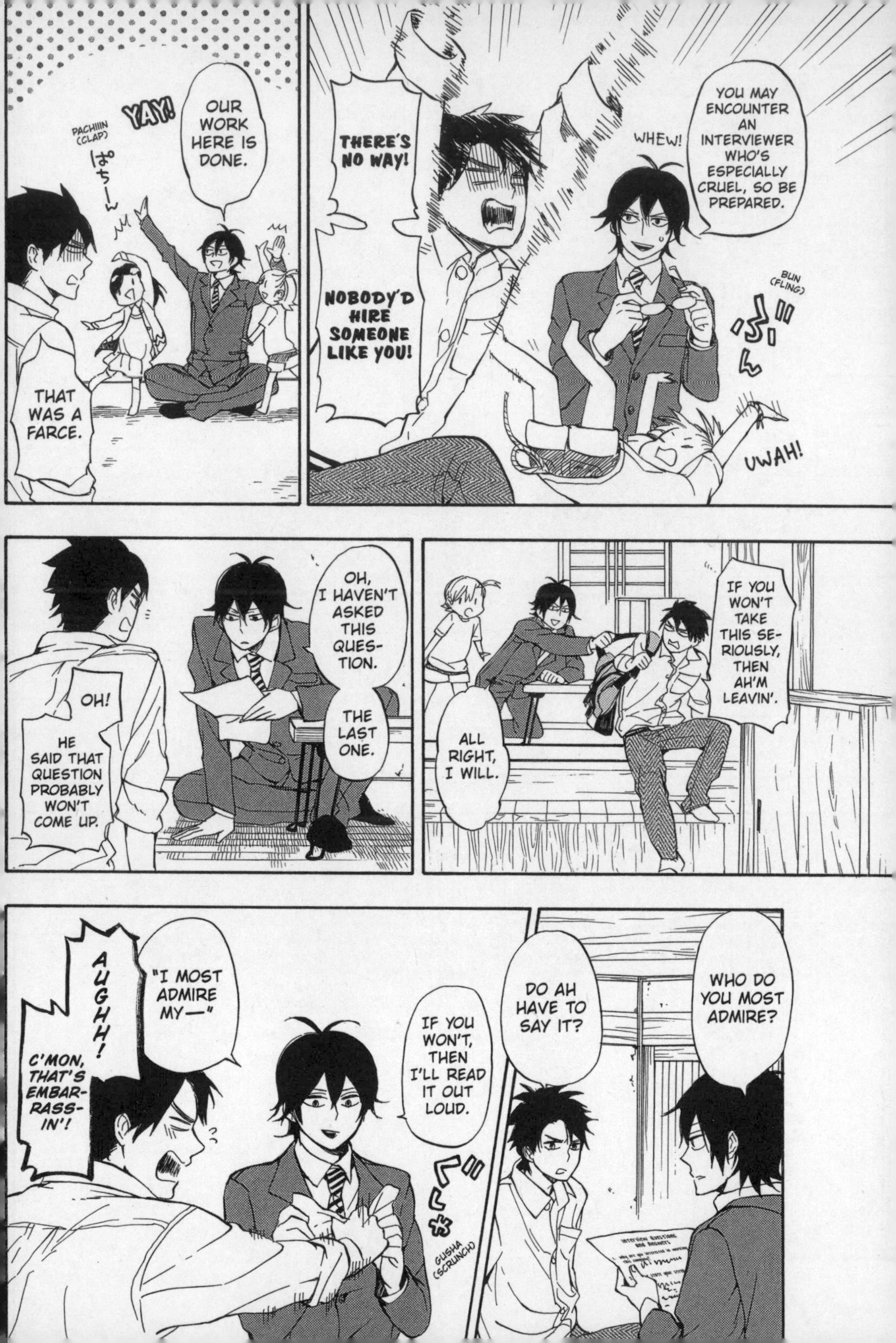
YOU MAY ENCOUNTER AN INTERVIEWER WHO'S ESPECIALLY CRUEL, SO BE PREPARED.
WHEW!
BUN (FLING)
ぶん
THERE'S NO WAY!
NOBODY'D HIRE SOMEONE LIKE YOU!
UWAH!
OUR WORK HERE IS DONE.
YAY!
PACHIIIN (CLAP)
ぱちーん
THAT WAS A FARCE.
IF YOU WON'T TAKE THIS SE-RIOUSLY, THEN AH'M LEAVIN'.
ALL RIGHT, I WILL.
OH, I HAVEN'T ASKED THIS QUES-TION.
THE LAST ONE.
OH!
HE SAID THAT QUESTION PROBABLY WON'T COME UP.
WHO DO YOU MOST ADMIRE?
DO AH HAVE TO SAY IT?
IF YOU WON'T, THEN I'LL READ IT OUT LOUD.
ぐしゃ
GUSHA (SCRUNCH)
"I MOST ADMIRE MY—"
AUGHH!
C'MON, THAT'S EMBAR-RASS-IN'!

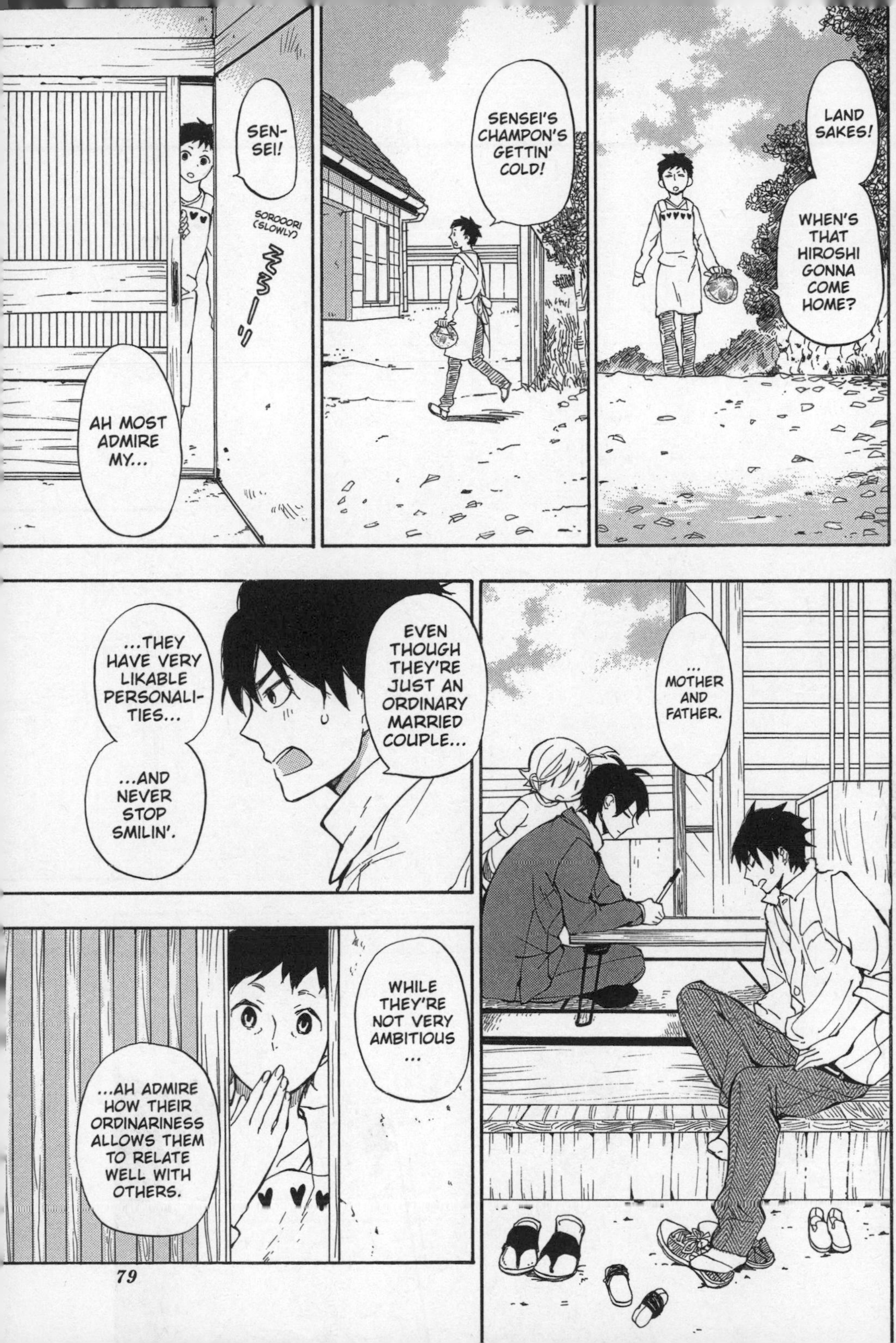
LAND SAKES!
WHEN'S THAT HIROSHI GONNA COME HOME?
SENSEI'S CHAMPON'S GETTIN' COLD!
SEN-SEI!
SOROOORI (SLOWLY)
AH MOST ADMIRE MY...
... MOTHER AND FATHER.
EVEN THOUGH THEY'RE JUST AN ORDINARY MARRIED COUPLE...
...THEY HAVE VERY LIKABLE PERSONALI-TIES...
...AND NEVER STOP SMILIN'.
WHILE THEY'RE NOT VERY AMBITIOUS ...
...AH ADMIRE HOW THEIR ORDINARINESS ALLOWS THEM TO RELATE WELL WITH OTHERS.

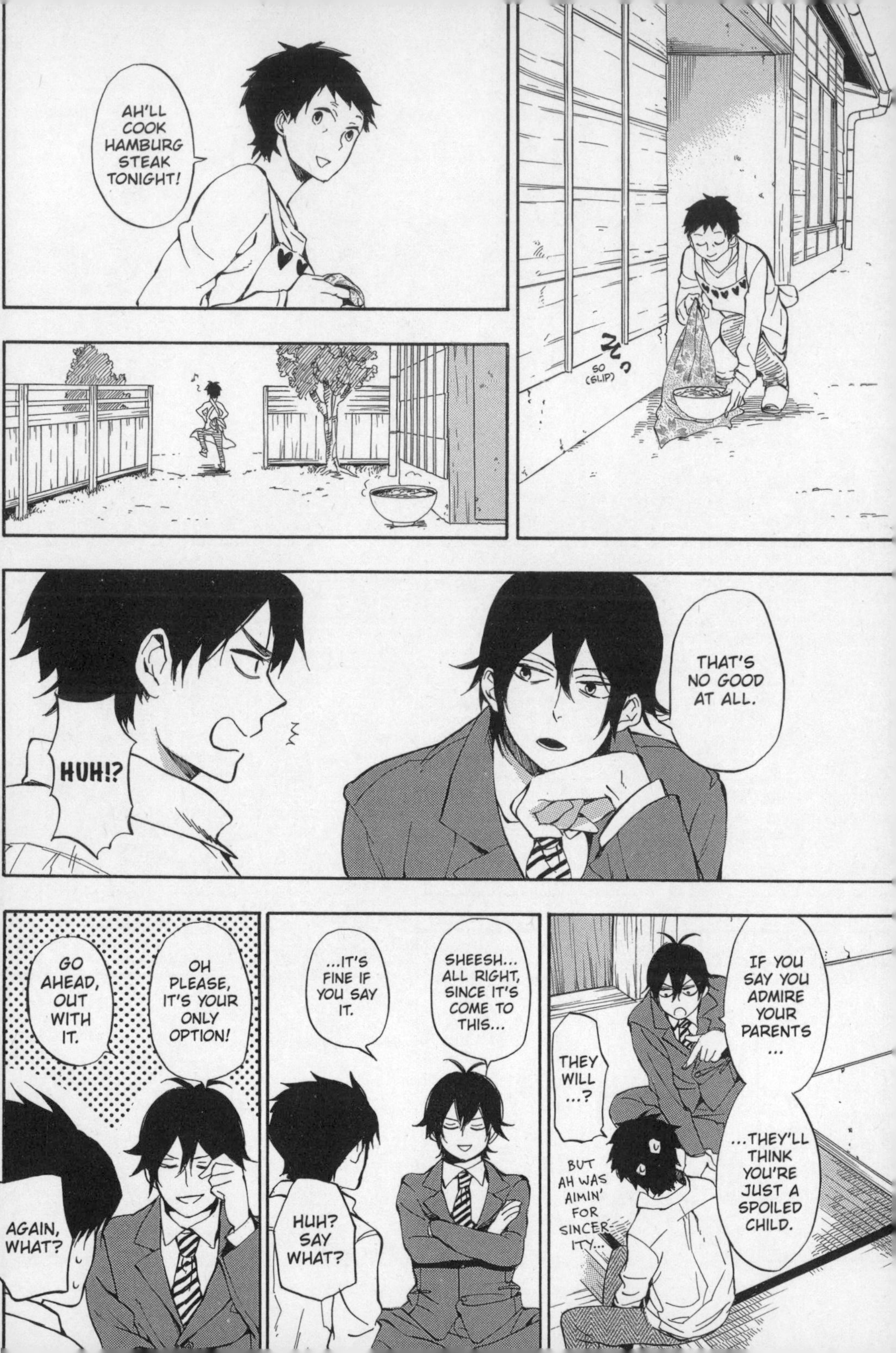
SO (SLIP)
AH'LL COOK HAMBURG STEAK TONIGHT!
THAT'S NO GOOD AT ALL.
HUH!?
IF YOU SAY YOU ADMIRE YOUR PARENTS ...
THEY WILL ...?
...THEY'LL THINK YOU'RE JUST A SPOILED CHILD.
BUT AH WAS AIMIN' FOR SINCER- ITY...
SHEESH... ALL RIGHT, SINCE IT'S COME TO THIS...
...IT'S FINE IF YOU SAY IT.
HUH? SAY WHAT?
OH PLEASE, IT'S YOUR ONLY OPTION!
GO AHEAD, OUT WITH IT.
AGAIN, WHAT?

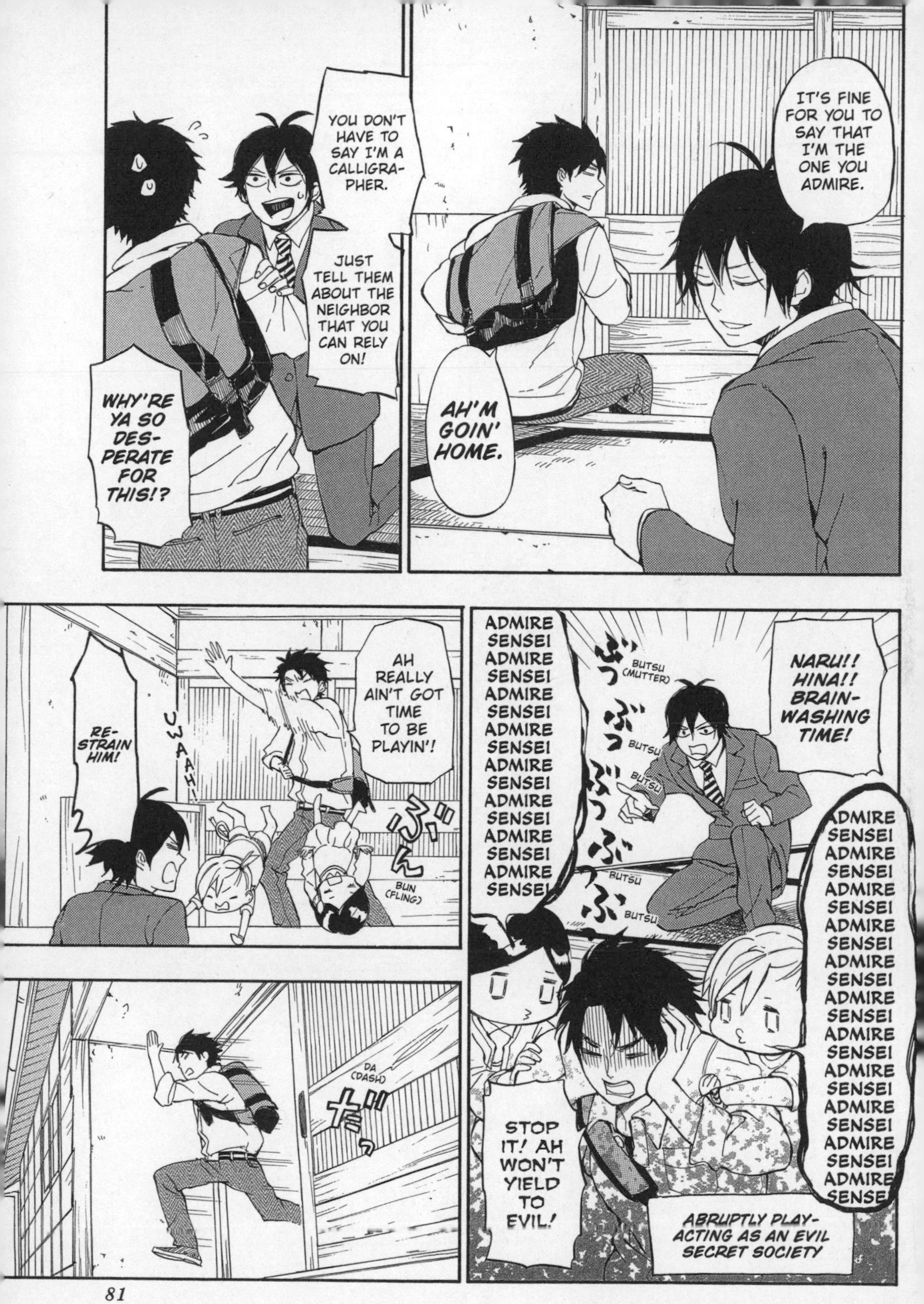

IT'S FINE FOR YOU TO SAY THAT I'M THE ONE YOU ADMIRE.
AH'M GOIN' HOME.
YOU DON'T HAVE TO SAY I'M A CALLIGRAPHER.
JUST TELL THEM ABOUT THE NEIGHBOR THAT YOU CAN RELY ON!
WHY'RE YA SO DESPERATE FOR THIS!?
NARU!! HINA!! BRAINWASHING TIME!
BUTSU (MUTTER)
BUTSU
BUTSU
BUTSU
BUTSU
ADMIRE SENSEI ADMIRE SENSEI ADMIRE SENSEI ADMIRE SENSEI ADMIRE SENSEI ADMIRE SENSEI ADMIRE SENSEI ADMIRE SENSEI ADMIRE SENSEI ADMIRE SENSEI ADMIRE SENSE
ADMIRE SENSEI ADMIRE SENSEI ADMIRE SENSEI ADMIRE SENSEI ADMIRE SENSEI ADMIRE SENSEI ADMIRE SENSEI
STOP IT! AH WON'T YIELD TO EVIL!
ABRUPTLY PLAY-ACTING AS AN EVIL SECRET SOCIETY
AH REALLY AIN'T GOT TIME TO BE PLAYIN'!
RE-STRAIN HIM!
UWAAAH!
BUN (FLING)
DA (DASH)

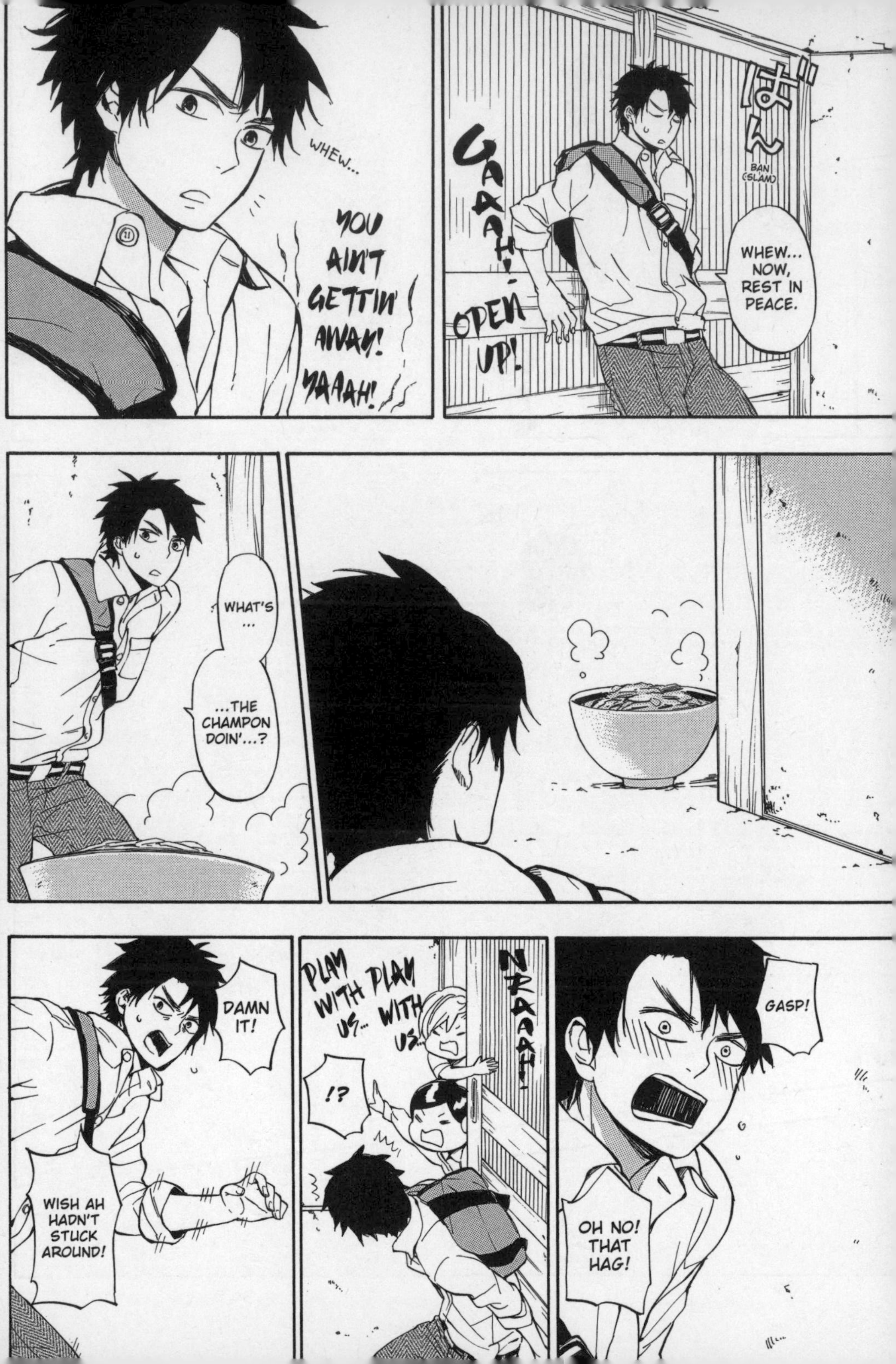
ばん
BAN (SLAM)
WHEW... NOW, REST IN PEACE.
UAAAH!- OPEN UP!
YOU AIN'T GETTIN' AWAY! YAAAH!
WHEW...
WHAT'S ...
...THE CHAMPON DOIN'...?
GASP!
OH NO! THAT HAG!
NRAAAAH!-
PLAY WITH US... PLAY WITH US...
!?
DAMN IT!
WISH AH HADN'T STUCK AROUND!

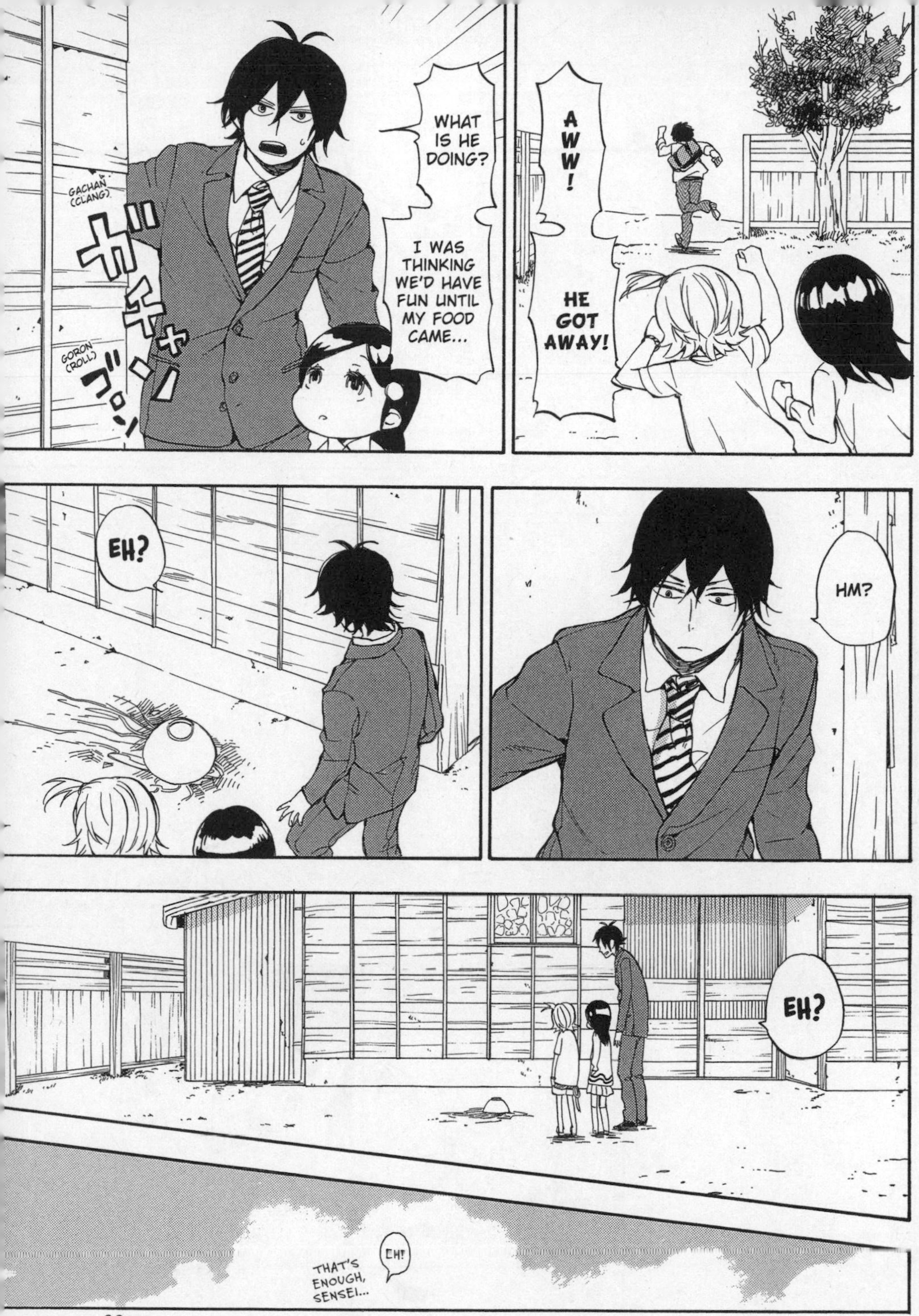
AWW!
HE GOT AWAY!
WHAT IS HE DOING?
I WAS THINKING WE'D HAVE FUN UNTIL MY FOOD CAME...
GACHAN (CLANG)
GORON (ROLL)
HM?
EH?
EH?
EH!
THAT'S ENOUGH, SENSEI...

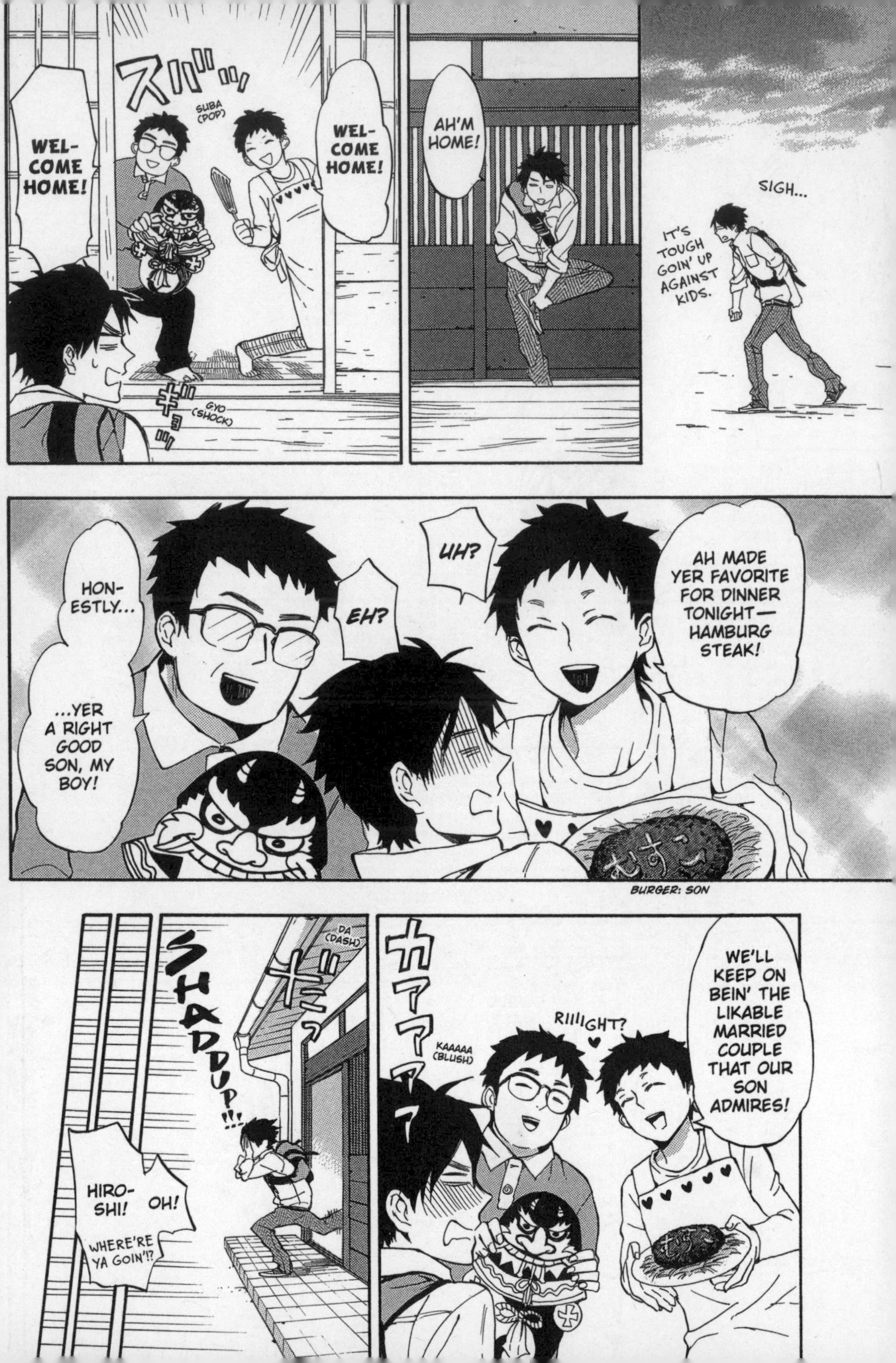

SIGH...
IT'S TOUGH GOIN' UP AGAINST KIDS.
AH'M HOME!
WEL-COME HOME!
スパッ
SUBA (POP)
WEL-COME HOME!
ギョッ
GYO (SHOCK)
AH MADE YER FAVORITE FOR DINNER TONIGHT— HAMBURG STEAK!
UH?
EH?
HON-ESTLY...
...YER A RIGHT GOOD SON, MY BOY!
BURGER: SON
WE'LL KEEP ON BEIN' THE LIKABLE MARRIED COUPLE THAT OUR SON ADMIRES!
RIIIIGHT? ♥
カァァァ
KAAAAA (BLUSH)
ダッ
DA (DASH)
SHADDUP!!!
HIRO-SHI!
OH!
WHERE'RE YA GOIN'!?

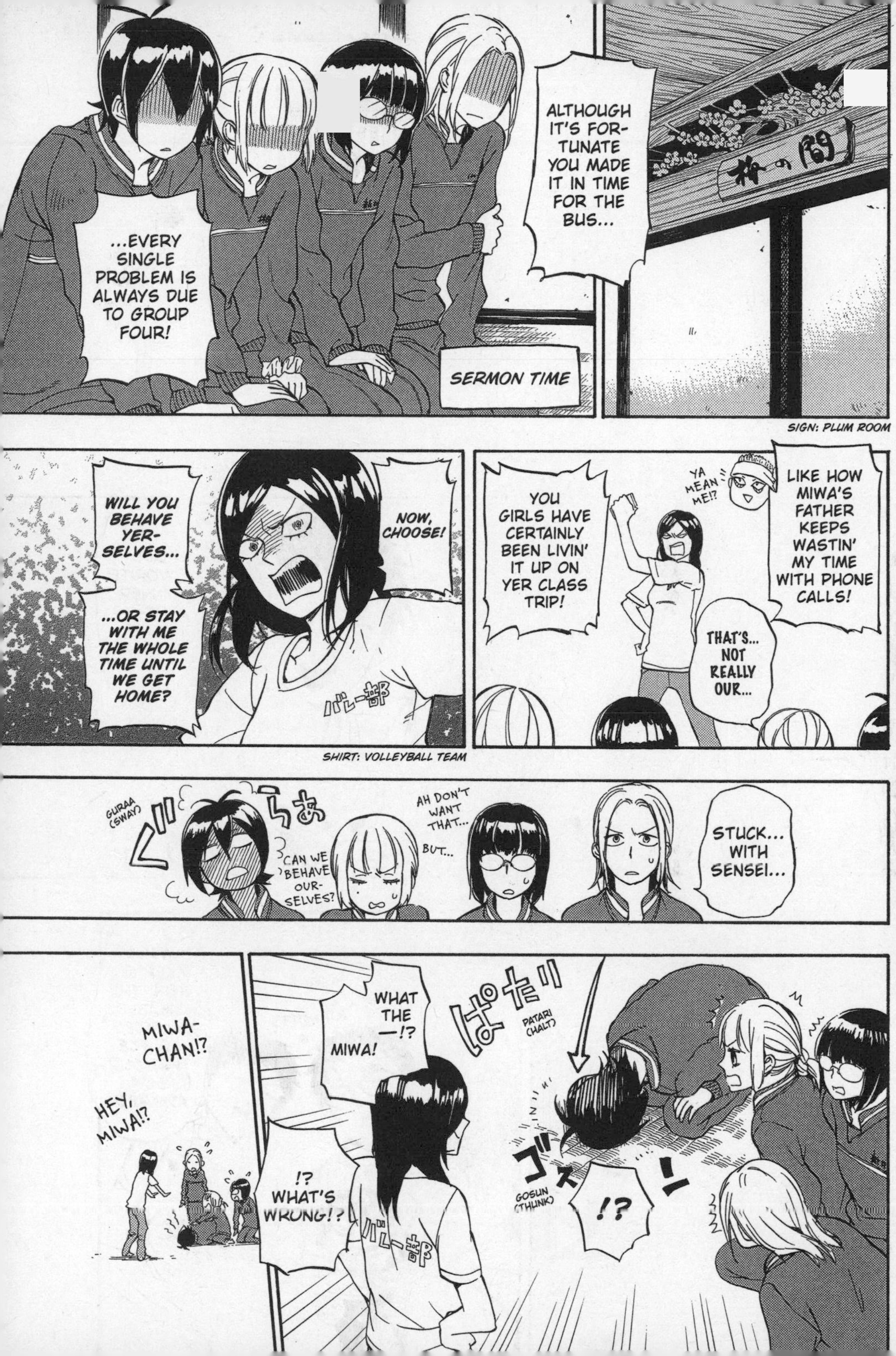
ALTHOUGH IT'S FORTUNATE YOU MADE IT IN TIME FOR THE BUS...
...EVERY SINGLE PROBLEM IS ALWAYS DUE TO GROUP FOUR!
SERMON TIME
SIGN: PLUM ROOM
LIKE HOW MIWA'S FATHER KEEPS WASTIN' MY TIME WITH PHONE CALLS!
YA MEAN ME!?
YOU GIRLS HAVE CERTAINLY BEEN LIVIN' IT UP ON YER CLASS TRIP!
THAT'S... NOT REALLY OUR...
NOW, CHOOSE!
WILL YOU BEHAVE YERSELVES...
...OR STAY WITH ME THE WHOLE TIME UNTIL WE GET HOME?
SHIRT: VOLLEYBALL TEAM
STUCK... WITH SENSEI...
AH DON'T WANT THAT...
BUT...
CAN WE BEHAVE OURSELVES?
GURAA (SWAY)
PATARI (HALT)
WHAT THE —!?
MIWA!
!
GOSUN (THUNK)
!?
!? WHAT'S WRONG!?
MIWA-CHAN!?
HEY, MIWA!?

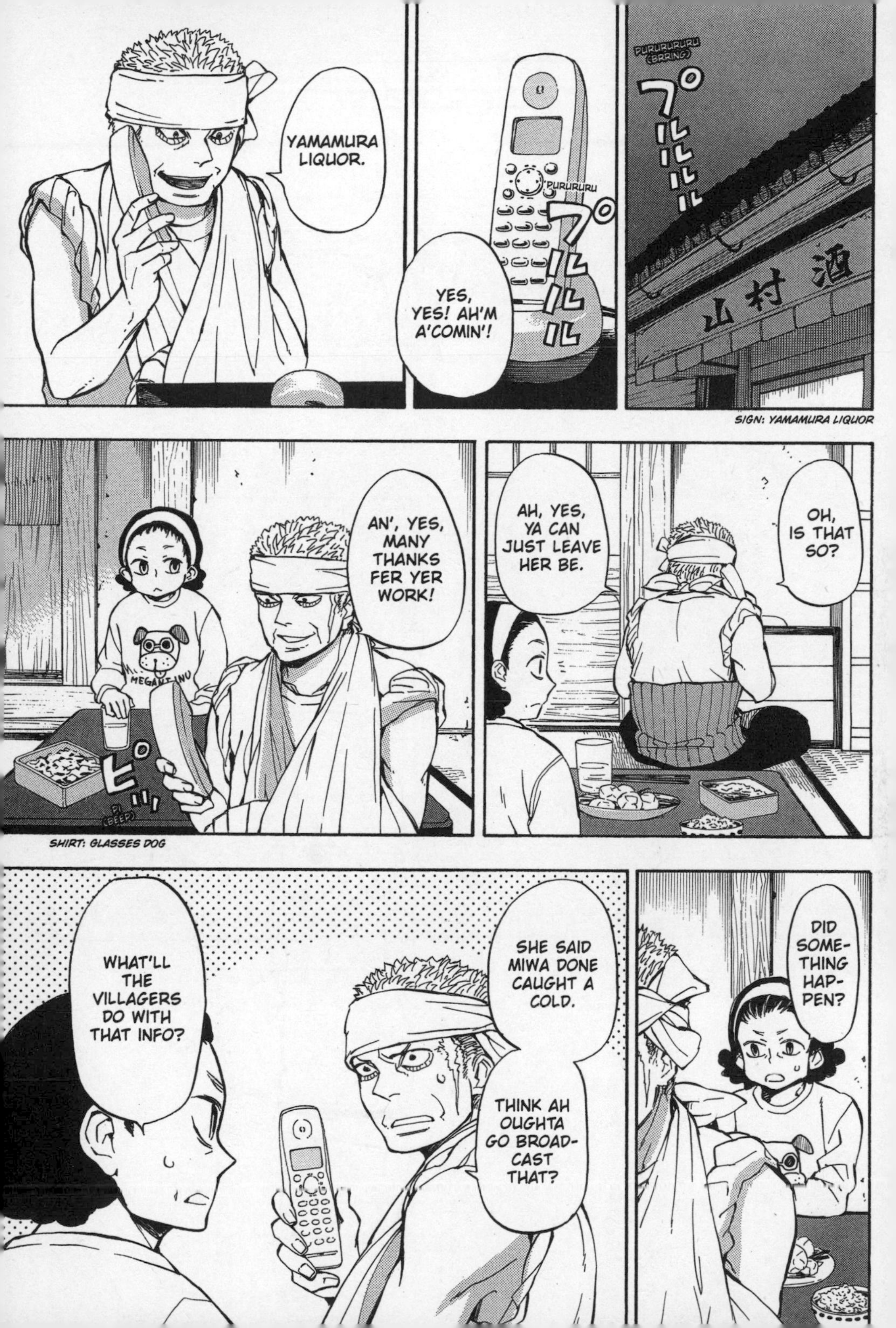
PURURURURU (BRRING)
プルルルルル
山村酒
SIGN: YAMAMURA LIQUOR
PURURURU
プルルル
YES, YES! AH'M A'COMIN'!
YAMAMURA LIQUOR.
OH, IS THAT SO?
AH, YES, YA CAN JUST LEAVE HER BE.
AN', YES, MANY THANKS FER YER WORK!
ピッ
PI (BEEP)
SHIRT: GLASSES DOG
DID SOMETHING HAPPEN?
SHE SAID MIWA DONE CAUGHT A COLD.
THINK AH OUGHTA GO BROADCAST THAT?
WHAT'LL THE VILLAGERS DO WITH THAT INFO?

ACT.64
THE CLASS TRIP

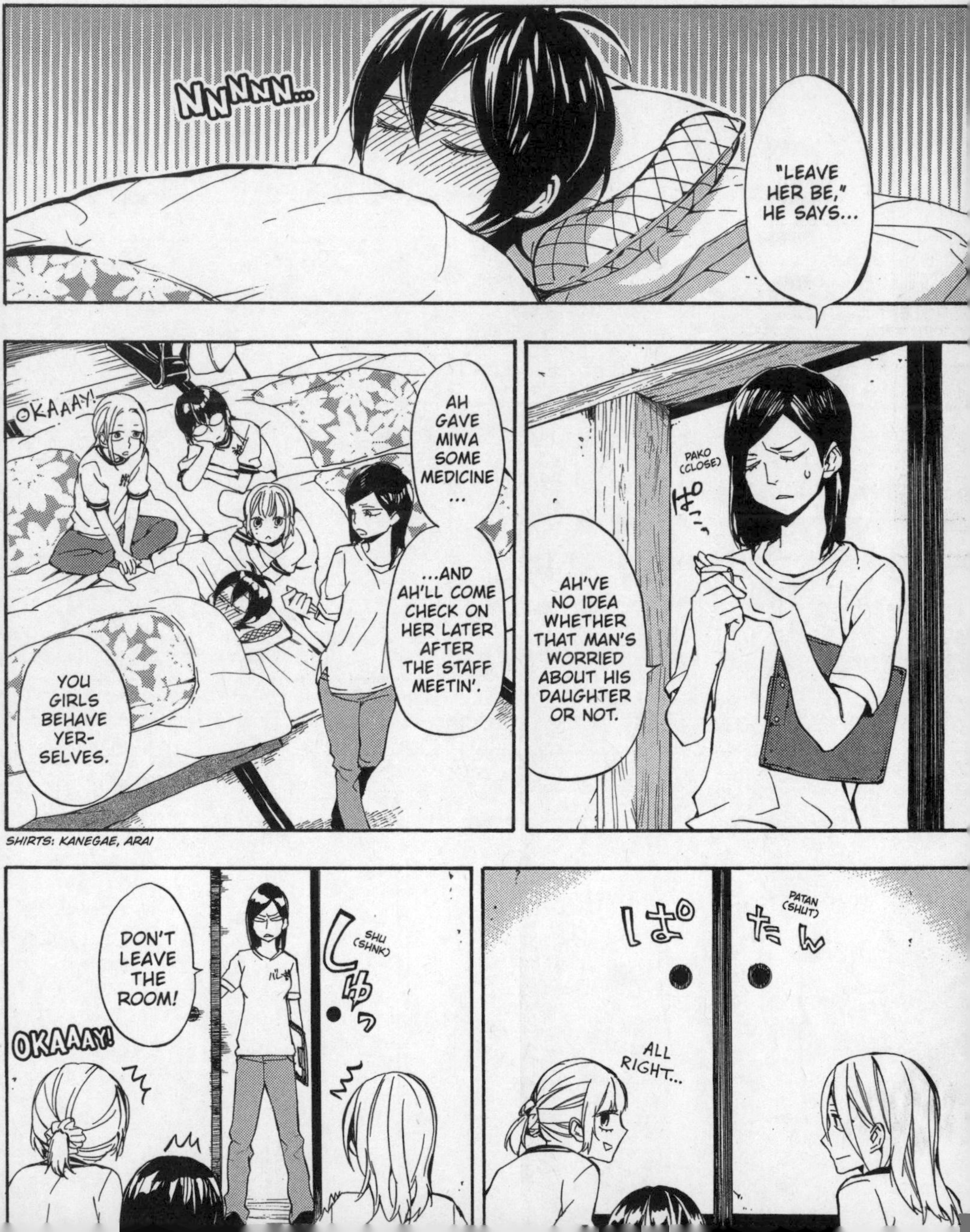
"LEAVE HER BE," HE SAYS...
NNNNN...
PAKO (CLOSE)
AH'VE NO IDEA WHETHER THAT MAN'S WORRIED ABOUT HIS DAUGHTER OR NOT.
AH GAVE MIWA SOME MEDICINE...
...AND AH'LL COME CHECK ON HER LATER AFTER THE STAFF MEETIN'.
YOU GIRLS BEHAVE YER-SELVES.
OKAAAY!
SHIRTS: KANEGAE, ARAI
PATAN (SHUT)
ALL RIGHT...
SHU (SHNK)
DON'T LEAVE THE ROOM!
OKAAAY!

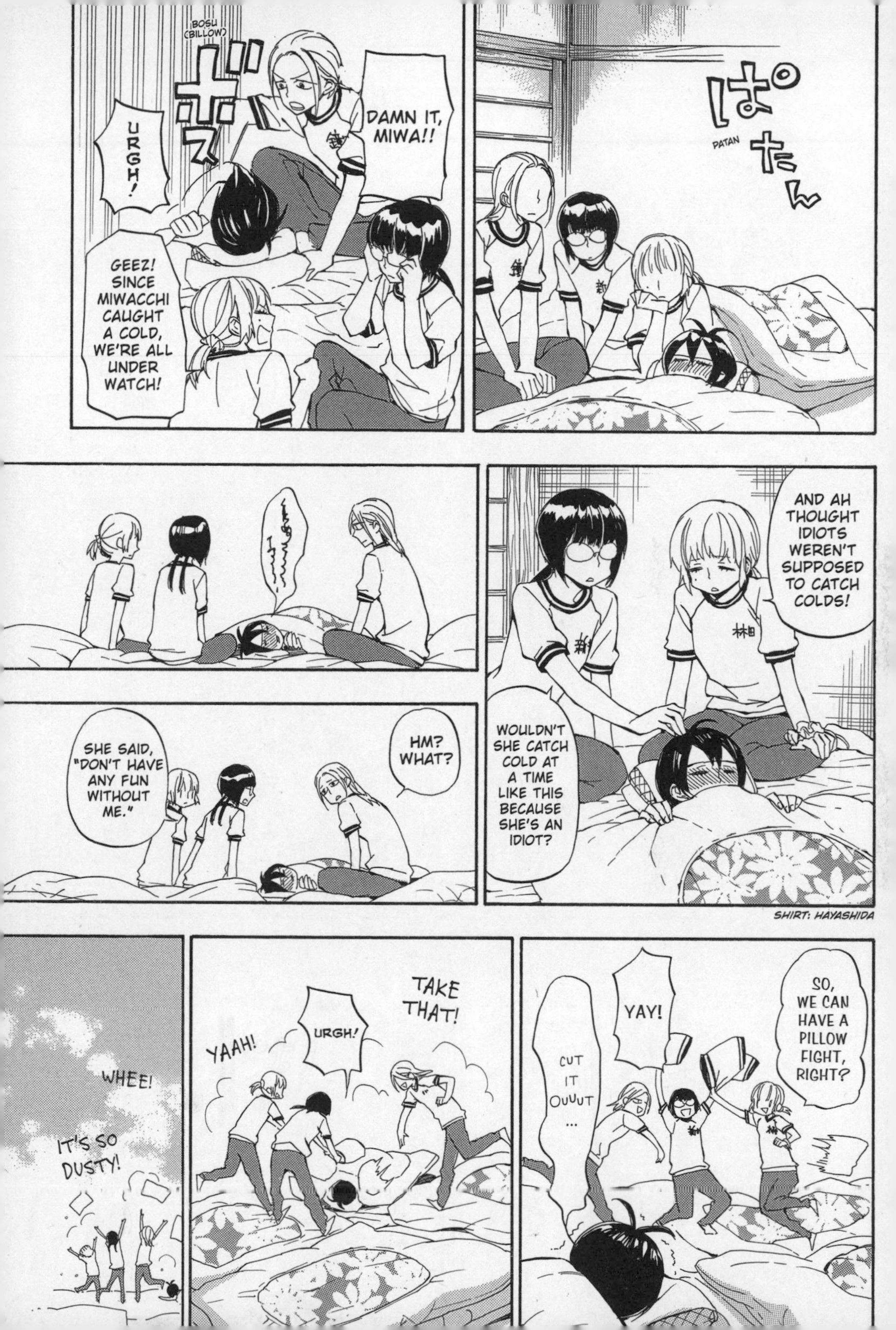
ぱたん
PATAN
DAMN IT, MIWA!!
BOSU (BILLOW)
URGH!
GEEZ! SINCE MIWACCHI CAUGHT A COLD, WE'RE ALL UNDER WATCH!
AND AH THOUGHT IDIOTS WEREN'T SUPPOSED TO CATCH COLDS!
WOULDN'T SHE CATCH COLD AT A TIME LIKE THIS BECAUSE SHE'S AN IDIOT?
HM? WHAT?
SHE SAID, "DON'T HAVE ANY FUN WITHOUT ME."
SHIRT: HAYASHIDA
SO, WE CAN HAVE A PILLOW FIGHT, RIGHT?
YAY!
CUT IT OUUUT ...
TAKE THAT!
URGH!
YAAH!
WHEE!
IT'S SO DUSTY!

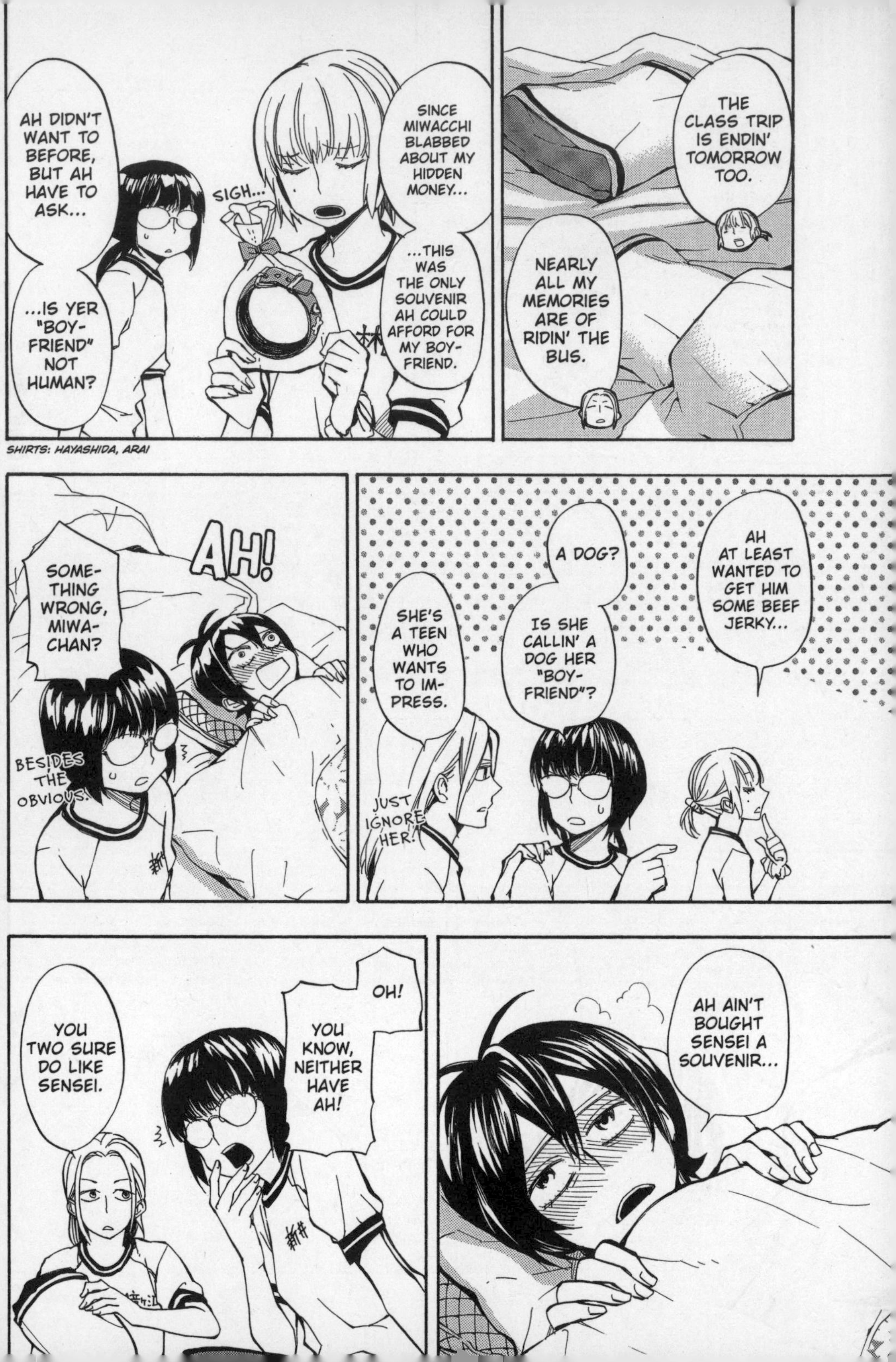
THE CLASS TRIP IS ENDIN' TOMORROW TOO.
NEARLY ALL MY MEMORIES ARE OF RIDIN' THE BUS.
SINCE MIWACCHI BLABBED ABOUT MY HIDDEN MONEY...
...THIS WAS THE ONLY SOUVENIR AH COULD AFFORD FOR MY BOY-FRIEND.
SIGH...
AH DIDN'T WANT TO BEFORE, BUT AH HAVE TO ASK...
...IS YER "BOY-FRIEND" NOT HUMAN?
SHIRTS: HAYASHIDA, ARAI
AH AT LEAST WANTED TO GET HIM SOME BEEF JERKY...
A DOG?
IS SHE CALLIN' A DOG HER "BOY-FRIEND"?
SHE'S A TEEN WHO WANTS TO IM-PRESS.
JUST IGNORE HER!
AH!
SOME-THING WRONG, MIWA-CHAN?
BESIDES THE OBVIOUS.
AH AIN'T BOUGHT SENSEI A SOUVENIR...
OH!
YOU KNOW, NEITHER HAVE AH!
YOU TWO SURE DO LIKE SENSEI.

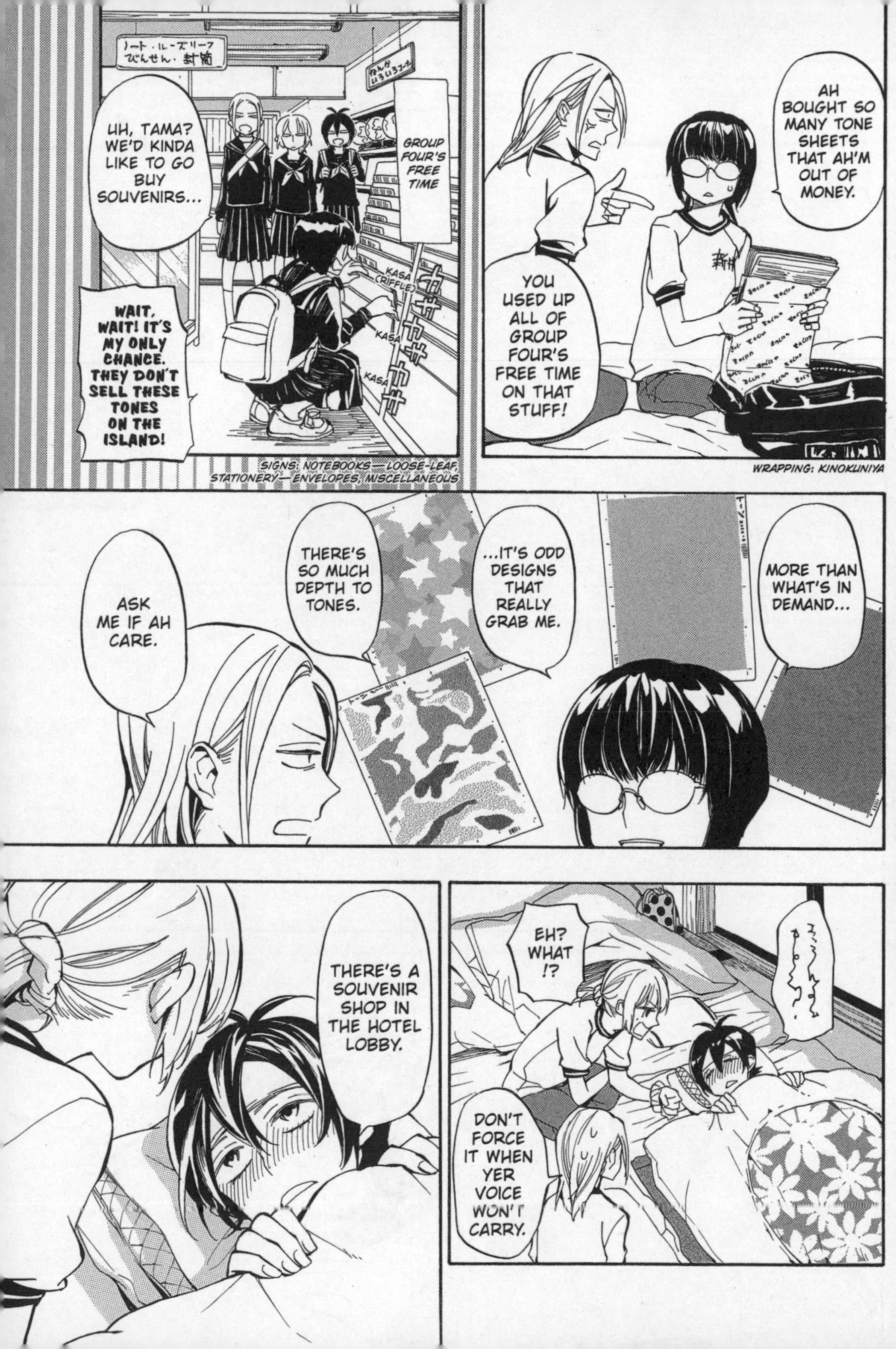
AH BOUGHT SO MANY TONE SHEETS THAT AH'M OUT OF MONEY.
YOU USED UP ALL OF GROUP FOUR'S FREE TIME ON THAT STUFF!
WRAPPING: KINOKUNIYA
ノート・ルーズリーフ びんせん・封筒
UH, TAMA? WE'D KINDA LIKE TO GO BUY SOUVENIRS...
GROUP FOUR'S FREE TIME
KASA (RIFFLE)
KASA
KASA
WAIT, WAIT! IT'S MY ONLY CHANCE. THEY DON'T SELL THESE TONES ON THE ISLAND!
SIGNS: NOTEBOOKS—LOOSE-LEAF, STATIONERY—ENVELOPES, MISCELLANEOUS
MORE THAN WHAT'S IN DEMAND...
...IT'S ODD DESIGNS THAT REALLY GRAB ME.
THERE'S SO MUCH DEPTH TO TONES.
ASK ME IF AH CARE.
EH? WHAT!?
DON'T FORCE IT WHEN YER VOICE WON'T CARRY.
THERE'S A SOUVENIR SHOP IN THE HOTEL LOBBY.

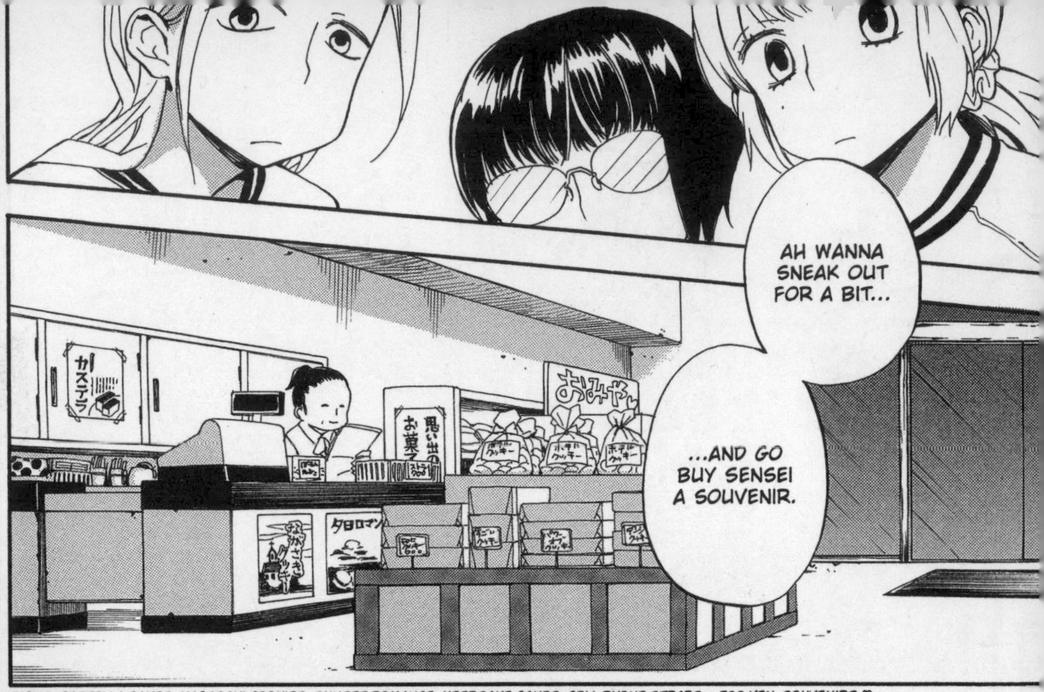
AH WANNA SNEAK OUT FOR A BIT...
...AND GO BUY SENSEI A SOUVENIR.

SIGNS: CASTELLA CAKES, NAGASAKI COOKIES, SUNSET ROMANCE, KEEPSAKE CAKES, CELL PHONE STRAPS—700 YEN, SOUVENIRS ♡
BAGS: HOTEL COOKIES / SMALL SIGNS: UTTERLY COOKIES, AMAZING COOKIES, POWER OF COOKIES, DANGER COOKIES

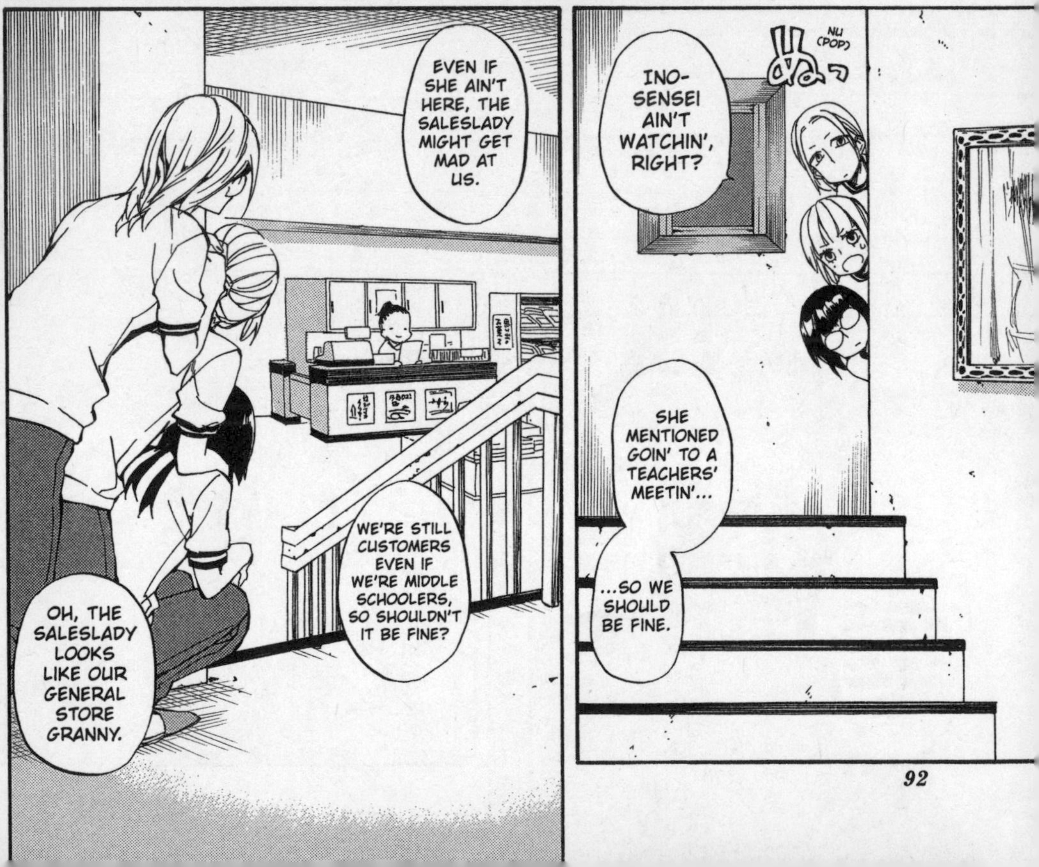
NU (POP)
INO-SENSEI AIN'T WATCHIN', RIGHT?
SHE MENTIONED GOIN' TO A TEACHERS' MEETIN'...
...SO WE SHOULD BE FINE.
EVEN IF SHE AIN'T HERE, THE SALESLADY MIGHT GET MAD AT US.
WE'RE STILL CUSTOMERS EVEN IF WE'RE MIDDLE SCHOOLERS, SO SHOULDN'T IT BE FINE?
OH, THE SALESLADY LOOKS LIKE OUR GENERAL STORE GRANNY.

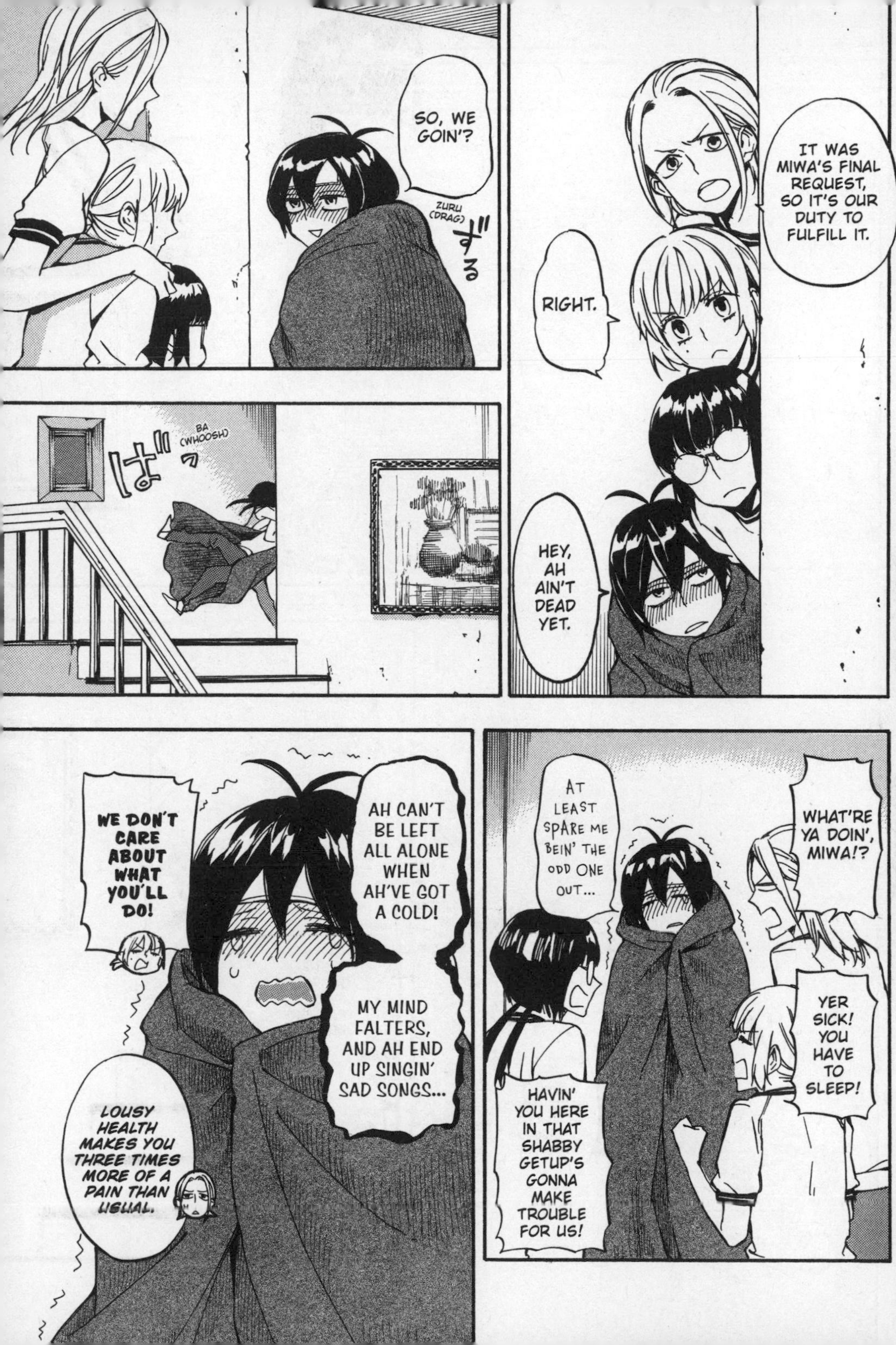
IT WAS MIWA'S FINAL REQUEST, SO IT'S OUR DUTY TO FULFILL IT.
RIGHT.
HEY, AH AIN'T DEAD YET.
SO, WE GOIN'?
ZURU (DRAG)
ずる
ばっ
BA (WHOOSH)
WHAT'RE YA DOIN', MIWA!?
AT LEAST SPARE ME BEIN' THE ODD ONE OUT...
YER SICK! YOU HAVE TO SLEEP!
HAVIN' YOU HERE IN THAT SHABBY GETUP'S GONNA MAKE TROUBLE FOR US!
AH CAN'T BE LEFT ALL ALONE WHEN AH'VE GOT A COLD!
WE DON'T CARE ABOUT WHAT YOU'LL DO!
MY MIND FALTERS, AND AH END UP SINGIN' SAD SONGS...
LOUSY HEALTH MAKES YOU THREE TIMES MORE OF A PAIN THAN USUAL.

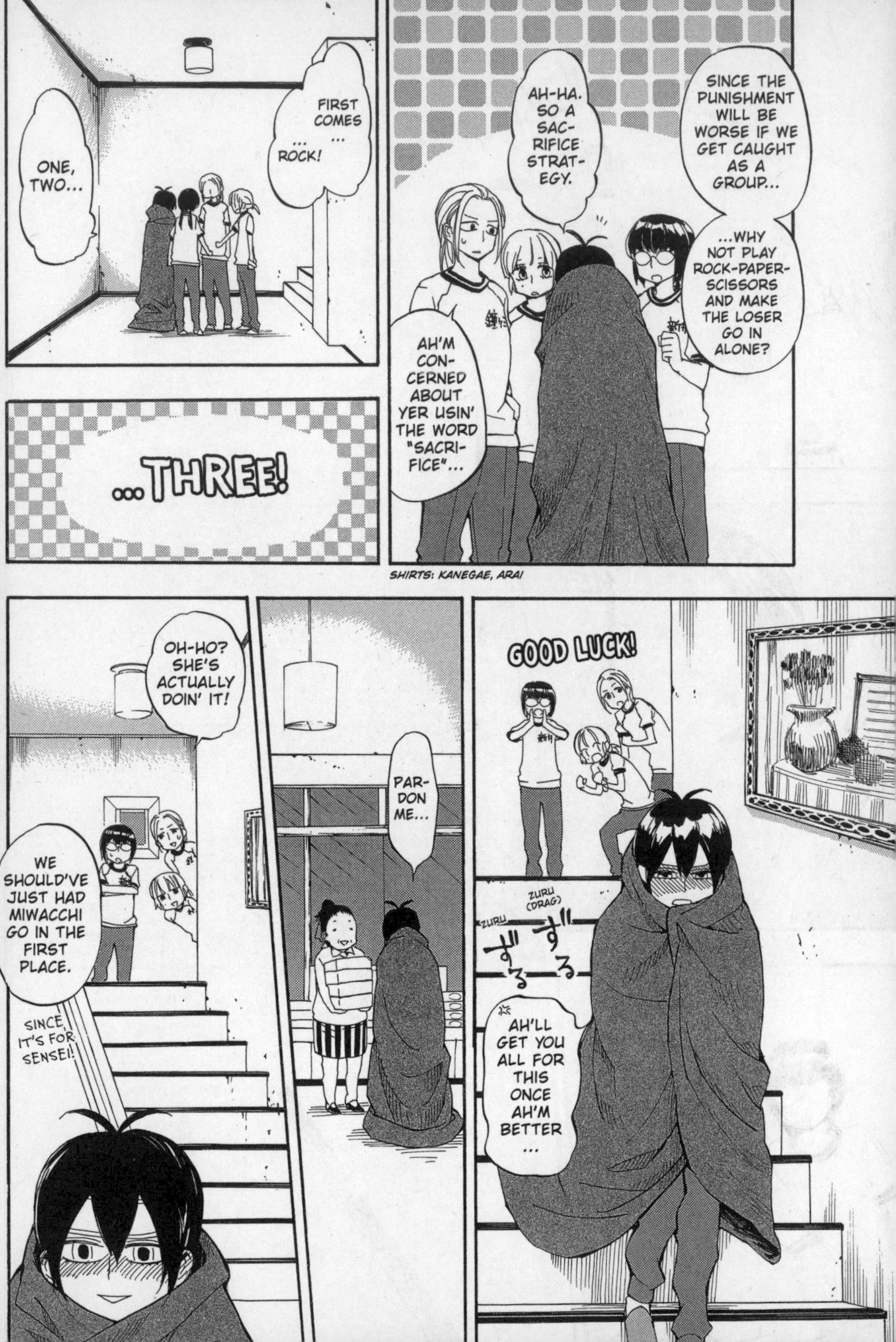
SINCE THE PUNISHMENT WILL BE WORSE IF WE GET CAUGHT AS A GROUP...
...WHY NOT PLAY ROCK-PAPER-SCISSORS AND MAKE THE LOSER GO IN ALONE?
AH-HA. SO A SAC-RIFICE STRAT-EGY.
AH'M CON-CERNED ABOUT YER USIN' THE WORD "SACRI-FICE"...
FIRST COMES ... ... ROCK!
ONE, TWO...
...THREE!
SHIRTS: KANEGAE, ARAI
GOOD LUCK!
ZURU (DRAG)
ZURU
ずる ずる
AH'LL GET YOU ALL FOR THIS ONCE AH'M BETTER ...
PAR-DON ME...
OH-HO? SHE'S ACTUALLY DOIN' IT!
WE SHOULD'VE JUST HAD MIWACCHI GO IN THE FIRST PLACE.
SINCE IT'S FOR SENSEI!

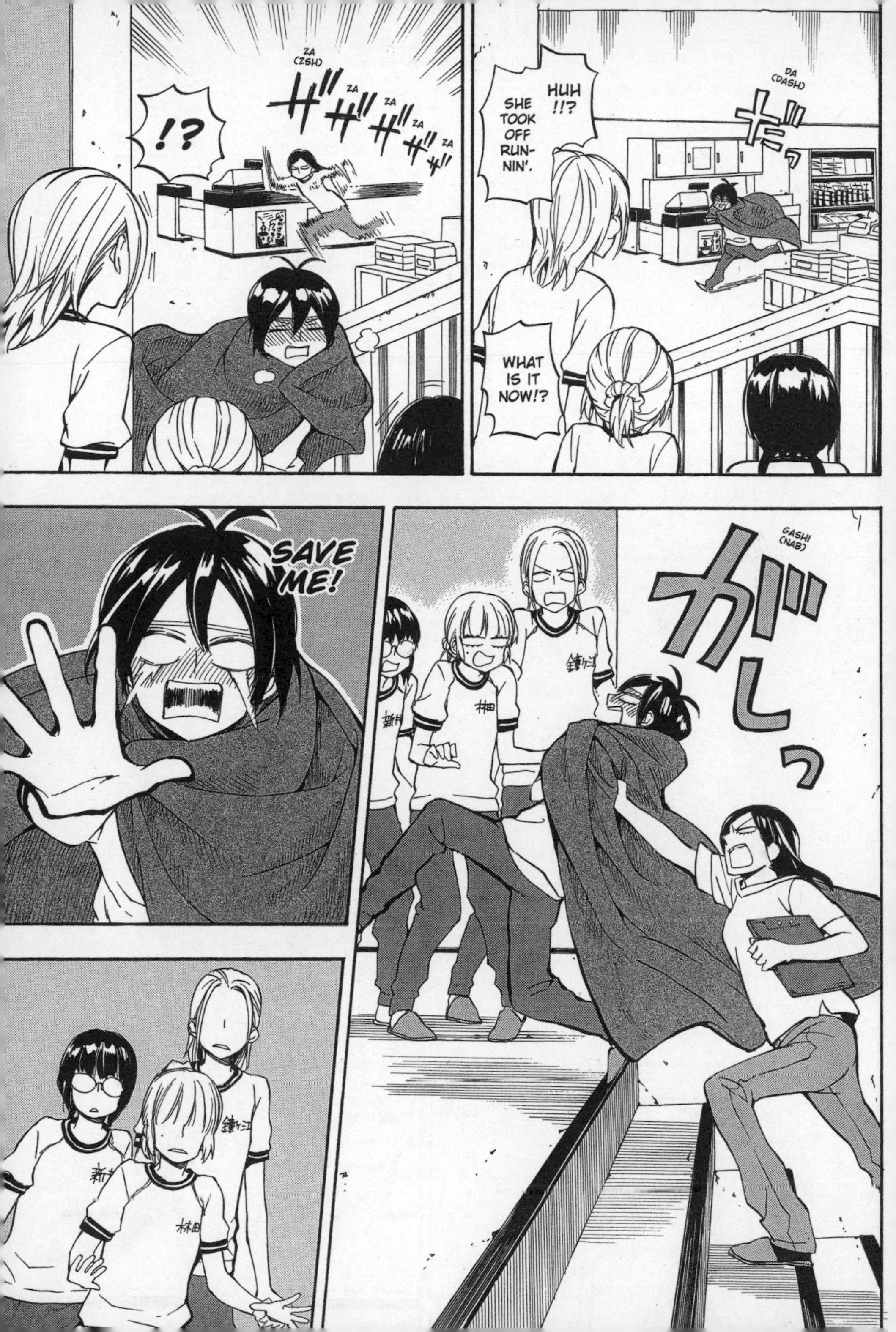
DA (DASH)
HUH !!?
SHE TOOK OFF RUN-NIN'.
WHAT IS IT NOW!?
ZA (ZSH)
ZA
ZA
ZA
ZA
!?
GASHI (NAB)
SAVE ME!

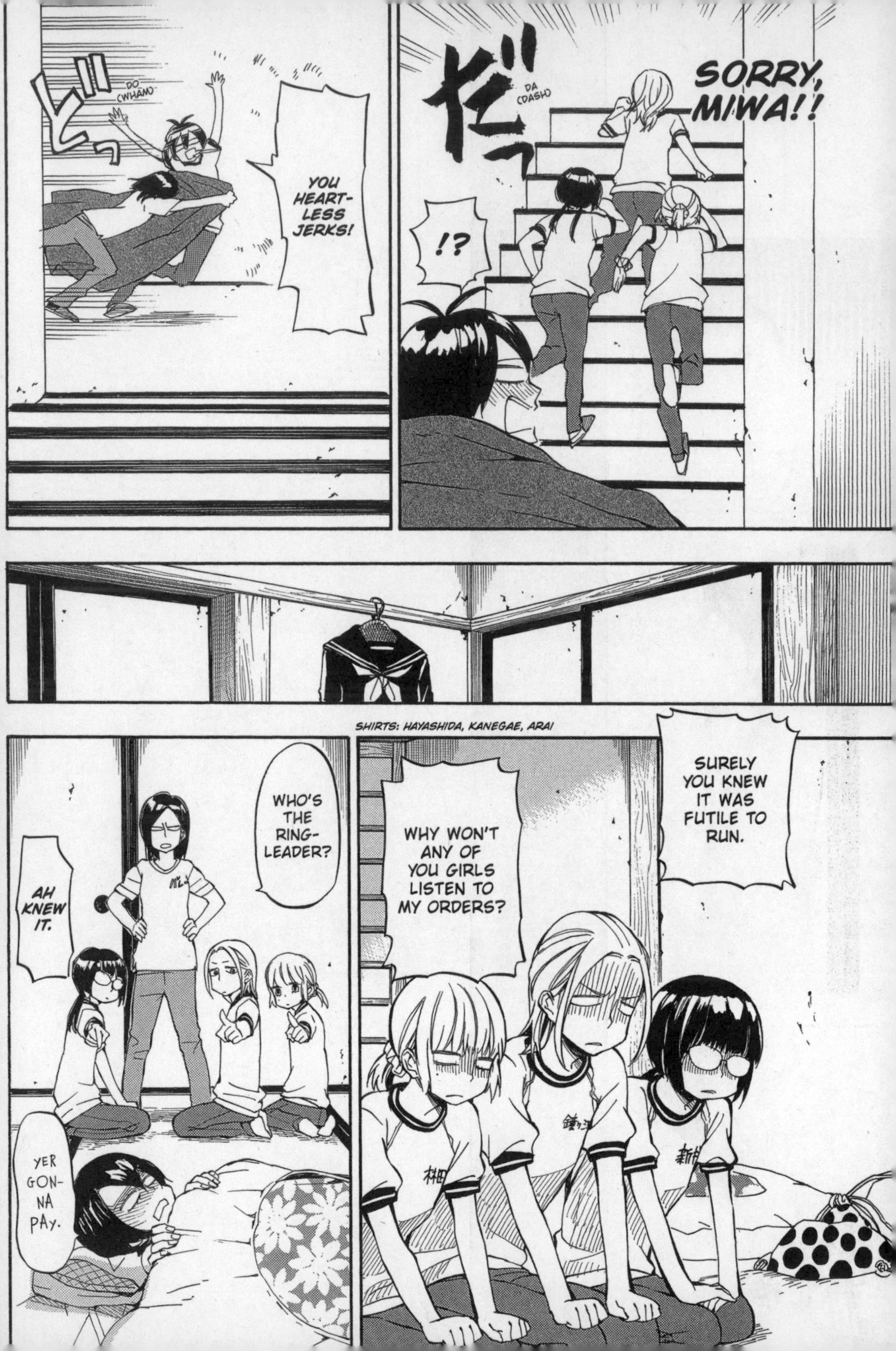
SORRY, MIWA!!
DA (DASH)
!?
DO (WHAM)
YOU HEARTLESS JERKS!
SHIRTS: HAYASHIDA, KANEGAE, ARAI
SURELY YOU KNEW IT WAS FUTILE TO RUN.
WHY WON'T ANY OF YOU GIRLS LISTEN TO MY ORDERS?
WHO'S THE RINGLEADER?
AH KNEW IT.
YER GONNA PAY.

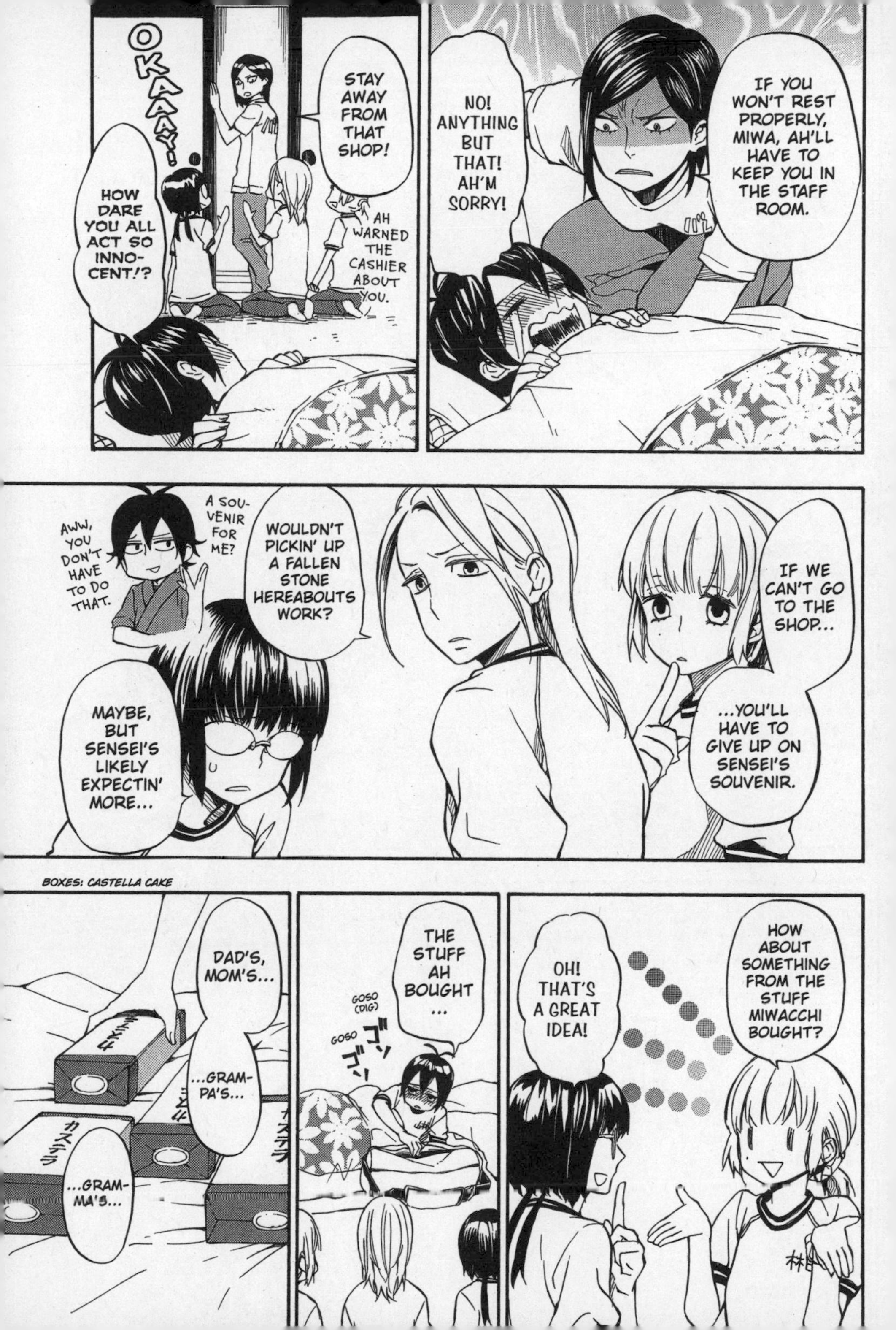
IF YOU WON'T REST PROPERLY, MIWA, AH'LL HAVE TO KEEP YOU IN THE STAFF ROOM.
NO! ANYTHING BUT THAT! AH'M SORRY!
STAY AWAY FROM THAT SHOP!
AH WARNED THE CASHIER ABOUT YOU.
OKAAAY!
HOW DARE YOU ALL ACT SO INNO-CENT!?
IF WE CAN'T GO TO THE SHOP...
...YOU'LL HAVE TO GIVE UP ON SENSEI'S SOUVENIR.
WOULDN'T PICKIN' UP A FALLEN STONE HEREABOUTS WORK?
A SOU-VENIR FOR ME?
AWW, YOU DON'T HAVE TO DO THAT.
MAYBE, BUT SENSEI'S LIKELY EXPECTIN' MORE...
BOXES: CASTELLA CAKE
HOW ABOUT SOMETHING FROM THE STUFF MIWACCHI BOUGHT?
OH! THAT'S A GREAT IDEA!
THE STUFF AH BOUGHT...
ゴソ GOSO (DIG)
ゴソ GOSO
DAD'S, MOM'S...
...GRAM-PA'S...
...GRAM-MA'S...
カステラ

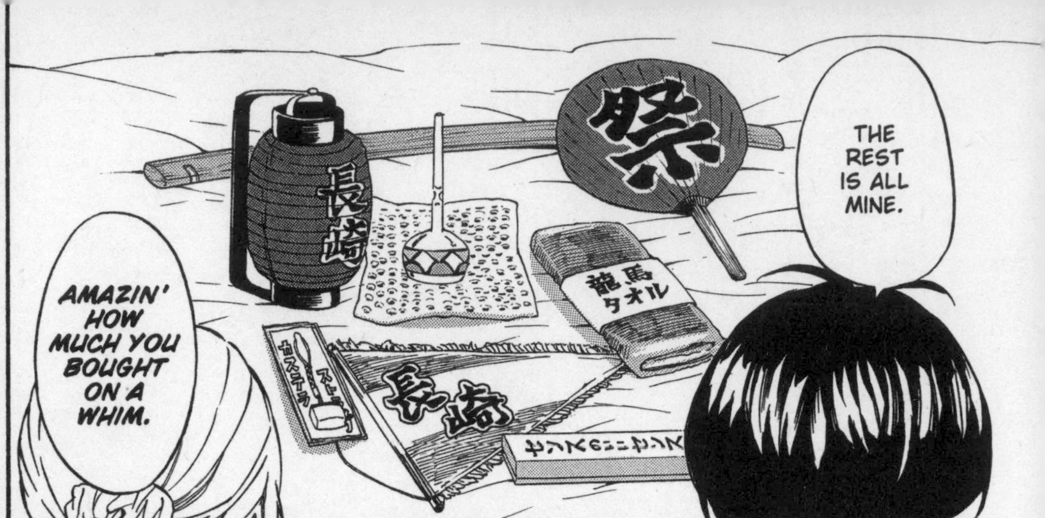
THE REST IS ALL MINE.
AMAZIN' HOW MUCH YOU BOUGHT ON A WHIM.
祭
長崎
龍馬タオル
カステラストラップ
長崎

LANTERN AND PENNANT: NAGASAKI / PACKET: CASTELLA CELL PHONE STRAP / FAN: FESTIVAL / TOWEL: RYOUMA TOWEL / THIN BOX: FANTASTIC FAN

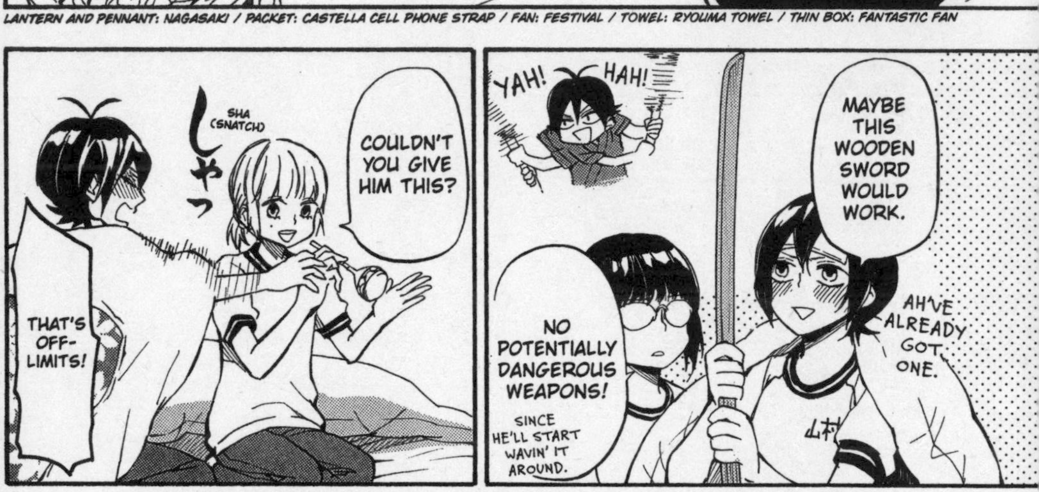
YAH!
HAH!
MAYBE THIS WOODEN SWORD WOULD WORK.
AH'VE ALREADY GOT ONE.
NO POTENTIALLY DANGEROUS WEAPONS!
SINCE HE'LL START WAVIN' IT AROUND.
COULDN'T YOU GIVE HIM THIS?
SHA (SNATCH)
しゃっ
THAT'S OFF-LIMITS!

TOWEL: ZEYO

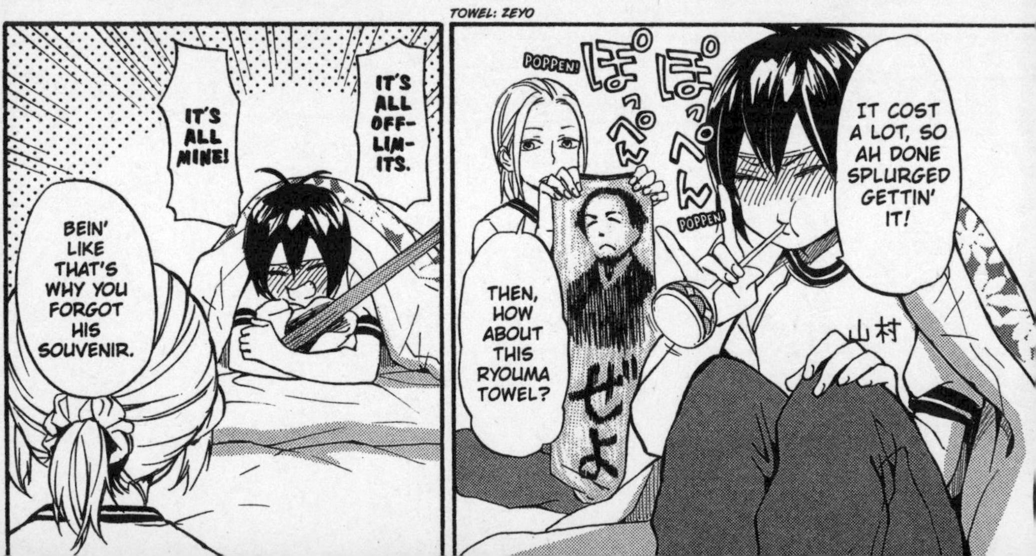
POPPEN!
ぽっぺん
POPPEN!
ぽっぺん
IT COST A LOT, SO AH DONE SPLURGED GETTIN' IT!
THEN, HOW ABOUT THIS RYOUMA TOWEL?
ぜよ
山村
IT'S ALL OFF-LIMITS.
IT'S ALL MINE!
BEIN' LIKE THAT'S WHY YOU FORGOT HIS SOUVENIR.

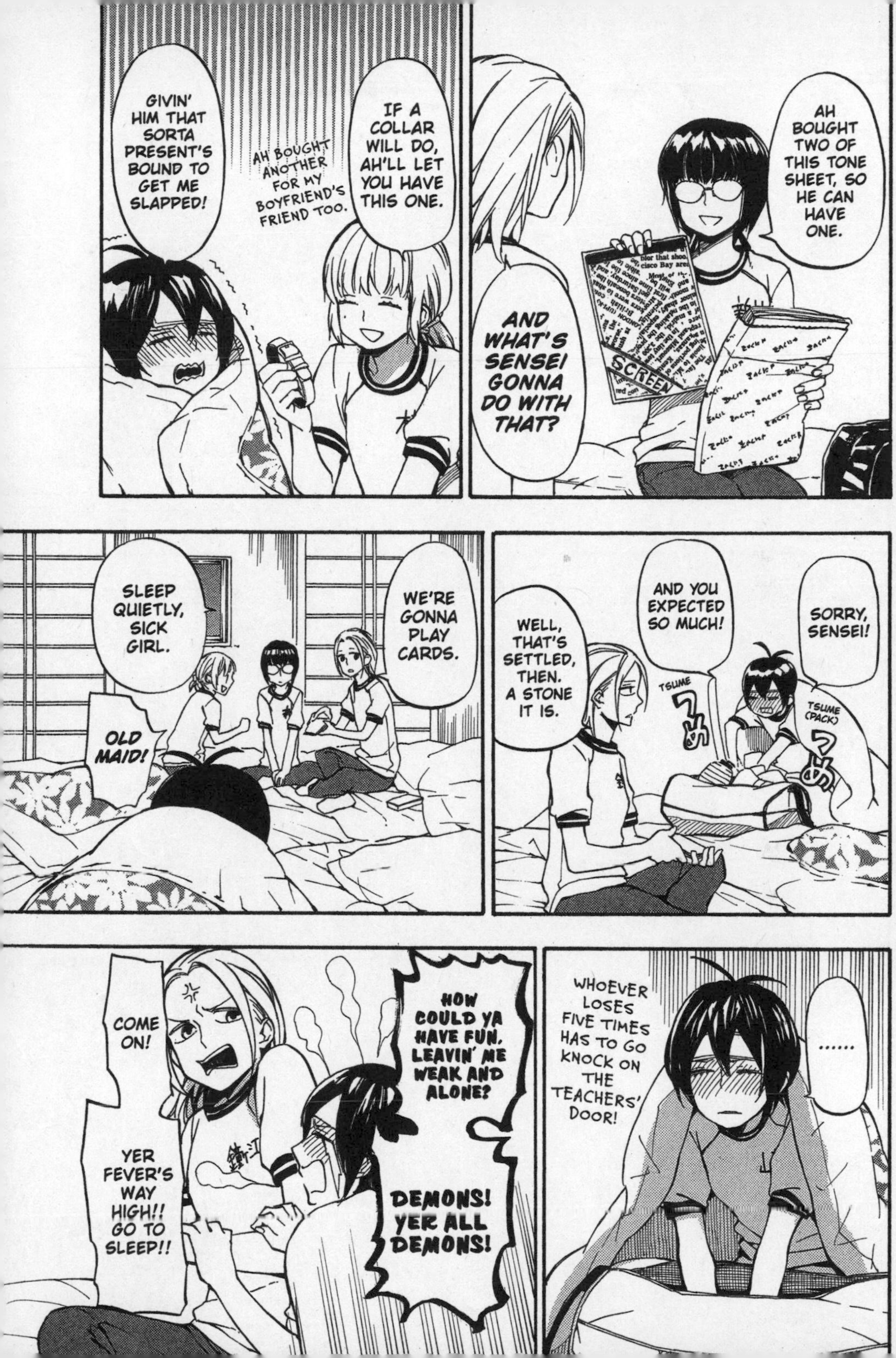
AH BOUGHT TWO OF THIS TONE SHEET, SO HE CAN HAVE ONE.
AND WHAT'S SENSEI GONNA DO WITH THAT?
SCREEN
IF A COLLAR WILL DO, AH'LL LET YOU HAVE THIS ONE.
AH BOUGHT ANOTHER FOR MY BOYFRIEND'S FRIEND TOO.
GIVIN' HIM THAT SORTA PRESENT'S BOUND TO GET ME SLAPPED!
SORRY, SENSEI!
AND YOU EXPECTED SO MUCH!
TSUME (PACK)
つめ
WELL, THAT'S SETTLED, THEN. A STONE IT IS.
TSUME
つめ
WE'RE GONNA PLAY CARDS.
SLEEP QUIETLY, SICK GIRL.
OLD MAID!
......
WHOEVER LOSES FIVE TIMES HAS TO GO KNOCK ON THE TEACHERS' DOOR!
HOW COULD YA HAVE FUN, LEAVIN' ME WEAK AND ALONE?
DEMONS! YER ALL DEMONS!
COME ON!
YER FEVER'S WAY HIGH!! GO TO SLEEP!!

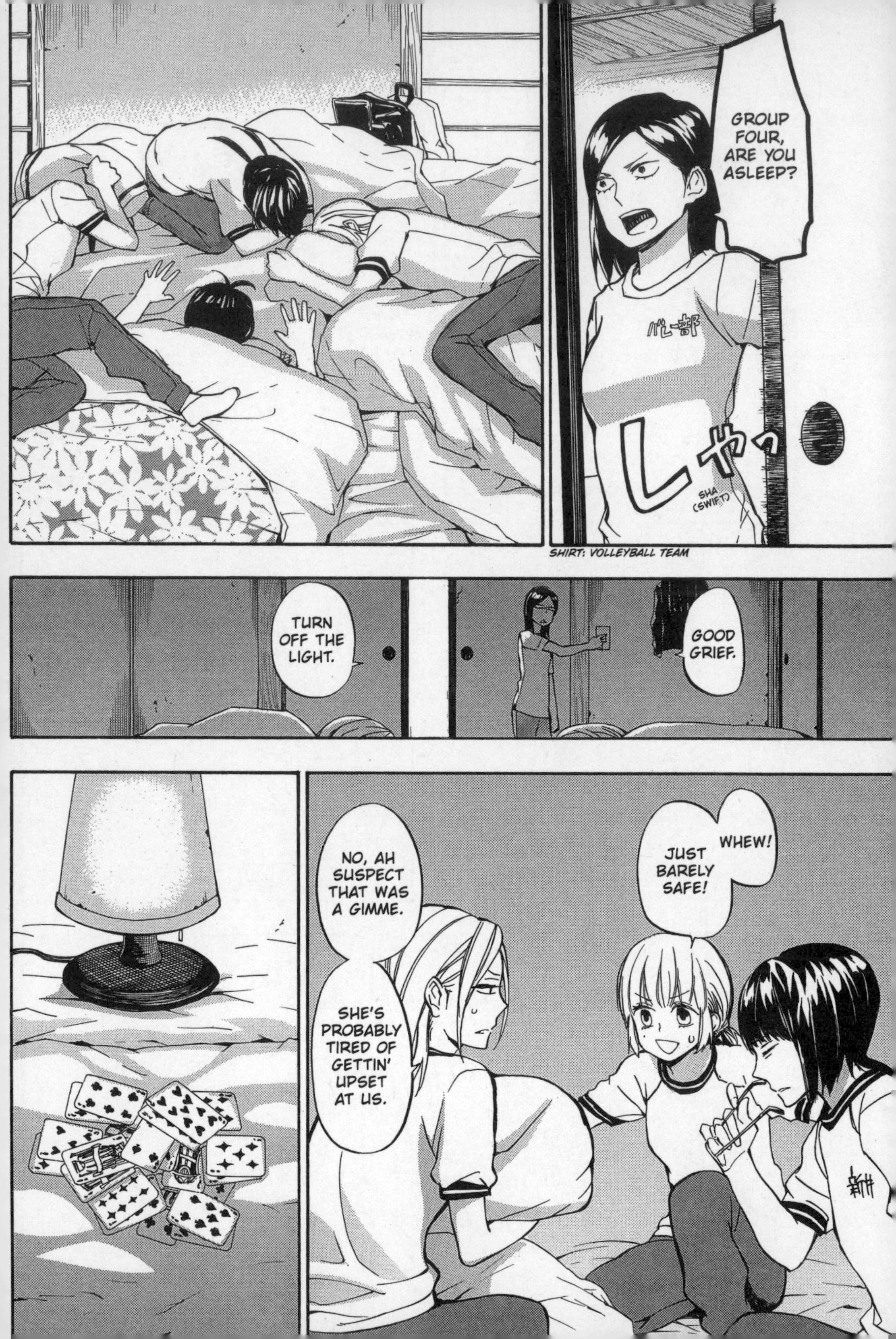
GROUP FOUR, ARE YOU ASLEEP?
バレー部
しゃっ
SHA (SWIFT)
SHIRT: VOLLEYBALL TEAM
GOOD GRIEF.
TURN OFF THE LIGHT.
WHEW!
JUST BARELY SAFE!
NO, AH SUSPECT THAT WAS A GIMME.
SHE'S PROBABLY TIRED OF GETTIN' UPSET AT US.
新井

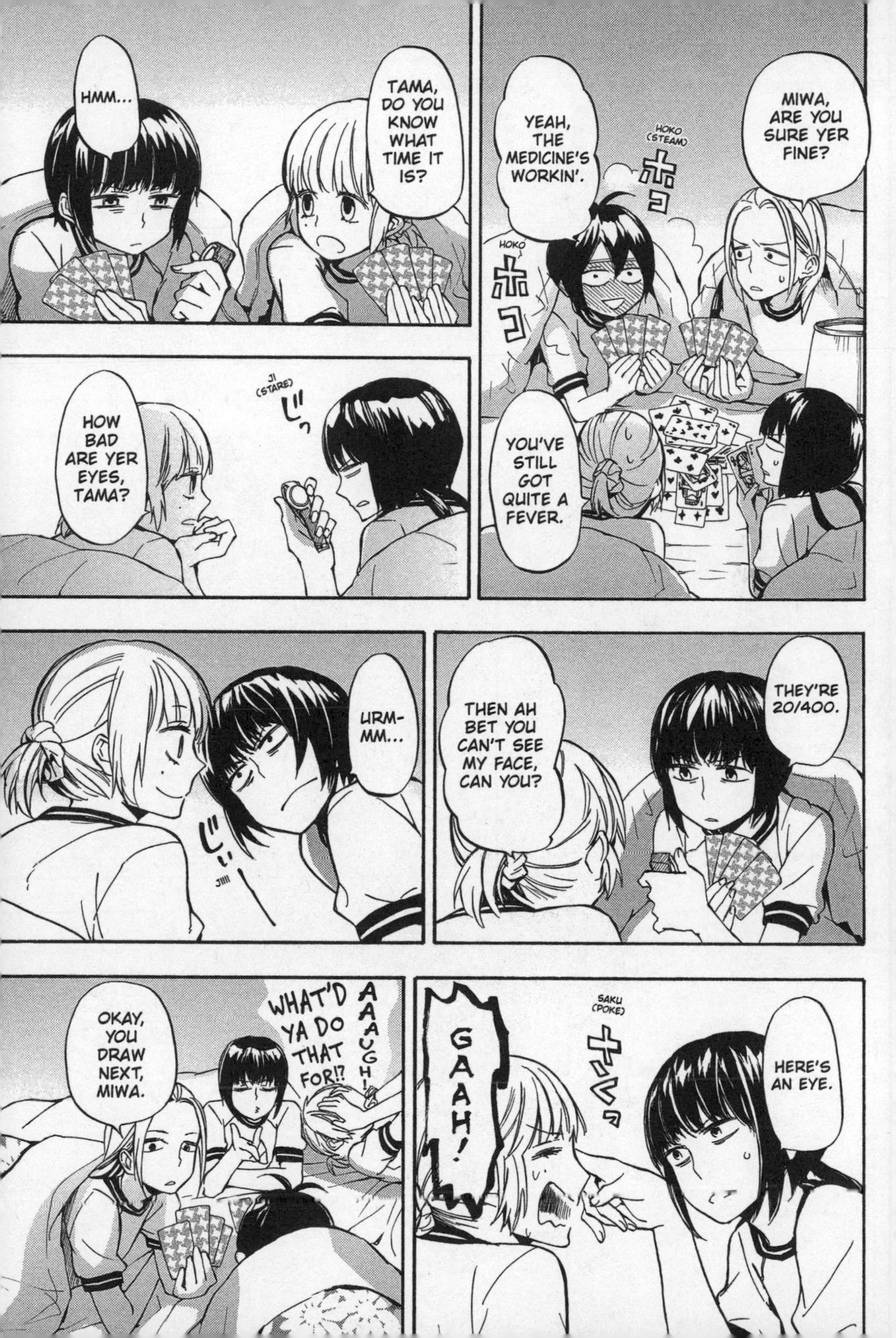
MIWA, ARE YOU SURE YER FINE?
HOKO (STEAM)
YEAH, THE MEDICINE'S WORKIN'.
HOKO
YOU'VE STILL GOT QUITE A FEVER.
TAMA, DO YOU KNOW WHAT TIME IT IS?
HMM...
JI (STARE)
HOW BAD ARE YER EYES, TAMA?
THEY'RE 20/400.
THEN AH BET YOU CAN'T SEE MY FACE, CAN YOU?
URM-MM...
JIIII
HERE'S AN EYE.
SAKU (POKE)
GAAH!
AAAAUGH!
WHAT'D YA DO THAT FOR!?
OKAY, YOU DRAW NEXT, MIWA.

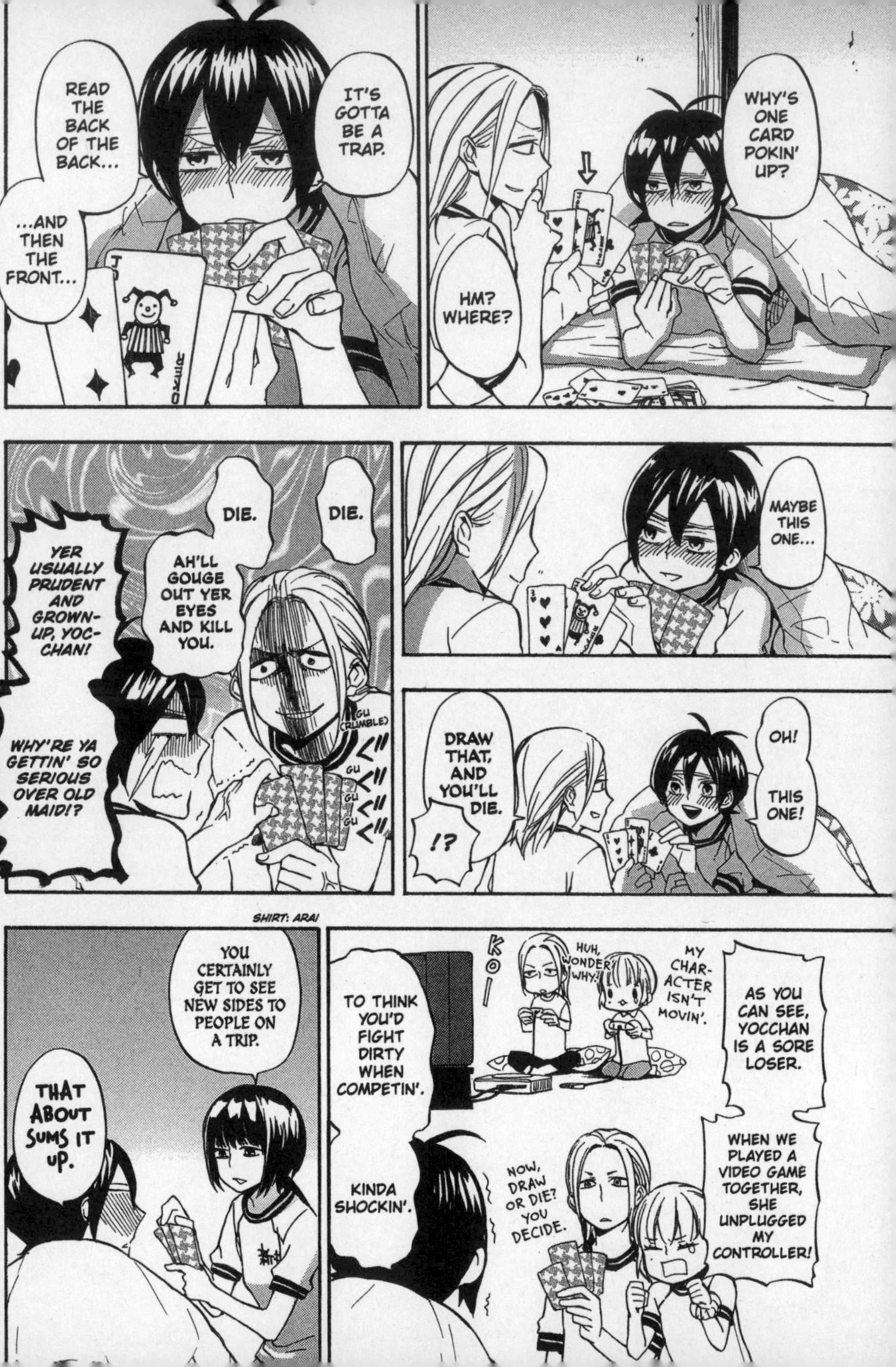
WHY'S ONE CARD POKIN' UP?
HM? WHERE?
IT'S GOTTA BE A TRAP.
READ THE BACK OF THE BACK...
...AND THEN THE FRONT...
MAYBE THIS ONE...
OH!
THIS ONE!
DRAW THAT, AND YOU'LL DIE.
!?
DIE.
DIE.
AH'LL GOUGE OUT YER EYES AND KILL YOU.
GU (CRUMBLE) GU GU GU
YER USUALLY PRUDENT AND GROWN-UP, YOC-CHAN!
WHY'RE YA GETTIN' SO SERIOUS OVER OLD MAID!?
SHIRT: ARAI
AS YOU CAN SEE, YOCCHAN IS A SORE LOSER.
MY CHAR-ACTER ISN'T MOVIN'.
HUH, WONDER WHY.
KOI
TO THINK YOU'D FIGHT DIRTY WHEN COMPETIN'.
WHEN WE PLAYED A VIDEO GAME TOGETHER, SHE UNPLUGGED MY CONTROLLER!
NOW, DRAW OR DIE? YOU DECIDE.
KINDA SHOCKIN'.
YOU CERTAINLY GET TO SEE NEW SIDES TO PEOPLE ON A TRIP.
THAT ABOUT SUMS IT UP.

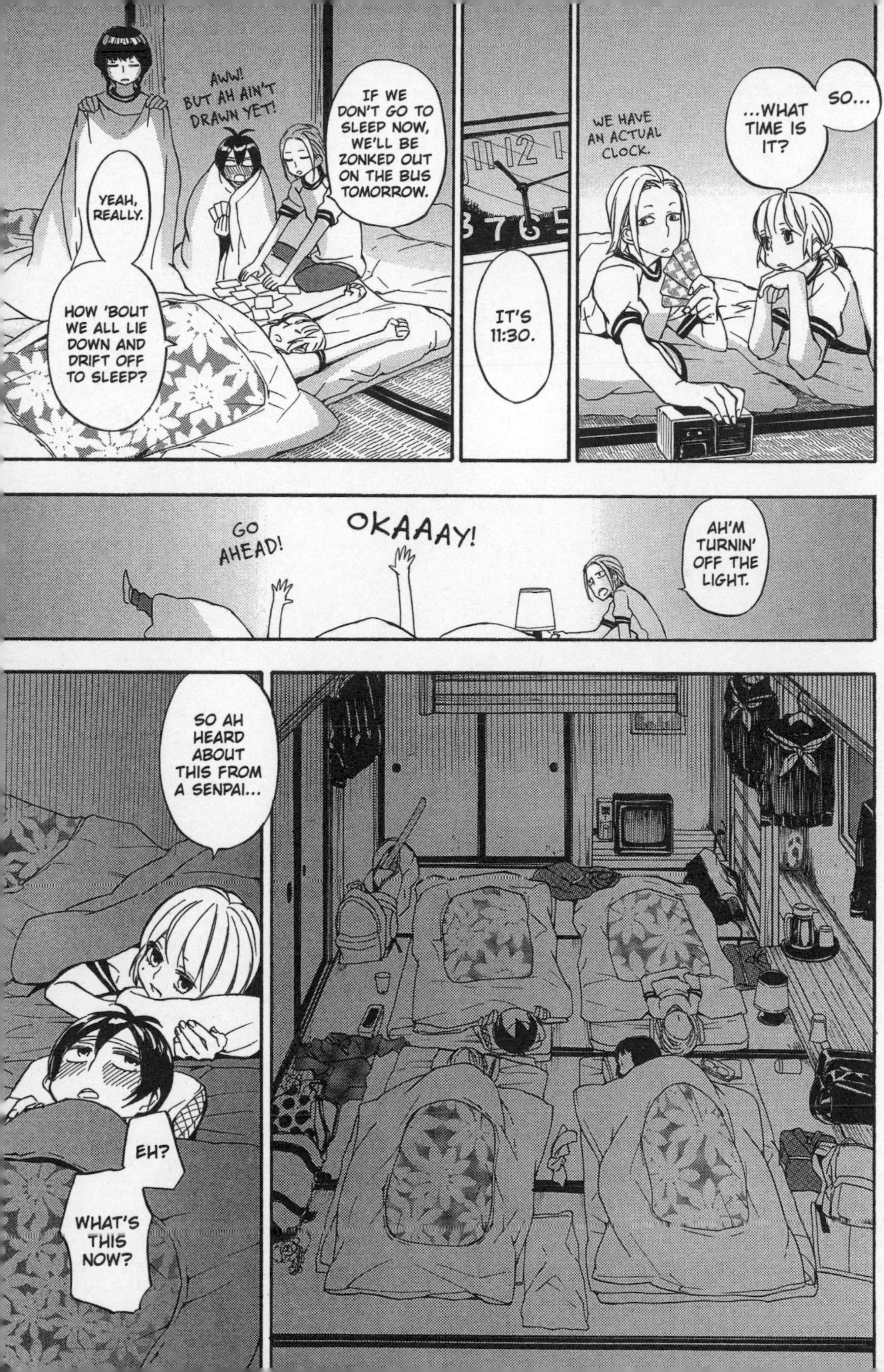
SO...
...WHAT TIME IS IT?
WE HAVE AN ACTUAL CLOCK.
IT'S 11:30.
IF WE DON'T GO TO SLEEP NOW, WE'LL BE ZONKED OUT ON THE BUS TOMORROW.
AWW! BUT AH AIN'T DRAWN YET!
YEAH, REALLY.
HOW 'BOUT WE ALL LIE DOWN AND DRIFT OFF TO SLEEP?
AH'M TURNIN' OFF THE LIGHT.
OKAAAY!
GO AHEAD!
SO AH HEARD ABOUT THIS FROM A SENPAI...
EH?
WHAT'S THIS NOW?

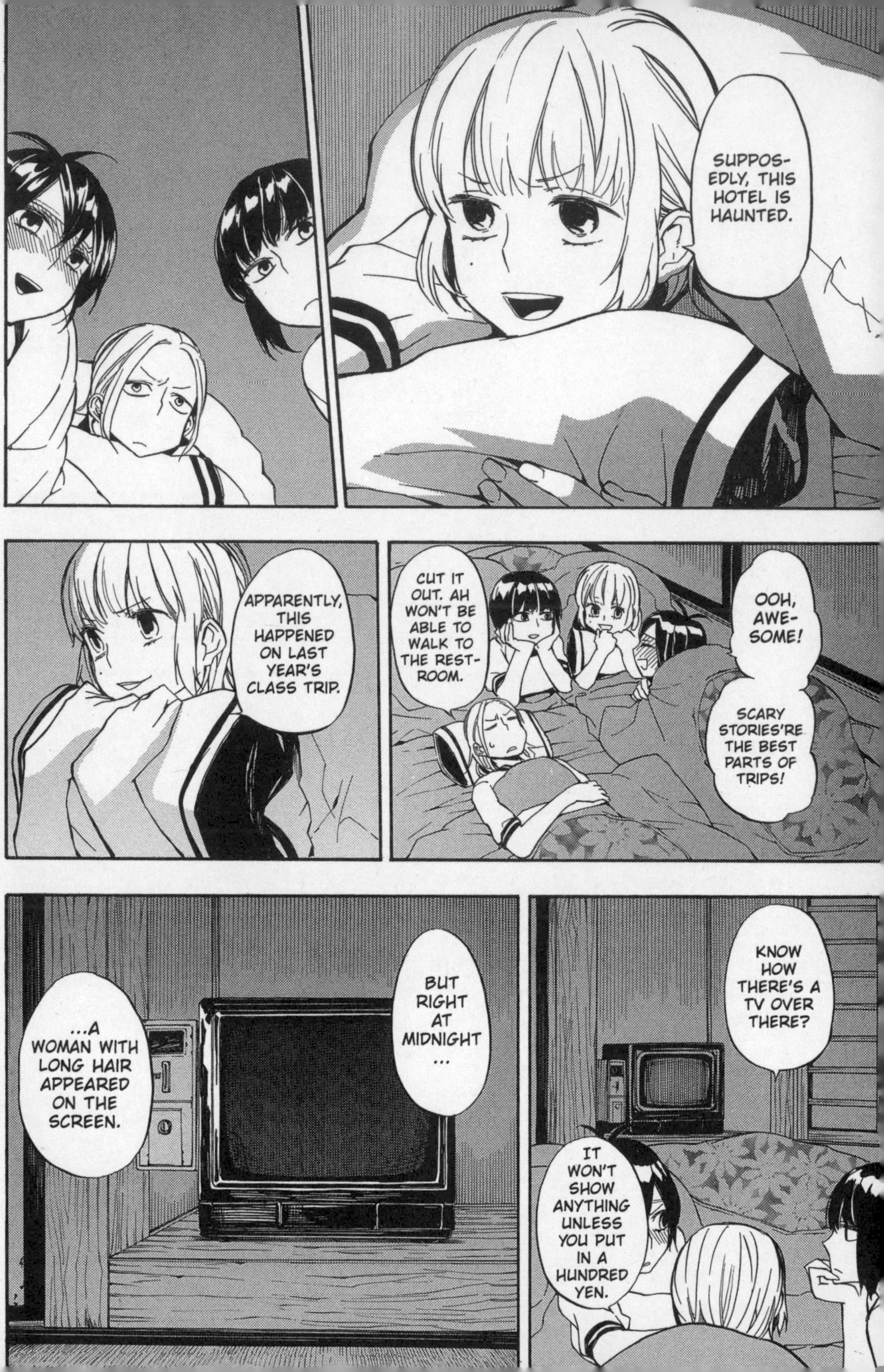
SUPPOSEDLY, THIS HOTEL IS HAUNTED.
OOH, AWESOME!
SCARY STORIES'RE THE BEST PARTS OF TRIPS!
CUT IT OUT. AH WON'T BE ABLE TO WALK TO THE RESTROOM.
APPARENTLY, THIS HAPPENED ON LAST YEAR'S CLASS TRIP.
KNOW HOW THERE'S A TV OVER THERE?
IT WON'T SHOW ANYTHING UNLESS YOU PUT IN A HUNDRED YEN.
BUT RIGHT AT MIDNIGHT...
...A WOMAN WITH LONG HAIR APPEARED ON THE SCREEN.

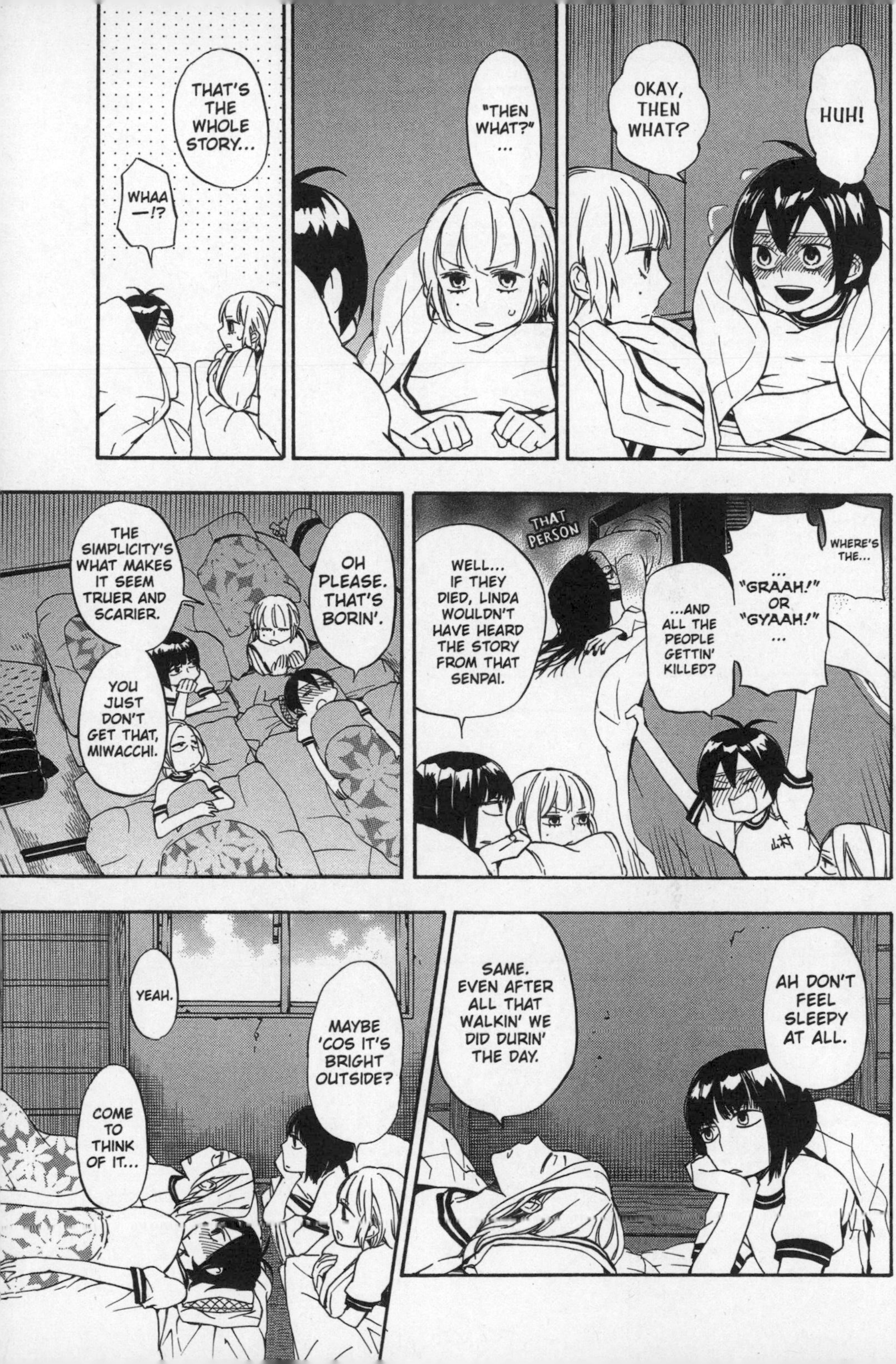
HUH!
OKAY, THEN WHAT?
"THEN WHAT?" ...
THAT'S THE WHOLE STORY...
WHAA—!?
WHERE'S THE...
... "GRAAH!" OR "GYAAH!" ...
...AND ALL THE PEOPLE GETTIN' KILLED?
THAT PERSON
WELL... IF THEY DIED, LINDA WOULDN'T HAVE HEARD THE STORY FROM THAT SENPAI.
OH PLEASE. THAT'S BORIN'.
THE SIMPLICITY'S WHAT MAKES IT SEEM TRUER AND SCARIER.
YOU JUST DON'T GET THAT, MIWACCHI.
AH DON'T FEEL SLEEPY AT ALL.
SAME. EVEN AFTER ALL THAT WALKIN' WE DID DURIN' THE DAY.
MAYBE 'COS IT'S BRIGHT OUTSIDE?
YEAH.
COME TO THINK OF IT...

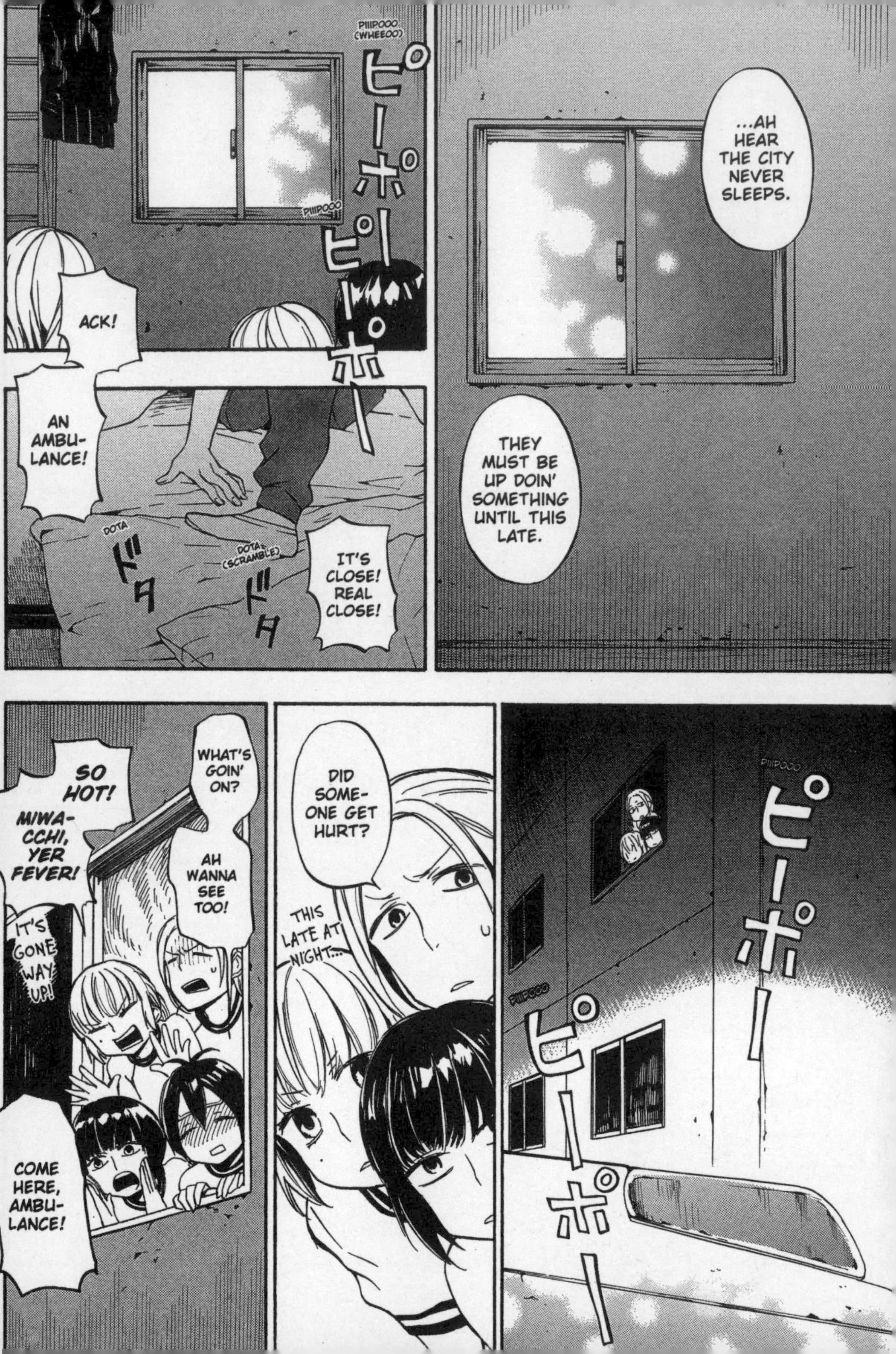
...AH HEAR THE CITY NEVER SLEEPS.
THEY MUST BE UP DOIN' SOMETHING UNTIL THIS LATE.
PIIIPOOO (WHEEOO)
ピーポーピーポー
PIIIPOOO
ACK!
AN AMBULANCE!
DOTA
ドタ
DOTA (SCRAMBLE)
ドタ
IT'S CLOSE! REAL CLOSE!
PIIIPOOO
ピーポー
PIIIPOOO
ピーポー
DID SOMEONE GET HURT?
THIS LATE AT NIGHT...
WHAT'S GOIN' ON?
SO HOT! MIWACCHI, YER FEVER!
AH WANNA SEE TOO!
IT'S GONE WAY UP!
COME HERE, AMBULANCE!

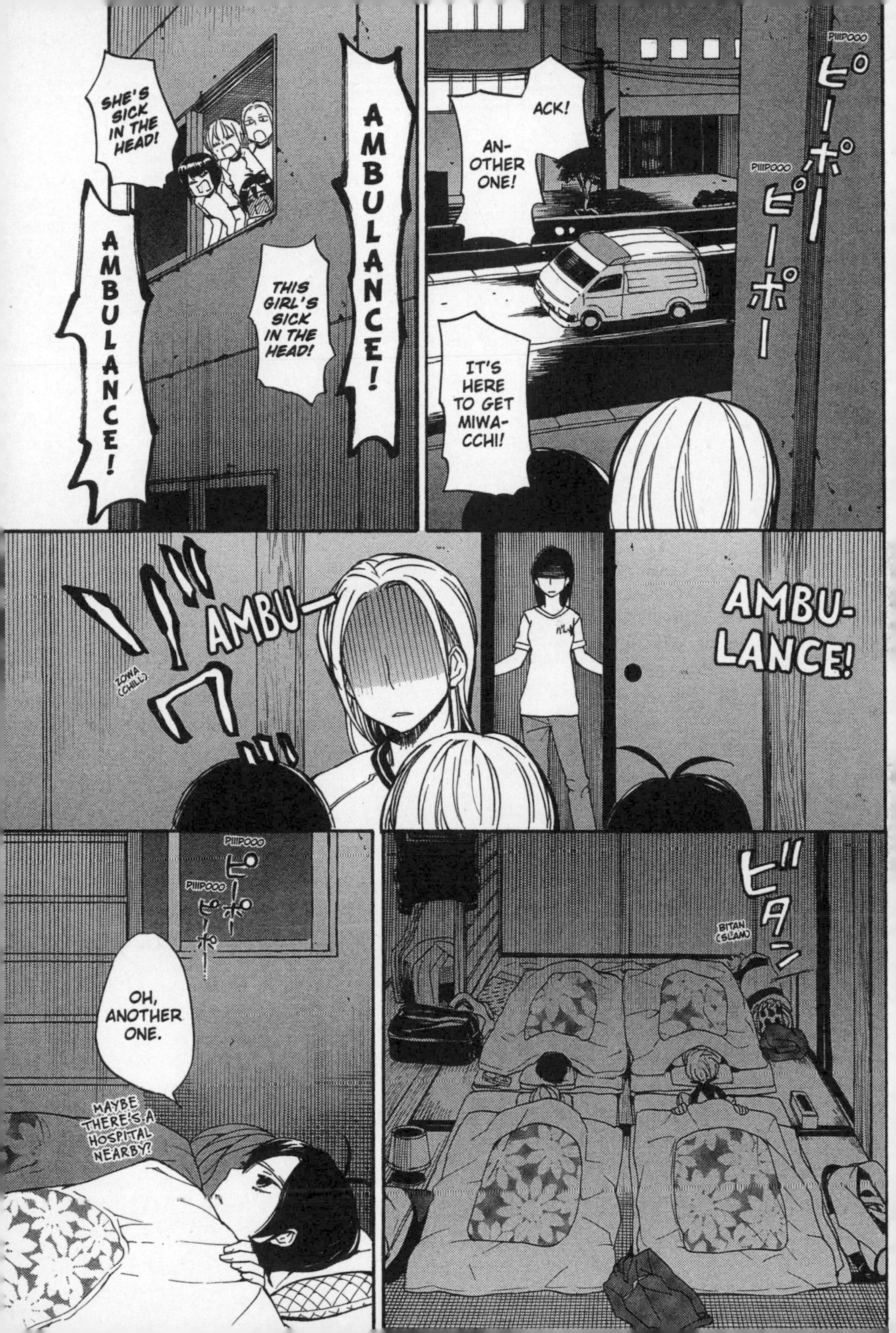
PIIIPOOO
ピーポー
PIIIPOOO
ピーポー
ACK!
AN-OTHER ONE!
IT'S HERE TO GET MIWACCHI!
AMBULANCE!
THIS GIRL'S SICK IN THE HEAD!
SHE'S SICK IN THE HEAD!
AMBULANCE!
AMBU-LANCE!
AMBU—
ZOWA (CHILL)
ビタン
BITAN (SLAM)
PIIIPOOO
ピーポー
PIIIPOOO
ピーポー
OH, ANOTHER ONE.
MAYBE THERE'S A HOSPITAL NEARBY?

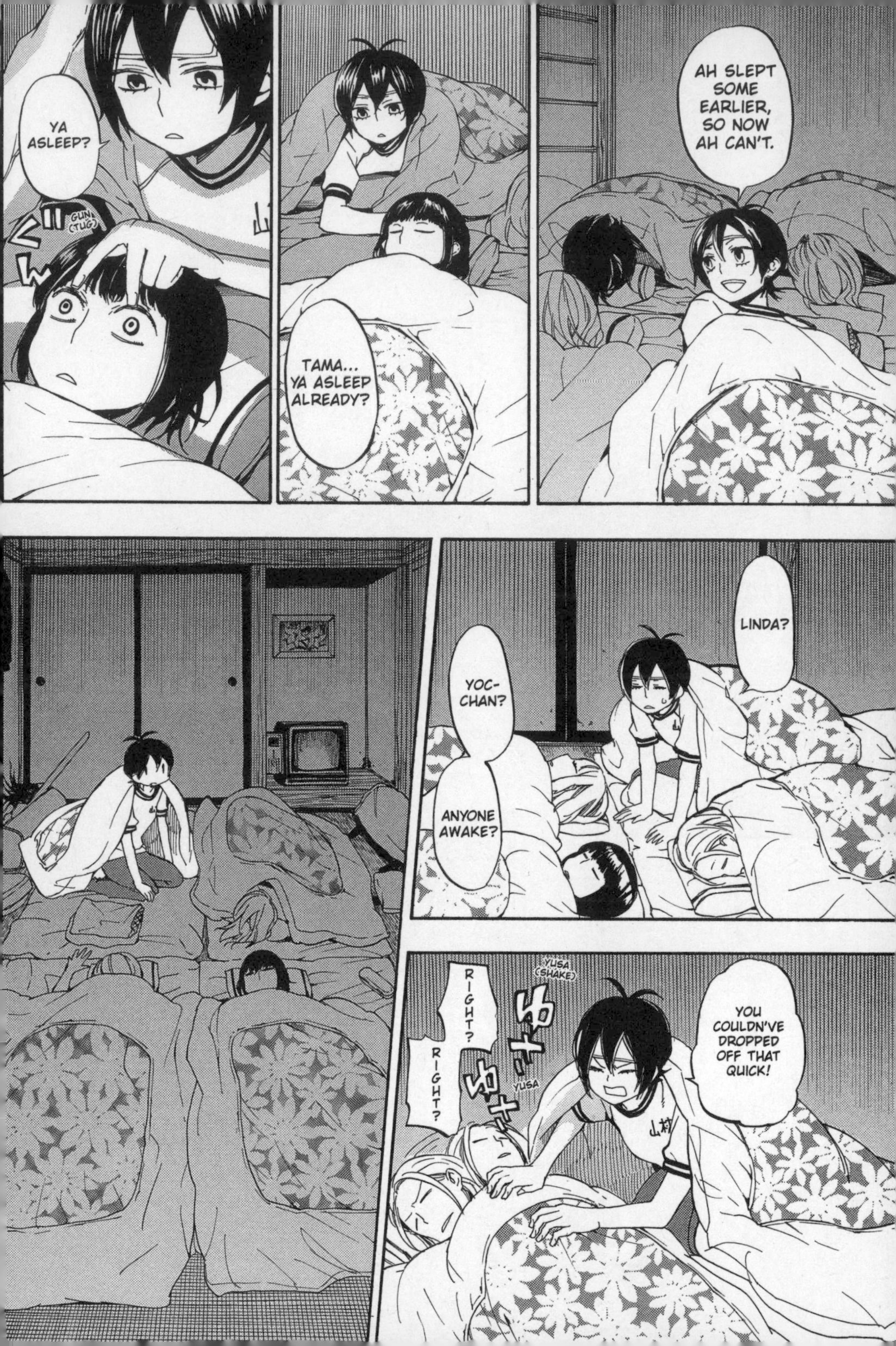
AH SLEPT SOME EARLIER, SO NOW AH CAN'T.
TAMA... YA ASLEEP ALREADY?
YA ASLEEP?
GUN (TUG)
LINDA?
YOC-CHAN?
ANYONE AWAKE?
YOU COULDN'VE DROPPED OFF THAT QUICK!
YUSA (SHAKE)
ゆさ
RIGHT?
ゆさ
YUSA
RIGHT?

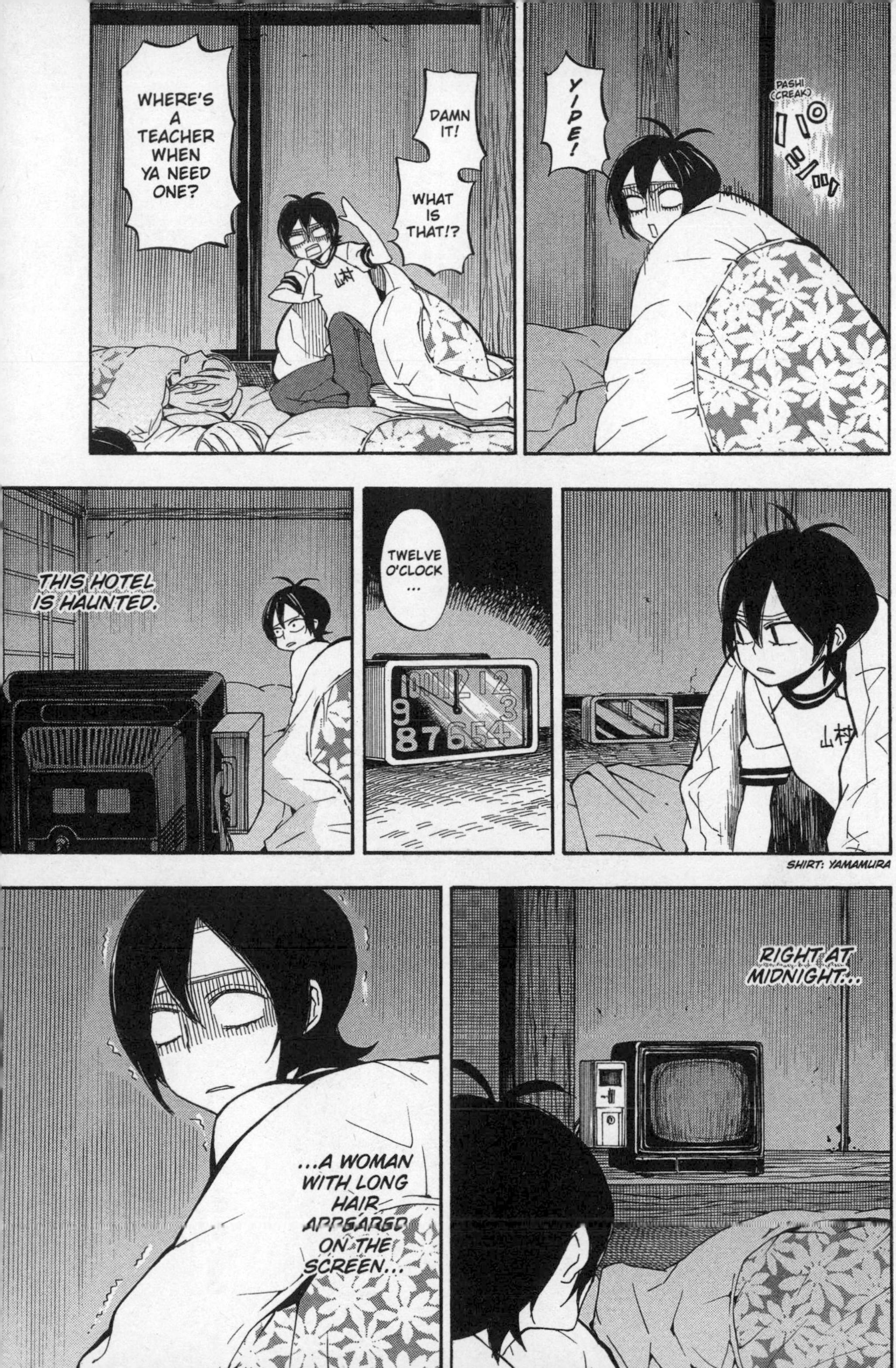
YIPE!
PASHI (CREAK)
DAMN IT!
WHAT IS THAT!?
WHERE'S A TEACHER WHEN YA NEED ONE?
SHIRT: YAMAMURA
TWELVE O'CLOCK...
THIS HOTEL IS HAUNTED.
RIGHT AT MIDNIGHT...
...A WOMAN WITH LONG HAIR APPEARED ON THE SCREEN...

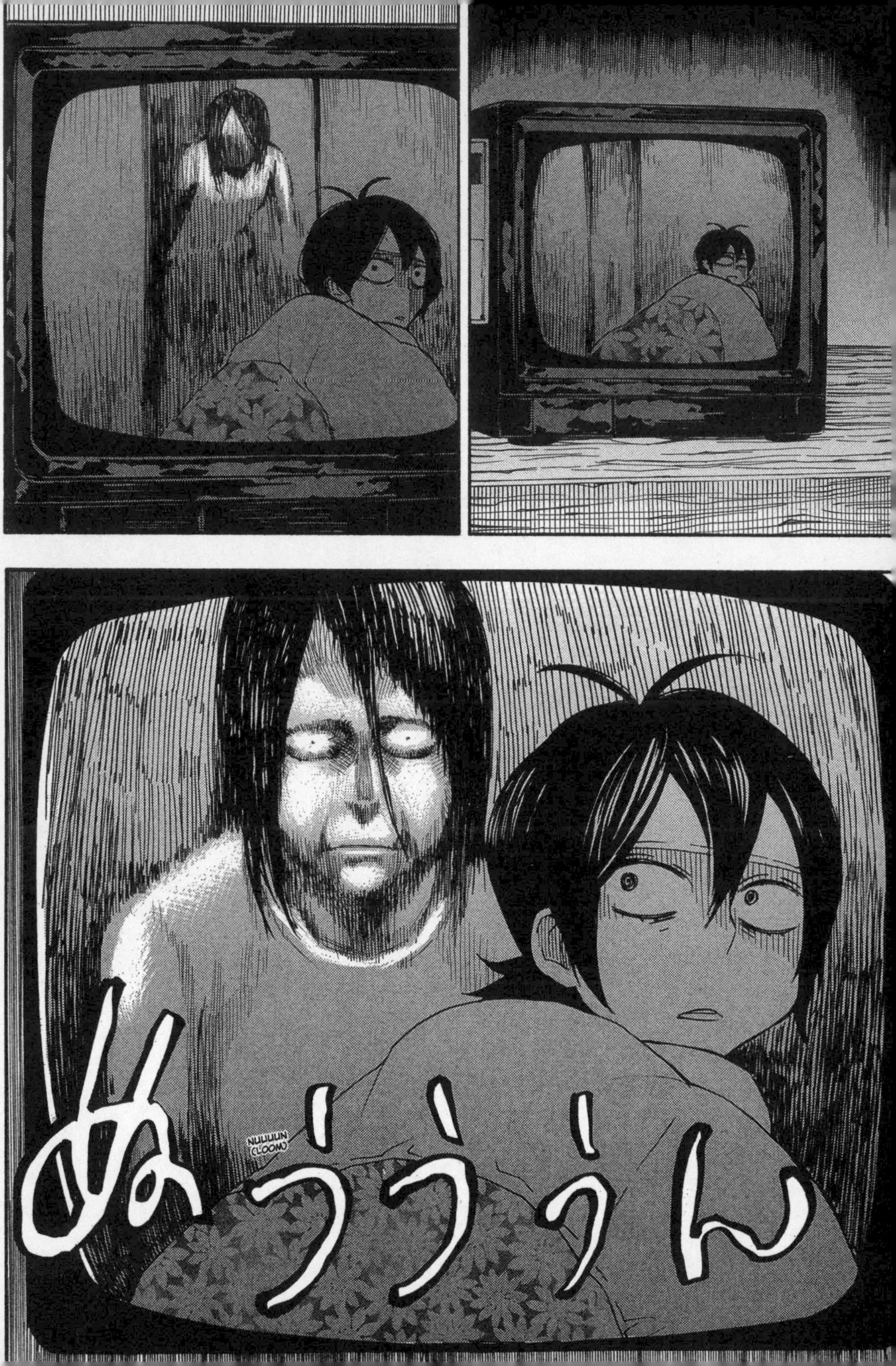
ぬううぅん
NUUUUN (LOOM)

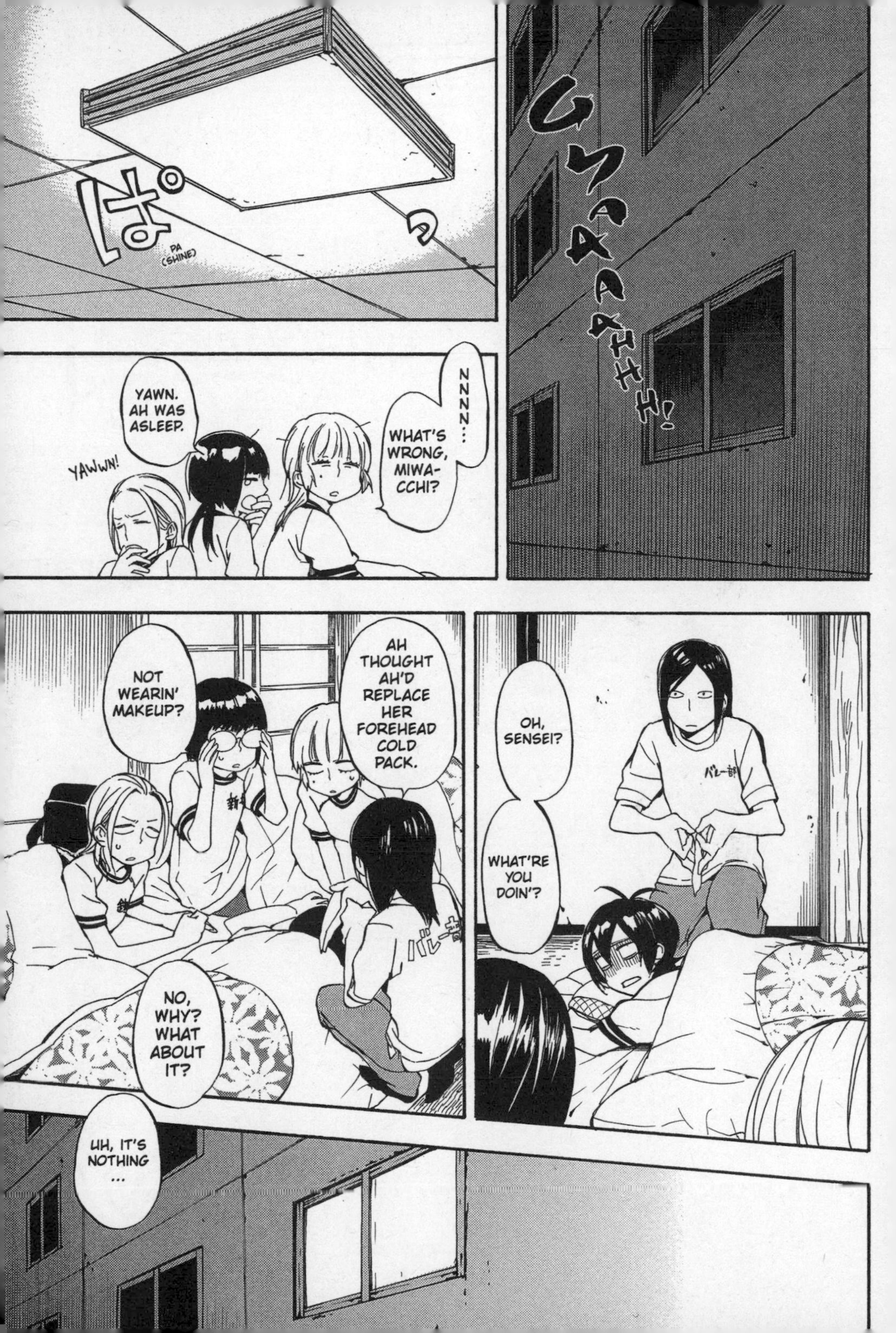

UMYAAAAHHHH!
ぱっ
PA (SHINE)
NNNN...
WHAT'S WRONG, MIWACCHI?
YAWN. AH WAS ASLEEP.
YAWWN!
OH, SENSEI?
WHAT'RE YOU DOIN'?
AH THOUGHT AH'D REPLACE HER FOREHEAD COLD PACK.
NOT WEARIN' MAKEUP?
NO, WHY? WHAT ABOUT IT?
UH, IT'S NOTHING ...

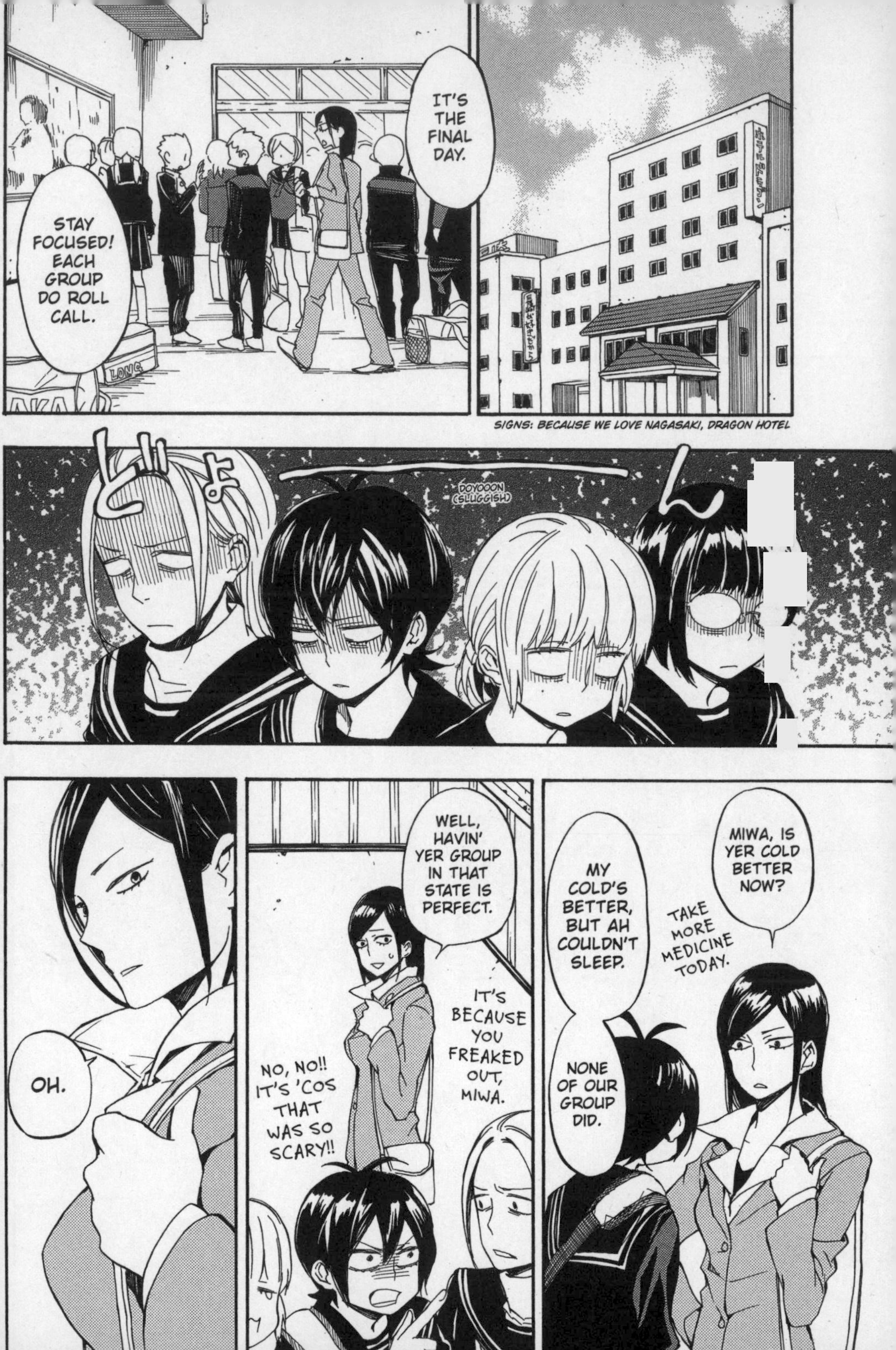
SIGNS: BECAUSE WE LOVE NAGASAKI, DRAGON HOTEL
IT'S THE FINAL DAY.
STAY FOCUSED! EACH GROUP DO ROLL CALL.
DOYOOON (SLUGGISH)
MIWA, IS YER COLD BETTER NOW?
TAKE MORE MEDICINE TODAY.
MY COLD'S BETTER, BUT AH COULDN'T SLEEP.
NONE OF OUR GROUP DID.
WELL, HAVIN' YER GROUP IN THAT STATE IS PERFECT.
IT'S BECAUSE YOU FREAKED OUT, MIWA.
NO, NO!! IT'S 'COS THAT WAS SO SCARY!!
OH.

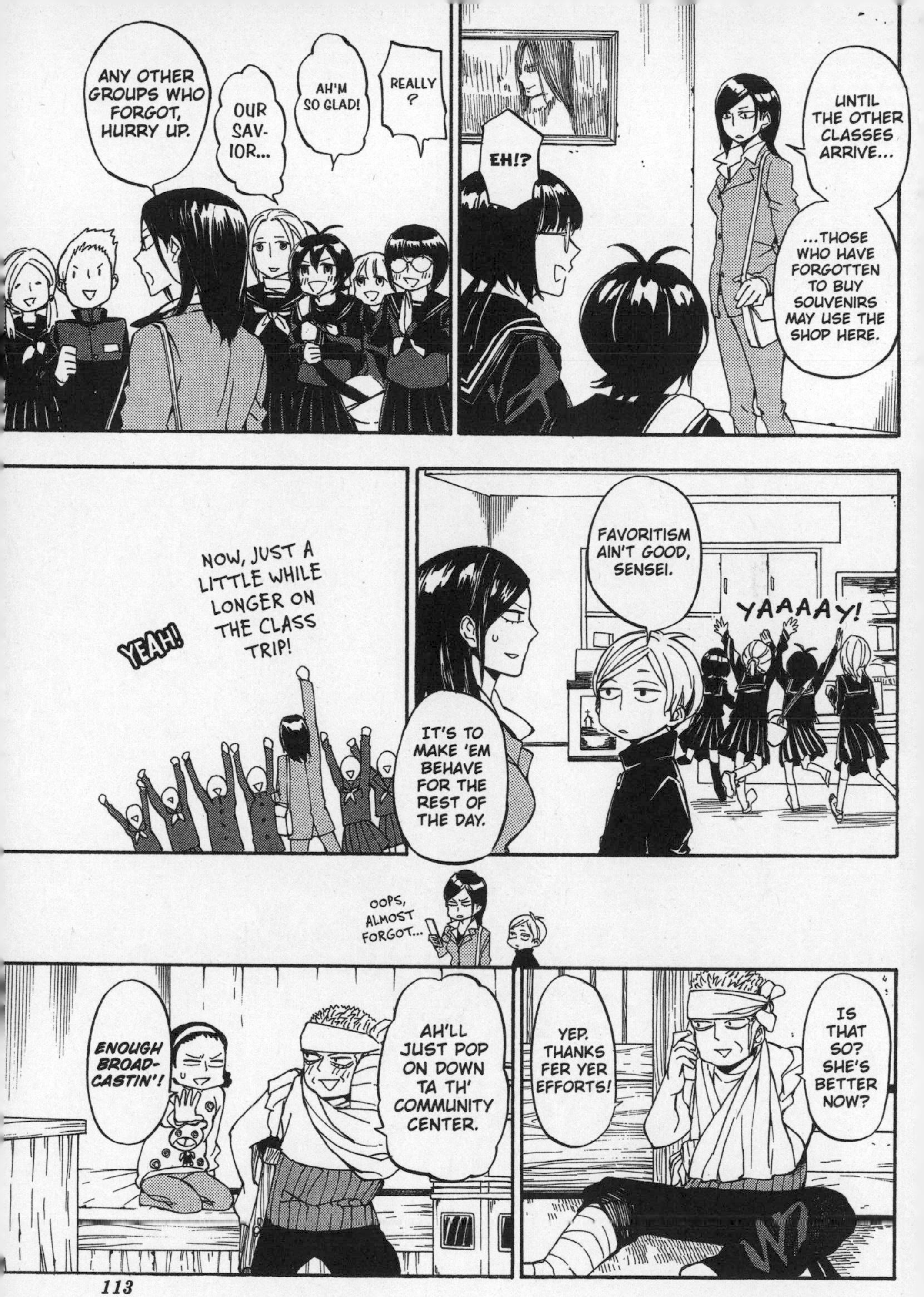
UNTIL THE OTHER CLASSES ARRIVE...
...THOSE WHO HAVE FORGOTTEN TO BUY SOUVENIRS MAY USE THE SHOP HERE.
EH!?
REALLY ?
AH'M SO GLAD!
OUR SAV-IOR...
ANY OTHER GROUPS WHO FORGOT, HURRY UP.
FAVORITISM AIN'T GOOD, SENSEI.
YAAAAY!
IT'S TO MAKE 'EM BEHAVE FOR THE REST OF THE DAY.
NOW, JUST A LITTLE WHILE LONGER ON THE CLASS TRIP!
YEAH!
OOPS, ALMOST FORGOT...
IS THAT SO? SHE'S BETTER NOW?
YEP. THANKS FER YER EFFORTS!
AH'LL JUST POP ON DOWN TA TH' COMMUNITY CENTER.
ENOUGH BROAD-CASTIN'!

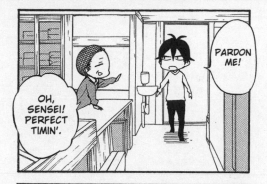

ACT.65 ABE

[Translation: Walk]

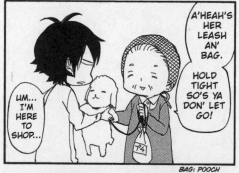

PARDON ME!
OH, SENSEI! PERFECT TIMIN'.
COULD YA TAKE POOCH A'HEAH FOAH A WALK?
EH? BUT I CAME TO SHOP...
A'HEAH'S HER LEASH AN' BAG.
HOLD TIGHT SO'S YA DON' LET GO!
UM... I'M HERE TO SHOP...
BAG: POOCH
HAVE A NICE WALK, NOW!
BUT MY SHOPPING ...

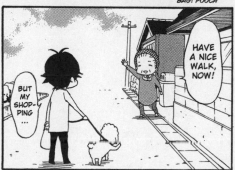

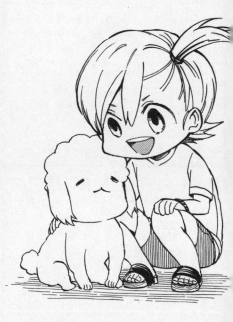

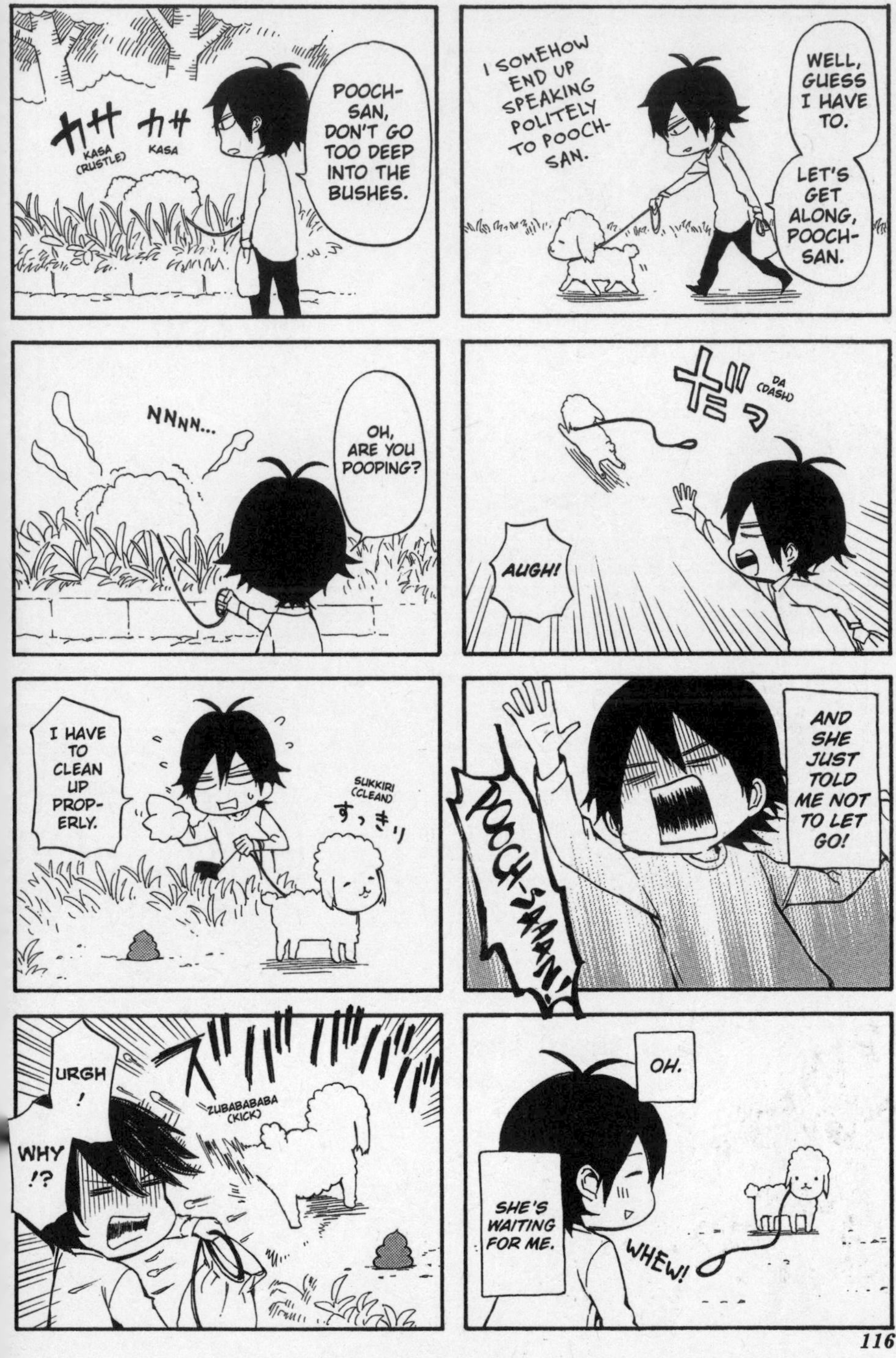
WELL, GUESS I HAVE TO.
LET'S GET ALONG, POOCH-SAN.
I SOMEHOW END UP SPEAKING POLITELY TO POOCH-SAN.
POOCH-SAN, DON'T GO TOO DEEP INTO THE BUSHES.
カサ カサ
KASA (RUSTLE) KASA
ダッ
DA (DASH)
AUGH!
OH, ARE YOU POOPING?
NNNN...
AND SHE JUST TOLD ME NOT TO LET GO!
POOCH-SAAAN!
すっきり
SUKKIRI (CLEAN)
I HAVE TO CLEAN UP PROPERLY.
OH.
SHE'S WAITING FOR ME.
WHEW!
ズババババ
ZUBABABABA (KICK)
URGH!
WHY!?

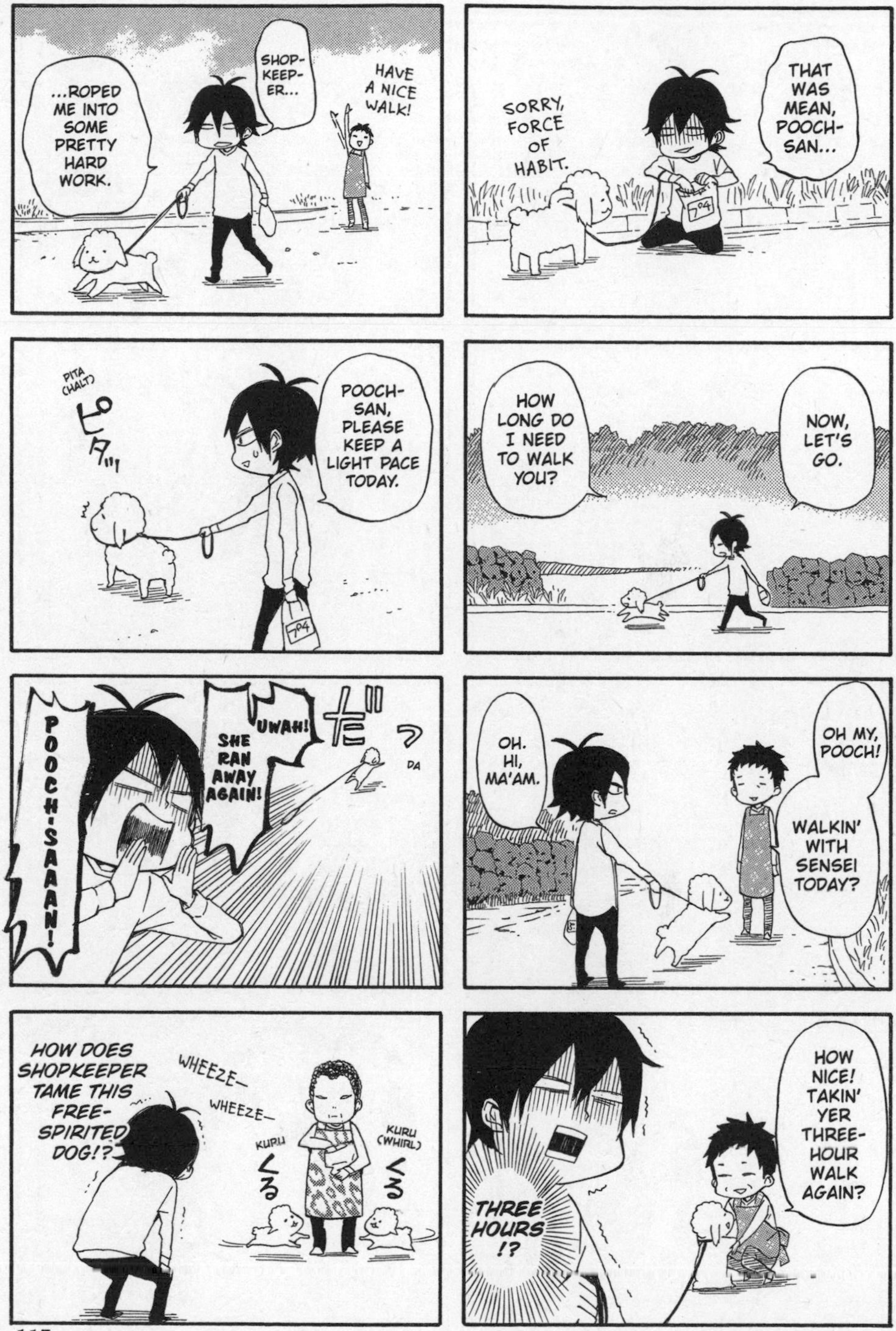
THAT WAS MEAN, POOCH-SAN...
SORRY, FORCE OF HABIT.
HAVE A NICE WALK!
SHOP-KEEP-ER...
...ROPED ME INTO SOME PRETTY HARD WORK.
NOW, LET'S GO.
HOW LONG DO I NEED TO WALK YOU?
POOCH-SAN, PLEASE KEEP A LIGHT PACE TODAY.
PITA (HALT)
ピタッ
OH MY, POOCH!
WALKIN' WITH SENSEI TODAY?
OH. HI, MA'AM.
だっ
DA
UWAH!
SHE RAN AWAY AGAIN!
POOCHI-SAAAAN!
HOW NICE! TAKIN' YER THREE-HOUR WALK AGAIN?
THREE HOURS !?
KURU (WHIRL)
くる
KURU
くる
WHEEZE—
WHEEZE—
HOW DOES SHOPKEEPER TAME THIS FREE-SPIRITED DOG!?

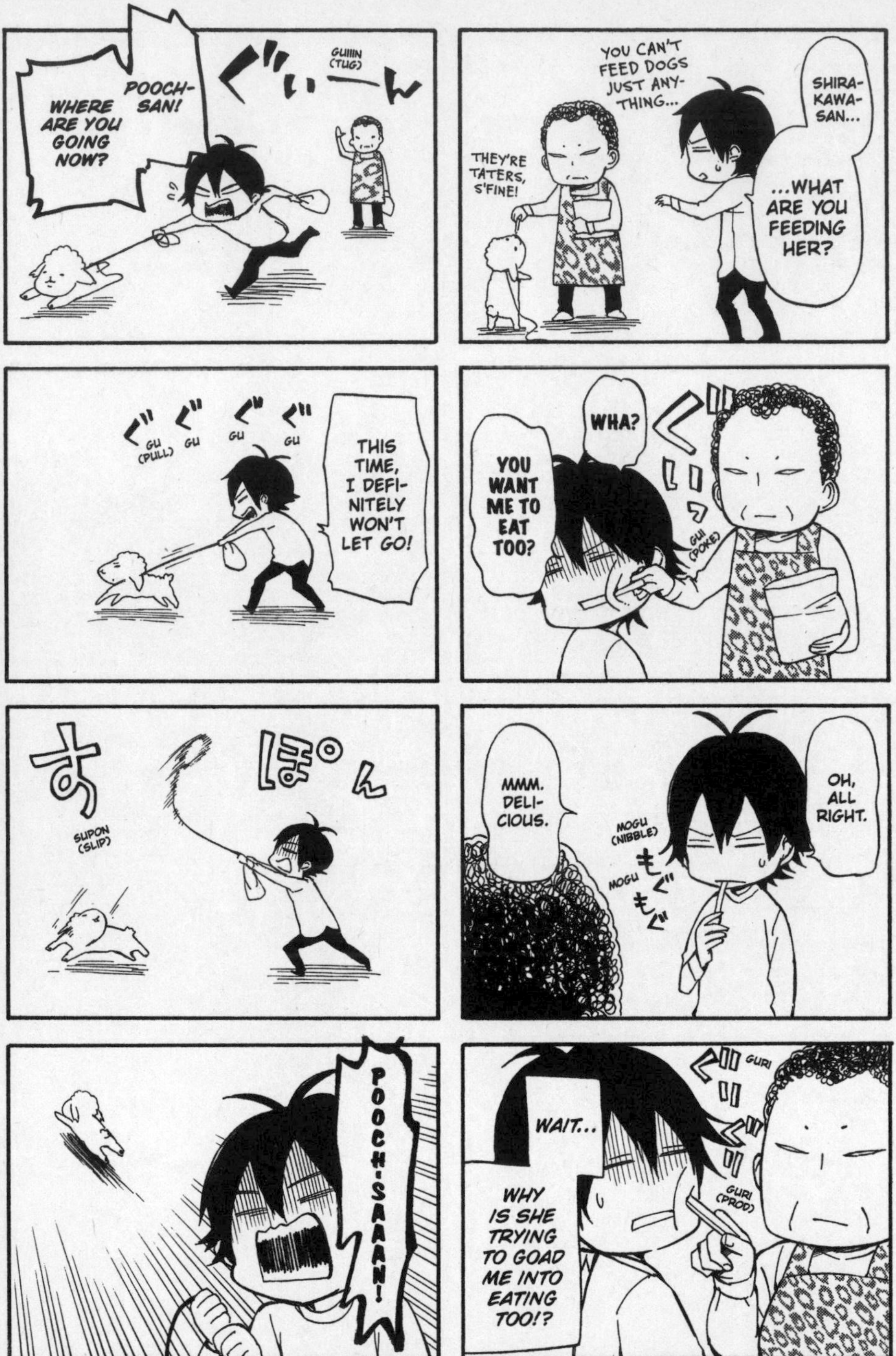
SHIRA-KAWA-SAN...
...WHAT ARE YOU FEEDING HER?
YOU CAN'T FEED DOGS JUST ANY-THING...
THEY'RE TATERS, S'FINE!
WHA?
YOU WANT ME TO EAT TOO?
GUI (POKE)
OH, ALL RIGHT.
MOGU (NIBBLE)
MOGU
MMM. DELI-CIOUS.
GURI
WAIT...
WHY IS SHE TRYING TO GOAD ME INTO EATING TOO!?
GURI (PROD)
GUIIIN (TUG)
POOCH-SAN!
WHERE ARE YOU GOING NOW?
THIS TIME, I DEFI-NITELY WON'T LET GO!
GU (PULL)
GU
GU
GU
SUPON (SLIP)
POOCH-SAAAN!

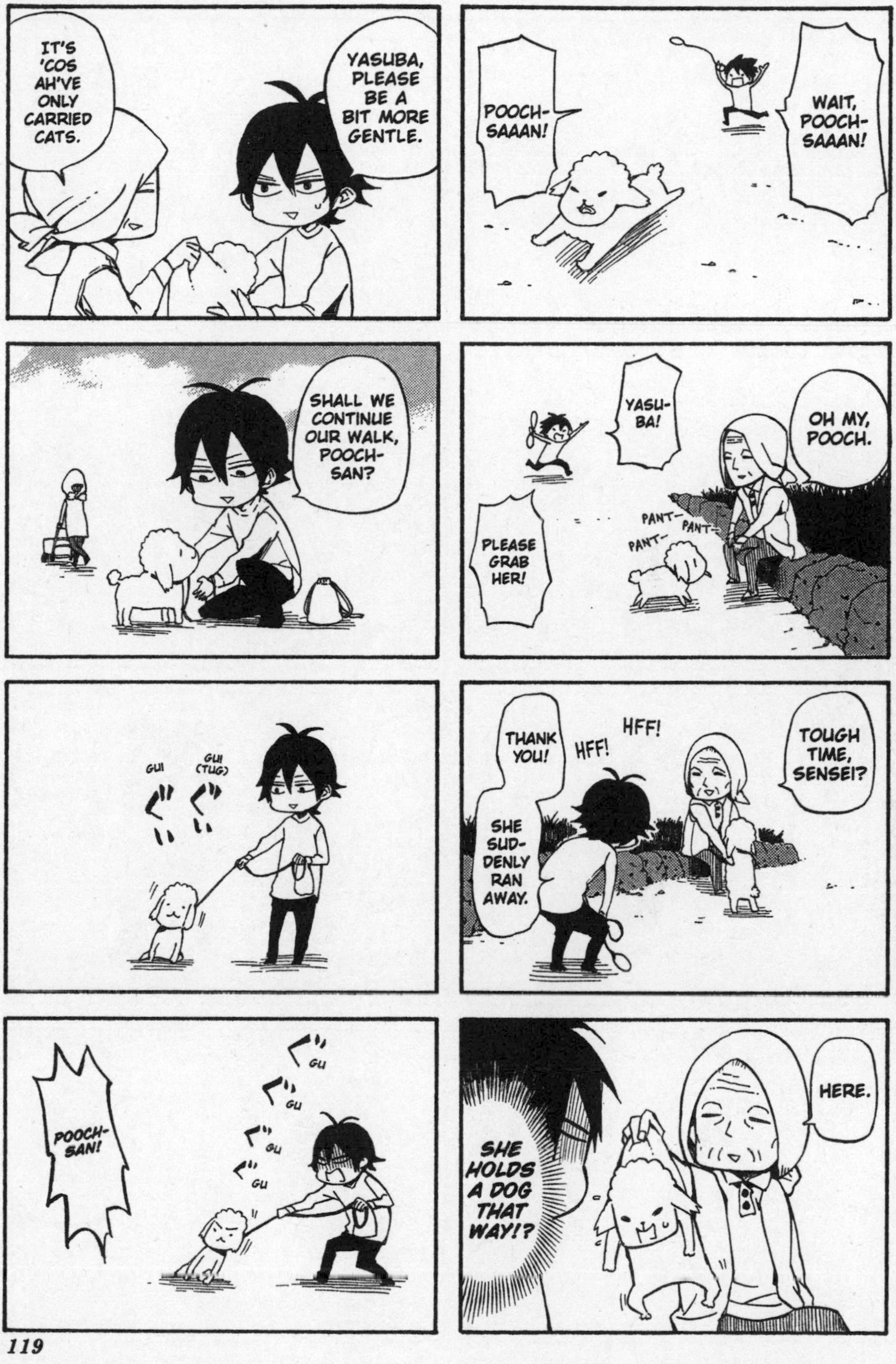
WAIT, POOCH-SAAAN!
POOCH-SAAAN!
OH MY, POOCH.
YASU-BA!
PLEASE GRAB HER!
PANT- PANT- PANT-
TOUGH TIME, SENSEI?
HFF! HFF!
THANK YOU!
SHE SUDDENLY RAN AWAY.
HERE.
SHE HOLDS A DOG THAT WAY!?
YASUBA, PLEASE BE A BIT MORE GENTLE.
IT'S 'COS AH'VE ONLY CARRIED CATS.
SHALL WE CONTINUE OUR WALK, POOCH-SAN?
ぐい GUI (TUG)
ぐい GUI
ぐ GU
ぐ GU
ぐ GU
ぐ GU
POOCH-SAN!

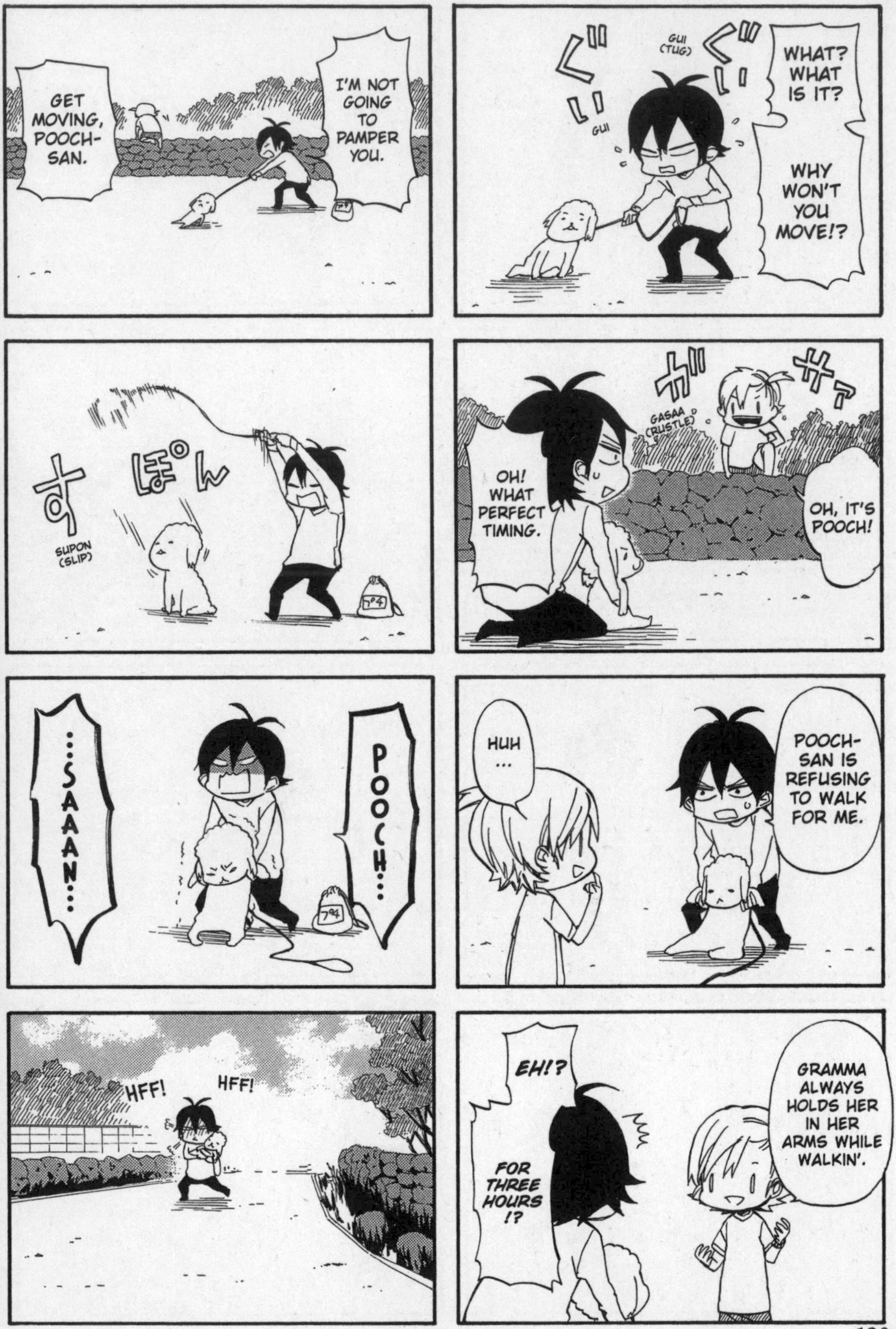
ぐい
GUI (TUG)
ぐい
GUI
WHAT? WHAT IS IT?
WHY WON'T YOU MOVE!?
I'M NOT GOING TO PAMPER YOU.
GET MOVING, POOCH-SAN.
ガサァ
GASAA (RUSTLE)
OH, IT'S POOCH!
OH! WHAT PERFECT TIMING.
すぽん
SUPON (SLIP)
POOCH-SAN IS REFUSING TO WALK FOR ME.
HUH ...
POOCH...
...SAAAN...
GRAMMA ALWAYS HOLDS HER IN HER ARMS WHILE WALKIN'.
EH!?
FOR THREE HOURS !?
HFF!
HFF!

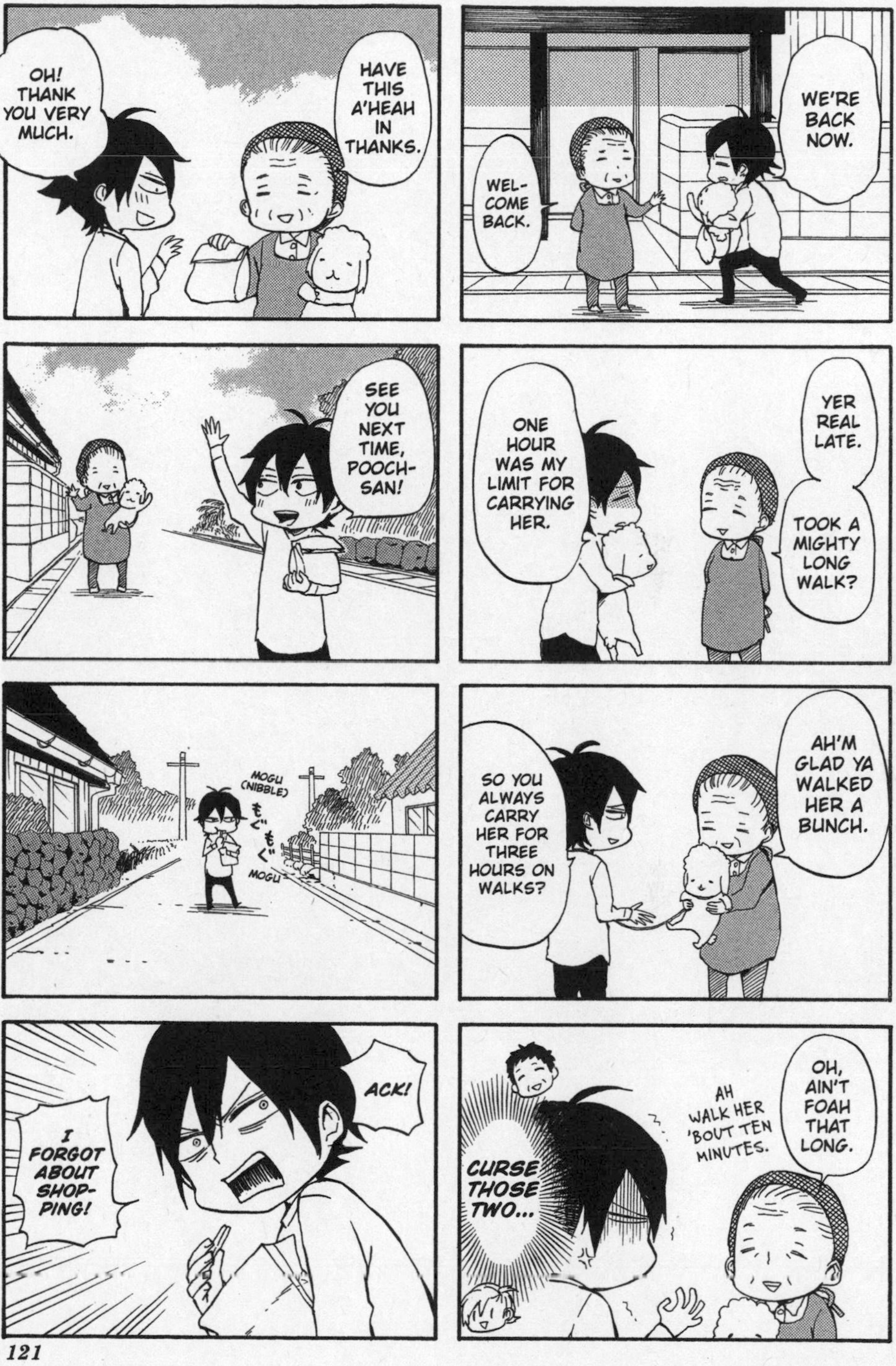
WE'RE BACK NOW.
WEL-COME BACK.
HAVE THIS A'HEAH IN THANKS.
OH! THANK YOU VERY MUCH.
YER REAL LATE.
TOOK A MIGHTY LONG WALK?
ONE HOUR WAS MY LIMIT FOR CARRYING HER.
SEE YOU NEXT TIME, POOCH-SAN!
AH'M GLAD YA WALKED HER A BUNCH.
SO YOU ALWAYS CARRY HER FOR THREE HOURS ON WALKS?
MOGU (NIBBLE)
もぐもぐ
MOGU
OH, AIN'T FOAH THAT LONG.
AH WALK HER 'BOUT TEN MINUTES.
CURSE THOSE TWO...
ACK!
I FORGOT ABOUT SHOP-PING!

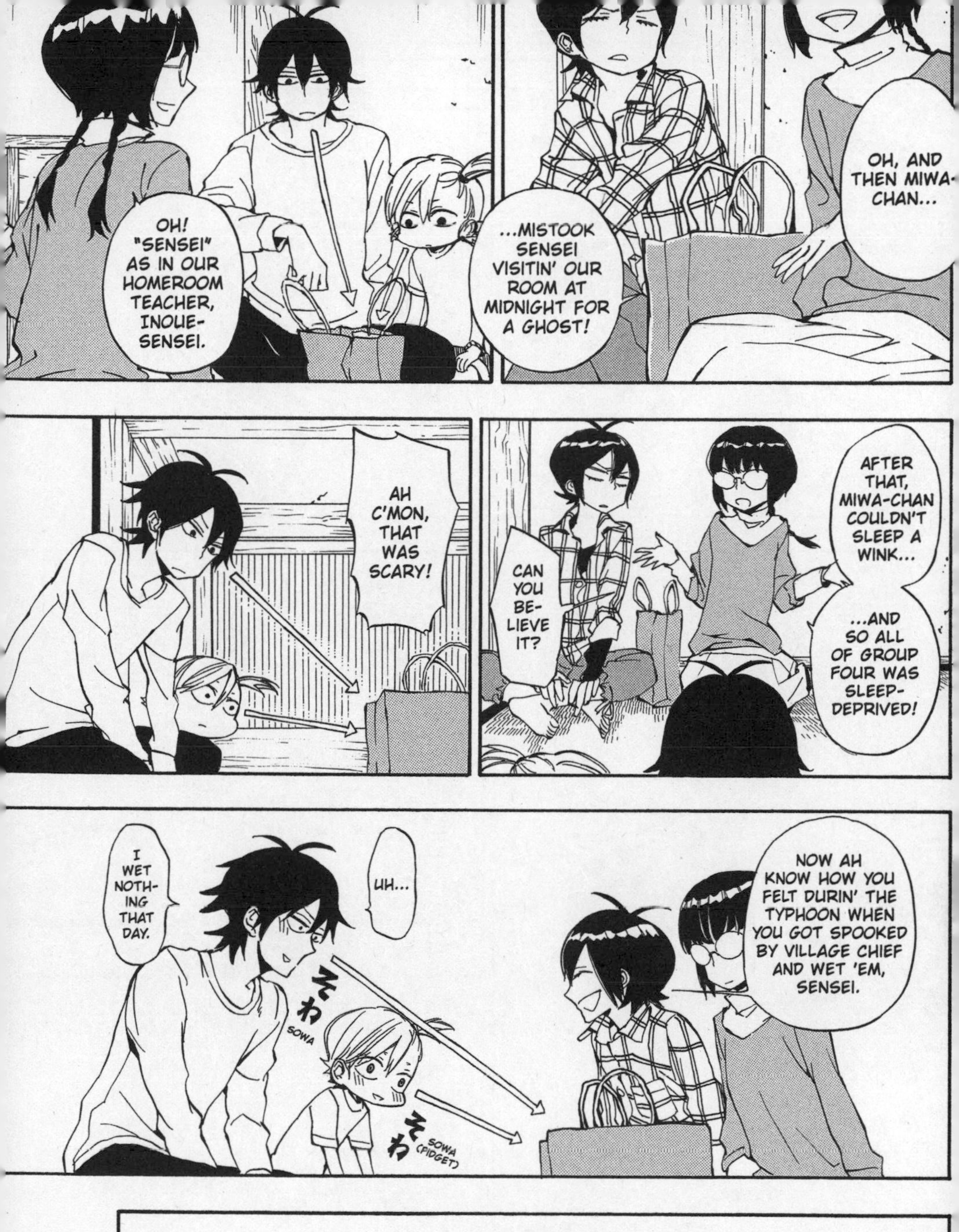
OH, AND THEN MIWA-CHAN...
...MISTOOK SENSEI VISITIN' OUR ROOM AT MIDNIGHT FOR A GHOST!
OH! "SENSEI" AS IN OUR HOMEROOM TEACHER, INOUE-SENSEI.
AFTER THAT, MIWA-CHAN COULDN'T SLEEP A WINK...
...AND SO ALL OF GROUP FOUR WAS SLEEP-DEPRIVED!
CAN YOU BE-LIEVE IT?
AH C'MON, THAT WAS SCARY!
NOW AH KNOW HOW YOU FELT DURIN' THE TYPHOON WHEN YOU GOT SPOOKED BY VILLAGE CHIEF AND WET 'EM, SENSEI.
UH...
I WET NOTHING THAT DAY.
そわ
SOWA
そわ
SOWA (FIDGET)

ACT.66
KICHIKURU

(Translation: I'll Listen)

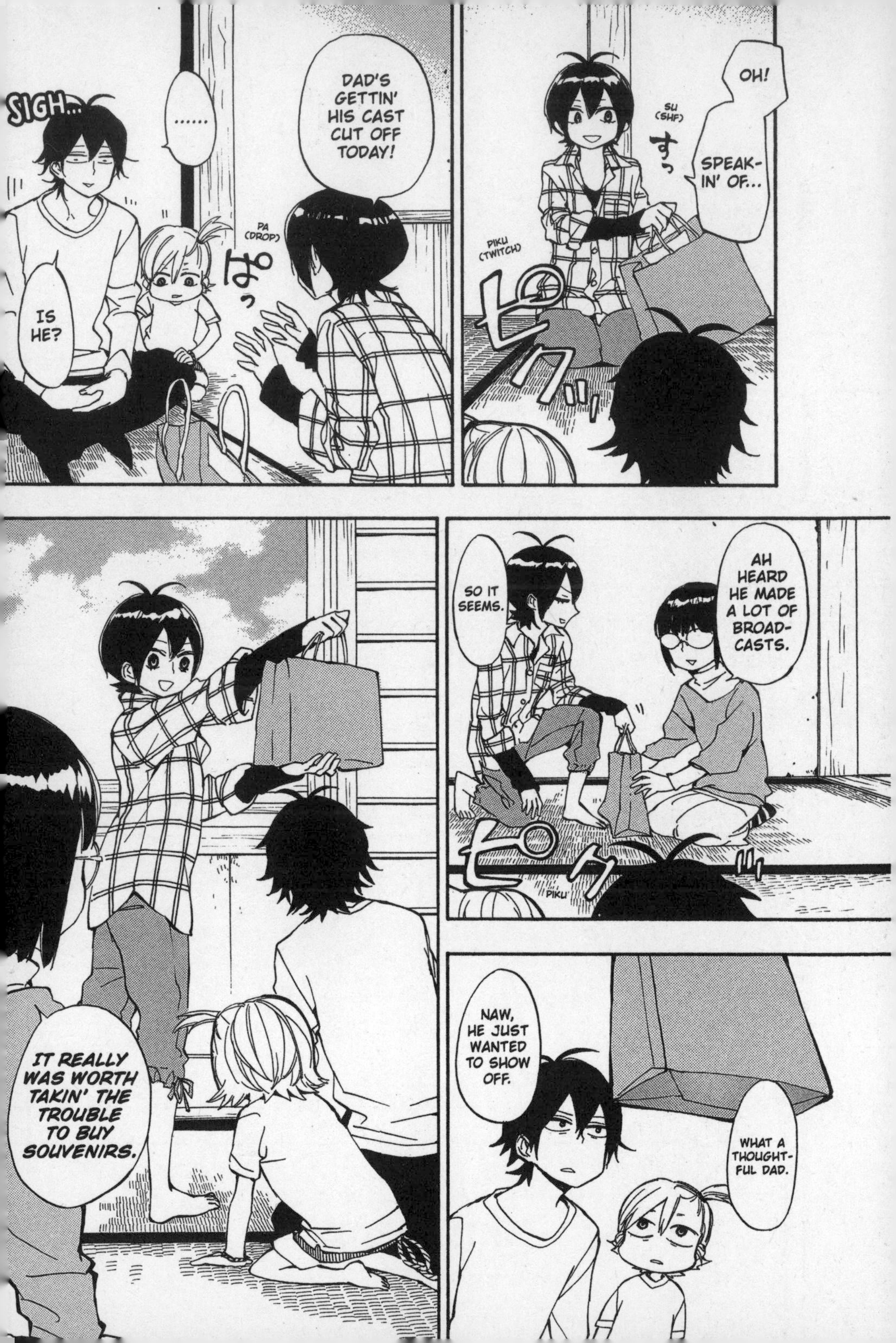
OH!
SPEAK-IN' OF...
SU (SHF)
すっ
PIKU (TWITCH)
ピクッ
DAD'S GETTIN' HIS CAST CUT OFF TODAY!
PA (DROP)
ぱっ
......
SIGH...
IS HE?
AH HEARD HE MADE A LOT OF BROAD-CASTS.
SO IT SEEMS.
ピクッ
PIKU
NAW, HE JUST WANTED TO SHOW OFF.
WHAT A THOUGHT-FUL DAD.
IT REALLY WAS WORTH TAKIN' THE TROUBLE TO BUY SOUVENIRS.

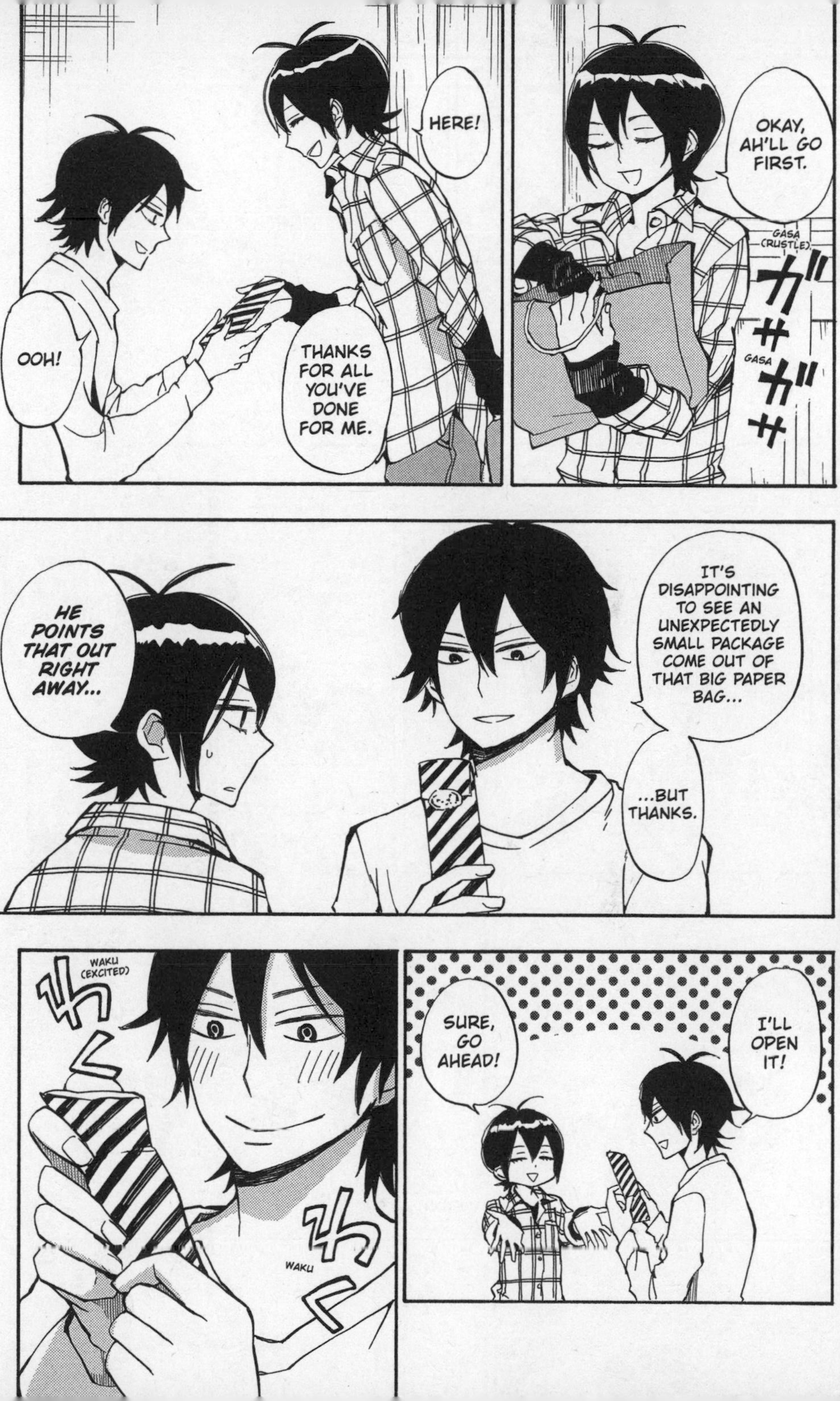
OKAY, AH'LL GO FIRST.
GASA (RUSTLE)
ガサ
GASA
ガサ
HERE!
THANKS FOR ALL YOU'VE DONE FOR ME.
OOH!
IT'S DISAPPOINTING TO SEE AN UNEXPECTEDLY SMALL PACKAGE COME OUT OF THAT BIG PAPER BAG...
...BUT THANKS.
HE POINTS THAT OUT RIGHT AWAY...
I'LL OPEN IT!
SURE, GO AHEAD!
WAKU (EXCITED)
わく
わく
WAKU

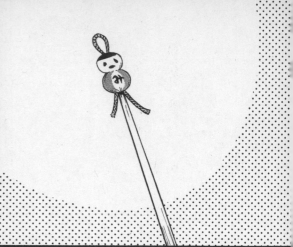

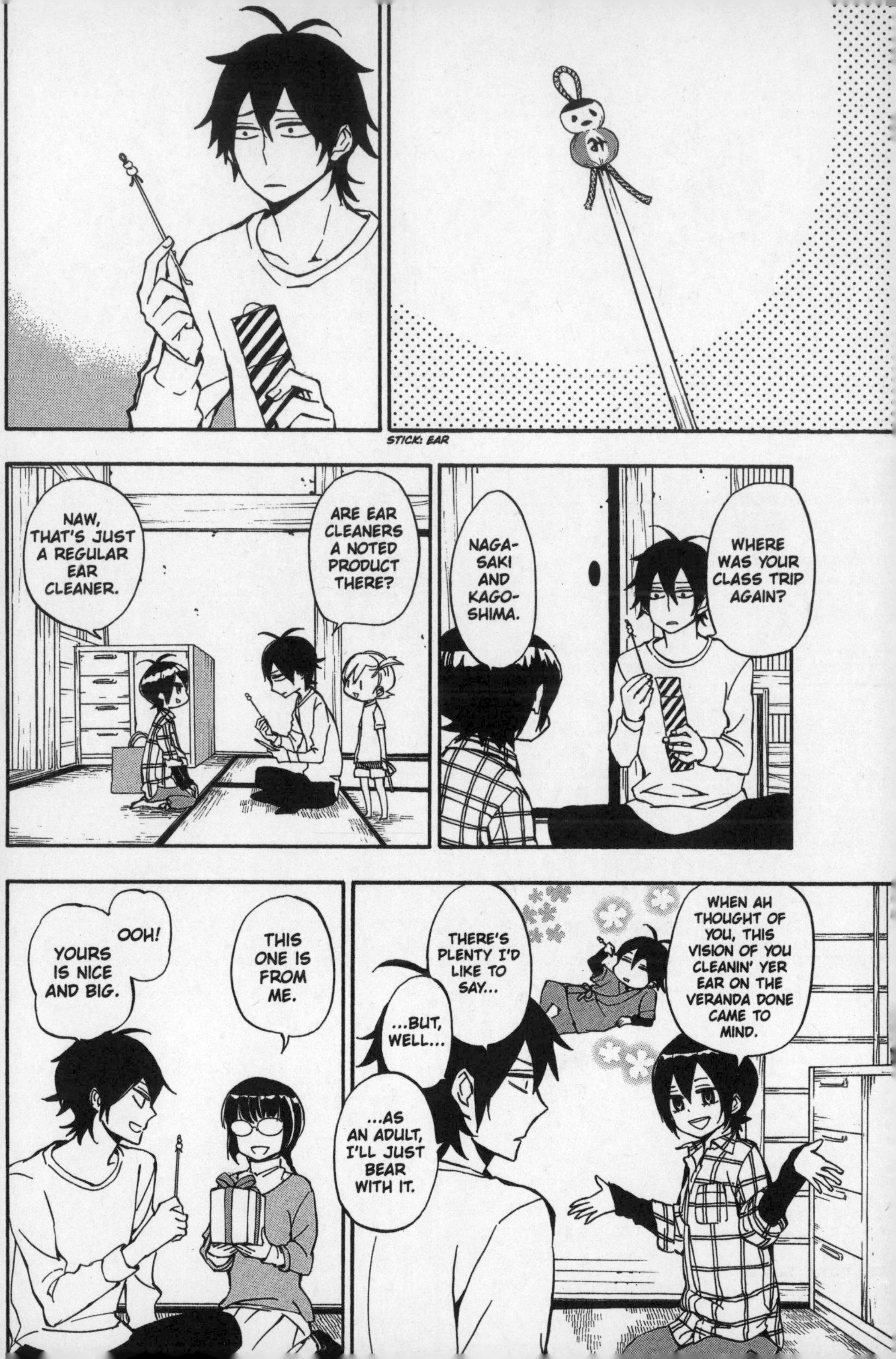
STICK: EAR
WHERE WAS YOUR CLASS TRIP AGAIN?
NAGA-SAKI AND KAGO-SHIMA.
ARE EAR CLEANERS A NOTED PRODUCT THERE?
NAW, THAT'S JUST A REGULAR EAR CLEANER.
WHEN AH THOUGHT OF YOU, THIS VISION OF YOU CLEANIN' YER EAR ON THE VERANDA DONE CAME TO MIND.
THERE'S PLENTY I'D LIKE TO SAY...
...BUT, WELL...
...AS AN ADULT, I'LL JUST BEAR WITH IT.
THIS ONE IS FROM ME.
OOH! YOURS IS NICE AND BIG.

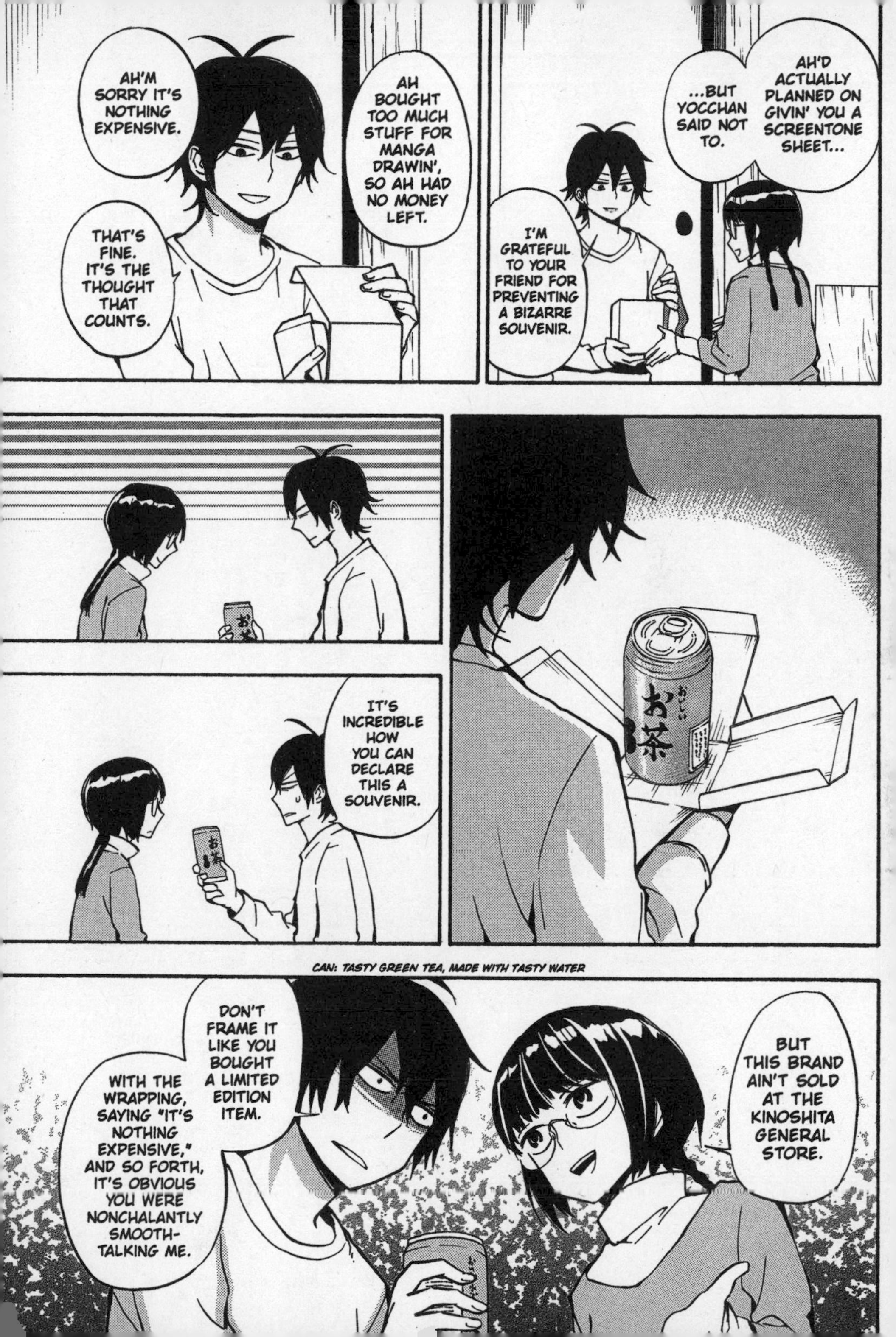
AH'D ACTUALLY PLANNED ON GIVIN' YOU A SCREENTONE SHEET...
...BUT YOCCHAN SAID NOT TO.
I'M GRATEFUL TO YOUR FRIEND FOR PREVENTING A BIZARRE SOUVENIR.
AH BOUGHT TOO MUCH STUFF FOR MANGA DRAWIN', SO AH HAD NO MONEY LEFT.
AH'M SORRY IT'S NOTHING EXPENSIVE.
THAT'S FINE. IT'S THE THOUGHT THAT COUNTS.
おいしい
お茶
IT'S INCREDIBLE HOW YOU CAN DECLARE THIS A SOUVENIR.
CAN: TASTY GREEN TEA, MADE WITH TASTY WATER
BUT THIS BRAND AIN'T SOLD AT THE KINOSHITA GENERAL STORE.
DON'T FRAME IT LIKE YOU BOUGHT A LIMITED EDITION ITEM.
WITH THE WRAPPING, SAYING "IT'S NOTHING EXPENSIVE," AND SO FORTH, IT'S OBVIOUS YOU WERE NONCHALANTLY SMOOTH-TALKING ME.

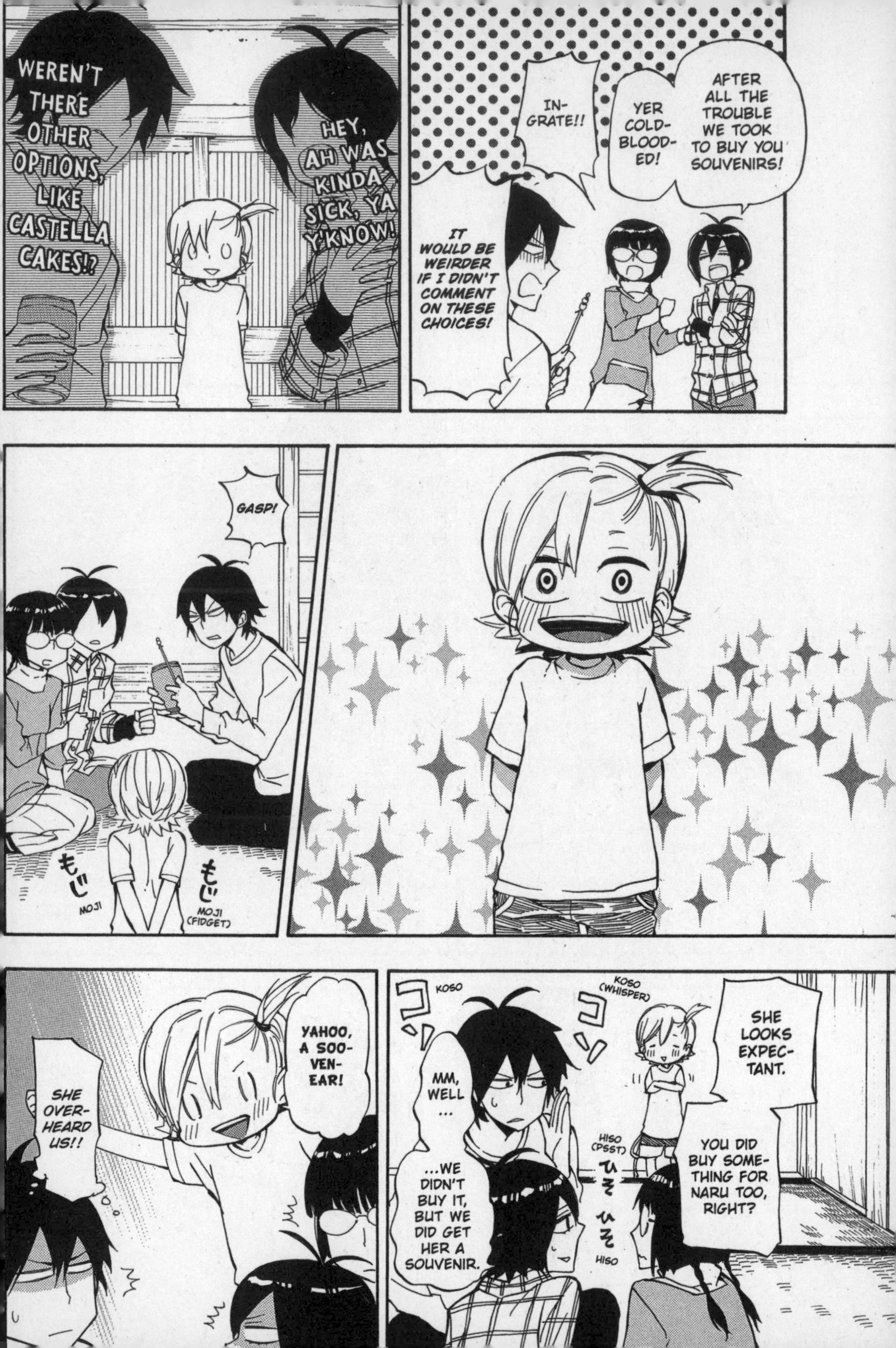
AFTER ALL THE TROUBLE WE TOOK TO BUY YOU SOUVENIRS!
YER COLD-BLOODED!
IN-GRATE!!
IT WOULD BE WEIRDER IF I DIDN'T COMMENT ON THESE CHOICES!
HEY, AH WAS KINDA SICK, YA Y'KNOW!
WEREN'T THERE OTHER OPTIONS, LIKE CASTELLA CAKES!?
GASP!
もじ MOJI (FIDGET)
もじ MOJI
KOSO (WHISPER)
KOSO
SHE LOOKS EXPECTANT.
MM, WELL ...
YOU DID BUY SOMETHING FOR NARU TOO, RIGHT?
ひそ HISO (PSST)
ひそ HISO
...WE DIDN'T BUY IT, BUT WE DID GET HER A SOUVENIR.
YAHOO, A SOOVENEAR!
SHE OVERHEARD US!!

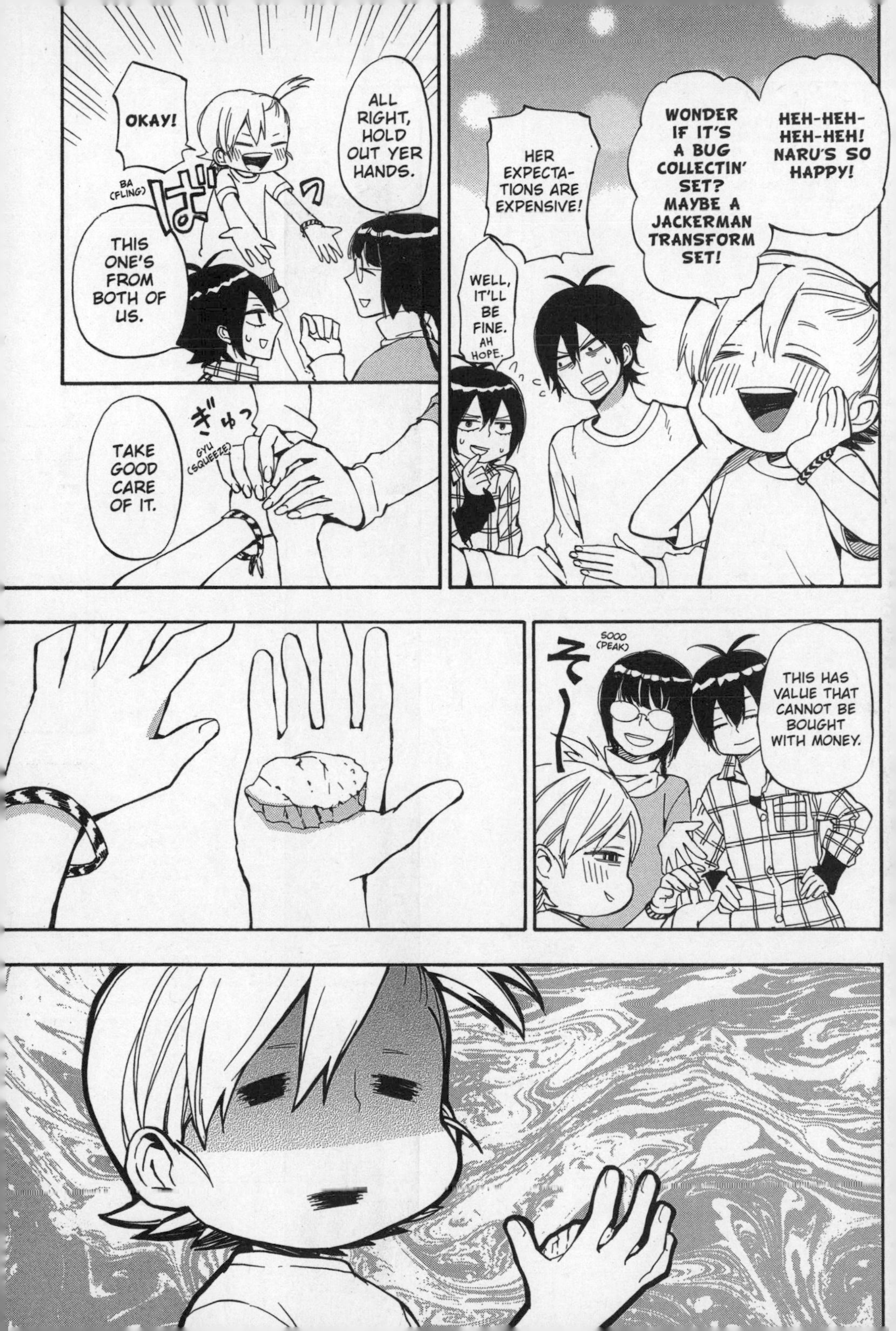
HEH-HEH-HEH-HEH! NARU'S SO HAPPY!
WONDER IF IT'S A BUG COLLECTIN' SET? MAYBE A JACKERMAN TRANSFORM SET!
HER EXPECTATIONS ARE EXPENSIVE!
WELL, IT'LL BE FINE. AH HOPE.
ALL RIGHT, HOLD OUT YER HANDS.
OKAY!
BA (FLING)
ばっ
THIS ONE'S FROM BOTH OF US.
ぎゅっ
GYU (SQUEEZE)
TAKE GOOD CARE OF IT.
SOOO (PEAK)
そ～
THIS HAS VALUE THAT CANNOT BE BOUGHT WITH MONEY.

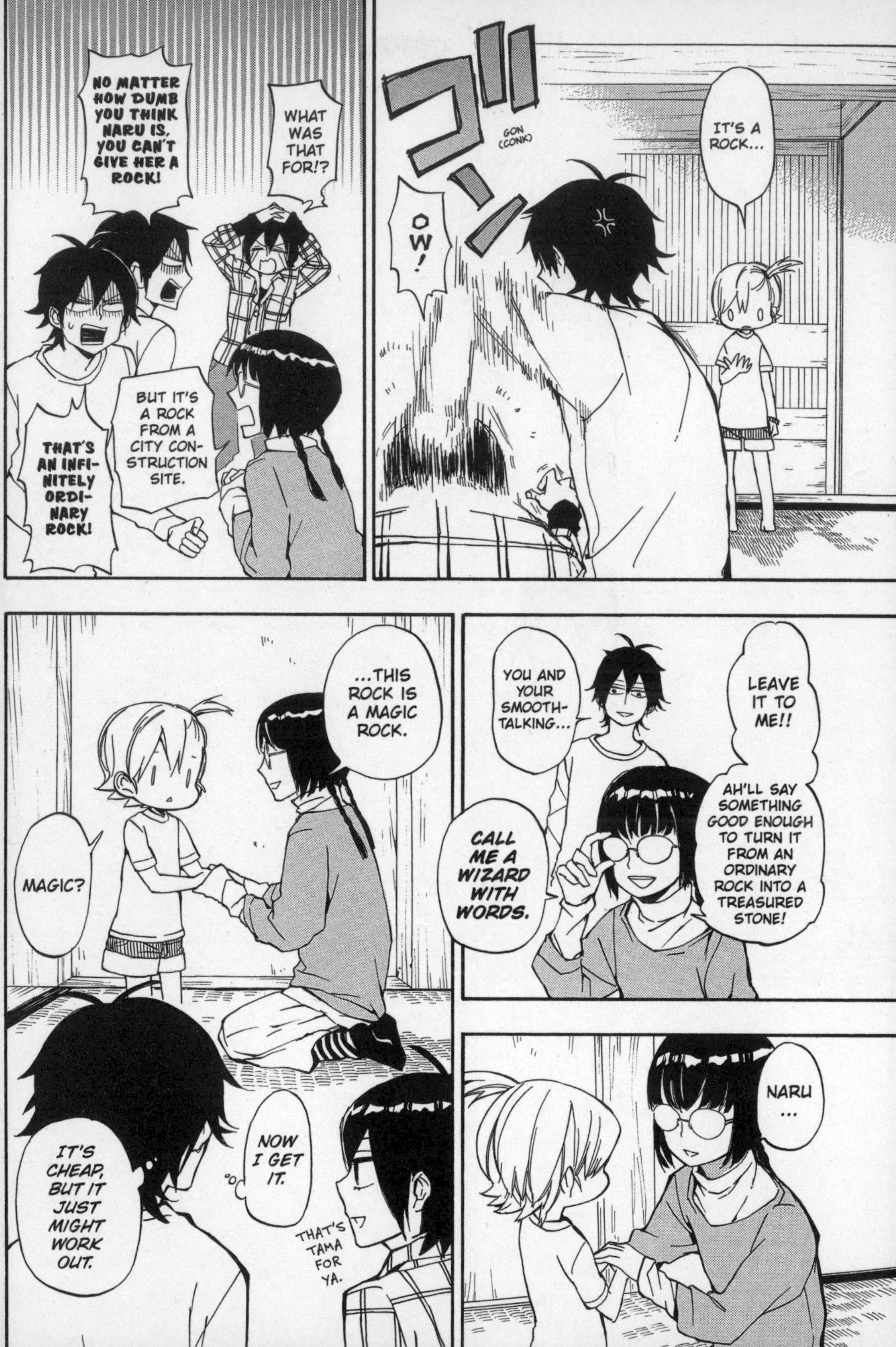
IT'S A ROCK...
GON (CONK)
OW!
WHAT WAS THAT FOR!?
NO MATTER HOW DUMB YOU THINK NARU IS, YOU CAN'T GIVE HER A ROCK!
BUT IT'S A ROCK FROM A CITY CONSTRUCTION SITE.
THAT'S AN INFINITELY ORDINARY ROCK!
LEAVE IT TO ME!!
YOU AND YOUR SMOOTH-TALKING...
AH'LL SAY SOMETHING GOOD ENOUGH TO TURN IT FROM AN ORDINARY ROCK INTO A TREASURED STONE!
CALL ME A WIZARD WITH WORDS.
NARU...
...THIS ROCK IS A MAGIC ROCK.
MAGIC?
NOW I GET IT.
THAT'S TAMA FOR YA.
IT'S CHEAP, BUT IT JUST MIGHT WORK OUT.

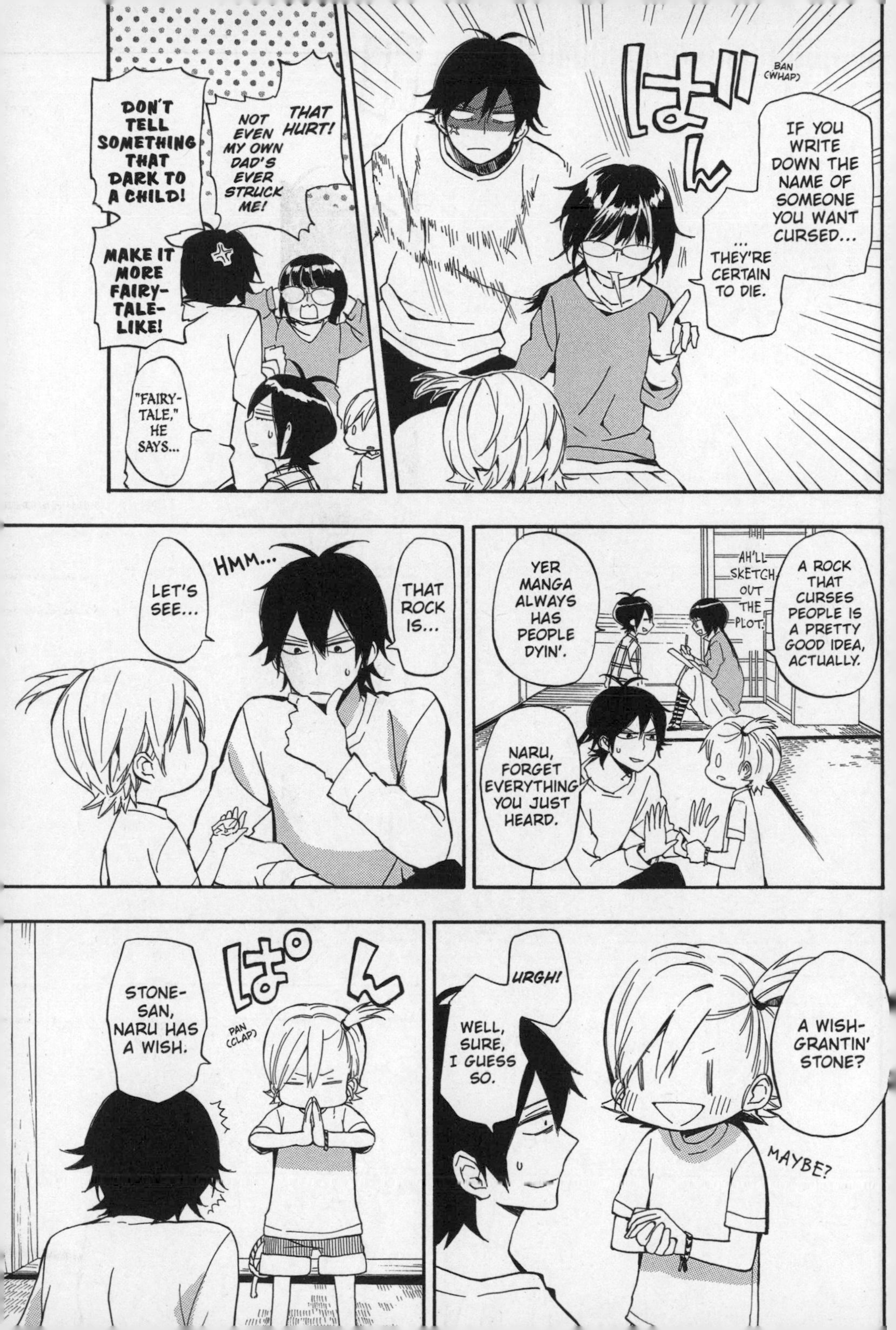
ばん
BAN (WHAP)
IF YOU WRITE DOWN THE NAME OF SOMEONE YOU WANT CURSED...
... THEY'RE CERTAIN TO DIE.
THAT HURT!
NOT EVEN MY OWN DAD'S EVER STRUCK ME!
DON'T TELL SOMETHING THAT DARK TO A CHILD!
MAKE IT MORE FAIRY-TALE-LIKE!
"FAIRY-TALE," HE SAYS...
A ROCK THAT CURSES PEOPLE IS A PRETTY GOOD IDEA, ACTUALLY.
AH'LL SKETCH OUT THE PLOT.
YER MANGA ALWAYS HAS PEOPLE DYIN'.
NARU, FORGET EVERYTHING YOU JUST HEARD.
THAT ROCK IS...
HMM...
LET'S SEE...
A WISH-GRANTIN' STONE?
MAYBE?
URGH!
WELL, SURE, I GUESS SO.
ぱん
PAN (CLAP)
STONE-SAN, NARU HAS A WISH.

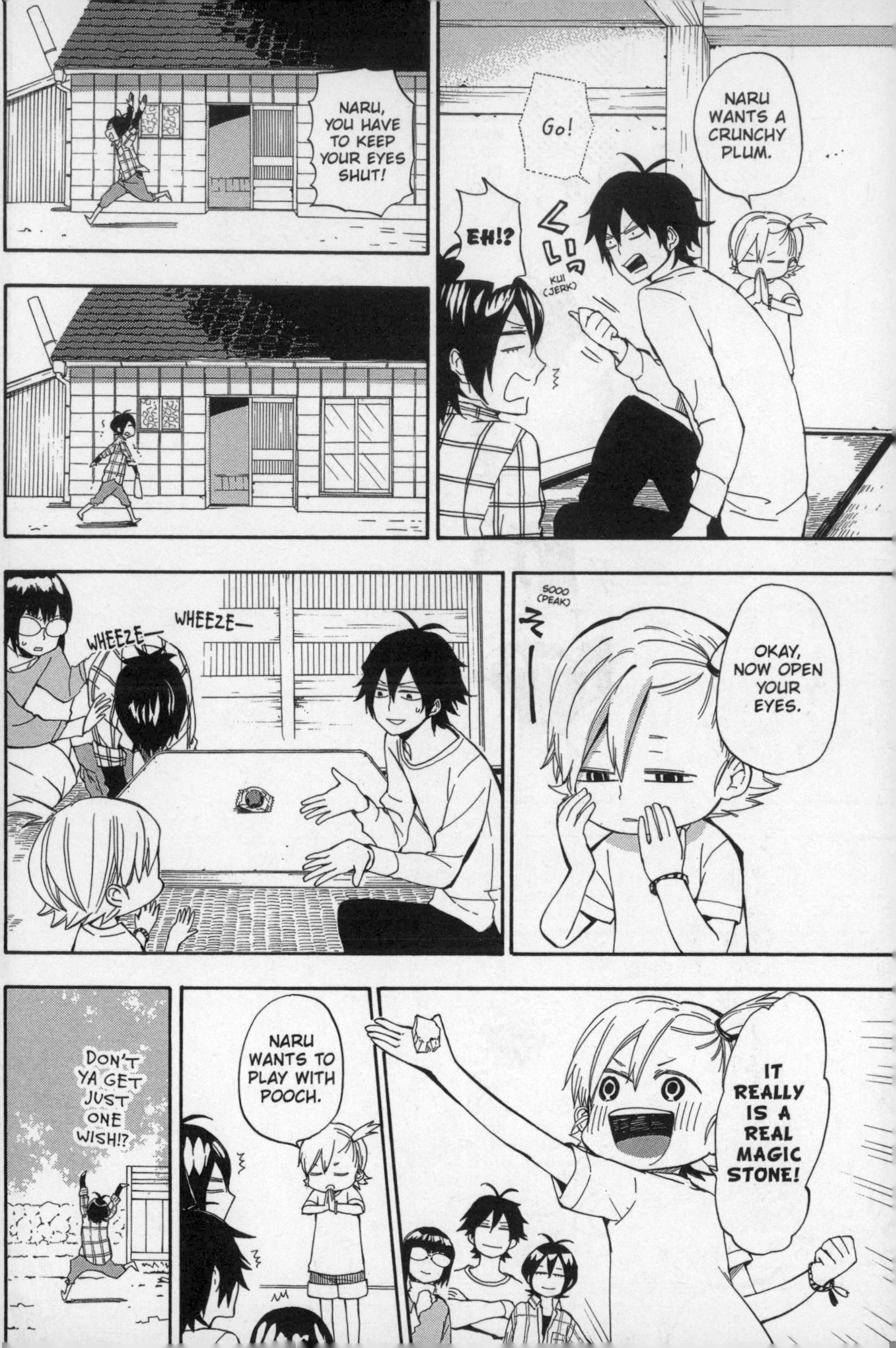
NARU WANTS A CRUNCHY PLUM.
Go!
EH!?
KUI (JERK)
NARU, YOU HAVE TO KEEP YOUR EYES SHUT!
SOOO (PEAK)
OKAY, NOW OPEN YOUR EYES.
WHEEZE—
WHEEZE—
IT REALLY IS A REAL MAGIC STONE!
NARU WANTS TO PLAY WITH POOCH.
DON'T YA GET JUST ONE WISH!?

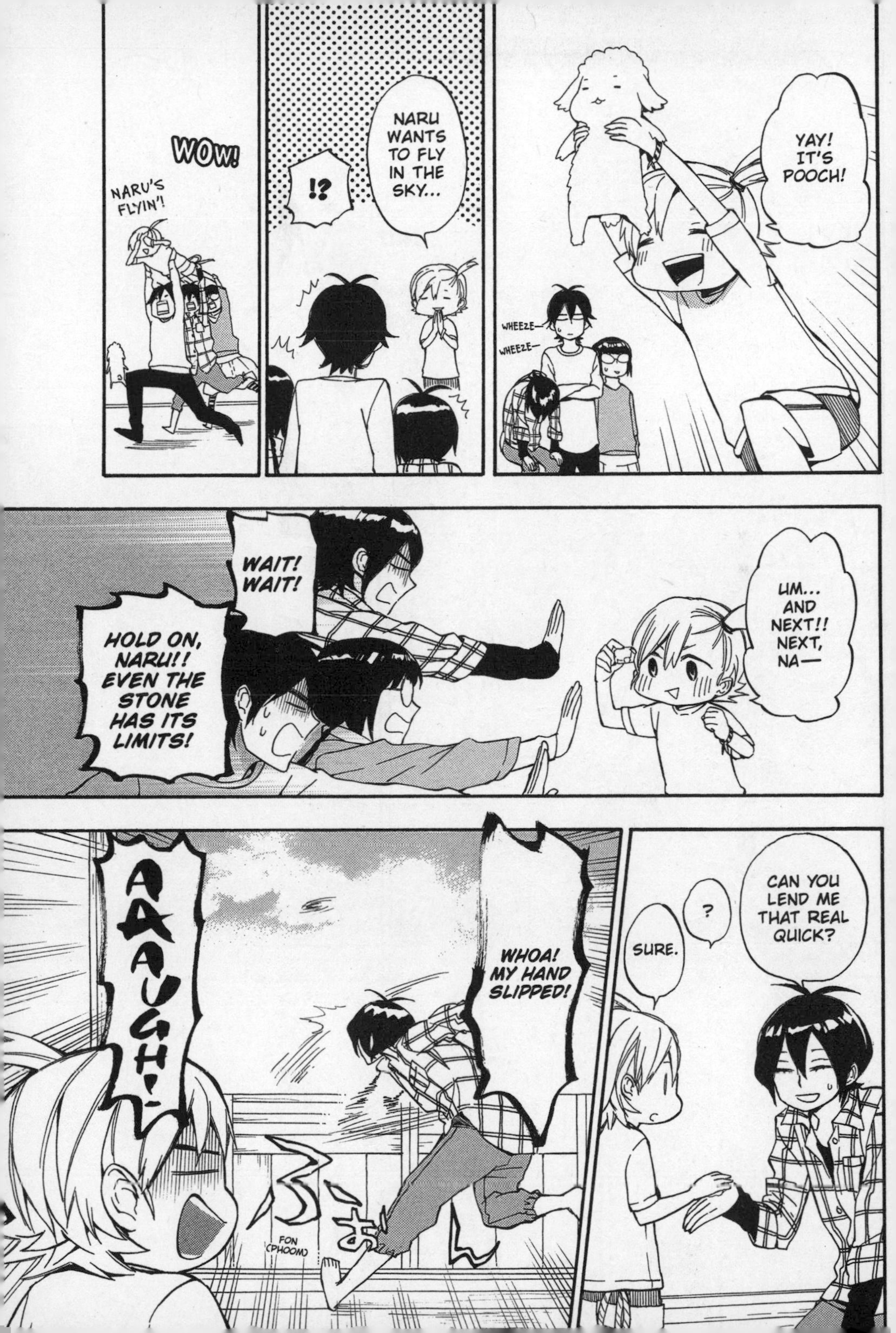

YAY! IT'S POOCH!
WHEEZE—
WHEEZE—
NARU WANTS TO FLY IN THE SKY...
!?
WOW!
NARU'S FLYIN'!
UM... AND NEXT!! NEXT, NA—
WAIT! WAIT!
HOLD ON, NARU!! EVEN THE STONE HAS ITS LIMITS!
CAN YOU LEND ME THAT REAL QUICK?
?
SURE.
WHOA! MY HAND SLIPPED!
AAAUGH!
FON (PHOOM)

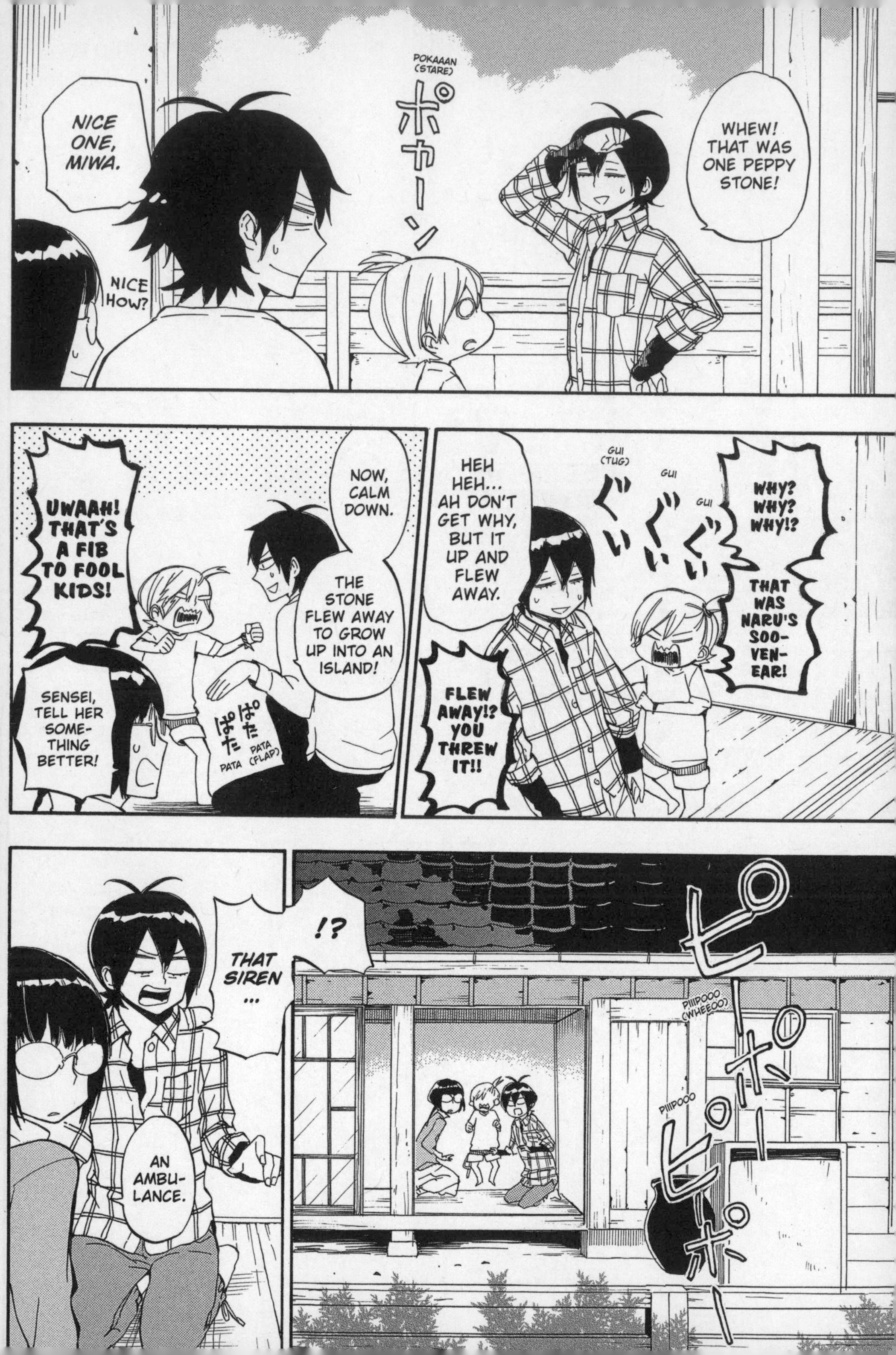

WHEW! THAT WAS ONE PEPPY STONE!
POKAAAN (STARE)
ポカーン
NICE ONE, MIWA.
NICE HOW?
WHY? WHY? WHY!?
GUI (TUG) GUI GUI
ぐいぐいぐい
THAT WAS NARU'S SOO-VEN-EAR!
HEH HEH... AH DON'T GET WHY, BUT IT UP AND FLEW AWAY.
FLEW AWAY!? YOU THREW IT!!
NOW, CALM DOWN.
THE STONE FLEW AWAY TO GROW UP INTO AN ISLAND!
UWAAH! THAT'S A FIB TO FOOL KIDS!
PATA PATA (FLAP)
ぱたぱた
SENSEI, TELL HER SOMETHING BETTER!
ピーポーピーポー
PIIIPOOO (WHEEOO)
PIIIPOOO
!?
THAT SIREN...
AN AMBULANCE.

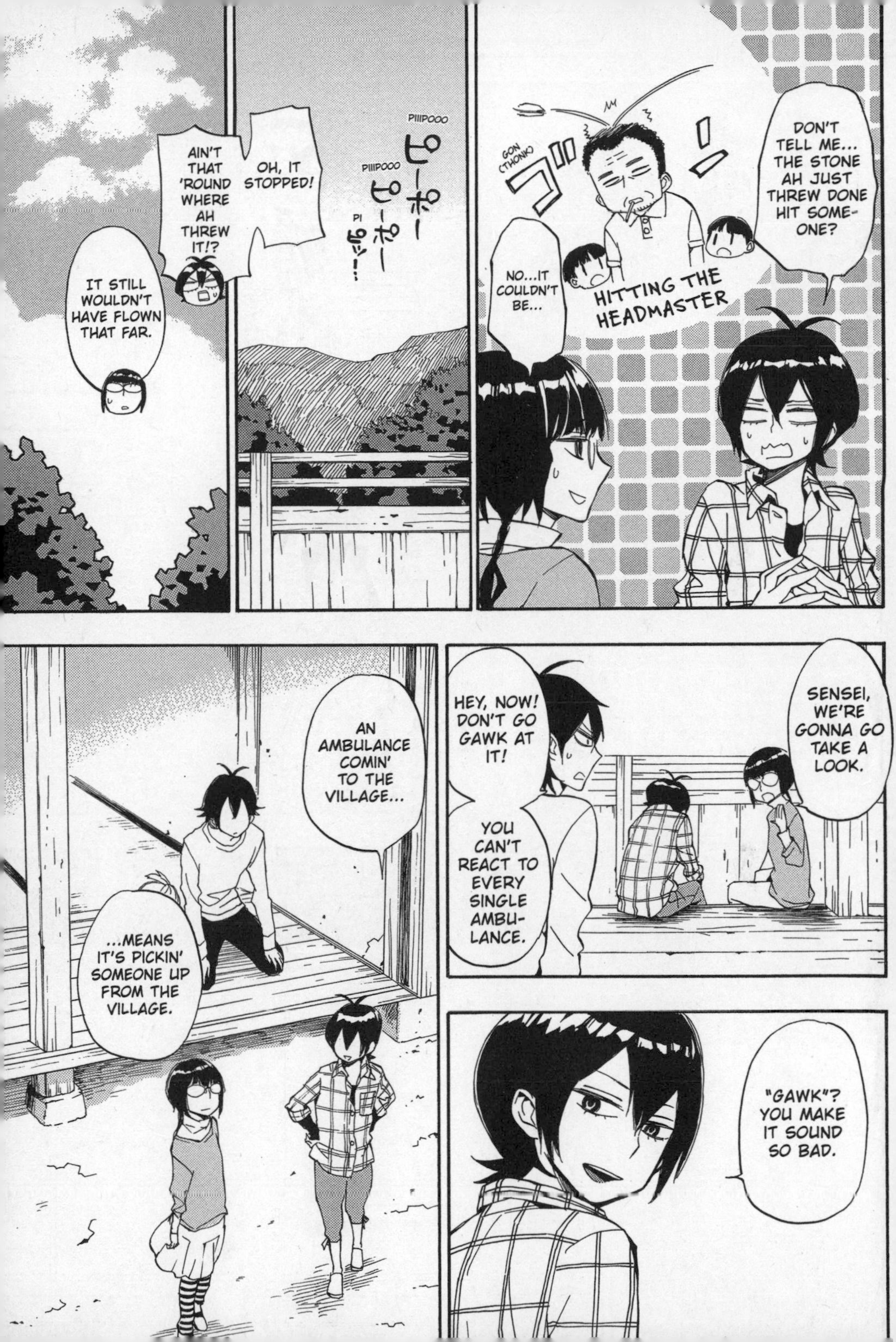
DON'T TELL ME... THE STONE AH JUST THREW DONE HIT SOME-ONE?
GON (THONK)
ゴッ
HITTING THE HEADMASTER
NO...IT COULDN'T BE...
PIIIPOOO
ピーポー
PIIIPOOO
ピーポー
PI
ピッ…!
OH, IT STOPPED!
AIN'T THAT 'ROUND WHERE AH THREW IT!?
IT STILL WOULDN'T HAVE FLOWN THAT FAR.
SENSEI, WE'RE GONNA GO TAKE A LOOK.
HEY, NOW! DON'T GO GAWK AT IT!
YOU CAN'T REACT TO EVERY SINGLE AMBULANCE.
"GAWK"? YOU MAKE IT SOUND SO BAD.
AN AMBULANCE COMIN' TO THE VILLAGE...
...MEANS IT'S PICKIN' SOMEONE UP FROM THE VILLAGE.

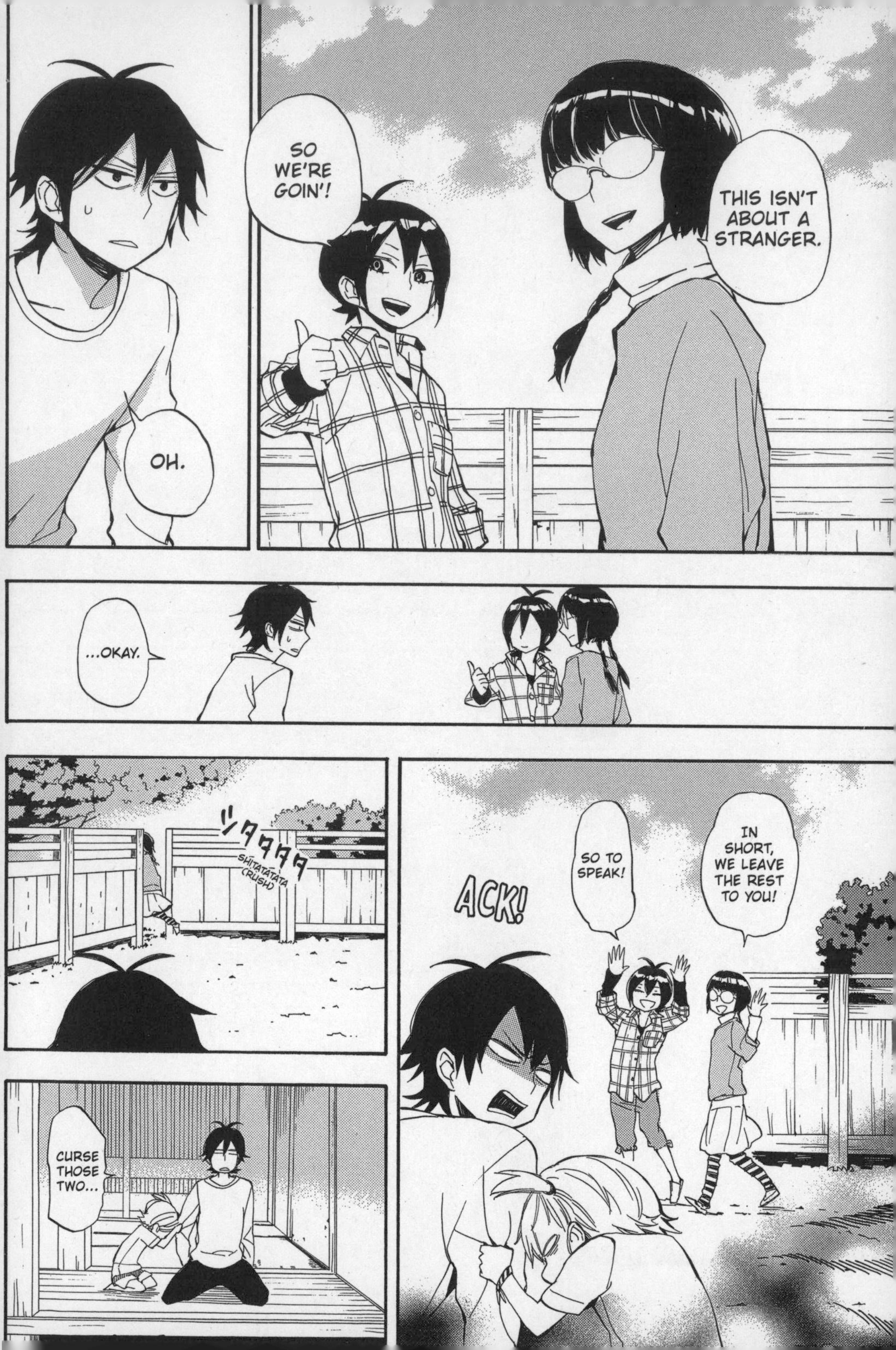
THIS ISN'T ABOUT A STRANGER.
SO WE'RE GOIN'!
OH.
...OKAY.
IN SHORT, WE LEAVE THE REST TO YOU!
SO TO SPEAK!
ACK!
ツタタタタ
SHITATATATA (RUSH)
CURSE THOSE TWO...

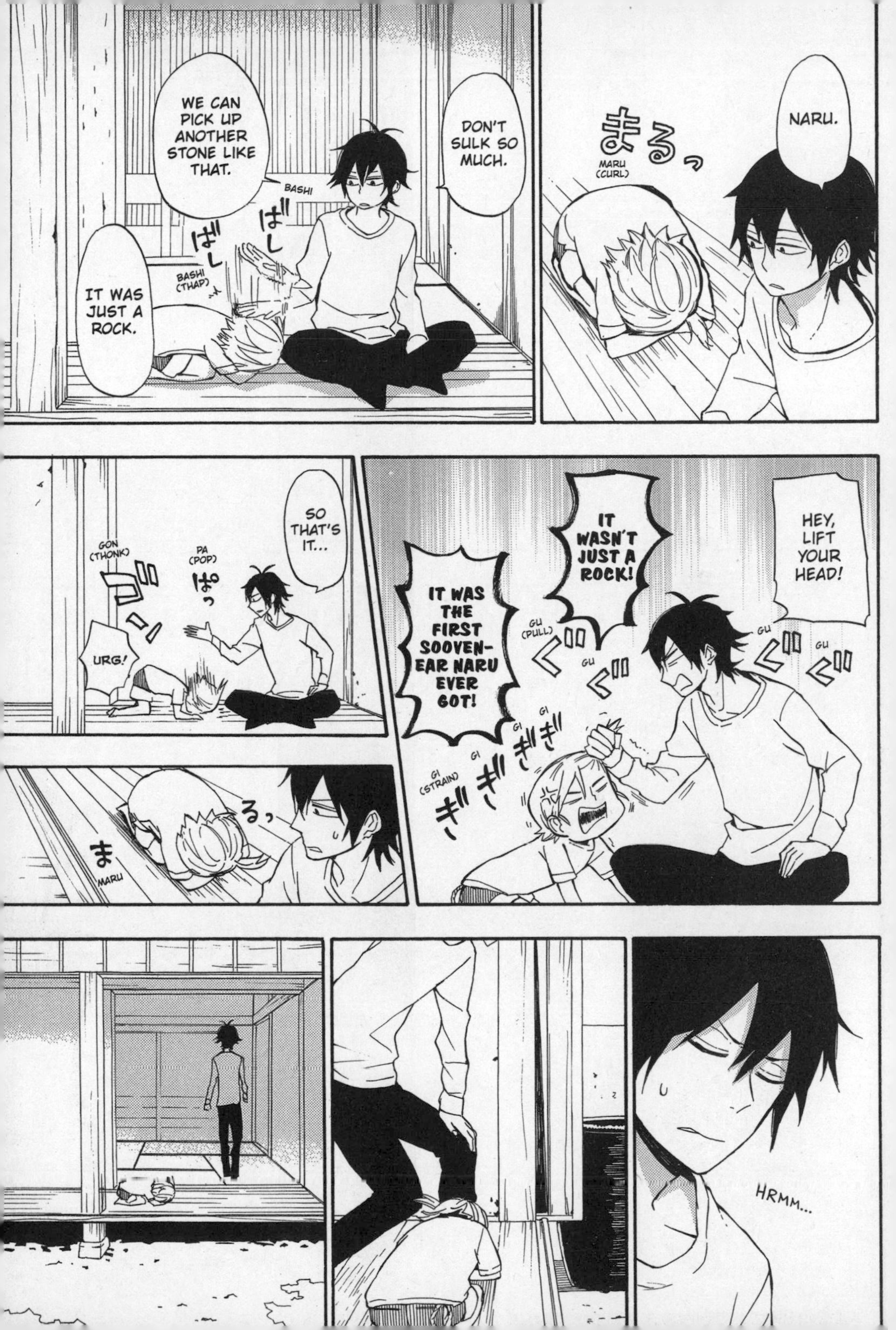
NARU.
まるっ
MARU (CURL)
DON'T SULK SO MUCH.
WE CAN PICK UP ANOTHER STONE LIKE THAT.
BASHI
ばし
ばし
BASHI (THAP)
IT WAS JUST A ROCK.
HEY, LIFT YOUR HEAD!
IT WASN'T JUST A ROCK!
IT WAS THE FIRST SOOVEN-EAR NARU EVER GOT!
GU
ぐッ
GU
ぐッ
GU
ぐッ
GU (PULL)
ぐッ
GI
ぎ
GI
ぎ
GI
ぎ
GI (STRAIN)
ぎ
SO THAT'S IT...
PA (POP)
ぱっ
GON (THONK)
ゴンッ
URG!
るっ
ま
MARU
HRMM...

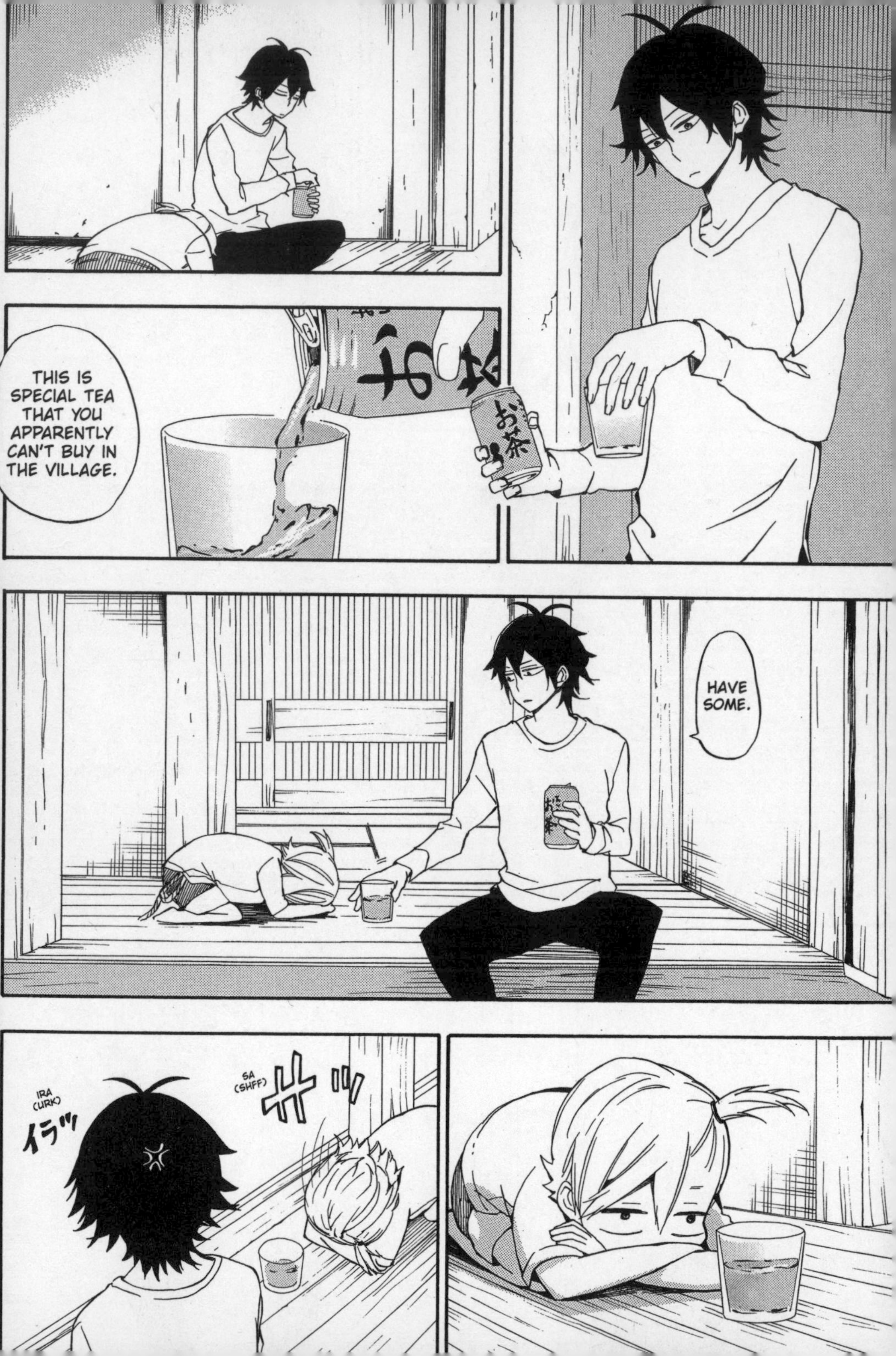

お茶
THIS IS SPECIAL TEA THAT YOU APPARENTLY CAN'T BUY IN THE VILLAGE.
HAVE SOME.
SA (SHFF)
ザッ
IRA (URK)
イラッ

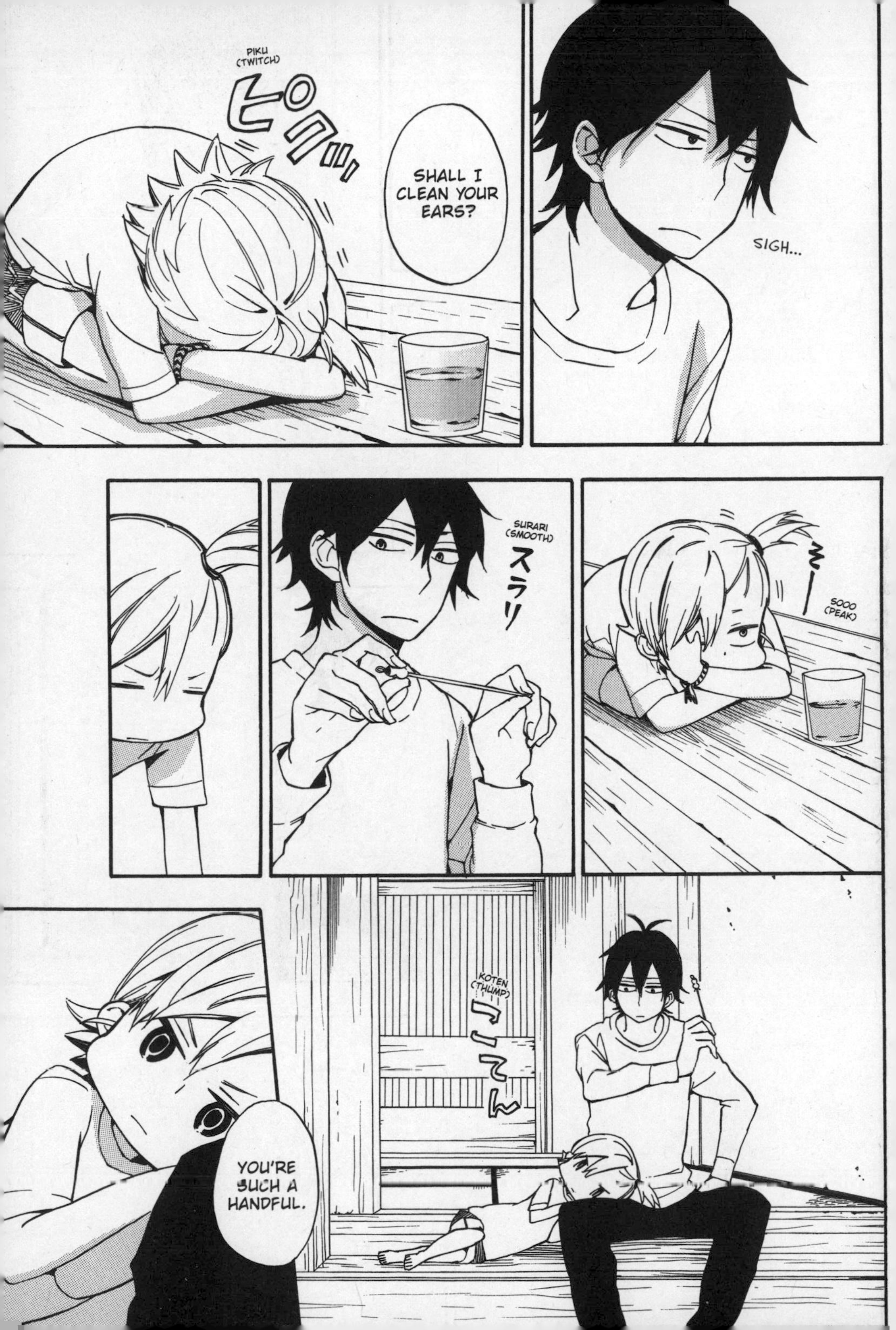
SIGH...
PIKU (TWITCH)
ピクッ
SHALL I CLEAN YOUR EARS?
SOOO (PEAK)
SURARI (SMOOTH)
スラリ
KOTEN (THUMP)
こてん
YOU'RE SUCH A HANDFUL.

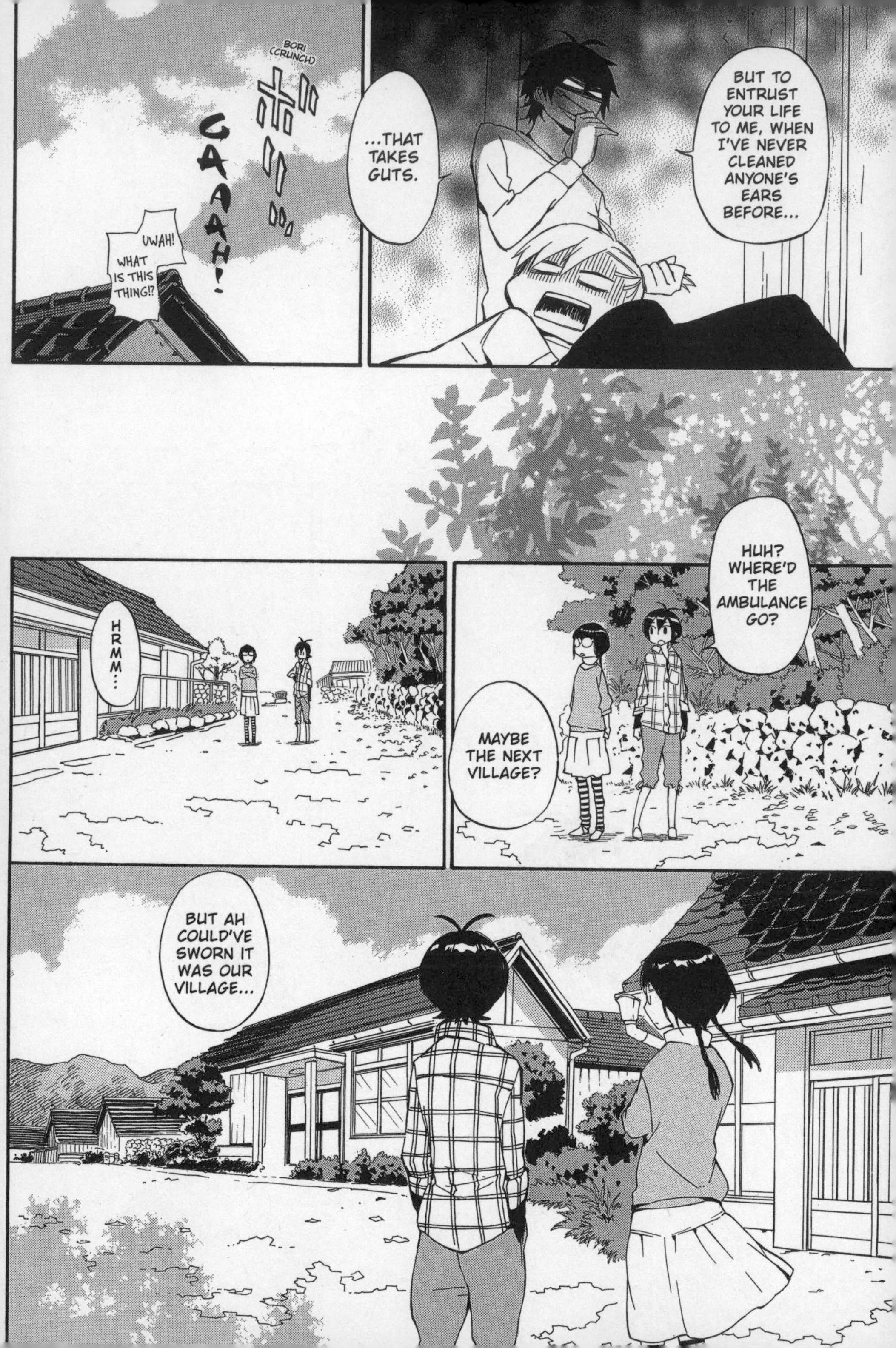
BUT TO ENTRUST YOUR LIFE TO ME, WHEN I'VE NEVER CLEANED ANYONE'S EARS BEFORE...
...THAT TAKES GUTS.
BORI (CRUNCH)
GAAAH!
UWAH! WHAT IS THIS THING!?
HUH? WHERE'D THE AMBULANCE GO?
MAYBE THE NEXT VILLAGE?
HRMM...
BUT AH COULD'VE SWORN IT WAS OUR VILLAGE...

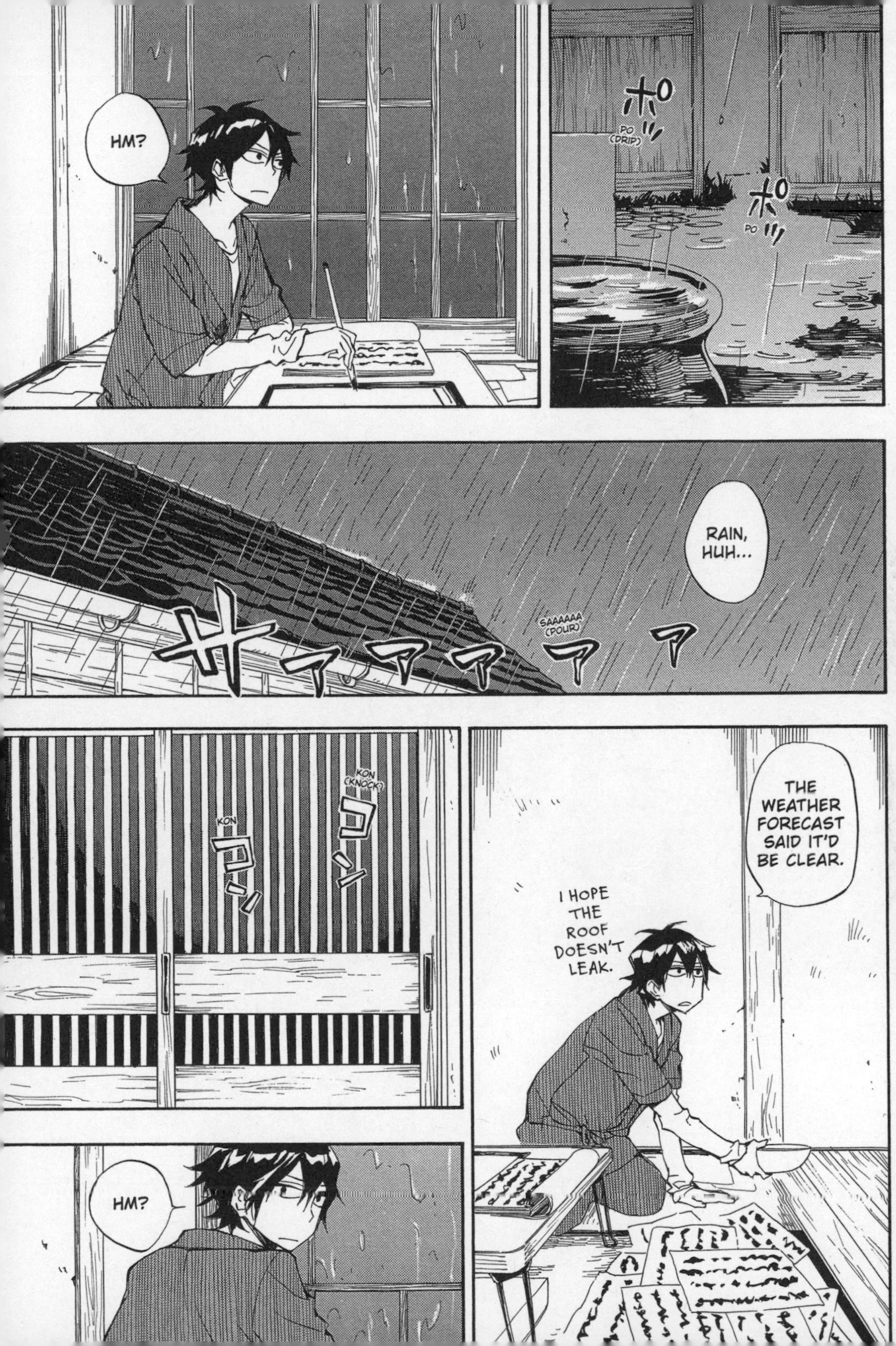
ポ
PO (DRIP)
ポ
PO
HM?
RAIN, HUH...
サァァァァ
SAAAAAA (POUR)
THE WEATHER FORECAST SAID IT'D BE CLEAR.
I HOPE THE ROOF DOESN'T LEAK.
コン
KON (KNOCK)
コン
KON
HM?

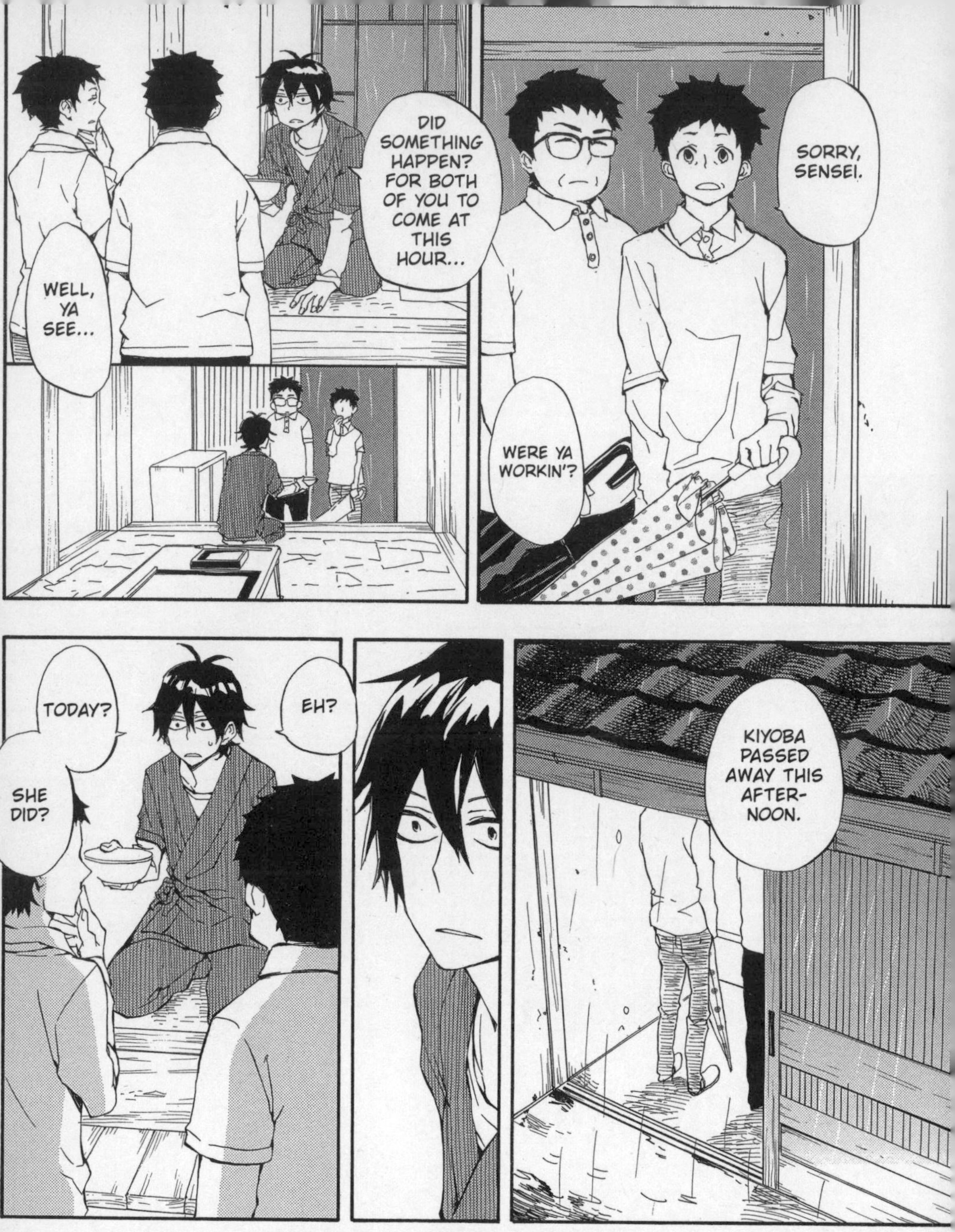
SORRY, SENSEI.
WERE YA WORKIN'?
DID SOMETHING HAPPEN? FOR BOTH OF YOU TO COME AT THIS HOUR...
WELL, YA SEE...
KIYOBA PASSED AWAY THIS AFTER-NOON.
EH?
TODAY?
SHE DID?

ACT.67 KUYAMI

(Translation: The Wake)

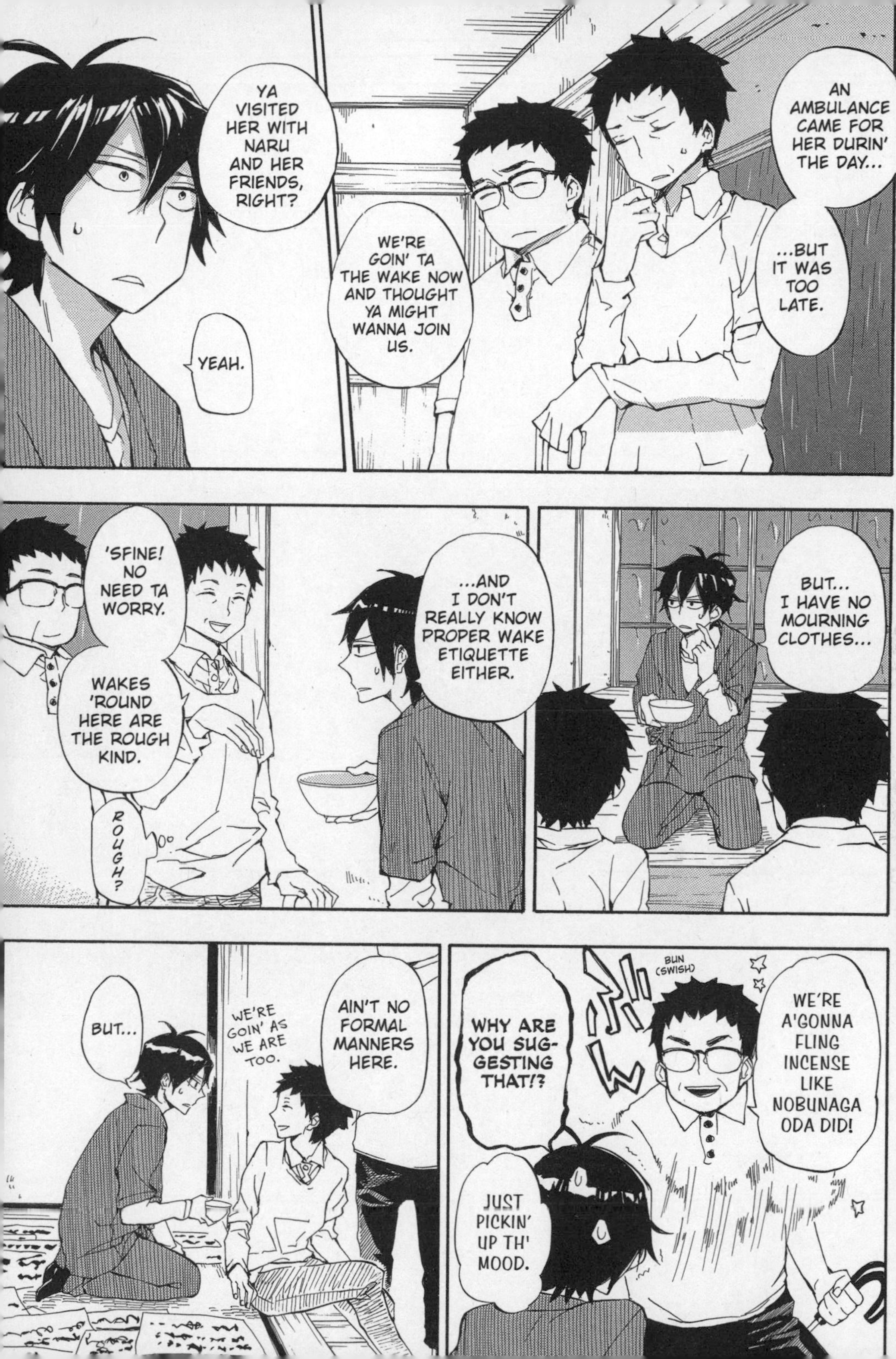
AN AMBULANCE CAME FOR HER DURIN' THE DAY...
...BUT IT WAS TOO LATE.
WE'RE GOIN' TA THE WAKE NOW AND THOUGHT YA MIGHT WANNA JOIN US.
YA VISITED HER WITH NARU AND HER FRIENDS, RIGHT?
YEAH.
BUT... I HAVE NO MOURNING CLOTHES...
...AND I DON'T REALLY KNOW PROPER WAKE ETIQUETTE EITHER.
'SFINE! NO NEED TA WORRY.
WAKES 'ROUND HERE ARE THE ROUGH KIND.
ROUGH?
BUN (SWISH)
WE'RE A'GONNA FLING INCENSE LIKE NOBUNAGA ODA DID!
WHY ARE YOU SUG-GESTING THAT!?
JUST PICKIN' UP TH' MOOD.
BUT...
AIN'T NO FORMAL MANNERS HERE.
WE'RE GOIN' AS WE ARE TOO.

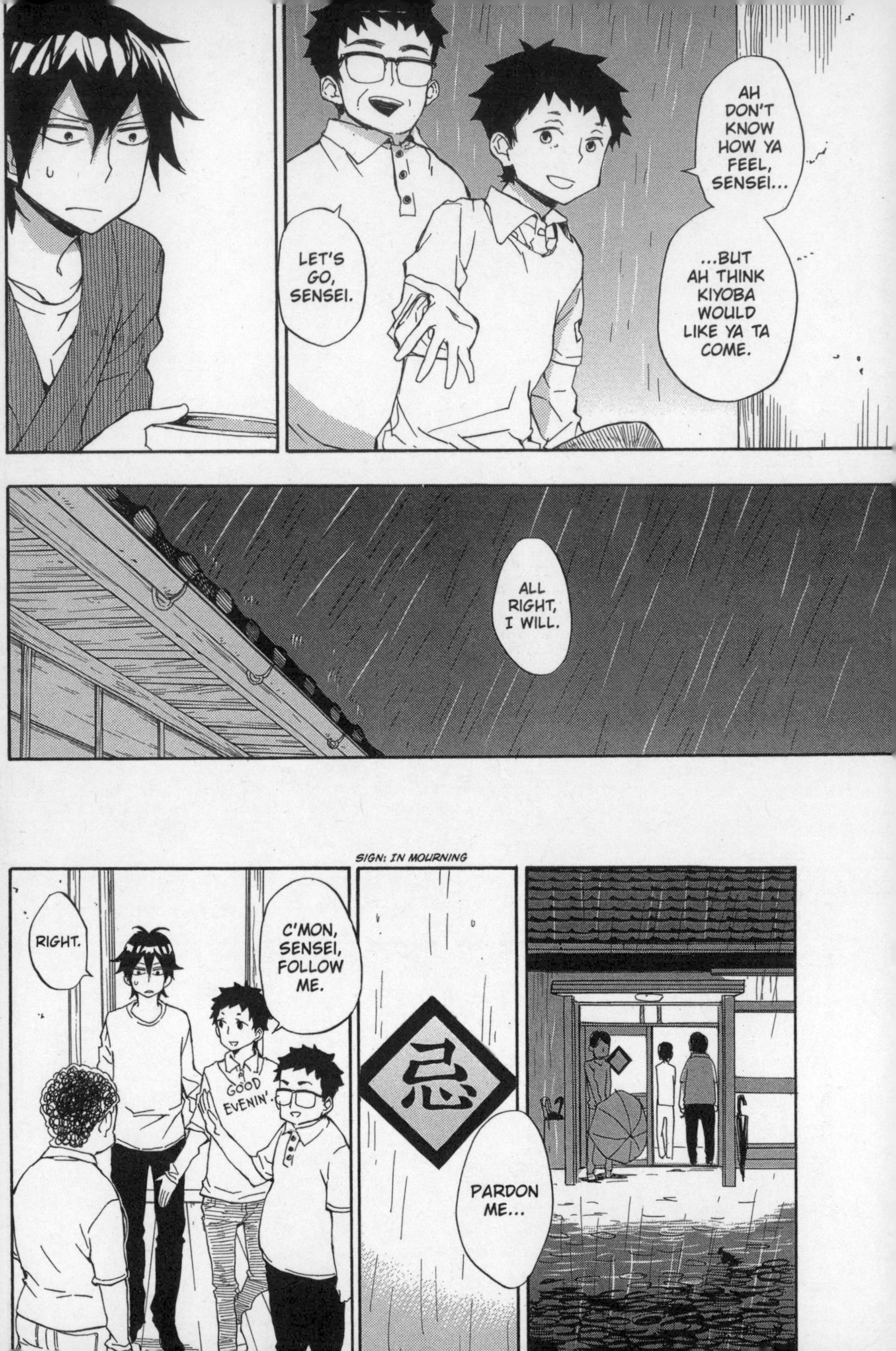
AH DON'T KNOW HOW YA FEEL, SENSEI...
...BUT AH THINK KIYOBA WOULD LIKE YA TA COME.
LET'S GO, SENSEI.
ALL RIGHT, I WILL.
PARDON ME...
SIGN: IN MOURNING
C'MON, SENSEI, FOLLOW ME.
RIGHT.
GOOD EVENIN'.

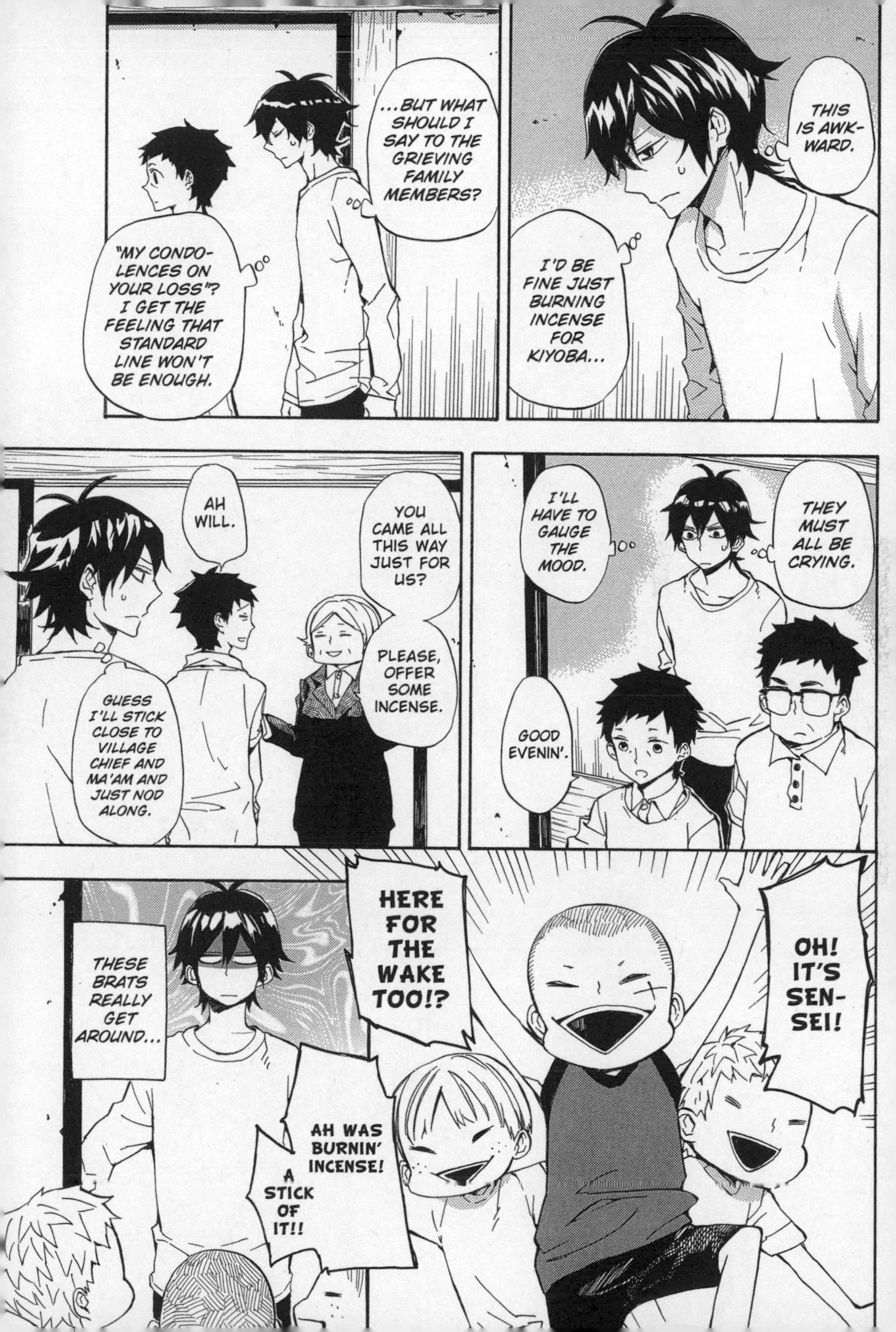
THIS IS AWKWARD.
I'D BE FINE JUST BURNING INCENSE FOR KIYOBA...
...BUT WHAT SHOULD I SAY TO THE GRIEVING FAMILY MEMBERS?
"MY CONDOLENCES ON YOUR LOSS"? I GET THE FEELING THAT STANDARD LINE WON'T BE ENOUGH.
THEY MUST ALL BE CRYING.
I'LL HAVE TO GAUGE THE MOOD.
GOOD EVENIN'.
YOU CAME ALL THIS WAY JUST FOR US?
PLEASE, OFFER SOME INCENSE.
AH WILL.
GUESS I'LL STICK CLOSE TO VILLAGE CHIEF AND MA'AM AND JUST NOD ALONG.
OH! IT'S SEN-SEI!
HERE FOR THE WAKE TOO!?
AH WAS BURNIN' INCENSE!
A STICK OF IT!!
THESE BRATS REALLY GET AROUND...

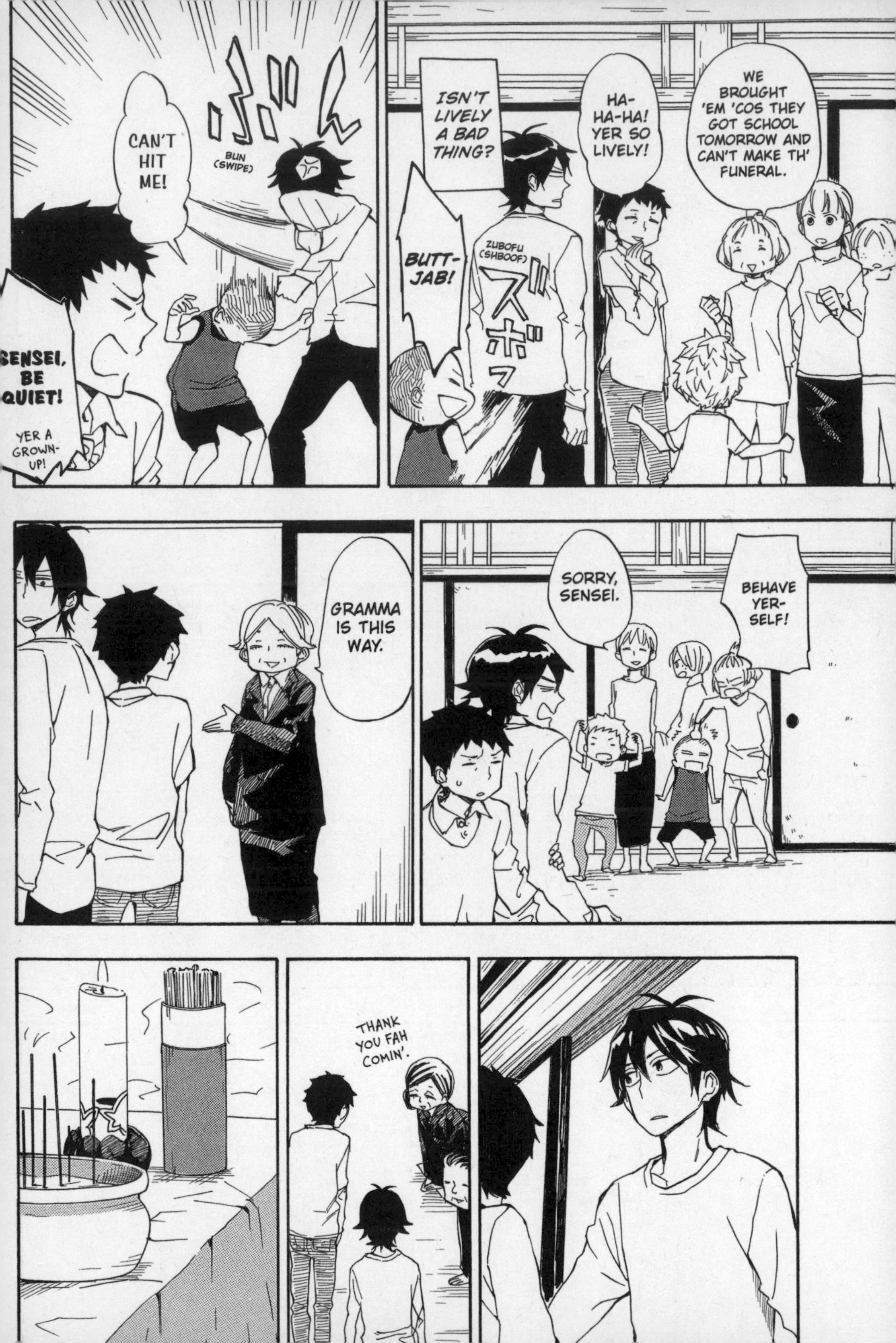
WE BROUGHT 'EM 'COS THEY GOT SCHOOL TOMORROW AND CAN'T MAKE TH' FUNERAL.
HA-HA-HA! YER SO LIVELY!
ISN'T LIVELY A BAD THING?
ZUBOFU (SHBOOF)
BUTT-JAB!
BUN (SWIPE)
CAN'T HIT ME!
SENSEI, BE QUIET!
YER A GROWN-UP!
BEHAVE YER-SELF!
SORRY, SENSEI.
GRAMMA IS THIS WAY.
THANK YOU FAH COMIN'.

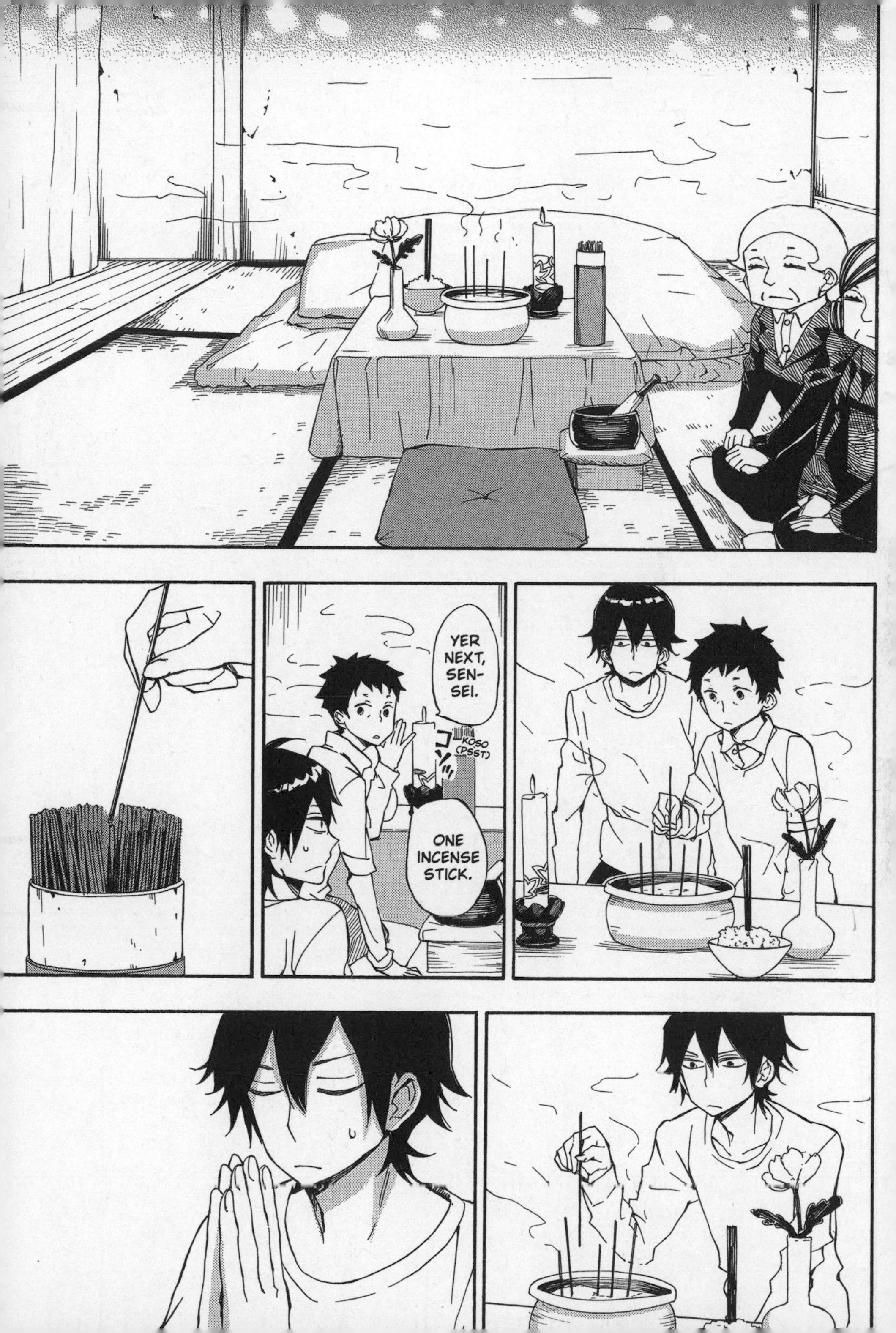
YER NEXT, SEN-SEI.
KOSO (PSST)
ONE INCENSE STICK.

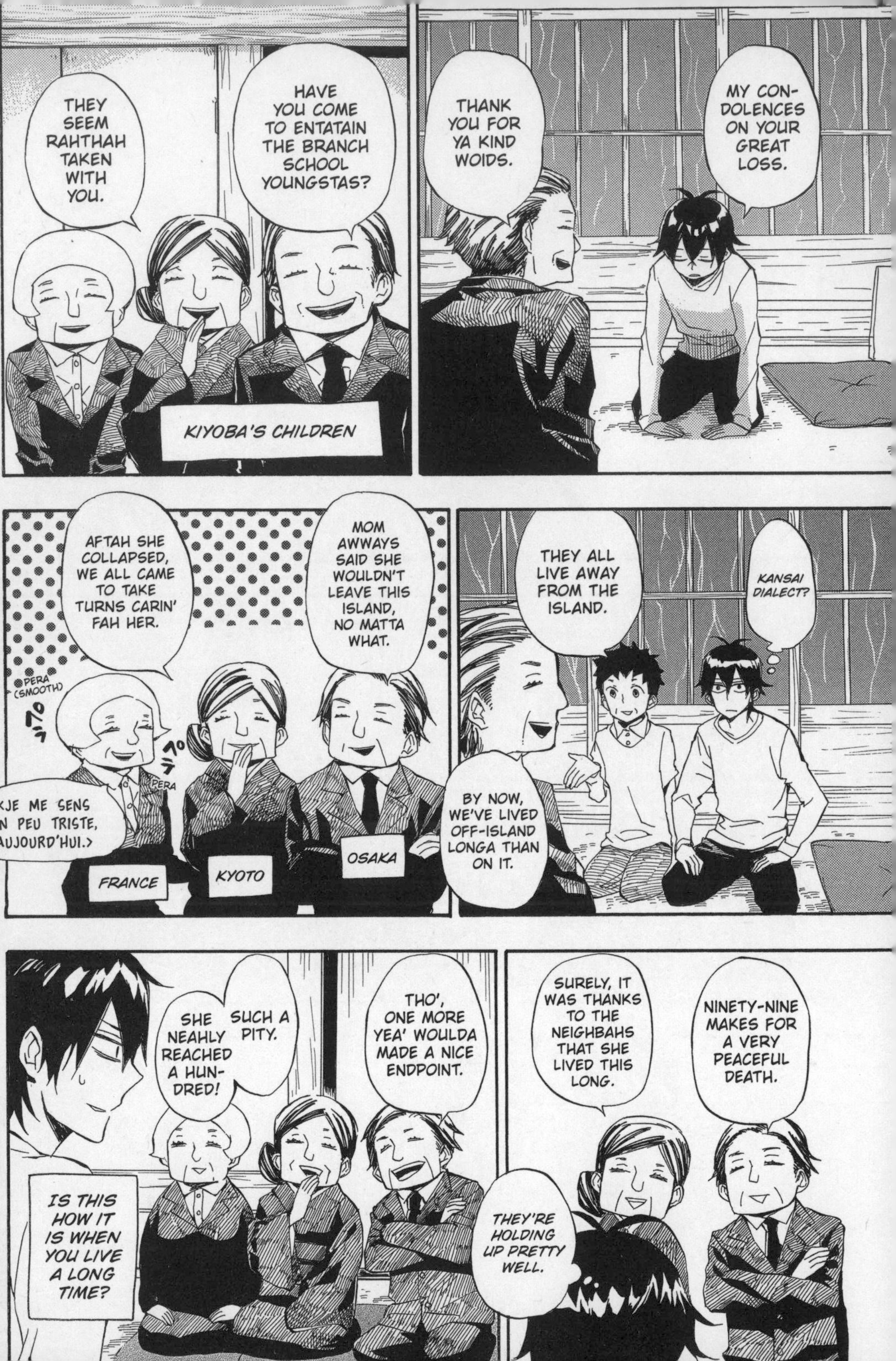
MY CONDOLENCES ON YOUR GREAT LOSS.
THANK YOU FOR YA KIND WOIDS.
HAVE YOU COME TO ENTATAIN THE BRANCH SCHOOL YOUNGSTAS?
THEY SEEM RAHTHAH TAKEN WITH YOU.
KIYOBA'S CHILDREN
KANSAI DIALECT?
THEY ALL LIVE AWAY FROM THE ISLAND.
BY NOW, WE'VE LIVED OFF-ISLAND LONGA THAN ON IT.
MOM AWWAYS SAID SHE WOULDN'T LEAVE THIS ISLAND, NO MATTA WHAT.
AFTAH SHE COLLAPSED, WE ALL CAME TO TAKE TURNS CARIN' FAH HER.
OSAKA
PERA
KYOTO
PERA (SMOOTH)
<JE ME SENS UN PEU TRISTE, AUJOURD'HUI.>
FRANCE
NINETY-NINE MAKES FOR A VERY PEACEFUL DEATH.
SURELY, IT WAS THANKS TO THE NEIGHBAHS THAT SHE LIVED THIS LONG.
THEY'RE HOLDING UP PRETTY WELL.
THO', ONE MORE YEA' WOULDA MADE A NICE ENDPOINT.
SUCH A PITY.
SHE NEAHLY REACHED A HUNDRED!
IS THIS HOW IT IS WHEN YOU LIVE A LONG TIME?

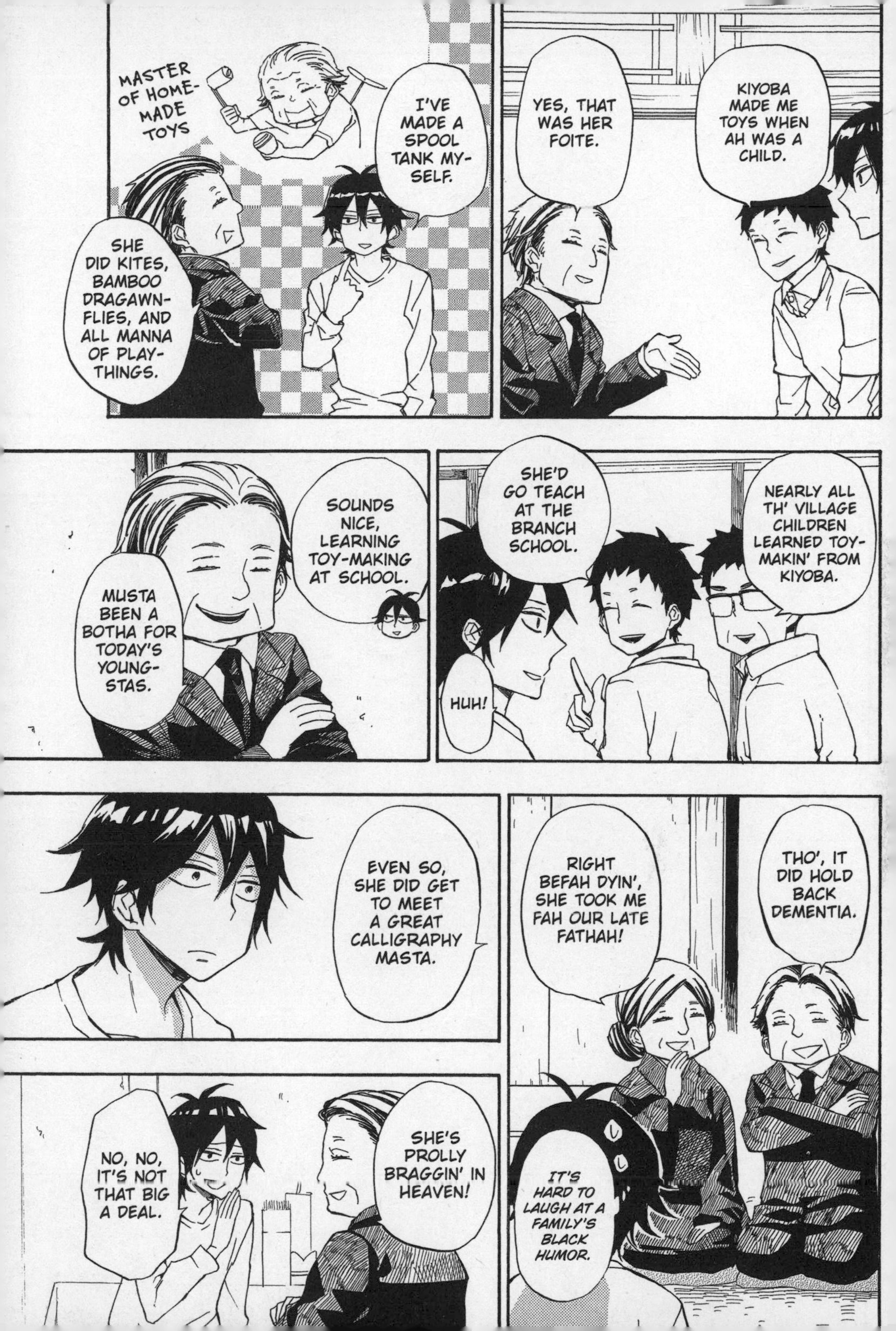
KIYOBA MADE ME TOYS WHEN AH WAS A CHILD.
YES, THAT WAS HER FOITE.
I'VE MADE A SPOOL TANK MY-SELF.
MASTER OF HOME-MADE TOYS
SHE DID KITES, BAMBOO DRAGAWN-FLIES, AND ALL MANNA OF PLAY-THINGS.
NEARLY ALL TH' VILLAGE CHILDREN LEARNED TOY-MAKIN' FROM KIYOBA.
SHE'D GO TEACH AT THE BRANCH SCHOOL.
HUH!
SOUNDS NICE, LEARNING TOY-MAKING AT SCHOOL.
MUSTA BEEN A BOTHA FOR TODAY'S YOUNG-STAS.
THO', IT DID HOLD BACK DEMENTIA.
RIGHT BEFAH DYIN', SHE TOOK ME FAH OUR LATE FATHAH!
IT'S HARD TO LAUGH AT A FAMILY'S BLACK HUMOR.
EVEN SO, SHE DID GET TO MEET A GREAT CALLIGRAPHY MASTA.
SHE'S PROLLY BRAGGIN' IN HEAVEN!
NO, NO, IT'S NOT THAT BIG A DEAL.

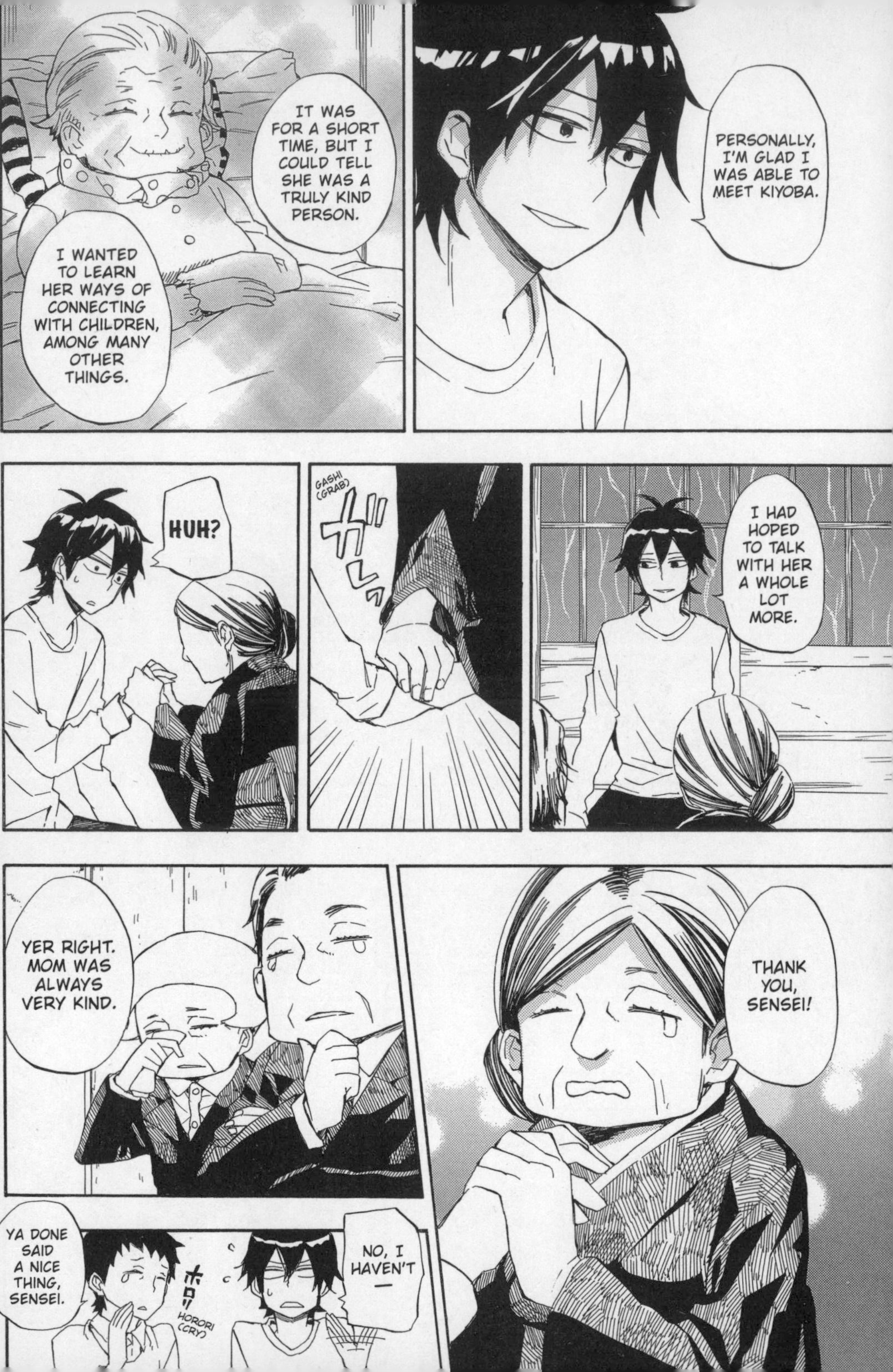
PERSONALLY, I'M GLAD I WAS ABLE TO MEET KIYOBA.
IT WAS FOR A SHORT TIME, BUT I COULD TELL SHE WAS A TRULY KIND PERSON.
I WANTED TO LEARN HER WAYS OF CONNECTING WITH CHILDREN, AMONG MANY OTHER THINGS.
I HAD HOPED TO TALK WITH HER A WHOLE LOT MORE.
GASHI (GRAB)
HUH?
THANK YOU, SENSEI!
YER RIGHT. MOM WAS ALWAYS VERY KIND.
NO, I HAVEN'T —
HORORI (CRY)
YA DONE SAID A NICE THING, SENSEI.

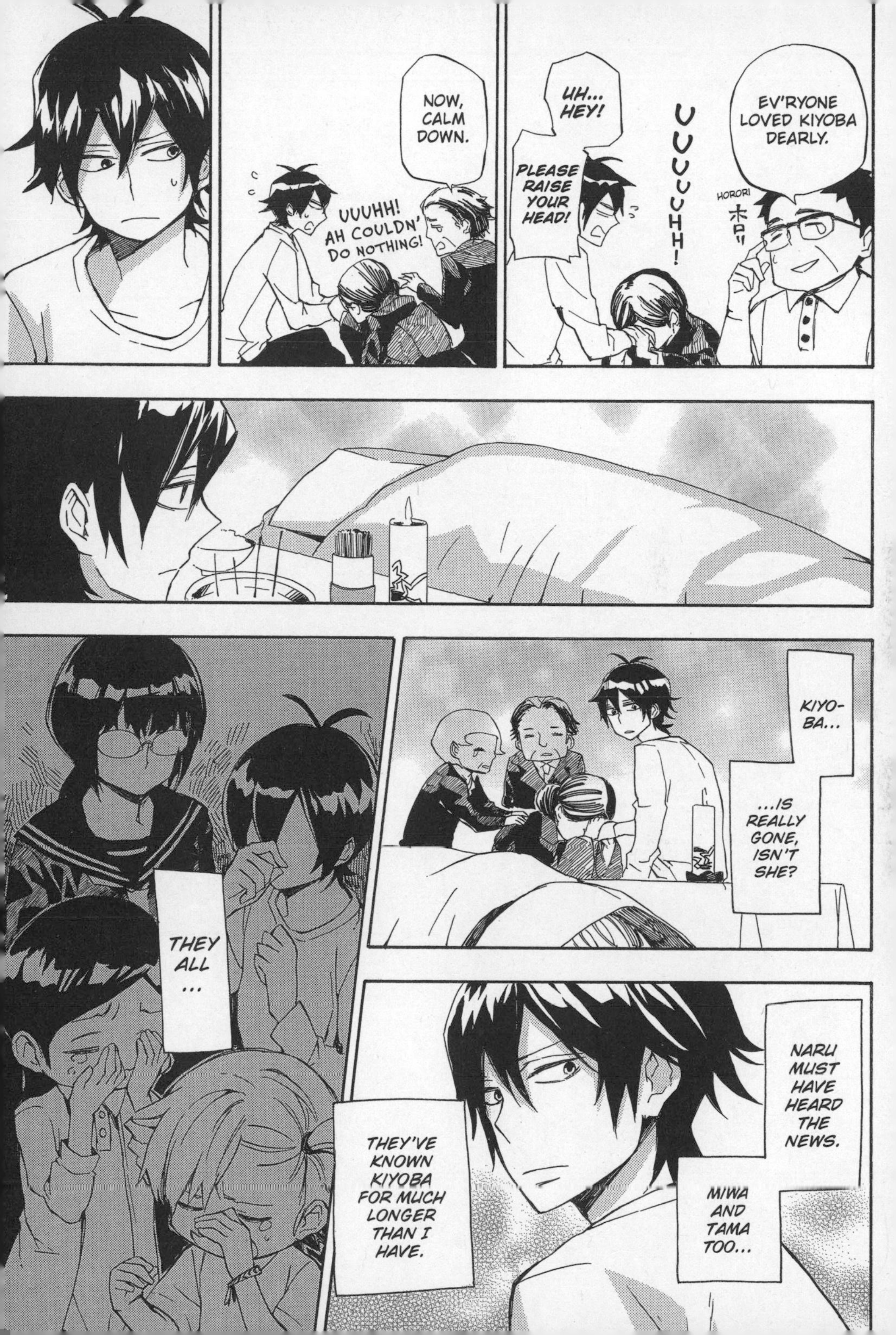

EV'RYONE LOVED KIYOBA DEARLY.
HORORI
ホロリ
UUUUUUHH!
UH... HEY!
PLEASE RAISE YOUR HEAD!
NOW, CALM DOWN.
UUUHH! AH COULDN' DO NOTHING!
KIYO-BA...
...IS REALLY GONE, ISN'T SHE?
NARU MUST HAVE HEARD THE NEWS.
MIWA AND TAMA TOO...
THEY'VE KNOWN KIYOBA FOR MUCH LONGER THAN I HAVE.
THEY ALL ...

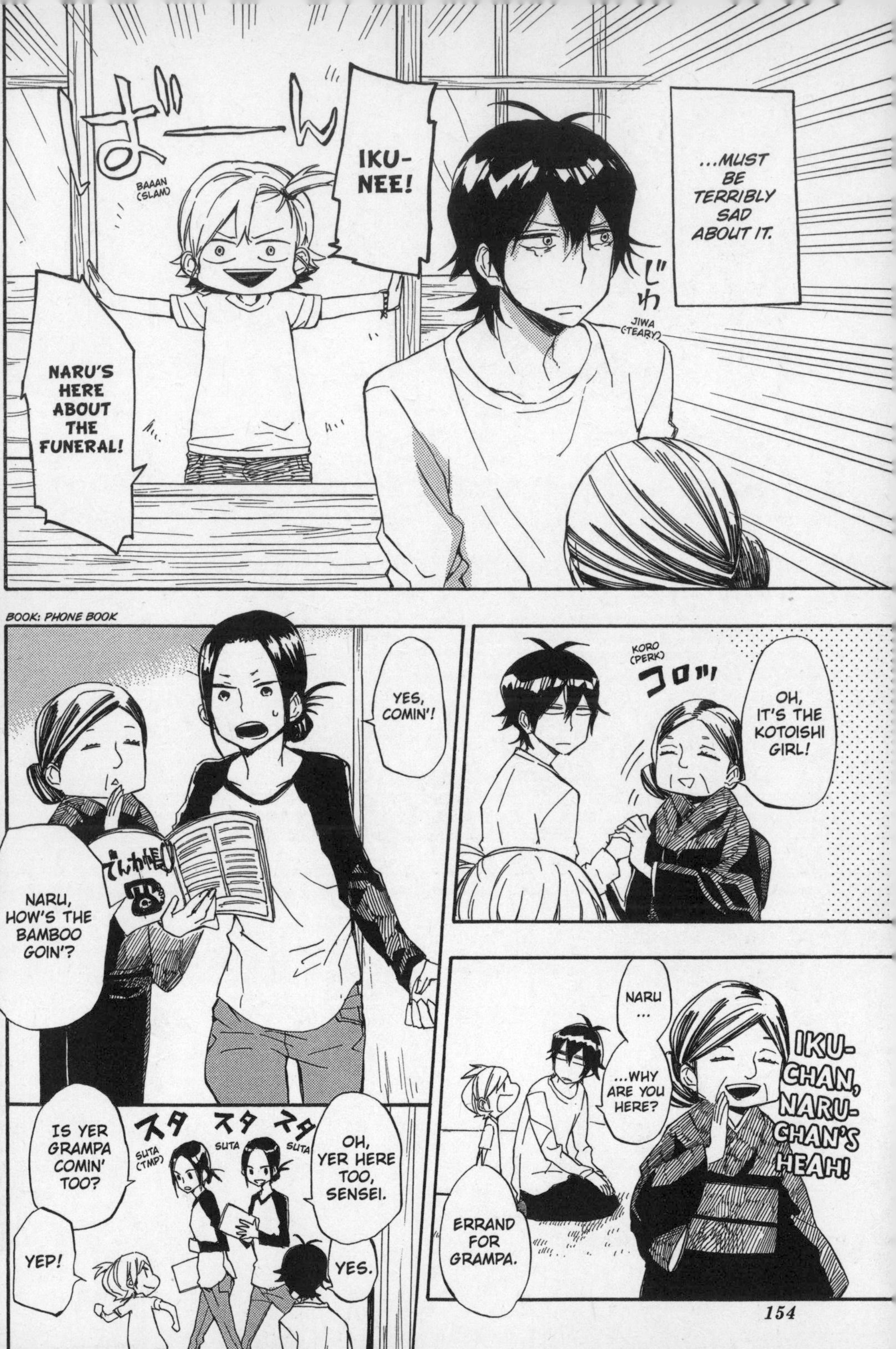
...MUST BE TERRIBLY SAD ABOUT IT.
じわ
JIWA (TEARY)
IKU-NEE!
ばーん
BAAAN (SLAM)
NARU'S HERE ABOUT THE FUNERAL!
KORO (PERK)
コロッ
OH, IT'S THE KOTOISHI GIRL!
IKU-CHAN, NARU-CHAN'S HEAH!
NARU ...
...WHY ARE YOU HERE?
ERRAND FOR GRAMPA.
BOOK: PHONE BOOK
YES, COMIN'!
NARU, HOW'S THE BAMBOO GOIN'?
OH, YER HERE TOO, SENSEI.
スタ スタ スタ
SUTA (TMP) SUTA SUTA
YES.
IS YER GRAMPA COMIN' TOO?
YEP!

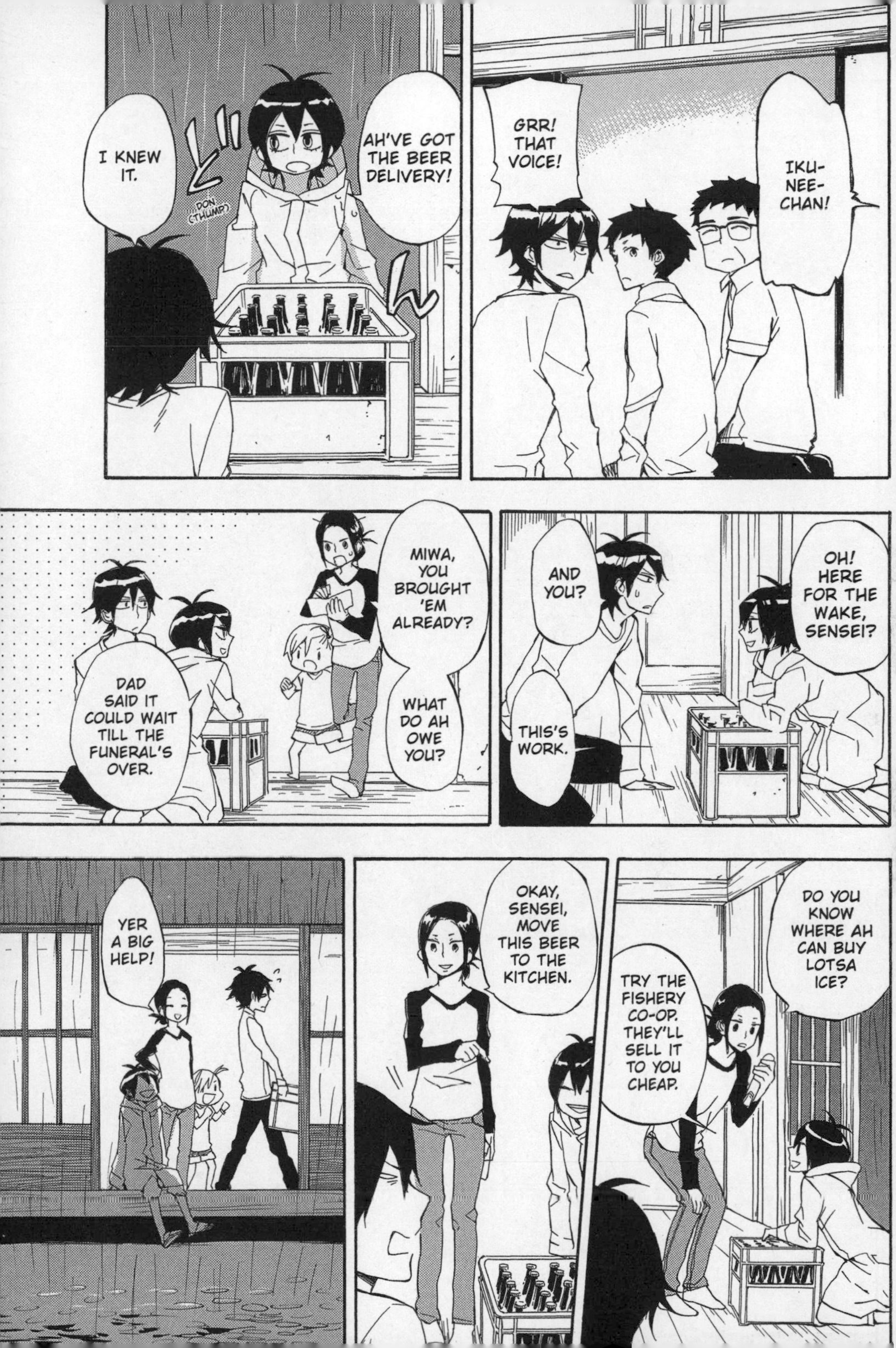
IKU-NEE-CHAN!
GRR! THAT VOICE!
AH'VE GOT THE BEER DELIVERY!
DON (THUMP)
I KNEW IT.
OH! HERE FOR THE WAKE, SENSEI?
AND YOU?
THIS'S WORK.
MIWA, YOU BROUGHT 'EM ALREADY?
WHAT DO AH OWE YOU?
DAD SAID IT COULD WAIT TILL THE FUNERAL'S OVER.
DO YOU KNOW WHERE AH CAN BUY LOTSA ICE?
TRY THE FISHERY CO-OP. THEY'LL SELL IT TO YOU CHEAP.
OKAY, SENSEI, MOVE THIS BEER TO THE KITCHEN.
YER A BIG HELP!

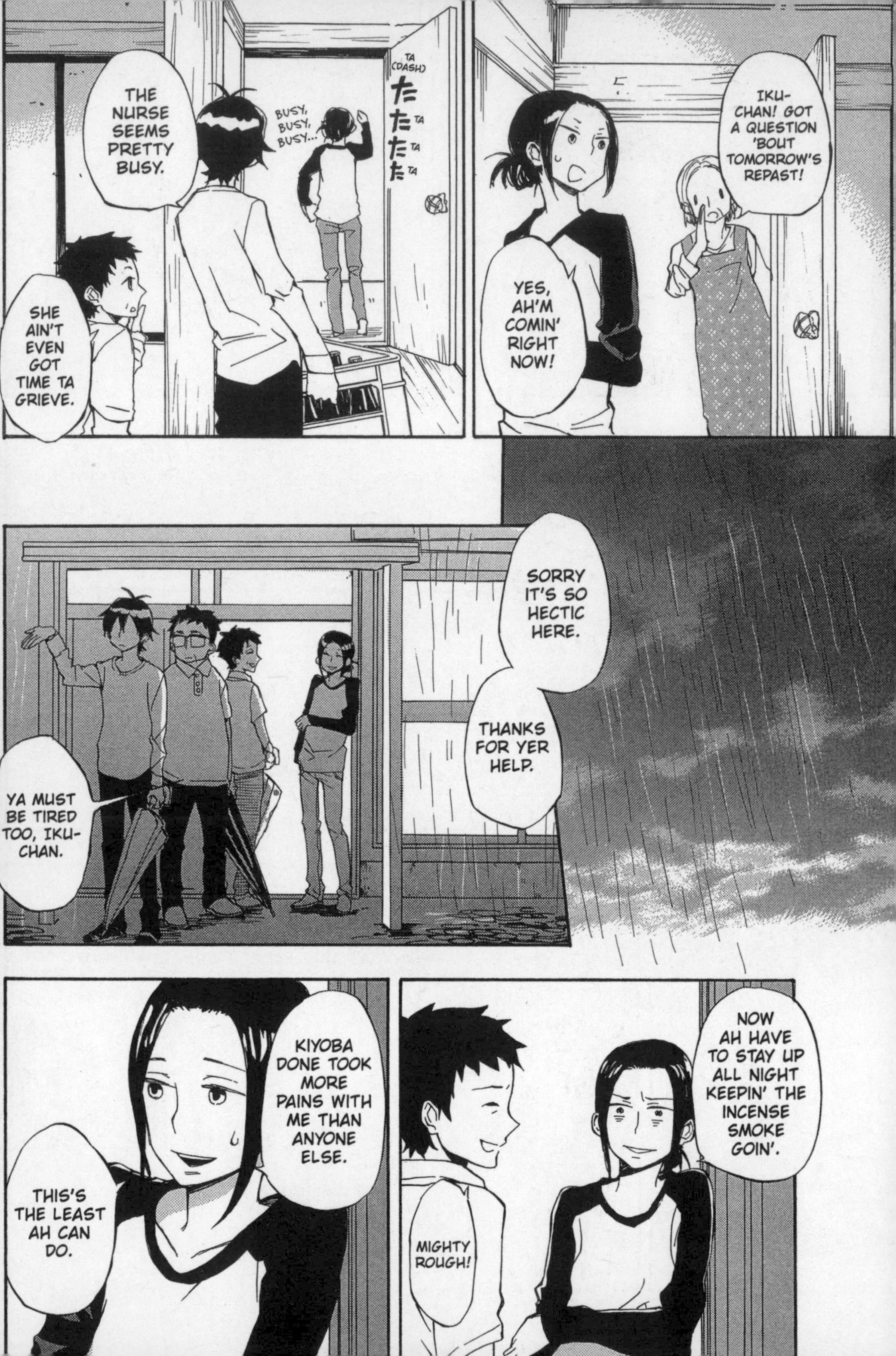
IKU-CHAN! GOT A QUESTION 'BOUT TOMORROW'S REPAST!
YES, AH'M COMIN' RIGHT NOW!
TA (DASH) たたたた TA TA TA
BUSY, BUSY, BUSY...
THE NURSE SEEMS PRETTY BUSY.
SHE AIN'T EVEN GOT TIME TA GRIEVE.
SORRY IT'S SO HECTIC HERE.
THANKS FOR YER HELP.
YA MUST BE TIRED TOO, IKU-CHAN.
NOW AH HAVE TO STAY UP ALL NIGHT KEEPIN' THE INCENSE SMOKE GOIN'.
MIGHTY ROUGH!
KIYOBA DONE TOOK MORE PAINS WITH ME THAN ANYONE ELSE.
THIS'S THE LEAST AH CAN DO.

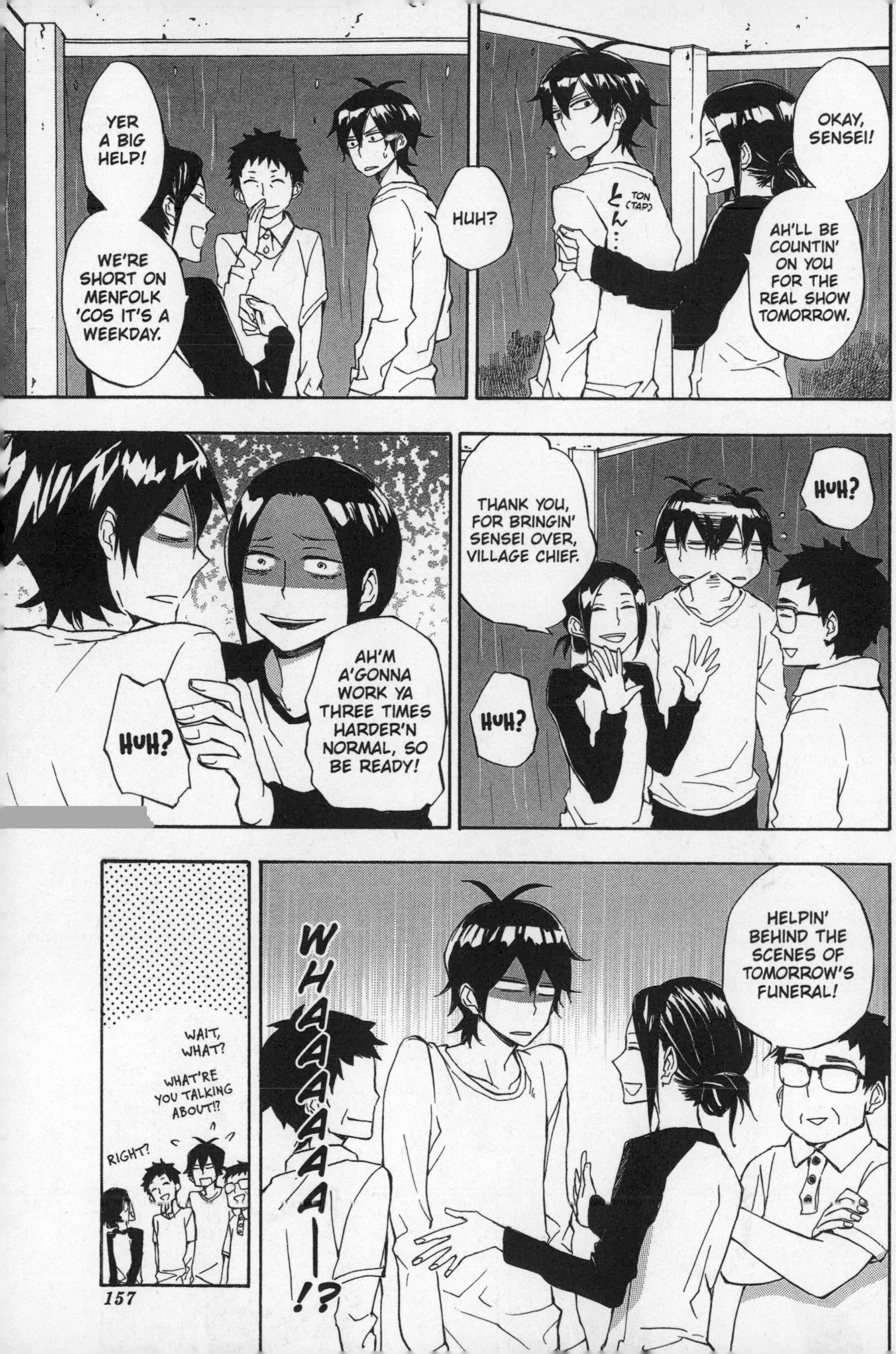
OKAY, SENSEI!
とん… TON (TAP)
AH'LL BE COUNTIN' ON YOU FOR THE REAL SHOW TOMORROW.
YER A BIG HELP!
WE'RE SHORT ON MENFOLK 'COS IT'S A WEEKDAY.
HUH?
THANK YOU, FOR BRINGIN' SENSEI OVER, VILLAGE CHIEF.
HUH?
HUH?
AH'M A'GONNA WORK YA THREE TIMES HARDER'N NORMAL, SO BE READY!
HUH?
HELPIN' BEHIND THE SCENES OF TOMORROW'S FUNERAL!
WHAAAAAA!?
WAIT, WHAT?
WHAT'RE YOU TALKING ABOUT!?
RIGHT?

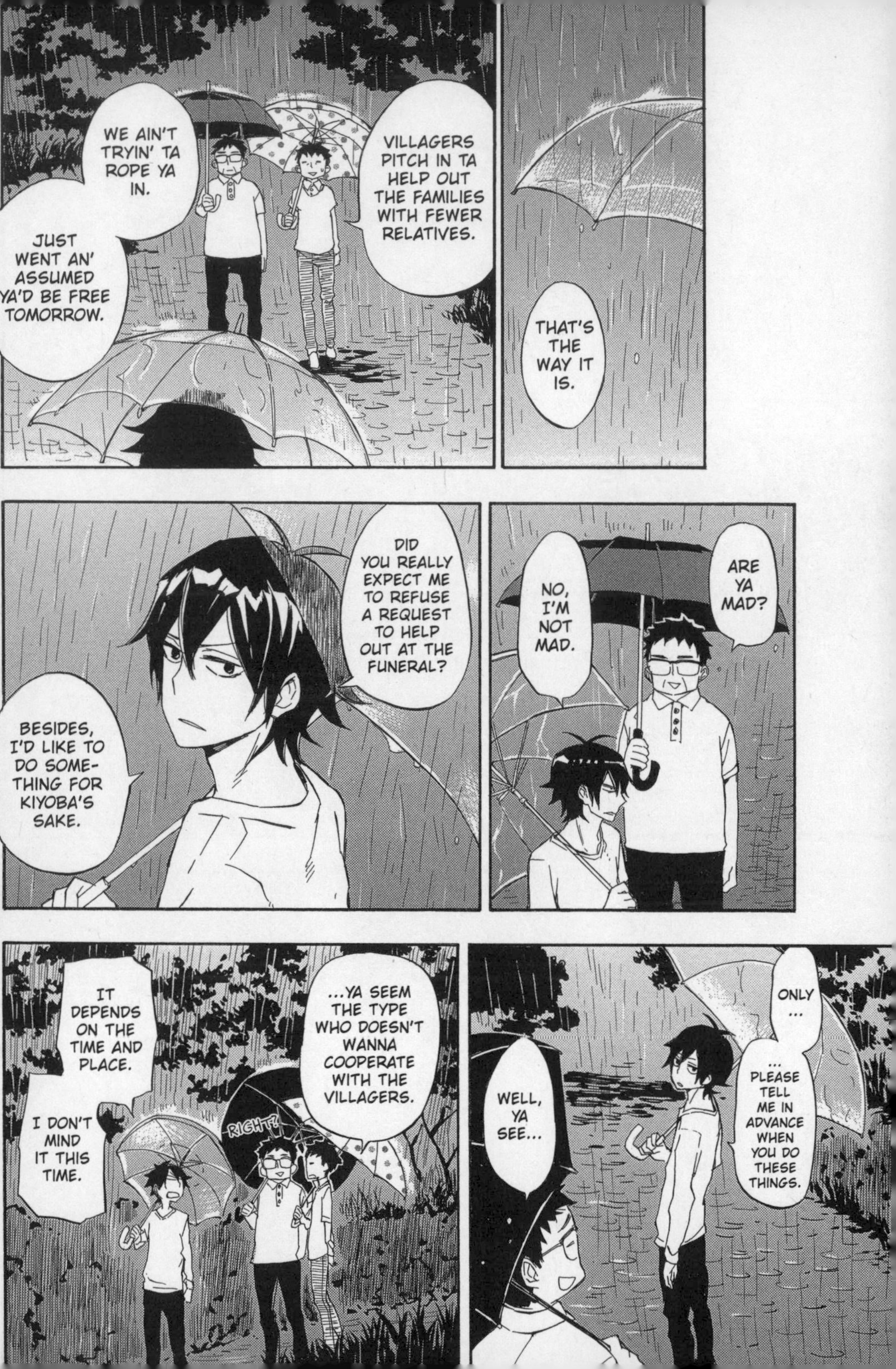
THAT'S THE WAY IT IS.
VILLAGERS PITCH IN TA HELP OUT THE FAMILIES WITH FEWER RELATIVES.
WE AIN'T TRYIN' TA ROPE YA IN.
JUST WENT AN' ASSUMED YA'D BE FREE TOMORROW.
ARE YA MAD?
NO, I'M NOT MAD.
DID YOU REALLY EXPECT ME TO REFUSE A REQUEST TO HELP OUT AT THE FUNERAL?
BESIDES, I'D LIKE TO DO SOME-THING FOR KIYOBA'S SAKE.
ONLY ...
... PLEASE TELL ME IN ADVANCE WHEN YOU DO THESE THINGS.
WELL, YA SEE...
...YA SEEM THE TYPE WHO DOESN'T WANNA COOPERATE WITH THE VILLAGERS.
RIGHT?
IT DEPENDS ON THE TIME AND PLACE.
I DON'T MIND IT THIS TIME.

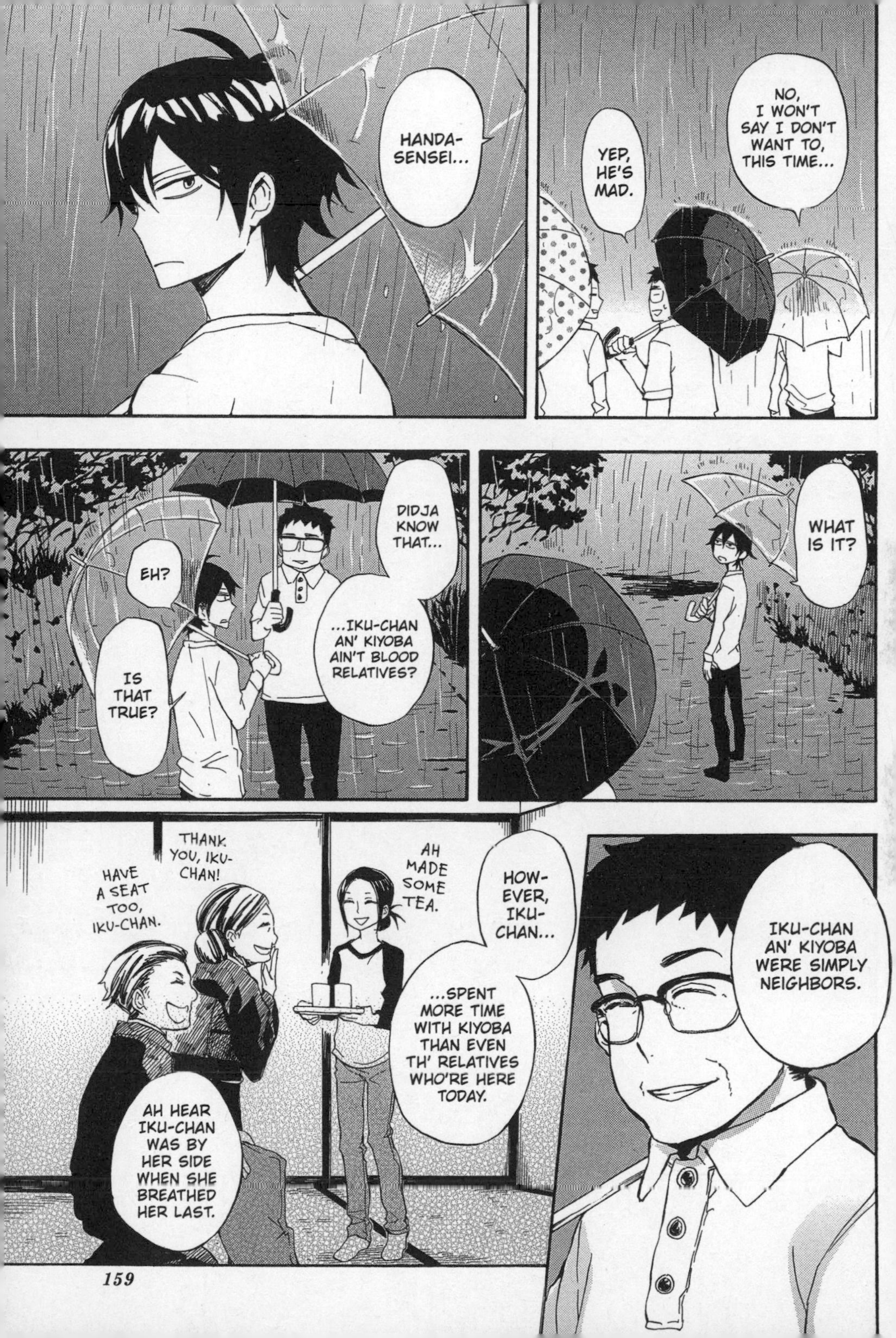
NO, I WON'T SAY I DON'T WANT TO, THIS TIME...
YEP, HE'S MAD.
HANDA-SENSEI...
WHAT IS IT?
DIDJA KNOW THAT...
EH?
...IKU-CHAN AN' KIYOBA AIN'T BLOOD RELATIVES?
IS THAT TRUE?
IKU-CHAN AN' KIYOBA WERE SIMPLY NEIGHBORS.
HOW-EVER, IKU-CHAN...
...SPENT MORE TIME WITH KIYOBA THAN EVEN TH' RELATIVES WHO'RE HERE TODAY.
AH MADE SOME TEA.
THANK YOU, IKU-CHAN!
HAVE A SEAT TOO, IKU-CHAN.
AH HEAR IKU-CHAN WAS BY HER SIDE WHEN SHE BREATHED HER LAST.

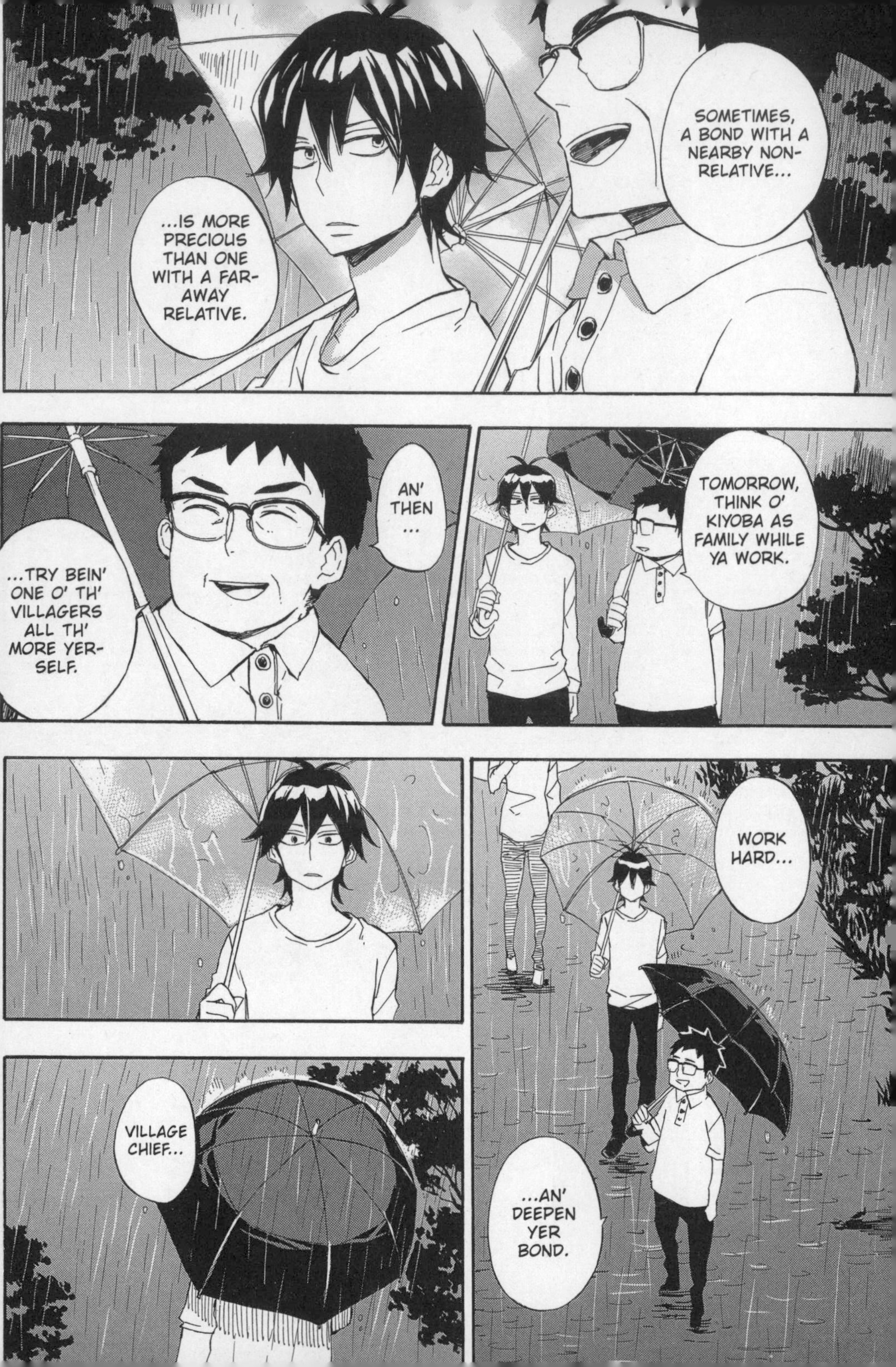
SOMETIMES, A BOND WITH A NEARBY NON-RELATIVE...
...IS MORE PRECIOUS THAN ONE WITH A FAR-AWAY RELATIVE.
TOMORROW, THINK O' KIYOBA AS FAMILY WHILE YA WORK.
AN' THEN ...
...TRY BEIN' ONE O' TH' VILLAGERS ALL TH' MORE YERSELF.
WORK HARD...
...AN' DEEPEN YER BOND.
VILLAGE CHIEF...

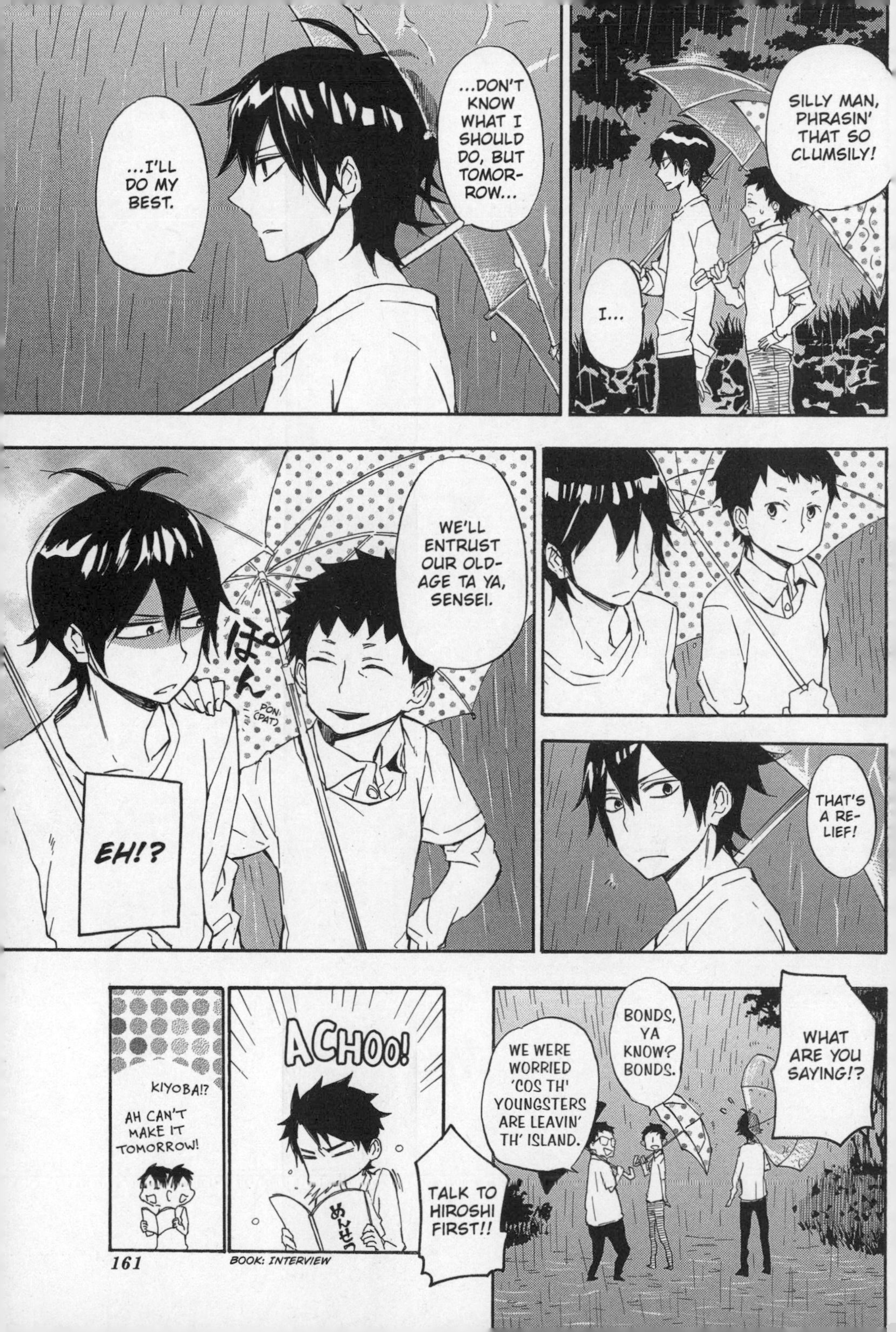
SILLY MAN, PHRASIN' THAT SO CLUMSILY!
I...
...DON'T KNOW WHAT I SHOULD DO, BUT TOMORROW...
...I'LL DO MY BEST.
THAT'S A RELIEF!
WE'LL ENTRUST OUR OLD-AGE TA YA, SENSEI.
ぽん
PON (PAT)
EH!?
WHAT ARE YOU SAYING!?
BONDS, YA KNOW? BONDS.
WE WERE WORRIED 'COS TH' YOUNGSTERS ARE LEAVIN' TH' ISLAND.
TALK TO HIROSHI FIRST!!
ACHOO!
めんせつ
BOOK: INTERVIEW
KIYOBA!?
AH CAN'T MAKE IT TOMORROW!

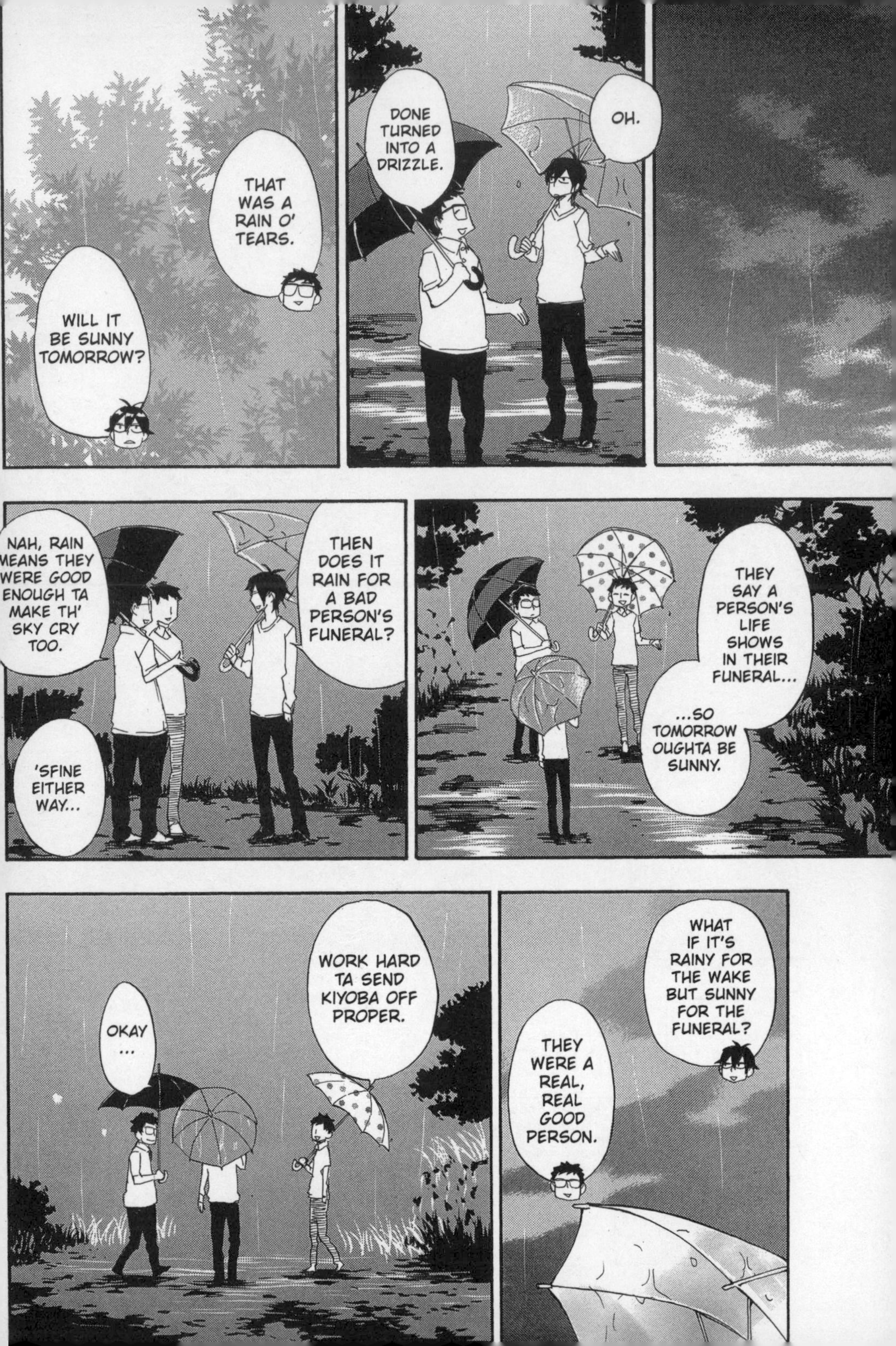
OH.
DONE TURNED INTO A DRIZZLE.
THAT WAS A RAIN O' TEARS.
WILL IT BE SUNNY TOMORROW?
THEY SAY A PERSON'S LIFE SHOWS IN THEIR FUNERAL...
...SO TOMORROW OUGHTA BE SUNNY.
THEN DOES IT RAIN FOR A BAD PERSON'S FUNERAL?
NAH, RAIN MEANS THEY WERE GOOD ENOUGH TA MAKE TH' SKY CRY TOO.
'SFINE EITHER WAY...
WHAT IF IT'S RAINY FOR THE WAKE BUT SUNNY FOR THE FUNERAL?
THEY WERE A REAL, REAL GOOD PERSON.
WORK HARD TA SEND KIYOBA OFF PROPER.
OKAY ...

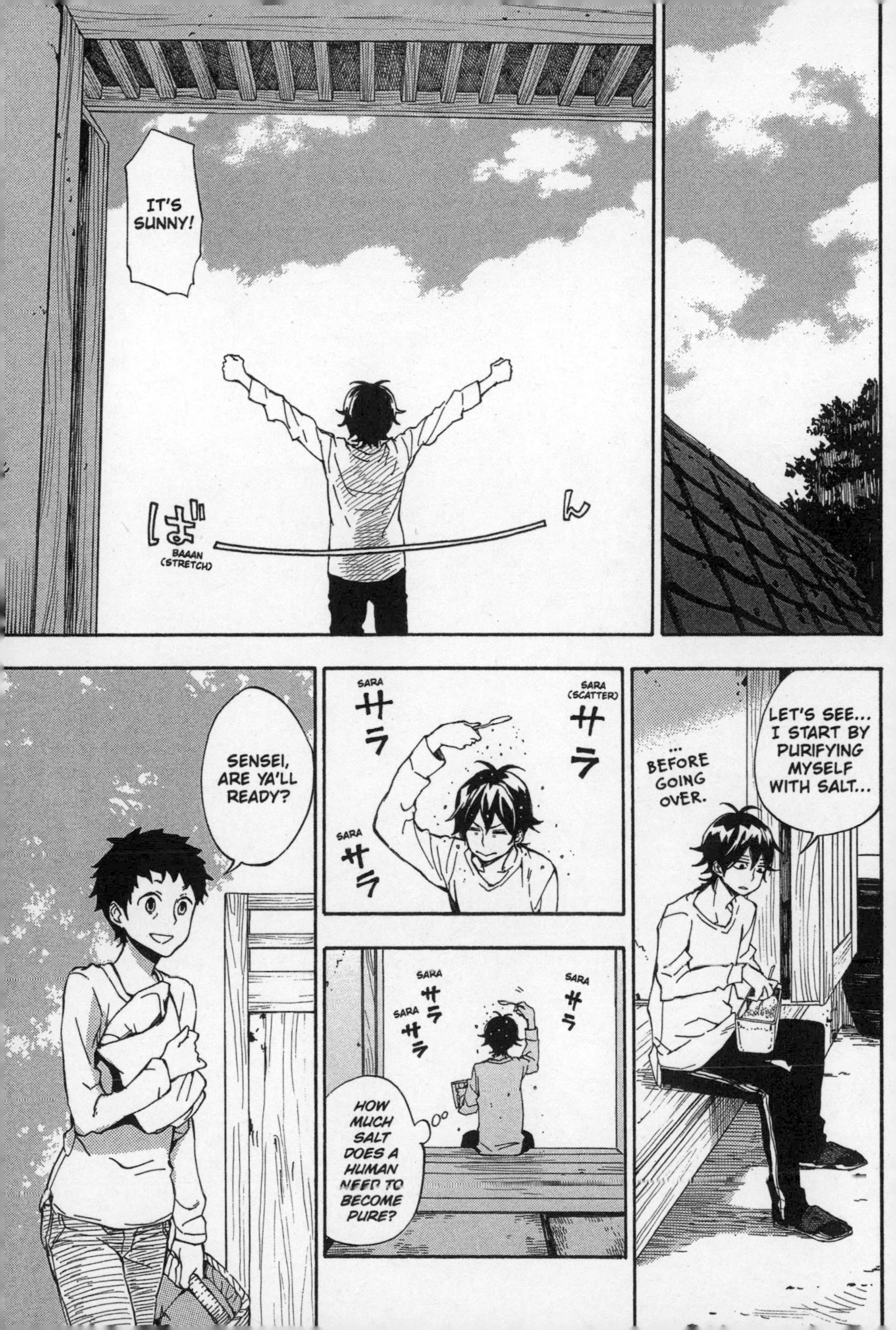
IT'S SUNNY!
ばぁ
ん
BAAAN (STRETCH)
LET'S SEE... I START BY PURIFYING MYSELF WITH SALT...
... BEFORE GOING OVER.
サラ
SARA (SCATTER)
サラ
SARA
サラ
SARA
サラ
SARA
サラ
SARA
サラ
SARA
HOW MUCH SALT DOES A HUMAN NEED TO BECOME PURE?
SENSEI, ARE YA'LL READY?

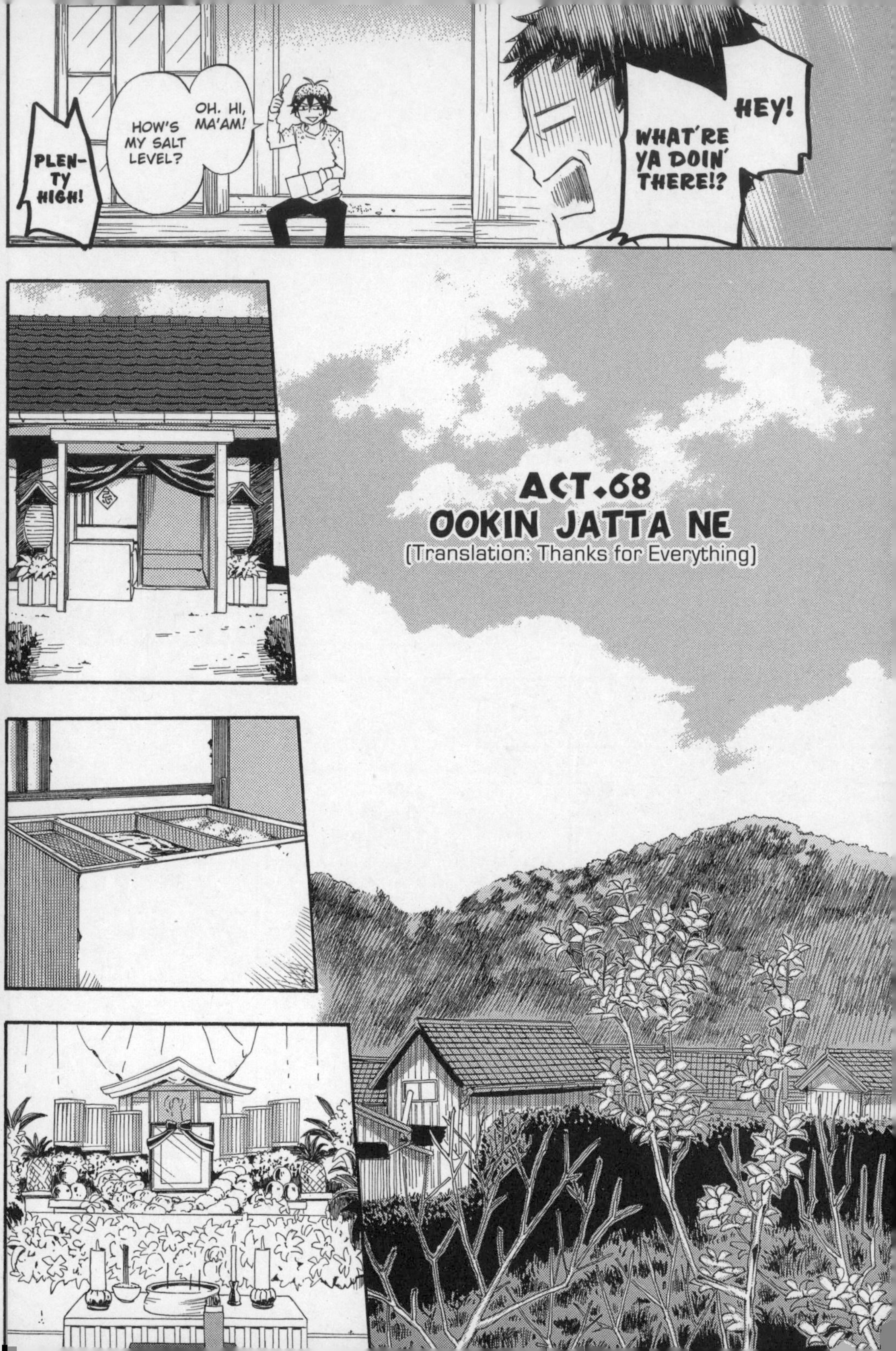
HEY!
WHAT'RE YA DOIN' THERE!?
OH. HI, MA'AM!
HOW'S MY SALT LEVEL?
PLEN-TY HIGH!
ACT.68
OOKIN JATTA NE
(Translation: Thanks for Everything)

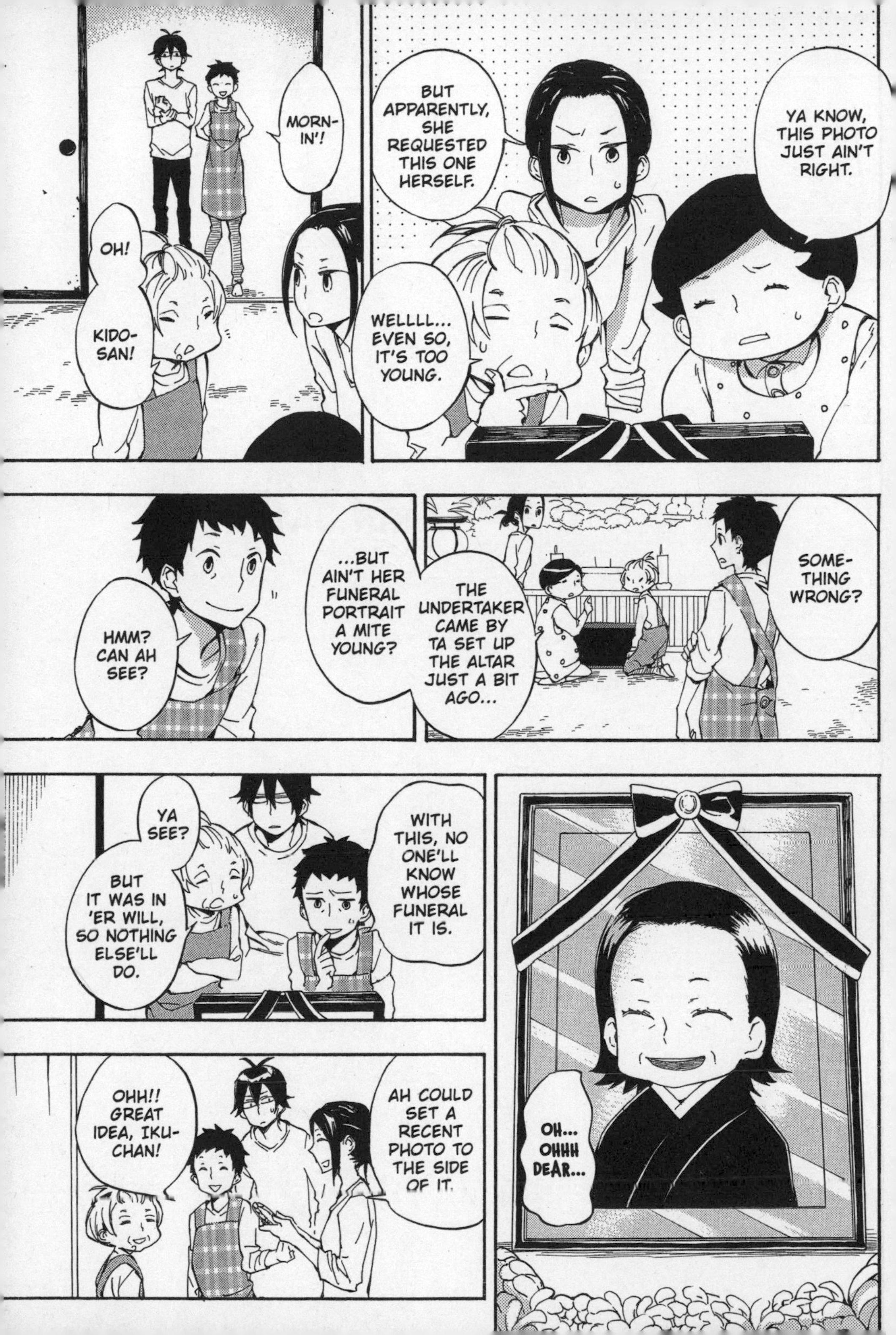
YA KNOW, THIS PHOTO JUST AIN'T RIGHT.
BUT APPARENTLY, SHE REQUESTED THIS ONE HERSELF.
WELLLL... EVEN SO, IT'S TOO YOUNG.
MORN-IN'!
OH!
KIDO-SAN!
SOME-THING WRONG?
THE UNDERTAKER CAME BY TA SET UP THE ALTAR JUST A BIT AGO...
...BUT AIN'T HER FUNERAL PORTRAIT A MITE YOUNG?
HMM? CAN AH SEE?
OH... OHHH DEAR...
WITH THIS, NO ONE'LL KNOW WHOSE FUNERAL IT IS.
YA SEE?
BUT IT WAS IN 'ER WILL, SO NOTHING ELSE'LL DO.
AH COULD SET A RECENT PHOTO TO THE SIDE OF IT.
OHH!! GREAT IDEA, IKU-CHAN!

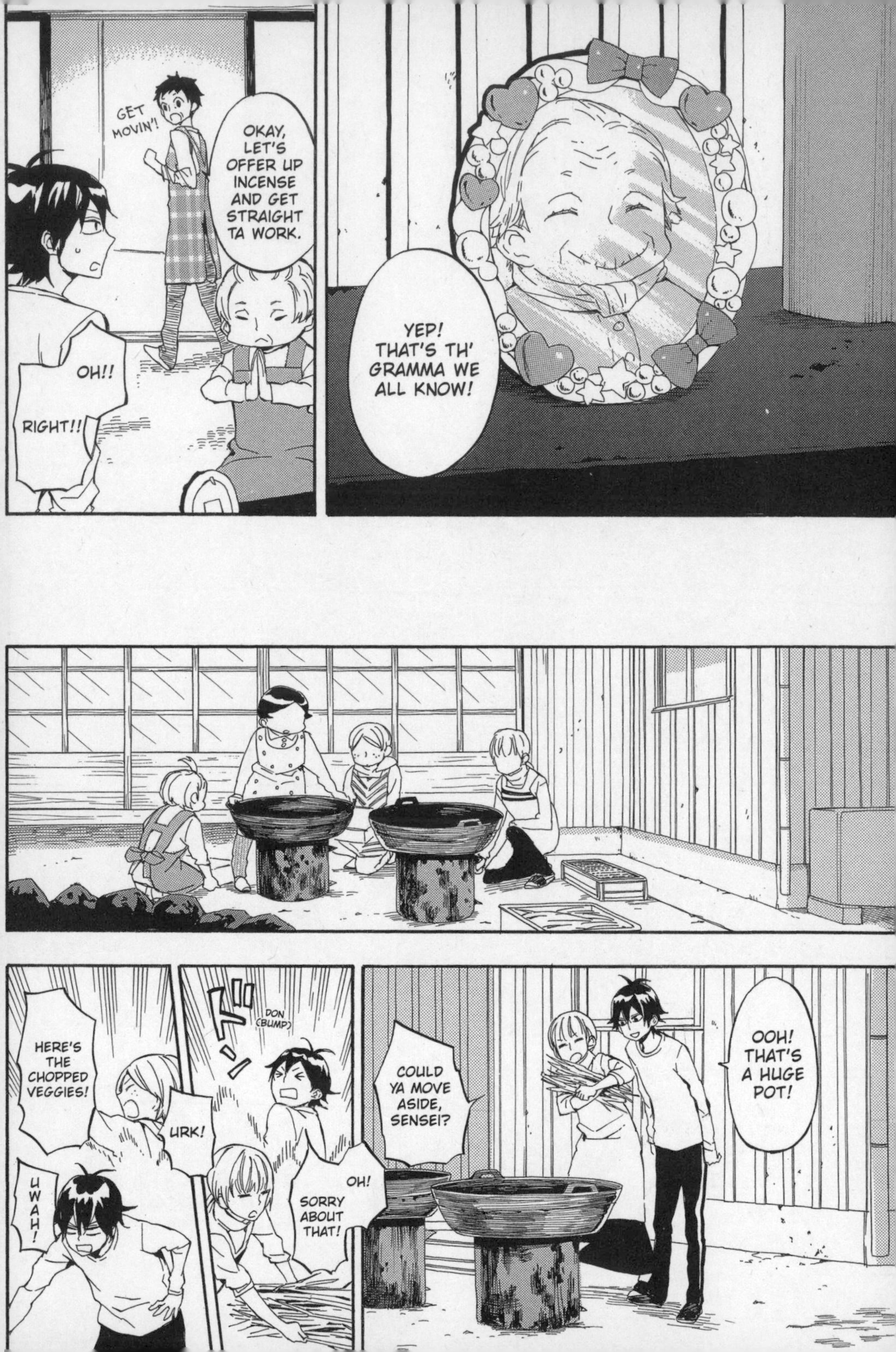
YEP! THAT'S TH' GRAMMA WE ALL KNOW!
OKAY, LET'S OFFER UP INCENSE AND GET STRAIGHT TA WORK.
GET MOVIN'!
OH!!
RIGHT!!
OOH! THAT'S A HUGE POT!
COULD YA MOVE ASIDE, SENSEI?
DON (BUMP)
URK!
OH!
SORRY ABOUT THAT!
HERE'S THE CHOPPED VEGGIES!
UWAH!

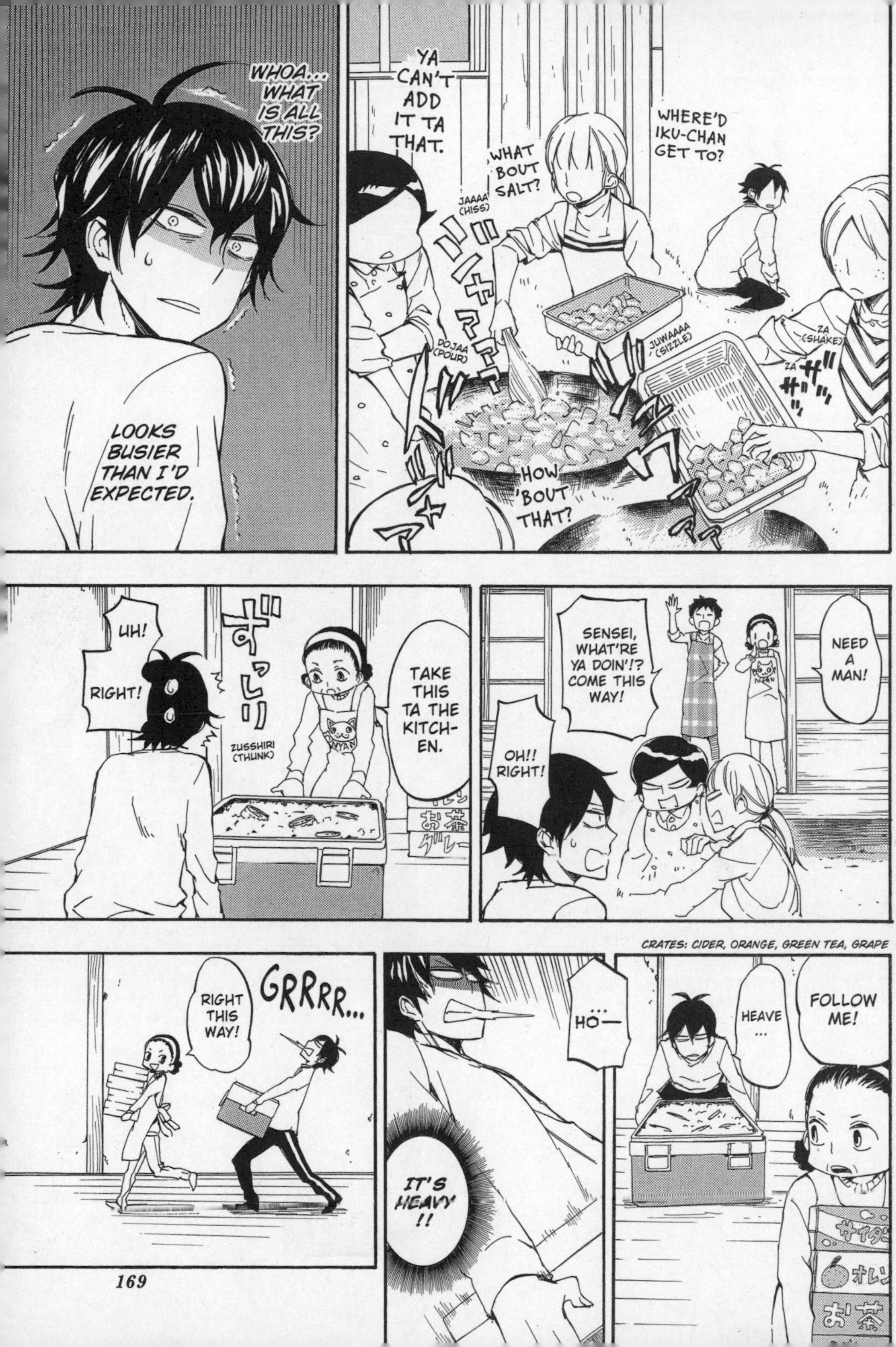
WHERE'D IKU-CHAN GET TO?
YA CAN'T ADD IT TA THAT.
WHAT BOUT SALT?
JAAAA (HISS)
ZA (SHAKE)
ZA
JUWAAAA (SIZZLE)
DOJAA (POUR)
HOW 'BOUT THAT?
WHOA... WHAT IS ALL THIS?
LOOKS BUSIER THAN I'D EXPECTED.
NEED A MAN!
SENSEI, WHAT'RE YA DOIN'!? COME THIS WAY!
OH!! RIGHT!
TAKE THIS TA THE KITCHEN.
ZUSSHIRI (THUNK)
UH!
RIGHT!
CRATES: CIDER, ORANGE, GREEN TEA, GRAPE
FOLLOW ME!
HEAVE...
...HO—
IT'S HEAVY!!
GRRRR...
RIGHT THIS WAY!

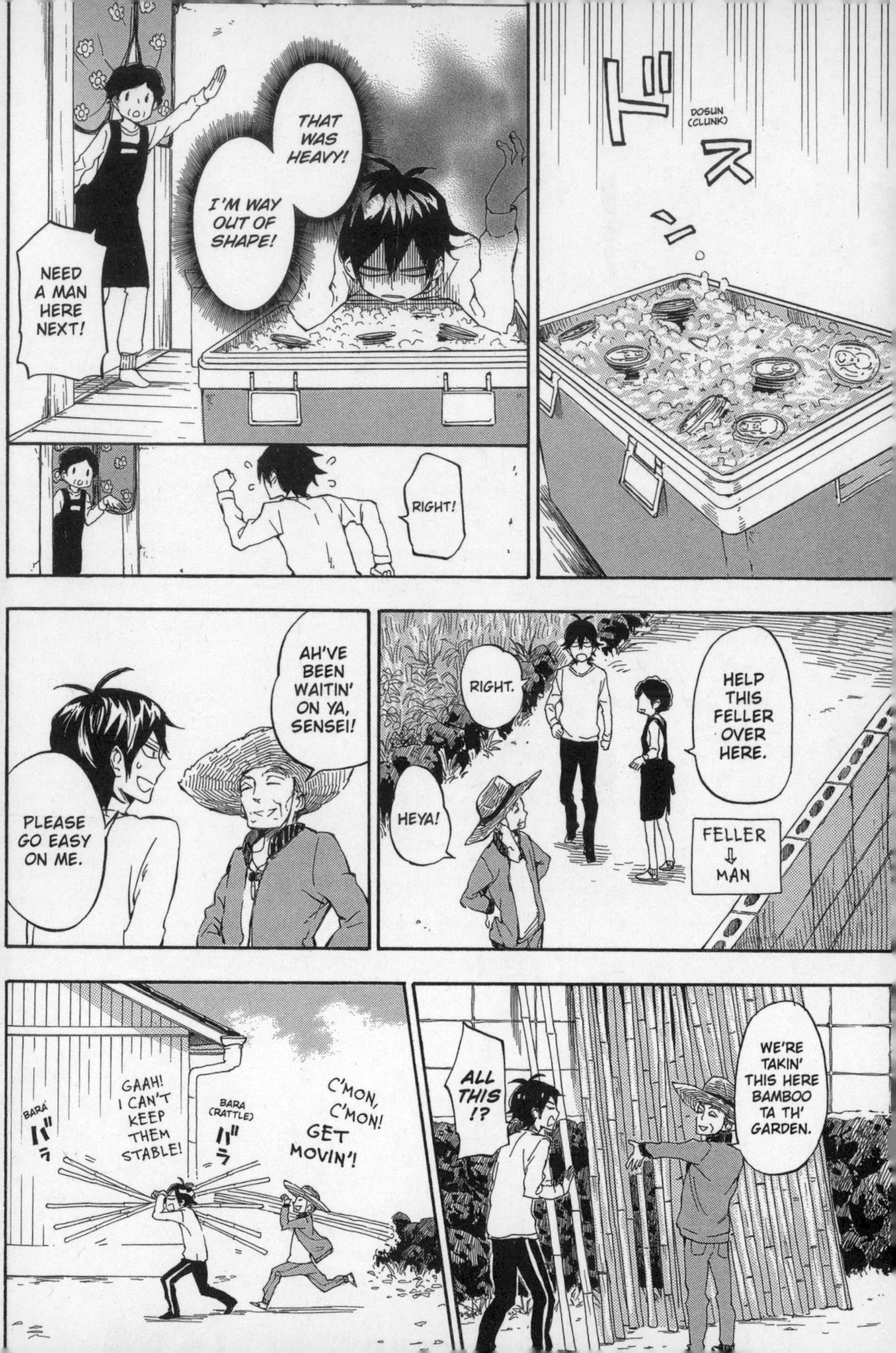
DOSUN (CLUNK)
ドスン
THAT WAS HEAVY!
I'M WAY OUT OF SHAPE!
NEED A MAN HERE NEXT!
RIGHT!
HELP THIS FELLER OVER HERE.
RIGHT.
HEYA!
FELLER ⇩ MAN
AH'VE BEEN WAITIN' ON YA, SENSEI!
PLEASE GO EASY ON ME.
WE'RE TAKIN' THIS HERE BAMBOO TA TH' GARDEN.
ALL THIS!?
C'MON, C'MON! GET MOVIN'!
BARA (RATTLE)
バラ
GAAH! I CAN'T KEEP THEM STABLE!
BARA
バラ

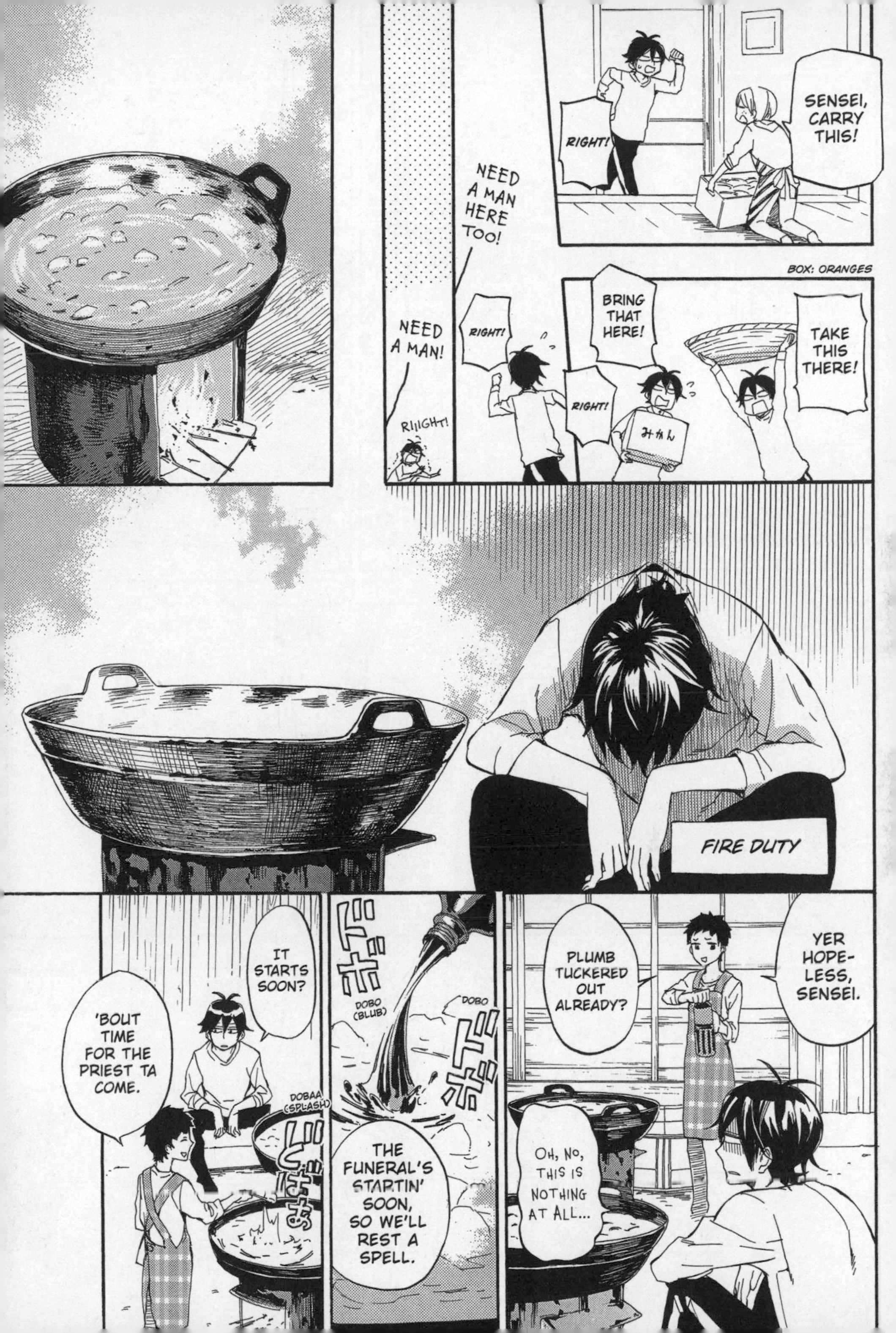
SENSEI, CARRY THIS!
RIGHT!
BOX: ORANGES
NEED A MAN HERE TOO!
TAKE THIS THERE!
BRING THAT HERE!
RIGHT!
みかん
RIGHT!
NEED A MAN!
RIIIGHT!
FIRE DUTY
YER HOPELESS, SENSEI.
PLUMB TUCKERED OUT ALREADY?
OH, NO, THIS IS NOTHING AT ALL...
DOBO (BLUB)
DOBO
THE FUNERAL'S STARTIN' SOON, SO WE'LL REST A SPELL.
DOBAA (SPLASH)
IT STARTS SOON?
'BOUT TIME FOR THE PRIEST TA COME.

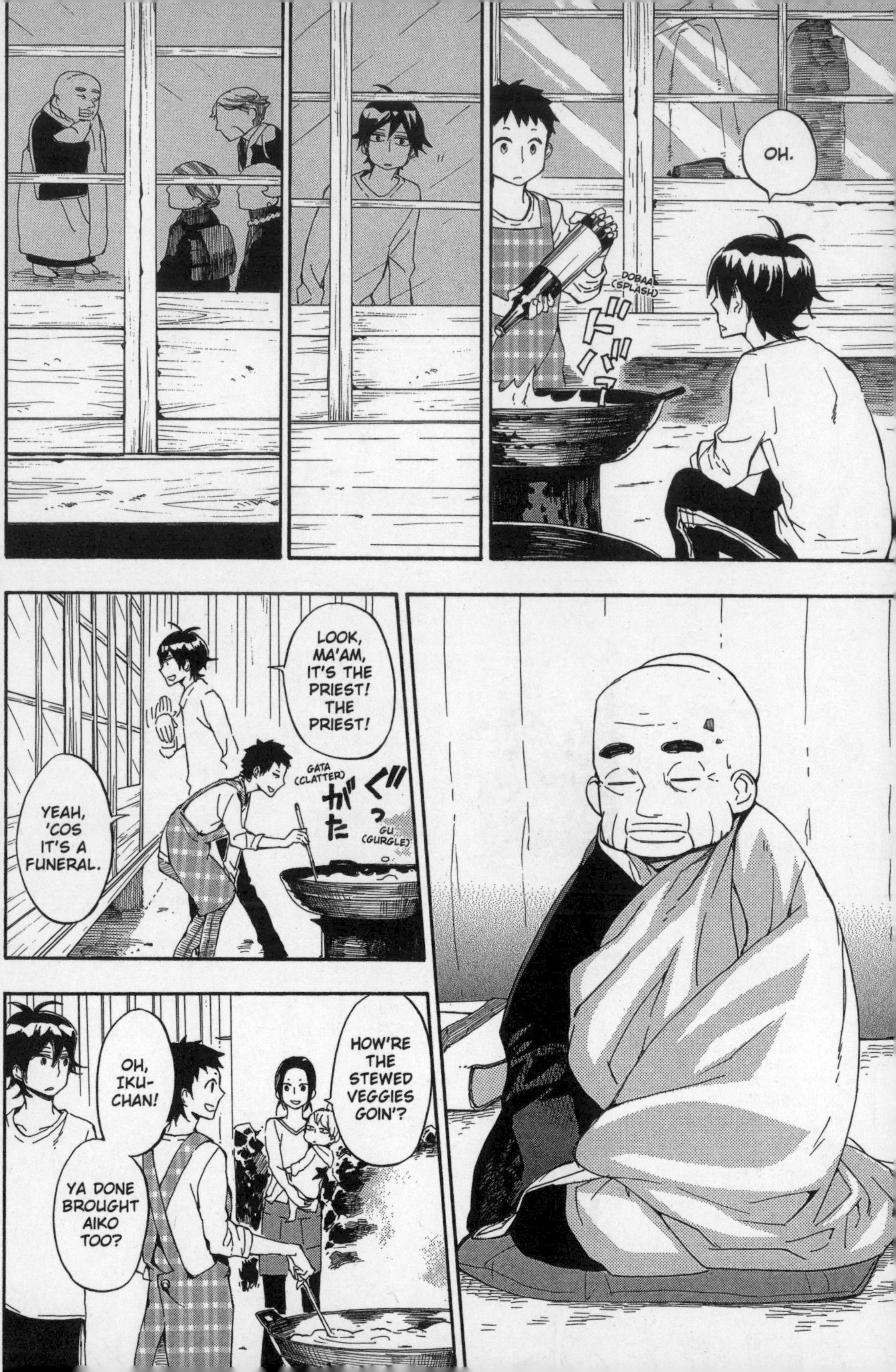
OH.
DOBAA (SPLASH)
ドバッ
LOOK, MA'AM, IT'S THE PRIEST! THE PRIEST!
GATA (CLATTER)
がた
ぐっ
GU (GURGLE)
YEAH, 'COS IT'S A FUNERAL.
HOW'RE THE STEWED VEGGIES GOIN'?
OH, IKU-CHAN!
YA DONE BROUGHT AIKO TOO?

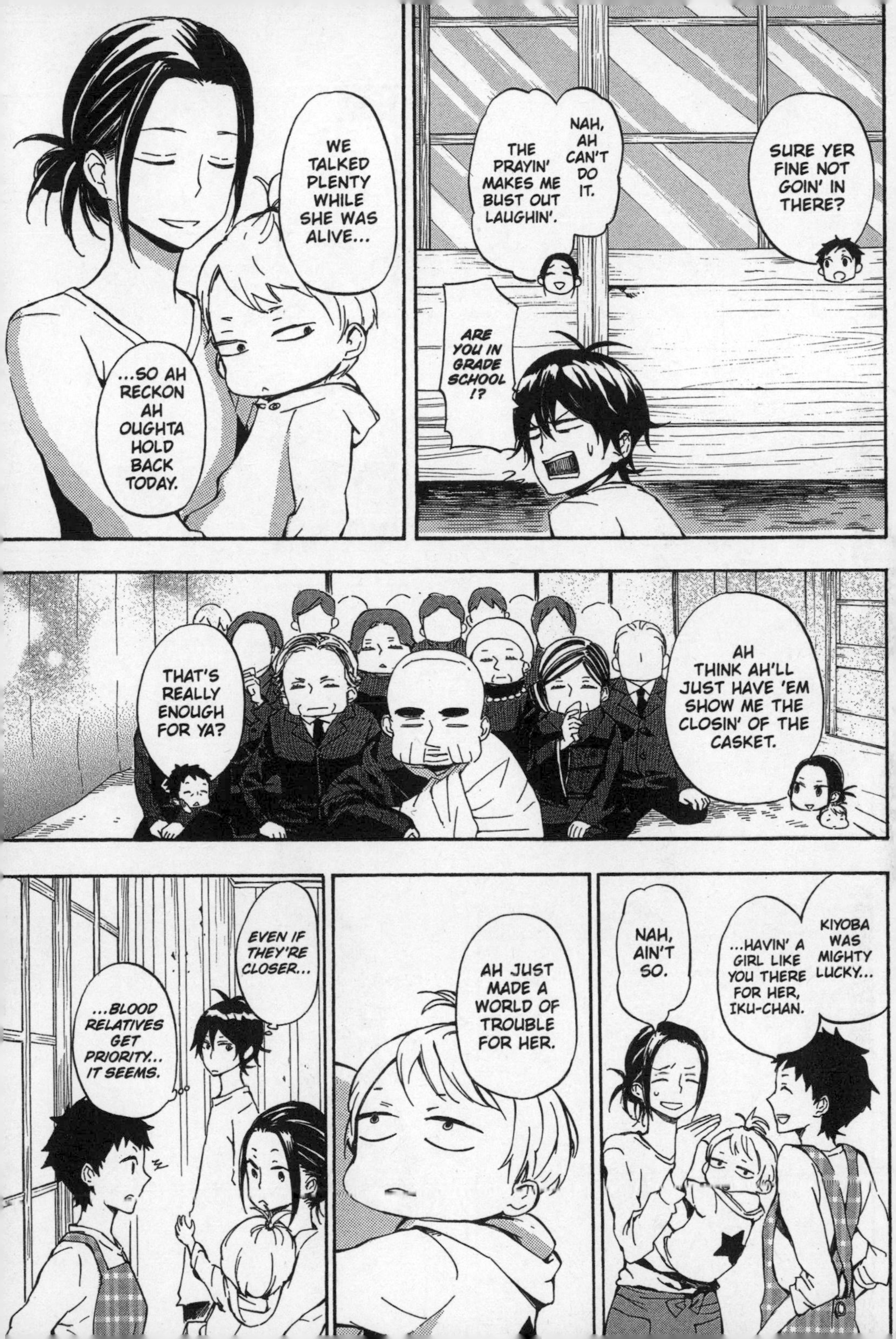
SURE YER FINE NOT GOIN' IN THERE?
NAH, AH CAN'T DO IT.
THE PRAYIN' MAKES ME BUST OUT LAUGHIN'.
ARE YOU IN GRADE SCHOOL !?
WE TALKED PLENTY WHILE SHE WAS ALIVE...
...SO AH RECKON AH OUGHTA HOLD BACK TODAY.
AH THINK AH'LL JUST HAVE 'EM SHOW ME THE CLOSIN' OF THE CASKET.
THAT'S REALLY ENOUGH FOR YA?
KIYOBA WAS MIGHTY LUCKY...
...HAVIN' A GIRL LIKE YOU THERE FOR HER, IKU-CHAN.
NAH, AIN'T SO.
AH JUST MADE A WORLD OF TROUBLE FOR HER.
EVEN IF THEY'RE CLOSER...
...BLOOD RELATIVES GET PRIORITY... IT SEEMS.

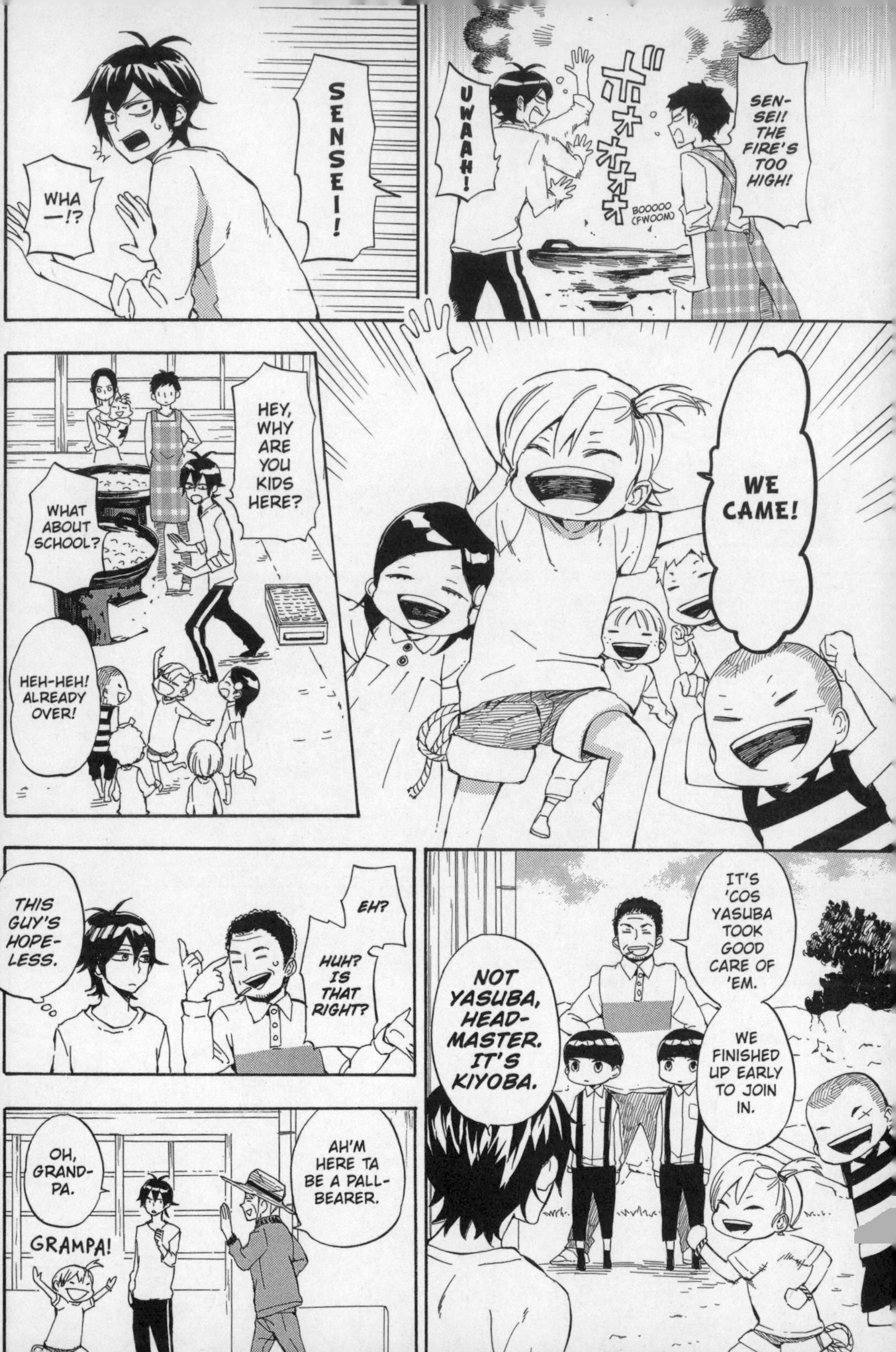
SEN-SEI! THE FIRE'S TOO HIGH!
UWAAH!
BOOOOO (FWOOM)
SENSEI!
WHA—!?
WE CAME!
HEY, WHY ARE YOU KIDS HERE?
WHAT ABOUT SCHOOL?
HEH-HEH! ALREADY OVER!
IT'S 'COS YASUBA TOOK GOOD CARE OF 'EM.
NOT YASUBA, HEAD-MASTER. IT'S KIYOBA.
WE FINISHED UP EARLY TO JOIN IN.
EH?
HUH? IS THAT RIGHT?
THIS GUY'S HOPE-LESS.
AH'M HERE TA BE A PALL-BEARER.
OH, GRAND-PA.
GRAMPA!

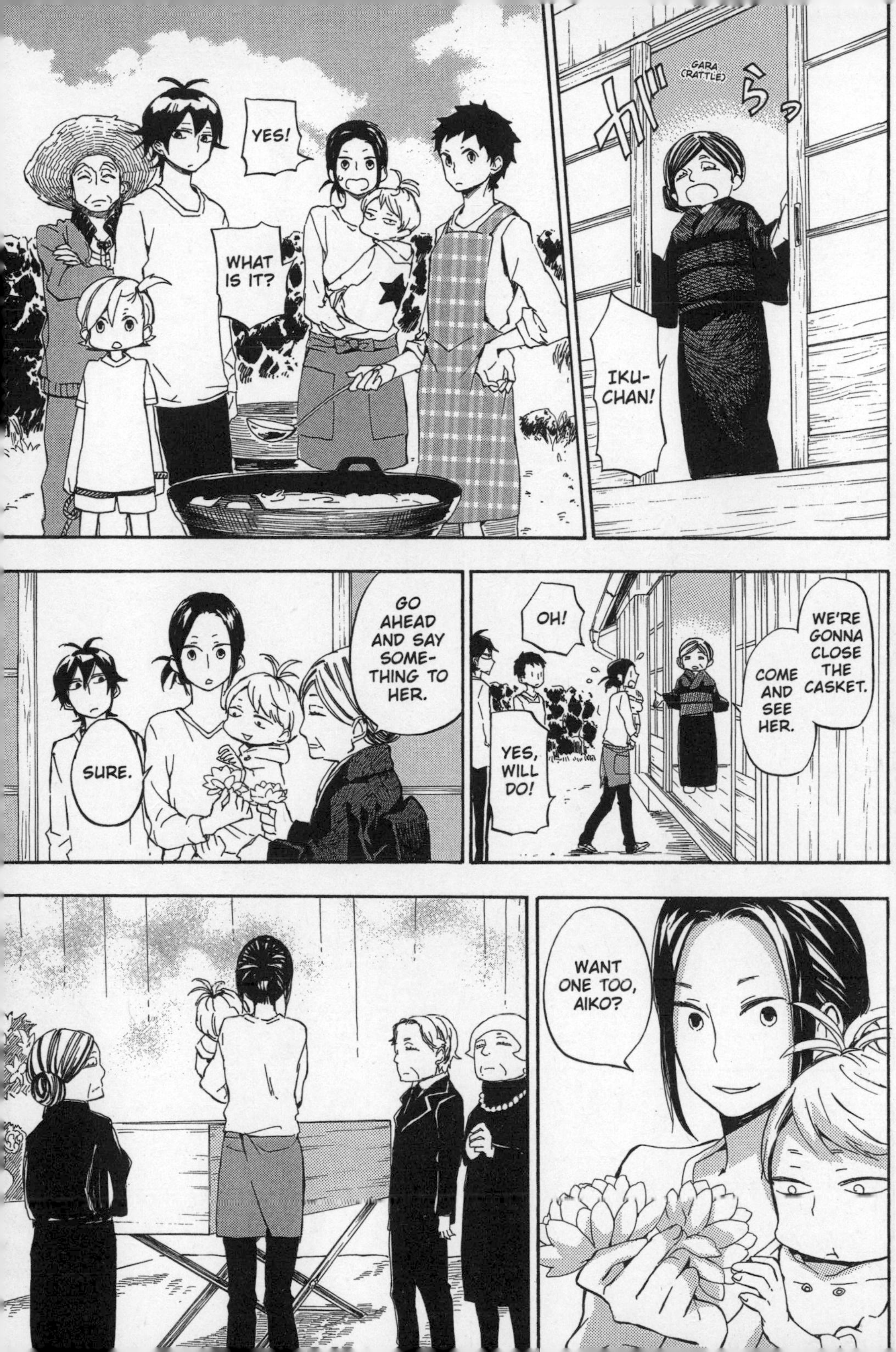
ガらっ
GARA (RATTLE)
IKU-CHAN!
YES!
WHAT IS IT?
WE'RE GONNA CLOSE THE CASKET.
COME AND SEE HER.
OH!
YES, WILL DO!
GO AHEAD AND SAY SOMETHING TO HER.
SURE.
WANT ONE TOO, AIKO?

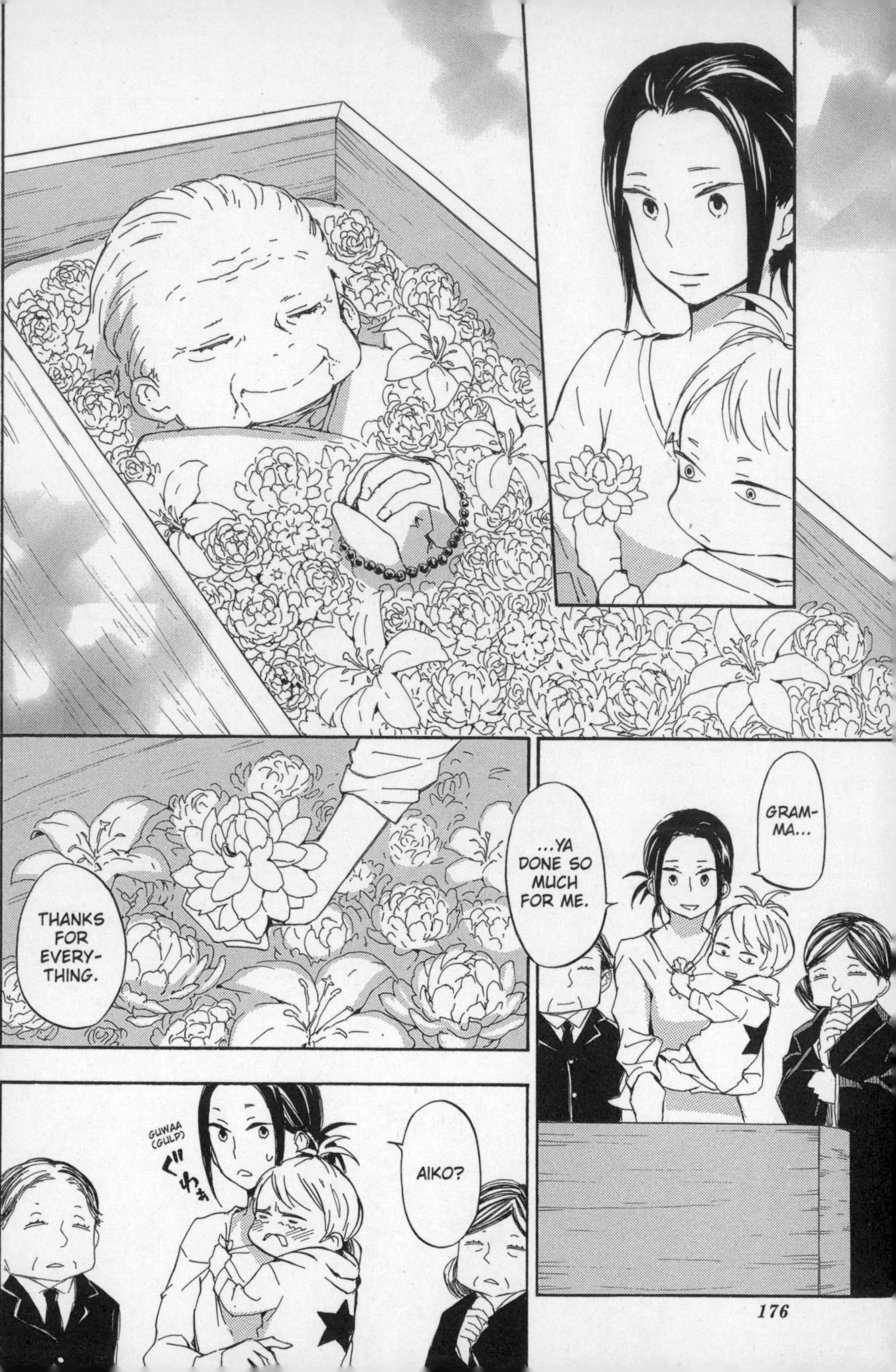
GRAM-MA...
...YA DONE SO MUCH FOR ME.
THANKS FOR EVERY-THING.
AIKO?
GUWAA (GULP)

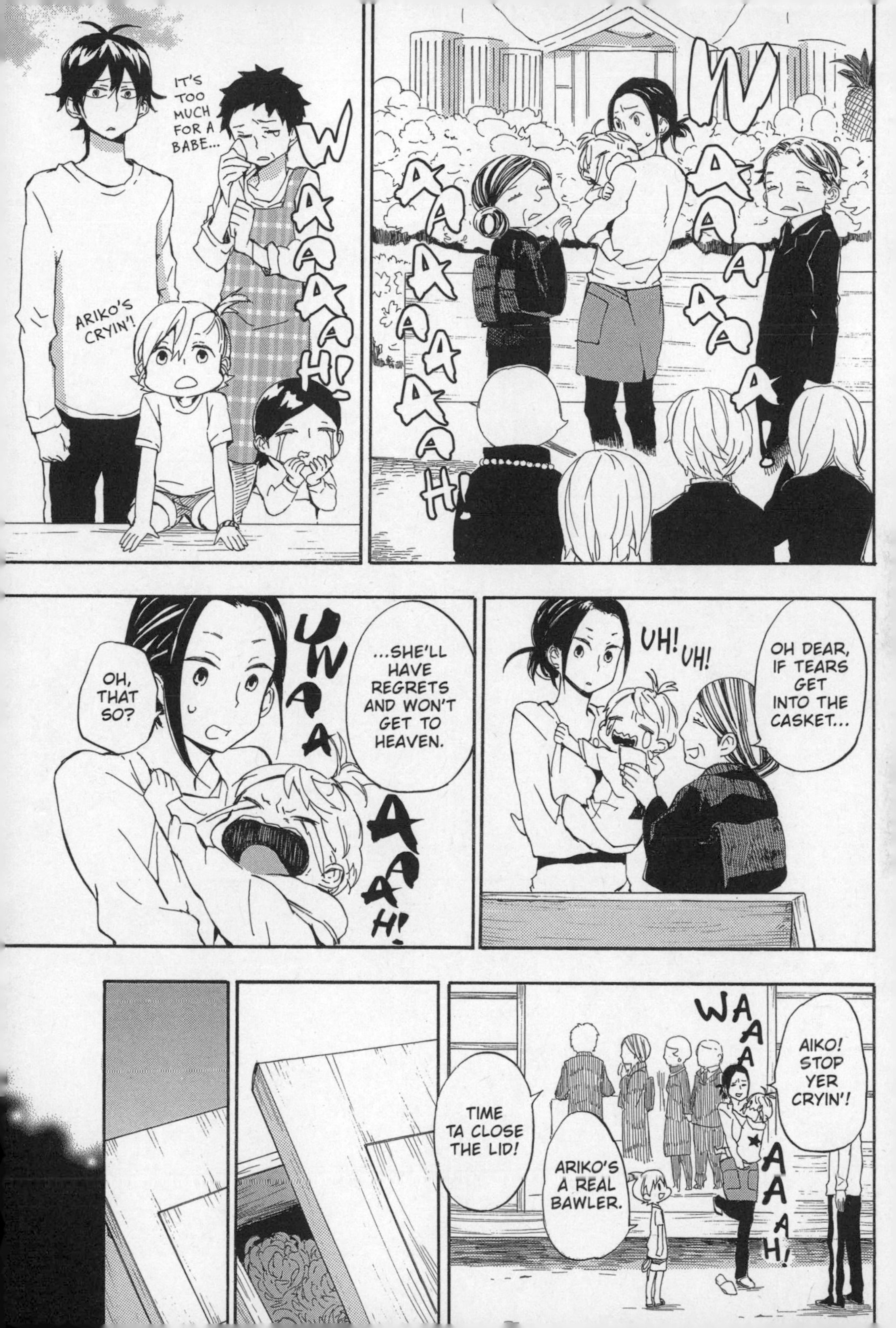
WAAAAAAH!
AAAAAAAH!
IT'S TOO MUCH FOR A BABE...
WAAAAAH!
ARIKO'S CRYIN'!
UH! UH!
OH DEAR, IF TEARS GET INTO THE CASKET...
...SHE'LL HAVE REGRETS AND WON'T GET TO HEAVEN.
UWAAAAAH!
OH, THAT SO?
AIKO! STOP YER CRYIN'!
WAAAAAAAH!
TIME TA CLOSE THE LID!
ARIKO'S A REAL BAWLER.

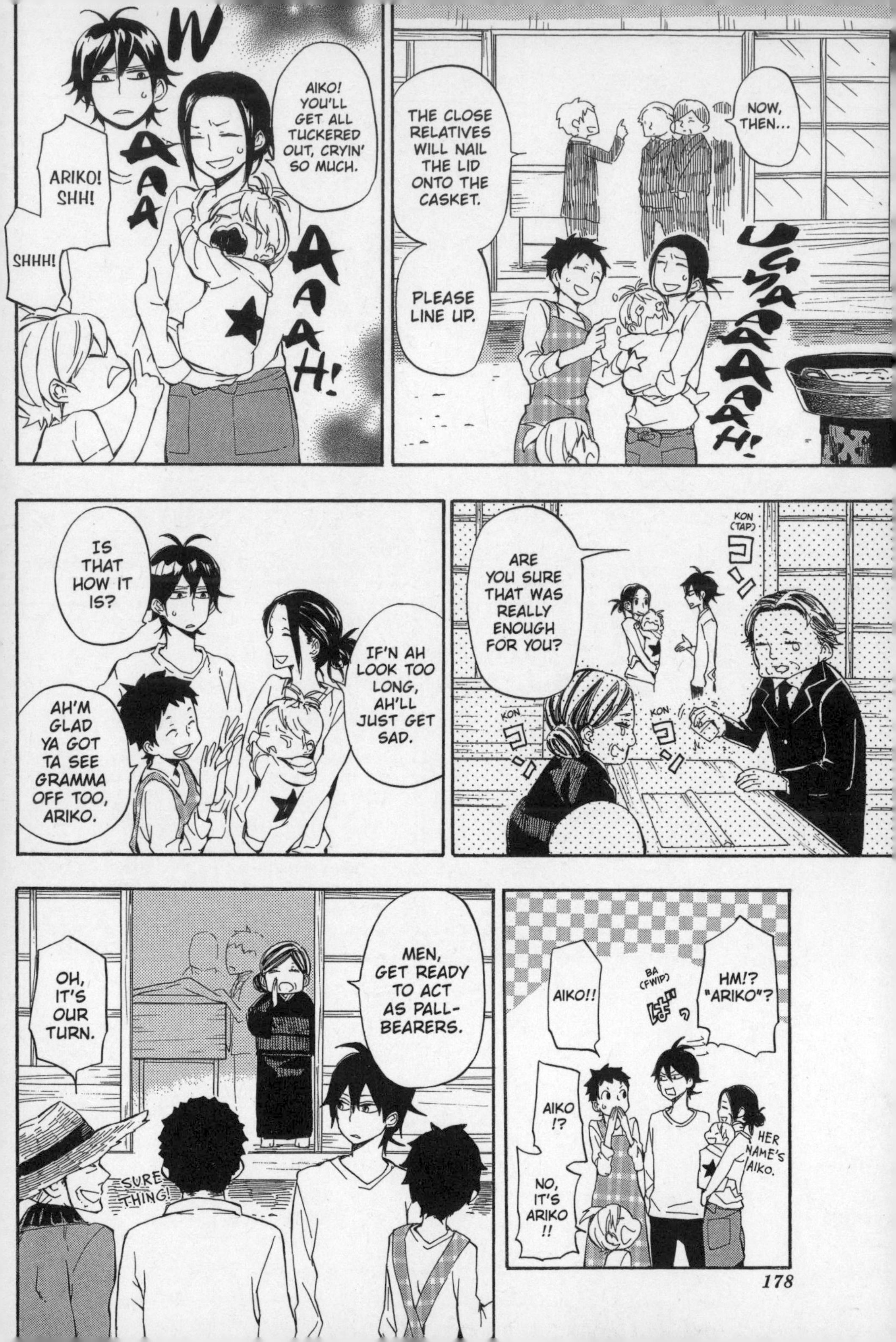
NOW, THEN...
THE CLOSE RELATIVES WILL NAIL THE LID ONTO THE CASKET.
PLEASE LINE UP.
UGYAAAAAAH!
AIKO! YOU'LL GET ALL TUCKERED OUT, CRYIN' SO MUCH.
WAAAAAAAH!
ARIKO! SHH!
SHHH!
KON (TAP)
ARE YOU SURE THAT WAS REALLY ENOUGH FOR YOU?
KON
KON
IS THAT HOW IT IS?
IF'N AH LOOK TOO LONG, AH'LL JUST GET SAD.
AH'M GLAD YA GOT TA SEE GRAMMA OFF TOO, ARIKO.
HM!? "ARIKO"?
BA (FWIP)
AIKO!!
HER NAME'S AIKO.
AIKO!?
NO, IT'S ARIKO!!
MEN, GET READY TO ACT AS PALL-BEARERS.
OH, IT'S OUR TURN.
SURE THING!

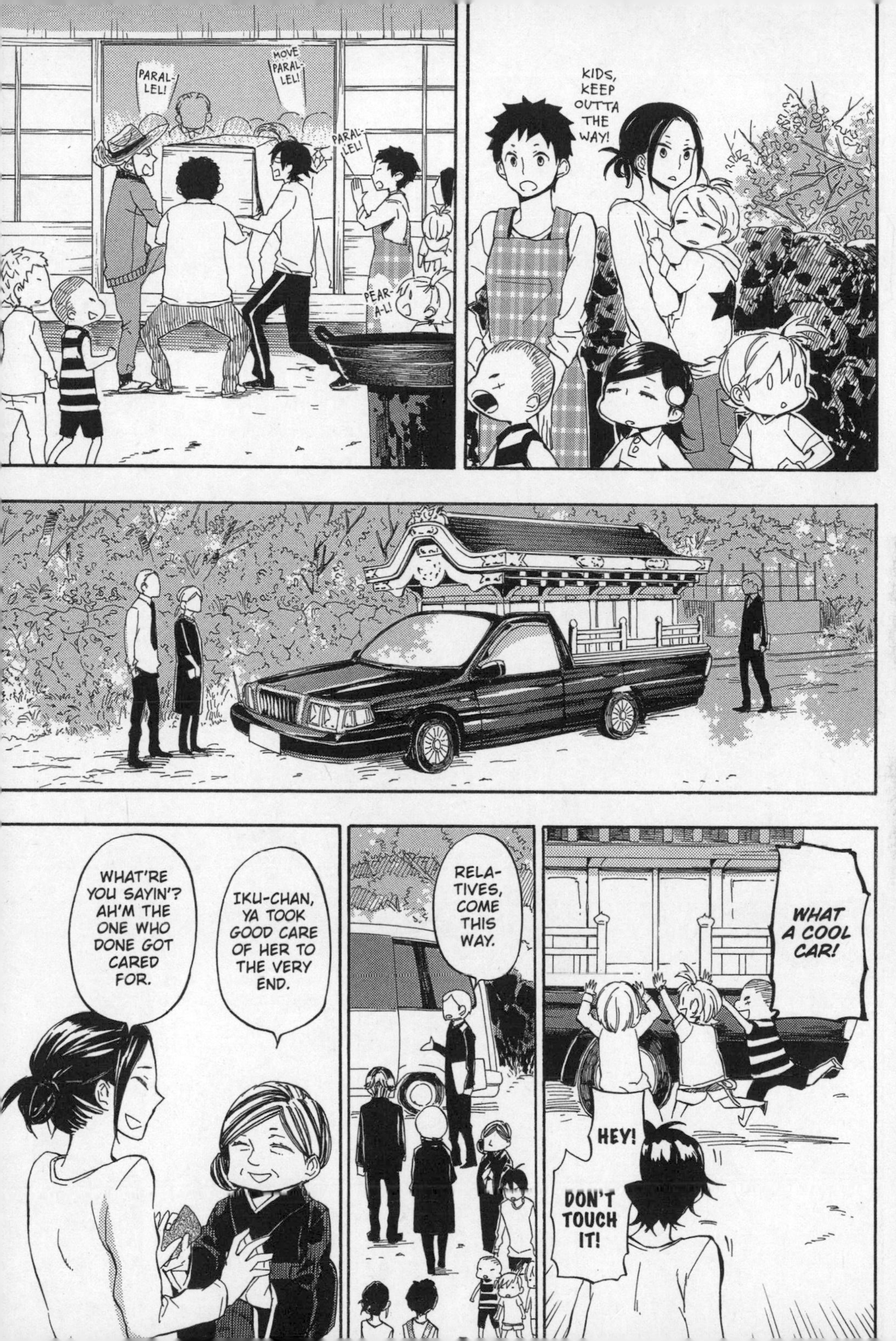
KIDS, KEEP OUTTA THE WAY!
MOVE PARAL-LEL!
PARAL-LEL!
PARAL-LEL!
PEAR-A-L!
WHAT A COOL CAR!
HEY!
DON'T TOUCH IT!
RELA-TIVES, COME THIS WAY.
IKU-CHAN, YA TOOK GOOD CARE OF HER TO THE VERY END.
WHAT'RE YOU SAYIN'? AH'M THE ONE WHO DONE GOT CARED FOR.

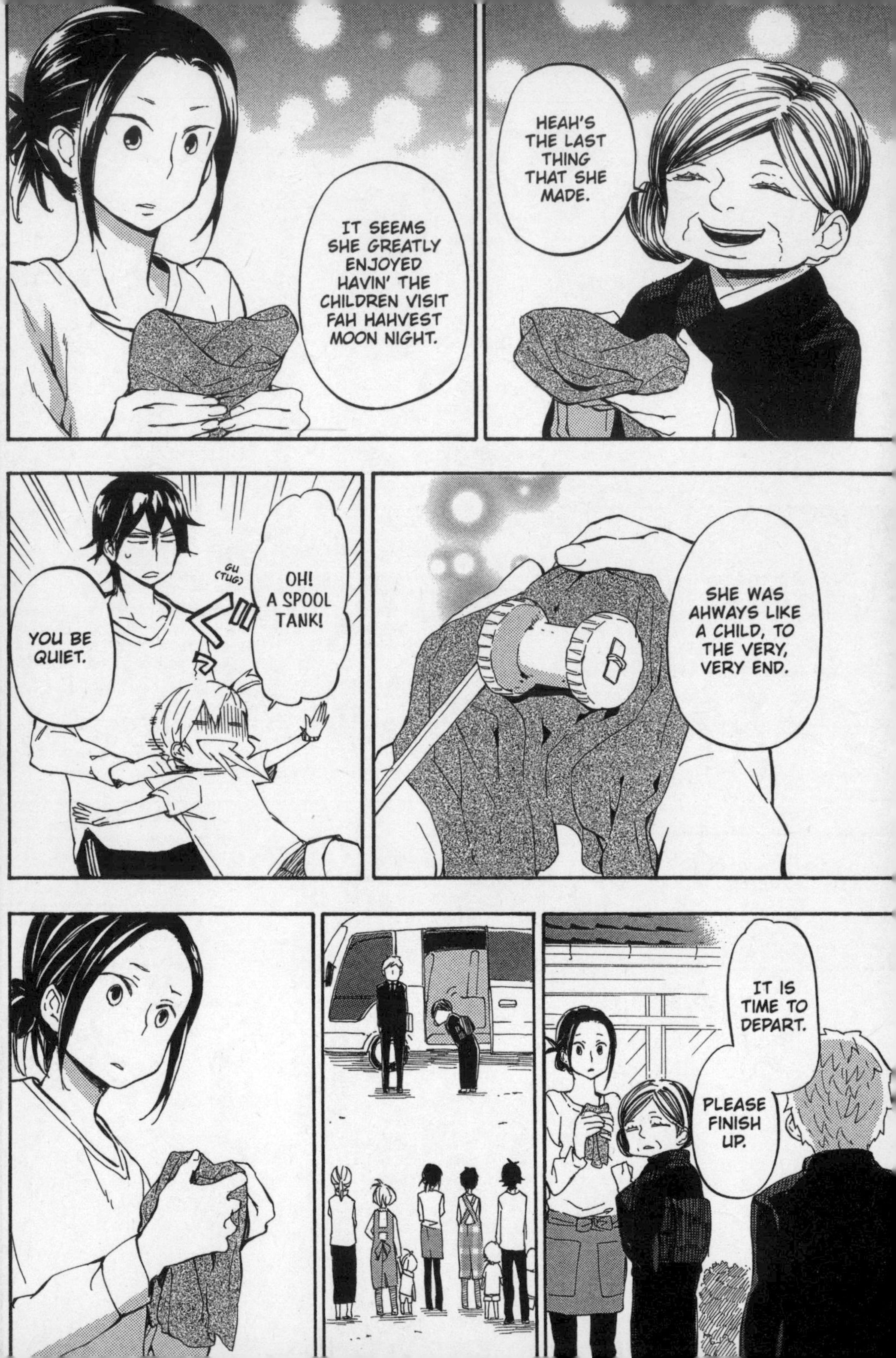
HEAH'S THE LAST THING THAT SHE MADE.
IT SEEMS SHE GREATLY ENJOYED HAVIN' THE CHILDREN VISIT FAH HAHVEST MOON NIGHT.
SHE WAS AHWAYS LIKE A CHILD, TO THE VERY, VERY END.
OH! A SPOOL TANK!
GU (TUG)
YOU BE QUIET.
IT IS TIME TO DEPART.
PLEASE FINISH UP.

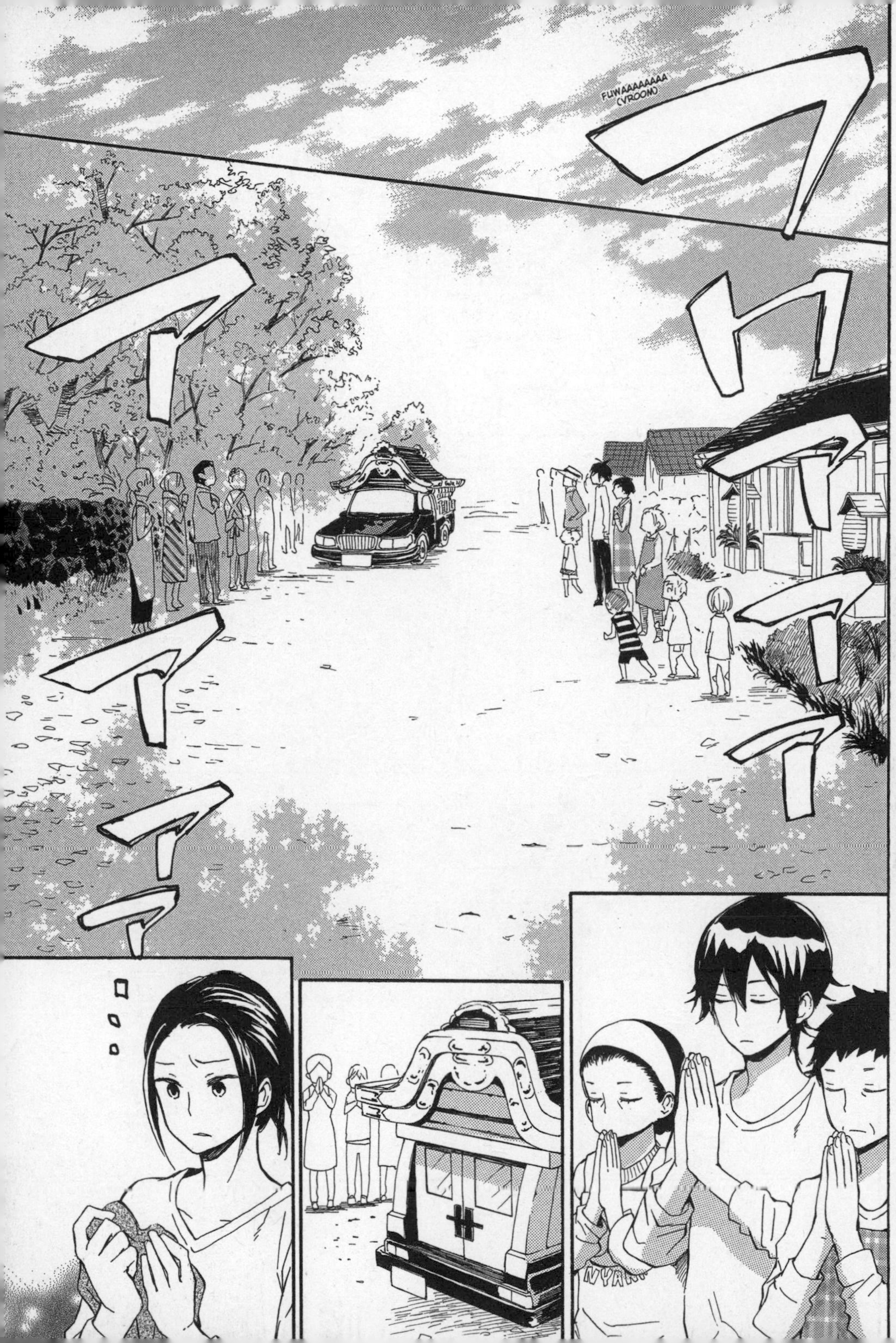
FUWAAAAAAAAA
(VROOM)

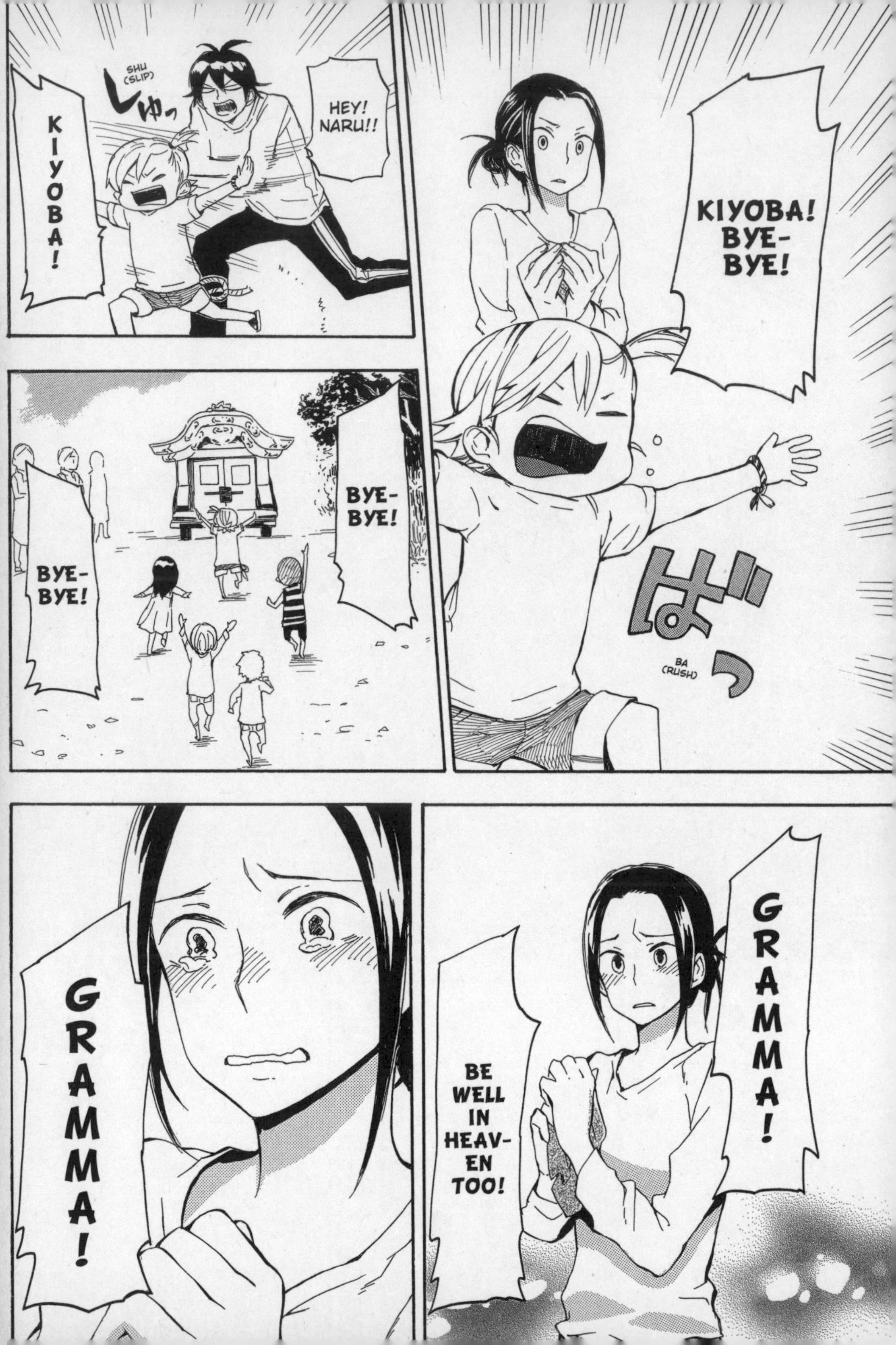
KIYOBA! BYE-BYE!
ばっ
BA (RUSH)
HEY! NARU!!
しゅっ
SHU (SLIP)
KIYOBA!
BYE-BYE!
BYE-BYE!
GRAMMA!
BE WELL IN HEAVEN TOO!
GRAMMA!

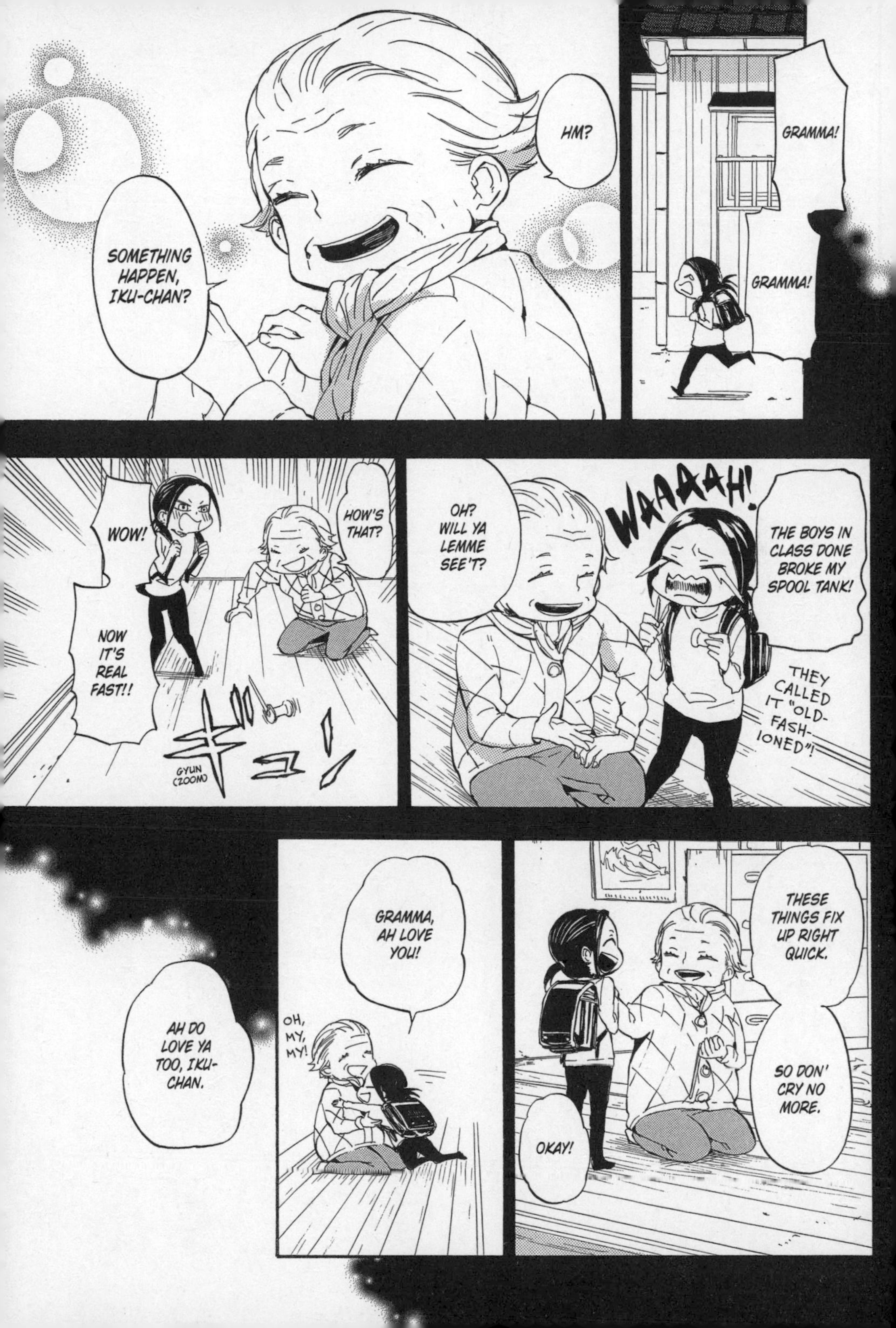
GRAMMA!
GRAMMA!
HM?
SOMETHING HAPPEN, IKU-CHAN?
WAAAAH!
THE BOYS IN CLASS DONE BROKE MY SPOOL TANK!
THEY CALLED IT "OLD-FASHIONED"!
OH? WILL YA LEMME SEE'T?
HOW'S THAT?
WOW!
NOW IT'S REAL FAST!!
GYUN (ZOOM)
THESE THINGS FIX UP RIGHT QUICK.
SO DON' CRY NO MORE.
OKAY!
GRAMMA, AH LOVE YOU!
OH, MY, MY!
AH DO LOVE YA TOO, IKU-CHAN.

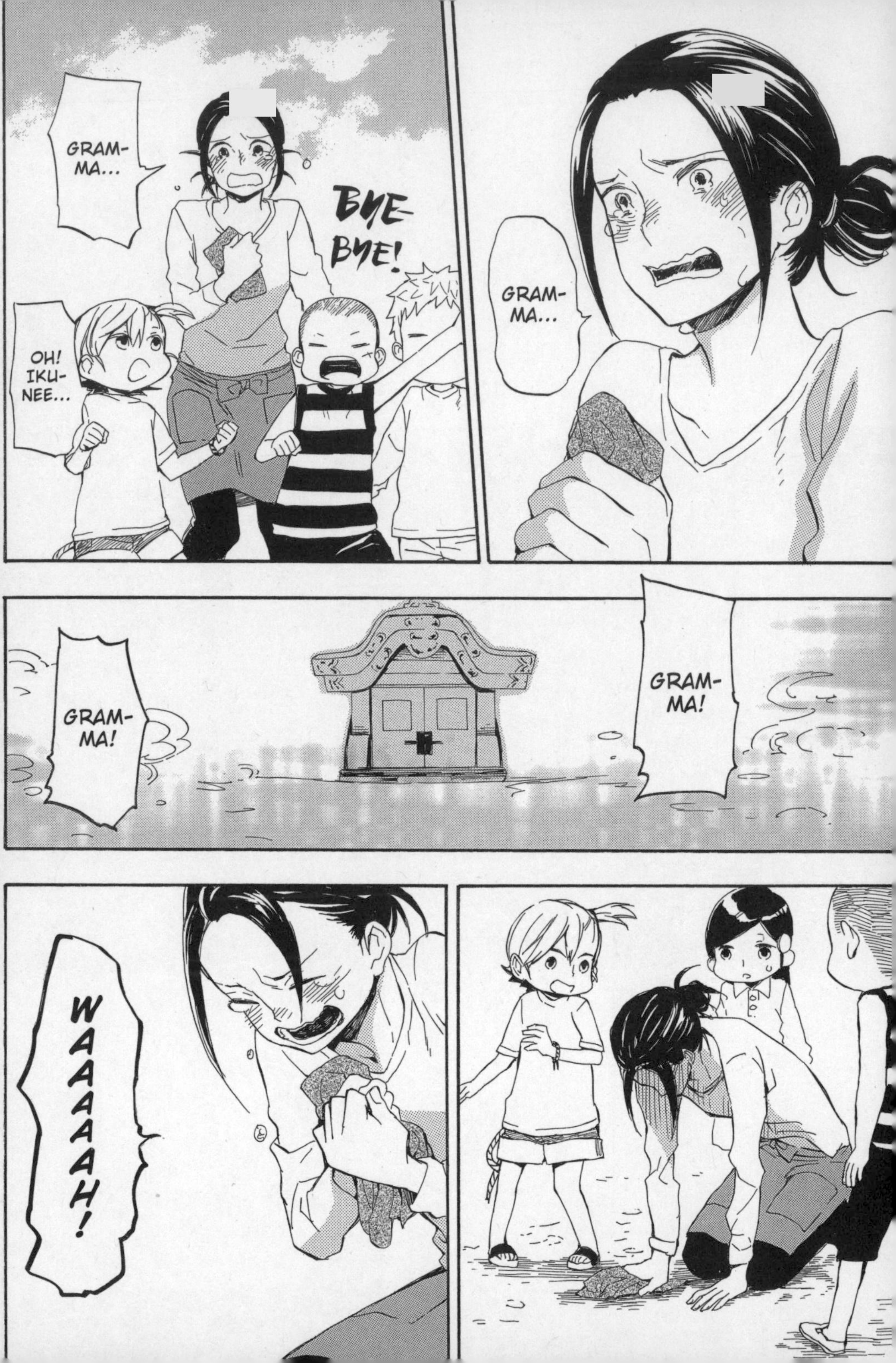
GRAM-MA...
GRAM-MA...
BYE-BYE!
OH! IKU-NEE...
GRAM-MA!
GRAM-MA!
WAAAAAAH!

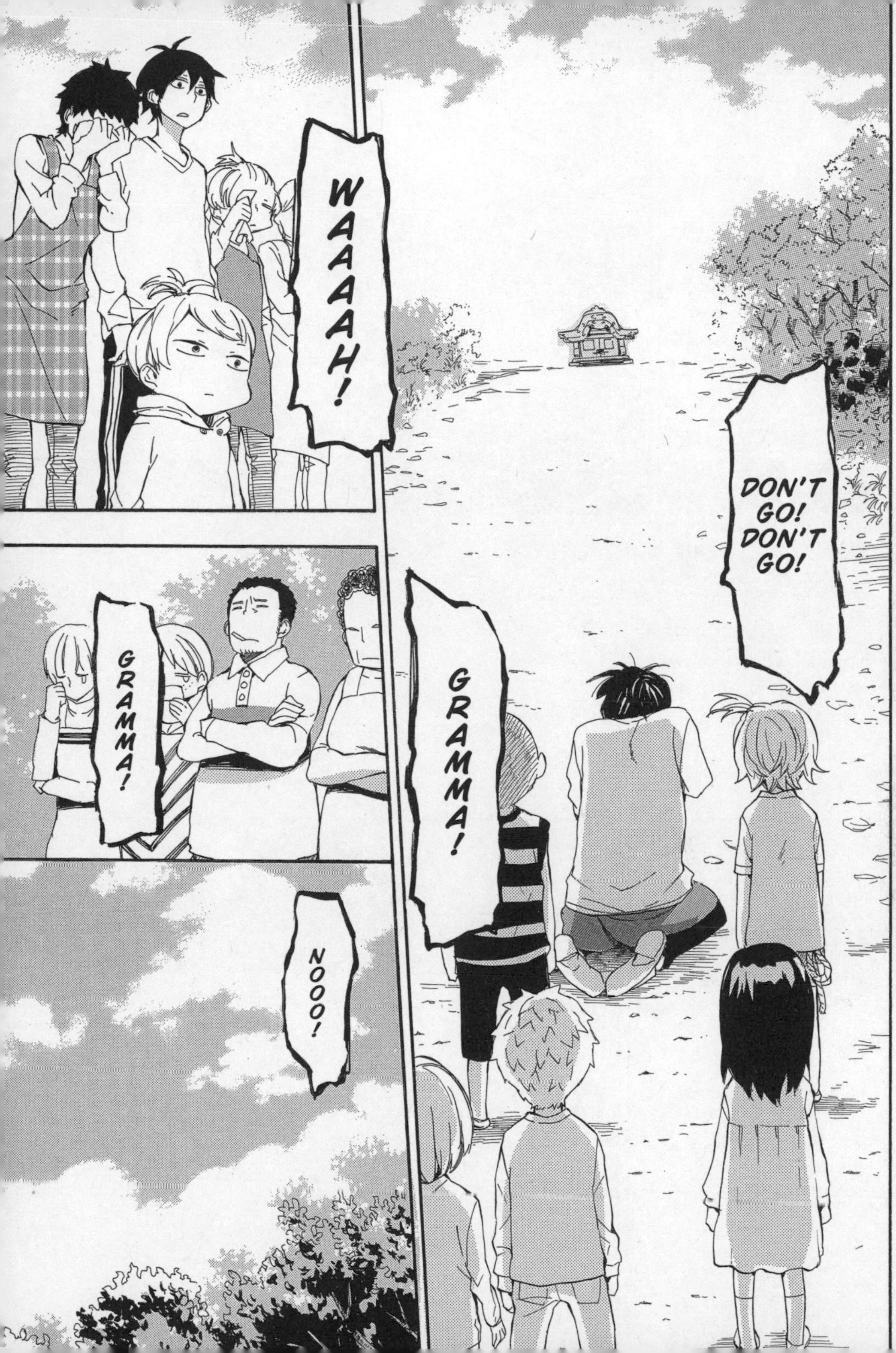
DON'T GO! DON'T GO!
GRAMMA!
WAAAAAH!
GRAMMA!
NOOOO!

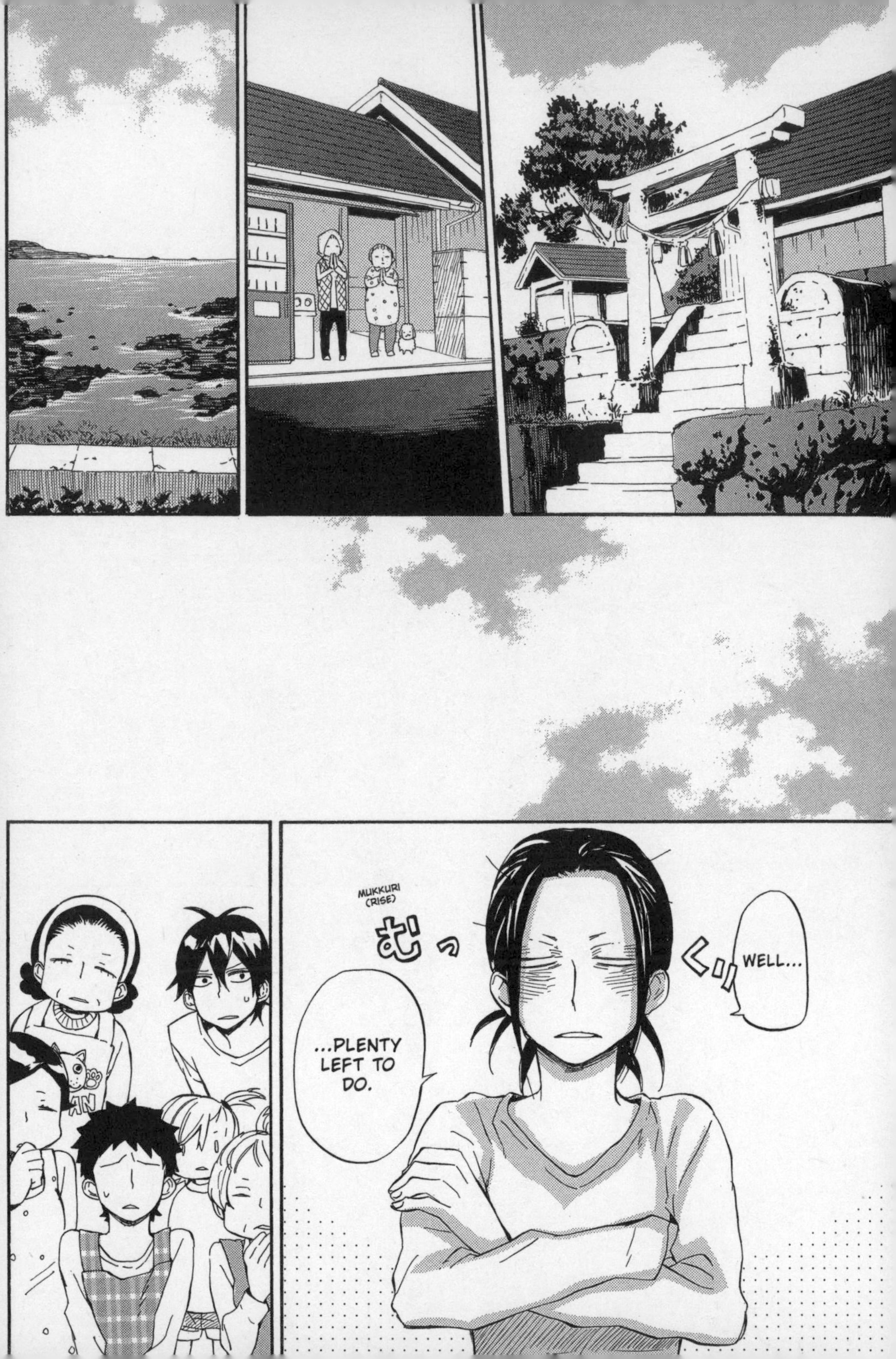
WELL...
MUKKURI (RISE)
むっ
...PLENTY LEFT TO DO.

GOODNESS! IS THAT IT?

'COS SHE'S SHORT?

AH'LL BE COUNTIN' ON YA!

FOR GRAMMA TO BE CREMATED, IT'LL TAKE...

...ABOUT TWO HOURS.

THOSE AREN'T THE WORDS OF SOMEONE WHO WAS JUST WAILING LOUDLY.

SORRY AH LOOKED UNSIGHTLY FOR A SPELL.

AH'LL MANAGE THIS RIGHT PROPER TO THE END.

IKU-CHAN, YA DON'T HAVE TA PUSH YERSELF.

EH?

RIGHT!

COUNT-IN' ON YA!

ASK NARU'S GRAMPA FOR THE DETAILS.

"INTER-MENT"?

SENSEI, YOU'LL HANDLE THE INTERMENT PREP.

YES, COM-ING!

SEN-SEI!

THIS'A WAY, THIS'A WAY!

SHE SWITCHES MODES QUICKLY.

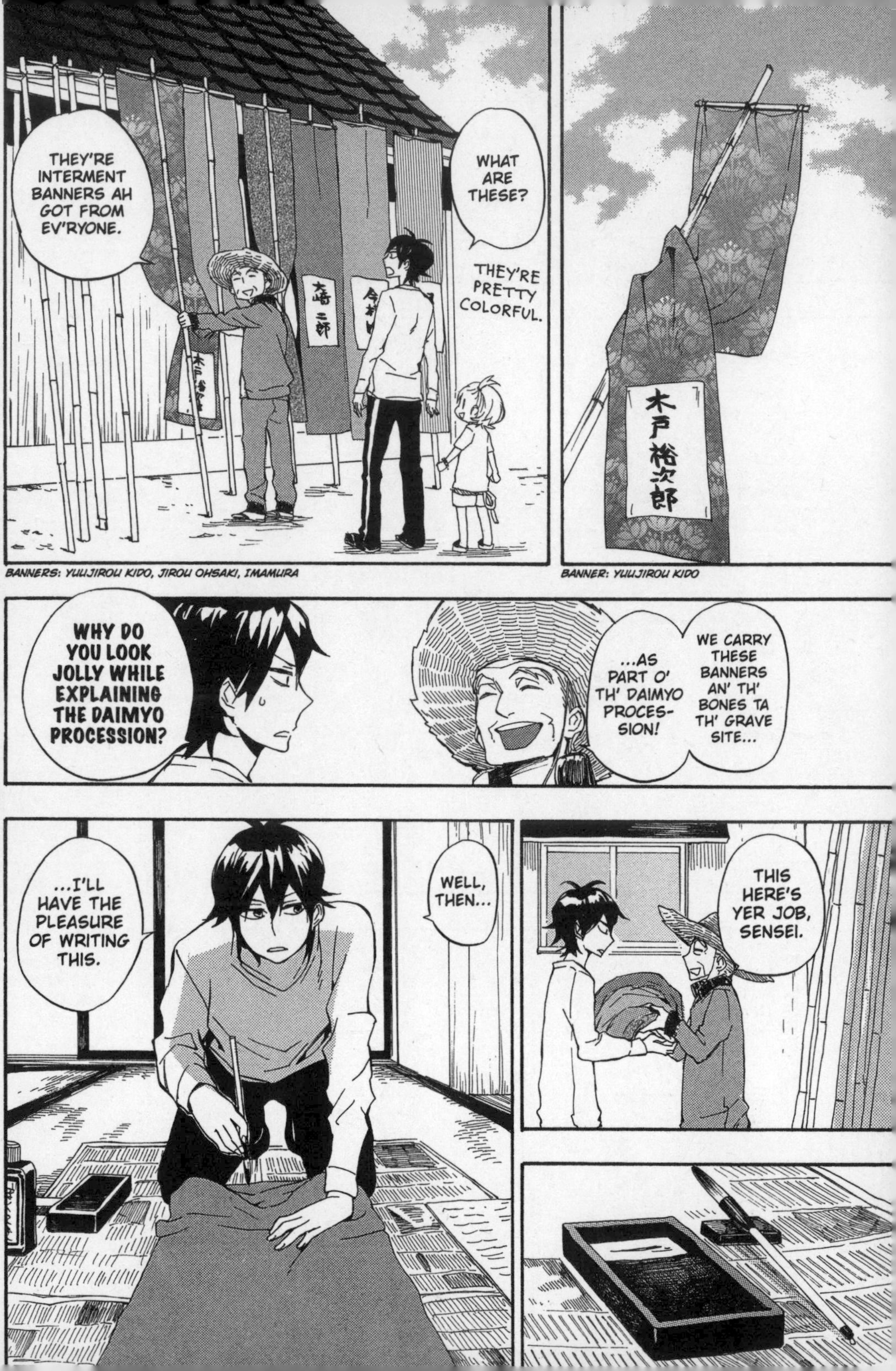
木戸裕次郎
BANNER: YUUJIROU KIDO
WHAT ARE THESE?
THEY'RE PRETTY COLORFUL.
THEY'RE INTERMENT BANNERS AH GOT FROM EV'RYONE.
BANNERS: YUUJIROU KIDO, JIROU OHSAKI, IMAMURA
WE CARRY THESE BANNERS AN' TH' BONES TA TH' GRAVE SITE...
...AS PART O' TH' DAIMYO PROCES-SION!
WHY DO YOU LOOK JOLLY WHILE EXPLAINING THE DAIMYO PROCESSION?
THIS HERE'S YER JOB, SENSEI.
WELL, THEN...
...I'LL HAVE THE PLEASURE OF WRITING THIS.

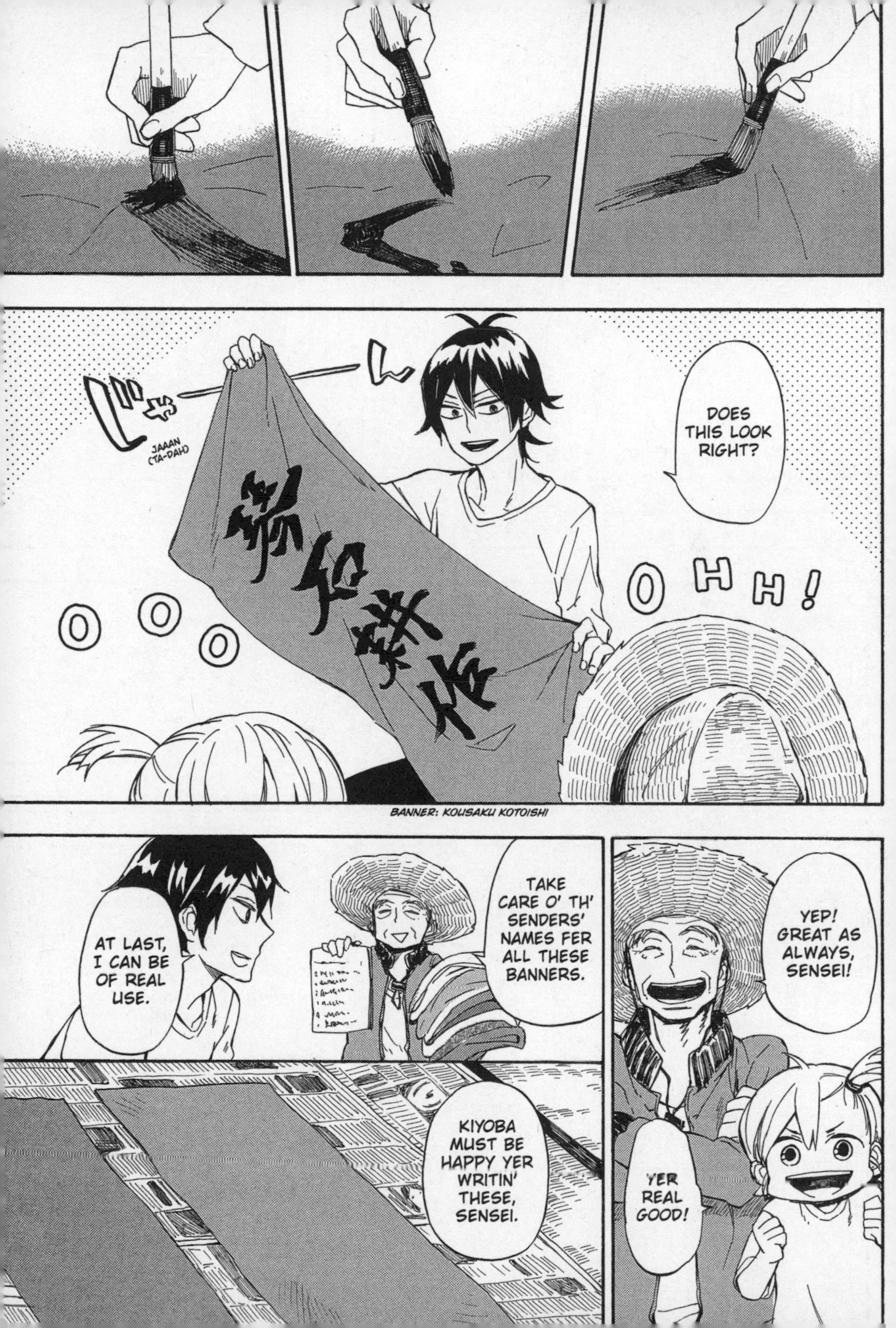
DOES THIS LOOK RIGHT?
JAAAN (TA-DAH)
OOOOHH!
BANNER: KOUSAKU KOTOISHI
YEP! GREAT AS ALWAYS, SENSEI!
YER REAL GOOD!
TAKE CARE O' TH' SENDERS' NAMES FER ALL THESE BANNERS.
AT LAST, I CAN BE OF REAL USE.
KIYOBA MUST BE HAPPY YER WRITIN' THESE, SENSEI.

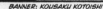

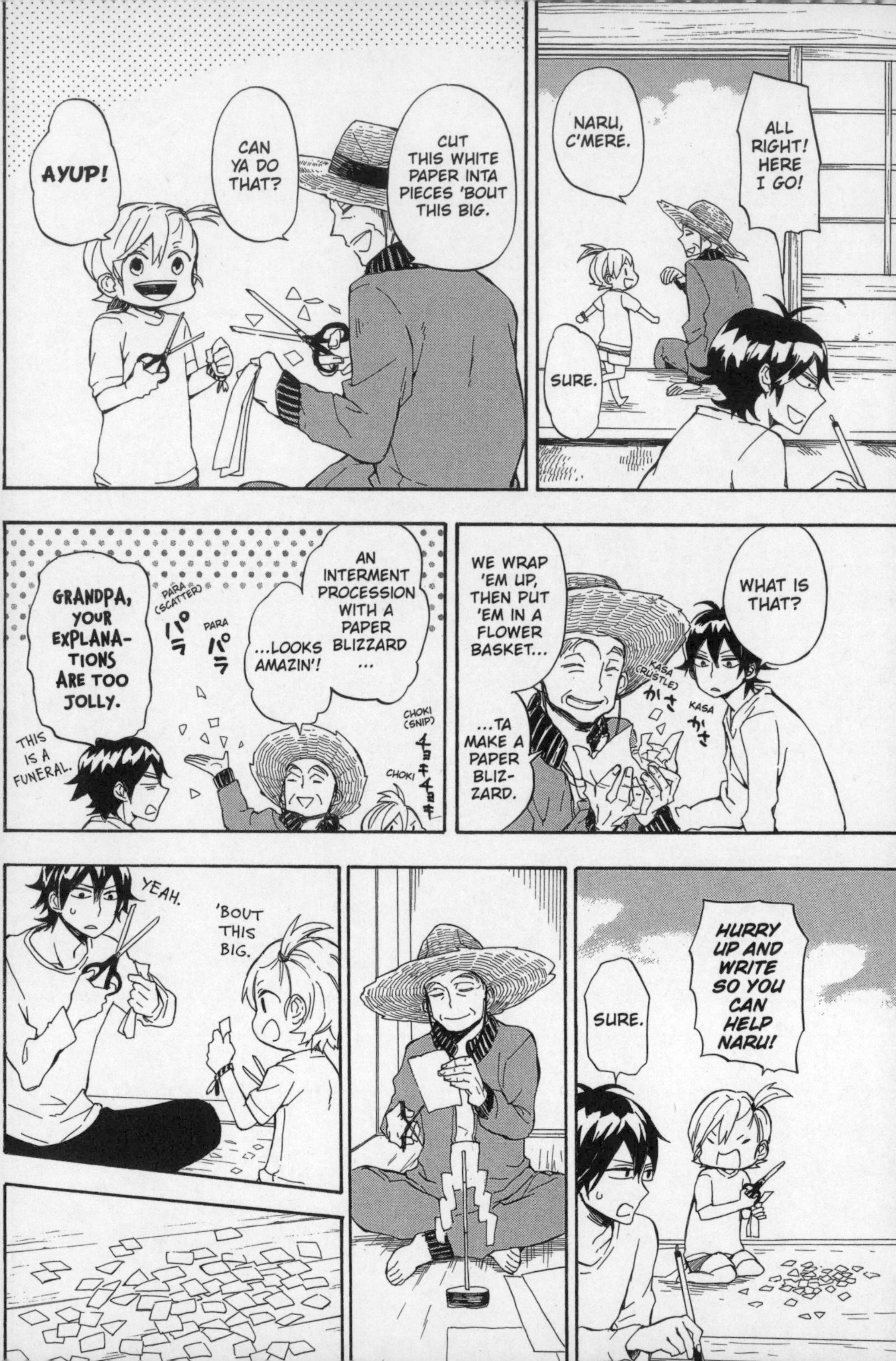
ALL RIGHT! HERE I GO!
NARU, C'MERE.
SURE.
CUT THIS WHITE PAPER INTA PIECES 'BOUT THIS BIG.
CAN YA DO THAT?
AYUP!
WHAT IS THAT?
WE WRAP 'EM UP, THEN PUT 'EM IN A FLOWER BASKET...
KASA かさ
KASA (RUSTLE) かさ
...TA MAKE A PAPER BLIZZARD.
AN INTERMENT PROCESSION WITH A PAPER BLIZZARD ...
...LOOKS AMAZIN'!
PARA パラ
PARA (SCATTER) パラ
GRANDPA, YOUR EXPLANATIONS ARE TOO JOLLY.
CHOKI (SNIP) チョキ
CHOKI チョキ
THIS IS A FUNERAL.
HURRY UP AND WRITE SO YOU CAN HELP NARU!
SURE.
'BOUT THIS BIG.
YEAH.

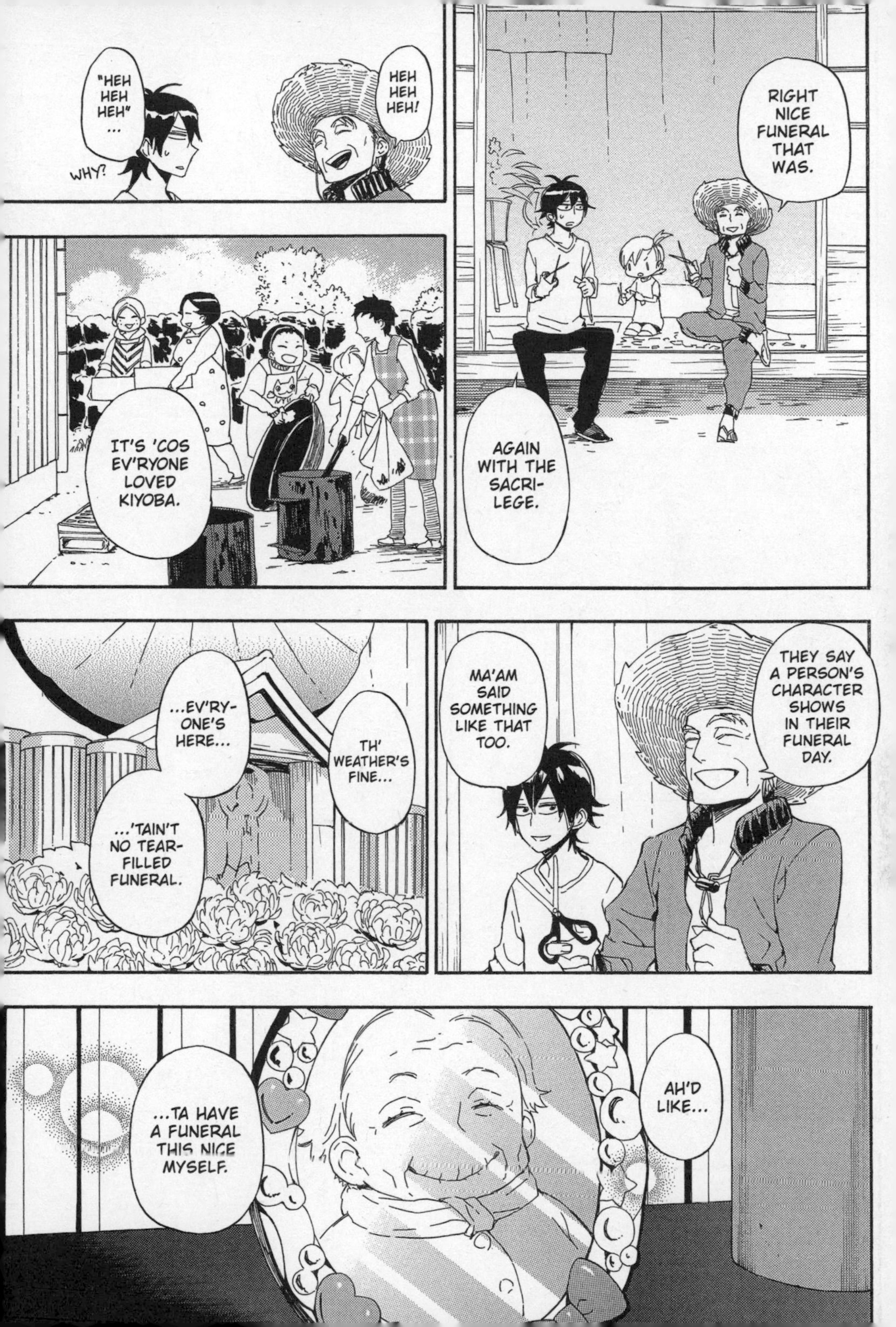
RIGHT NICE FUNERAL THAT WAS.
AGAIN WITH THE SACRI-LEGE.
HEH HEH HEH!
"HEH HEH HEH" ...
WHY?
IT'S 'COS EV'RYONE LOVED KIYOBA.
THEY SAY A PERSON'S CHARACTER SHOWS IN THEIR FUNERAL DAY.
MA'AM SAID SOMETHING LIKE THAT TOO.
TH' WEATHER'S FINE...
...EV'RY-ONE'S HERE...
...'TAIN'T NO TEAR-FILLED FUNERAL.
AH'D LIKE...
...TA HAVE A FUNERAL THIS NICE MYSELF.

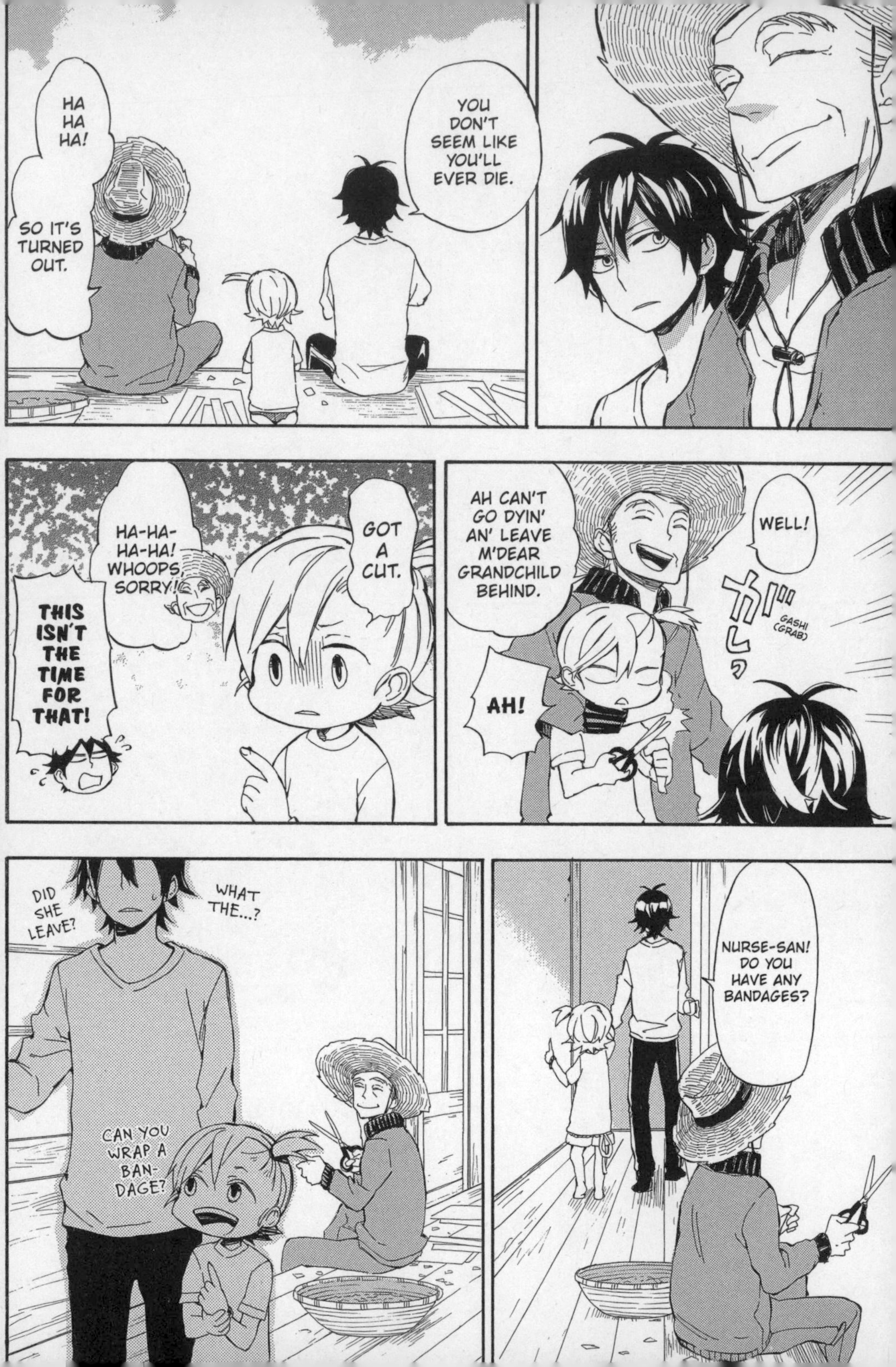
YOU DON'T SEEM LIKE YOU'LL EVER DIE.
HA HA HA!
SO IT'S TURNED OUT.
WELL!
AH CAN'T GO DYIN' AN' LEAVE M'DEAR GRANDCHILD BEHIND.
ガシッ
GASHI (GRAB)
AH!
GOT A CUT.
HA-HA-HA-HA! WHOOPS, SORRY!
THIS ISN'T THE TIME FOR THAT!
NURSE-SAN! DO YOU HAVE ANY BANDAGES?
WHAT THE...?
DID SHE LEAVE?
CAN YOU WRAP A BAN-DAGE?

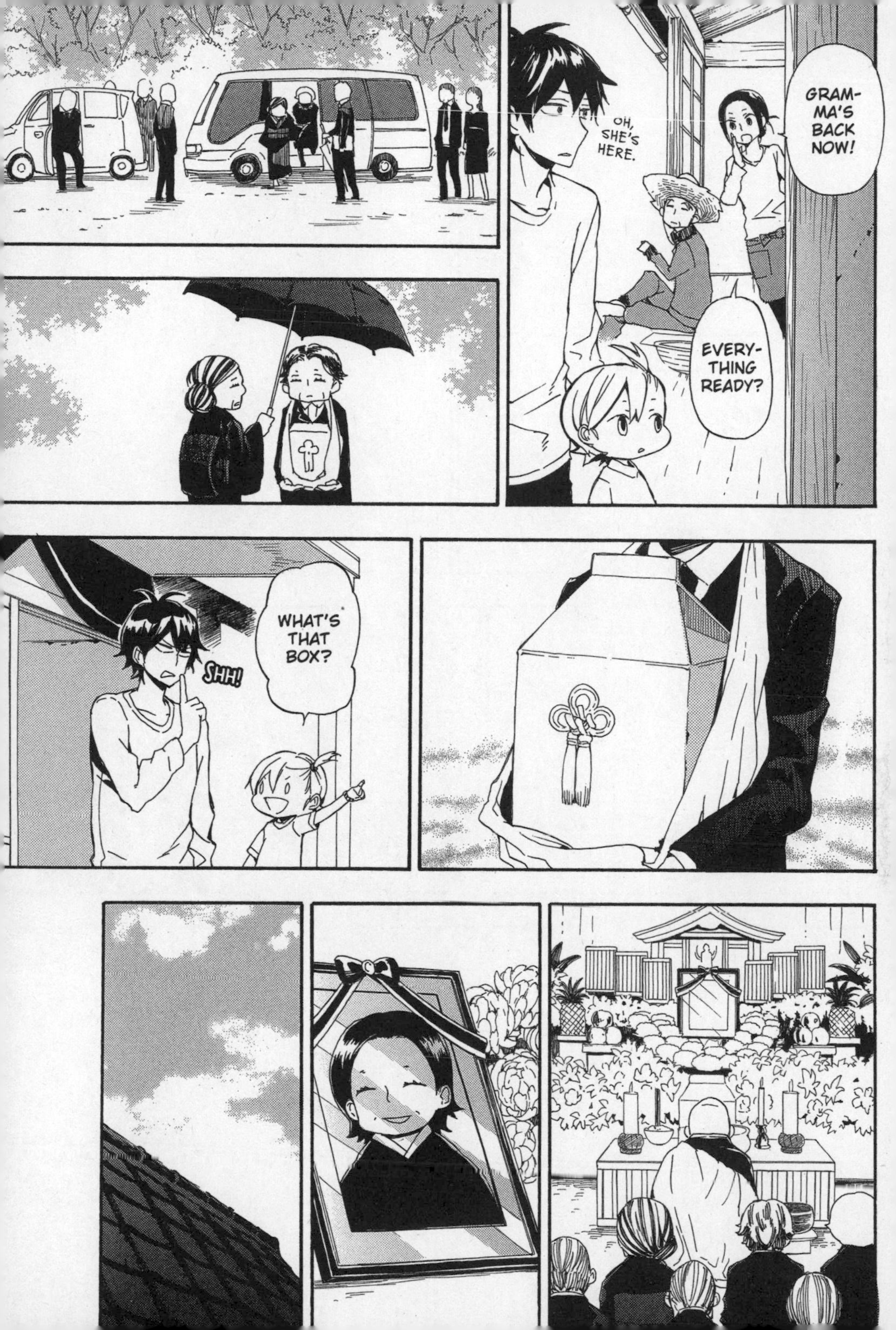
GRAM-MA'S BACK NOW!
OH, SHE'S HERE.
EVERY-THING READY?
WHAT'S THAT BOX?
SHH!

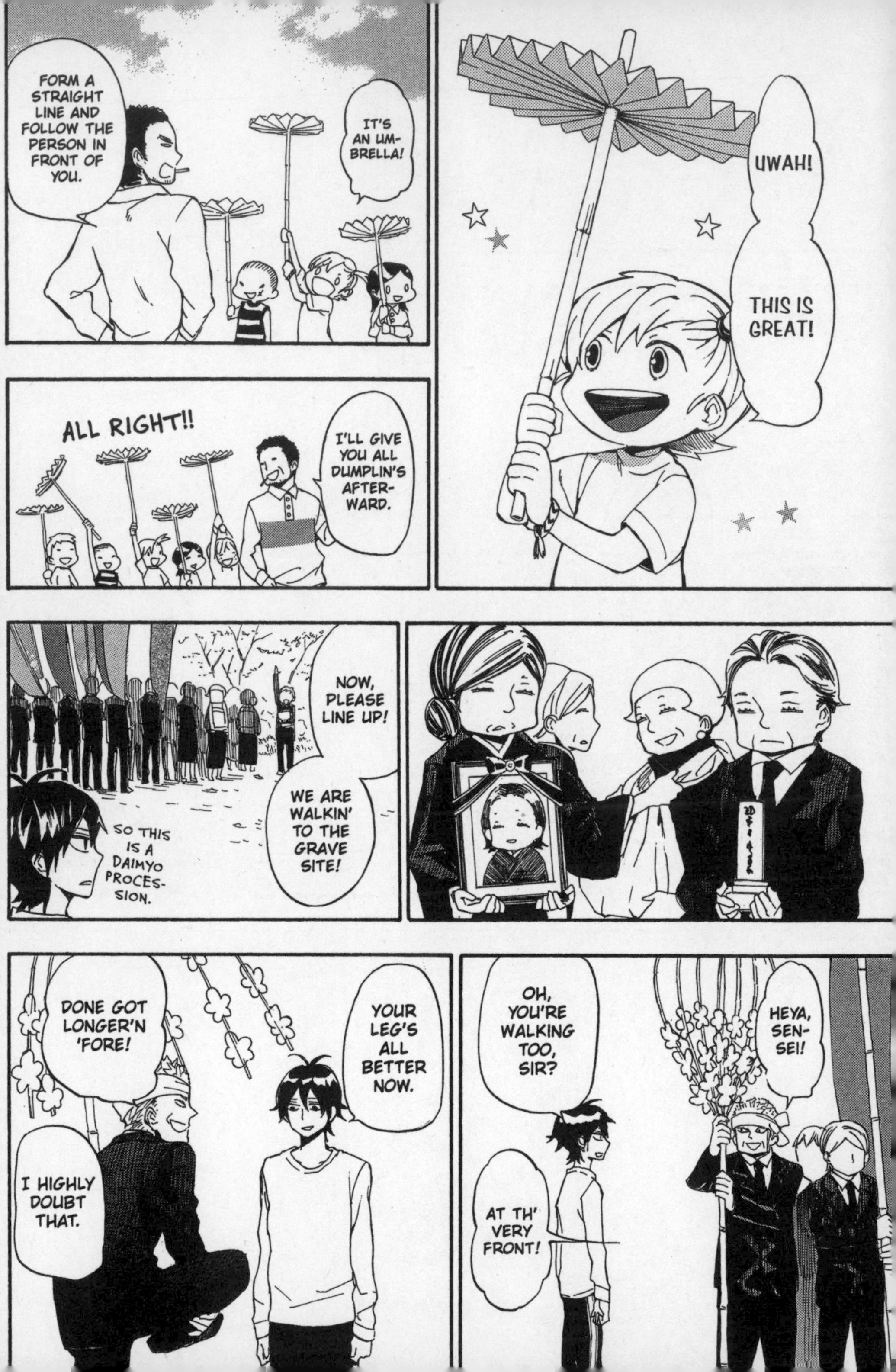
UWAH!
THIS IS GREAT!
IT'S AN UMBRELLA!
FORM A STRAIGHT LINE AND FOLLOW THE PERSON IN FRONT OF YOU.
I'LL GIVE YOU ALL DUMPLIN'S AFTERWARD.
ALL RIGHT!!
NOW, PLEASE LINE UP!
WE ARE WALKIN' TO THE GRAVE SITE!
SO THIS IS A DAIMYO PROCESSION.
HEYA, SENSEI!
OH, YOU'RE WALKING TOO, SIR?
AT TH' VERY FRONT!
YOUR LEG'S ALL BETTER NOW.
DONE GOT LONGER'N 'FORE!
I HIGHLY DOUBT THAT.

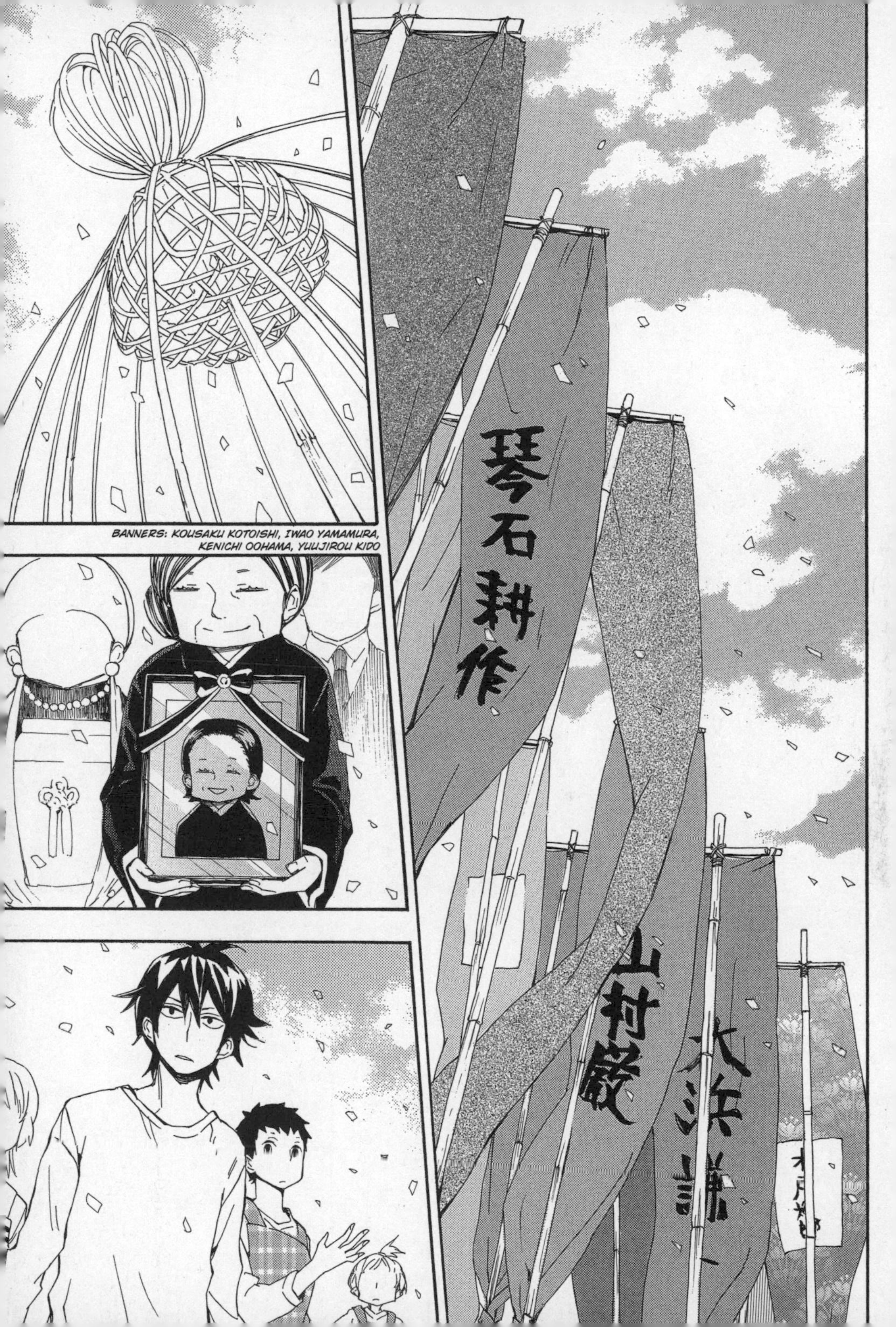
琴石耕作
BANNERS: KOUSAKU KOTOISHI, IWAO YAMAMURA, KENICHI OOHAMA, YUUJIROU KIDO

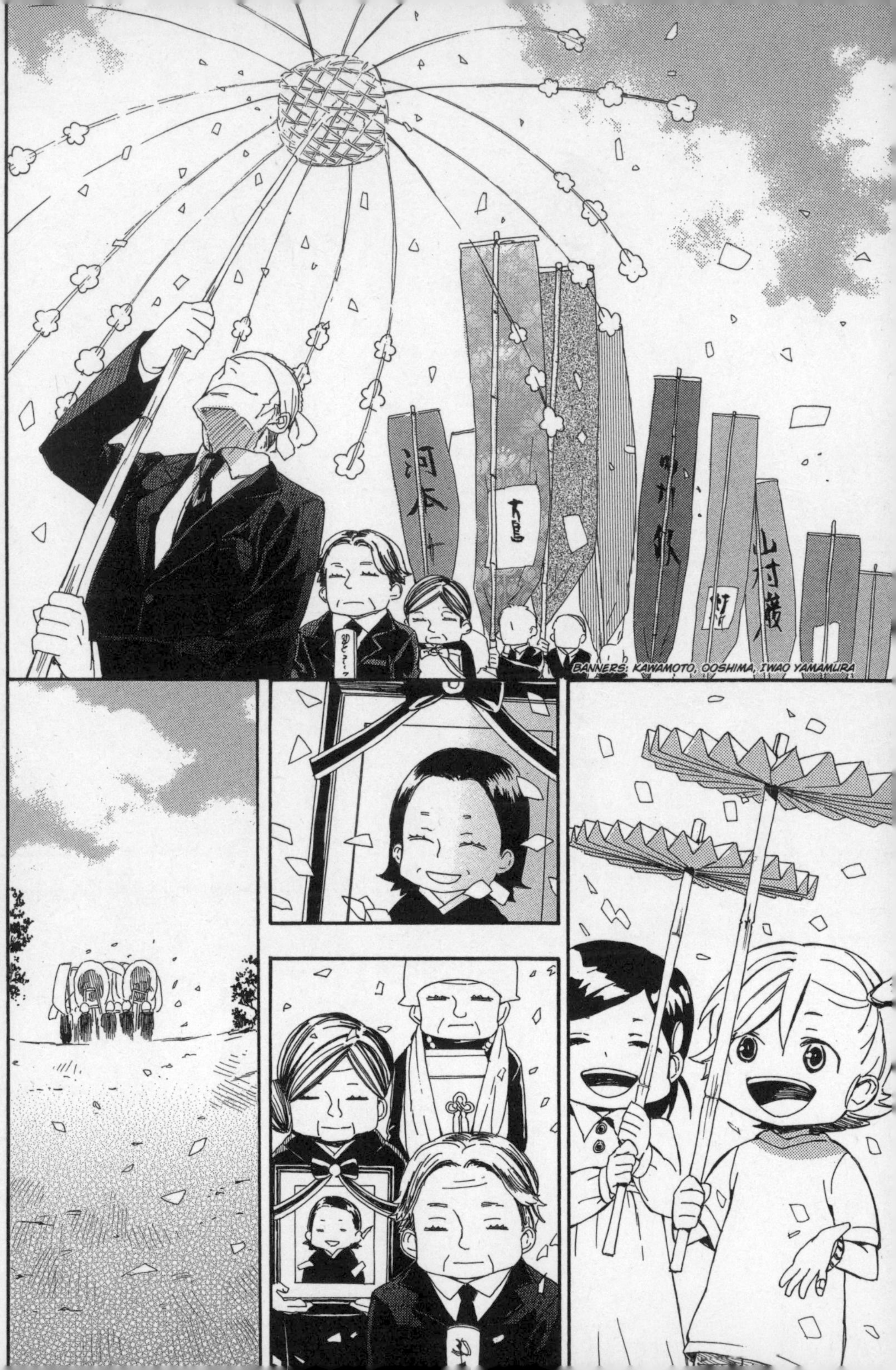
BANNERS: KAWAMOTO, OOSHIMA, IWAO YAMAMURA

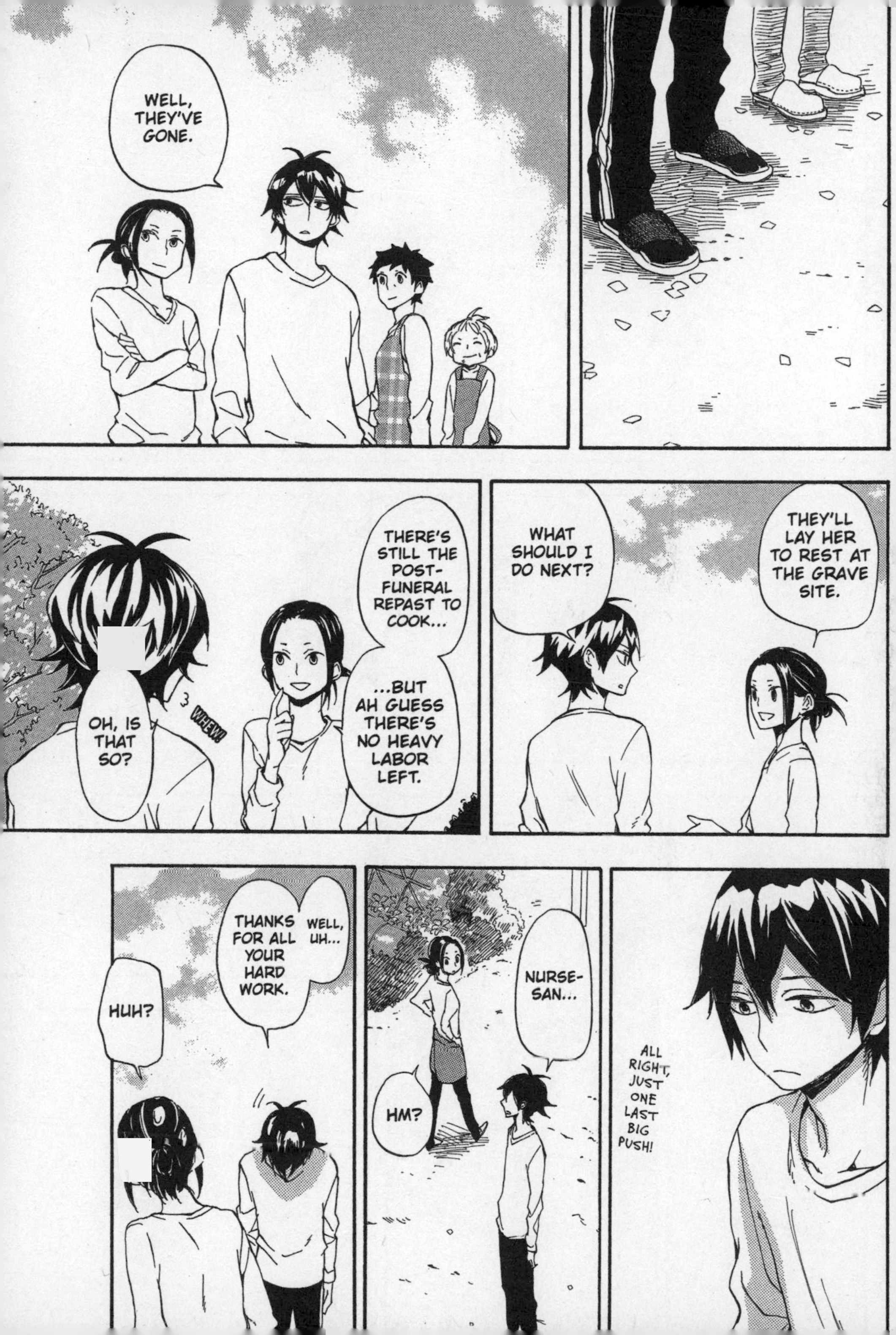
WELL, THEY'VE GONE.
THEY'LL LAY HER TO REST AT THE GRAVE SITE.
WHAT SHOULD I DO NEXT?
THERE'S STILL THE POST-FUNERAL REPAST TO COOK...
...BUT AH GUESS THERE'S NO HEAVY LABOR LEFT.
WHEW!
OH, IS THAT SO?
ALL RIGHT, JUST ONE LAST BIG PUSH!
NURSE-SAN...
HM?
WELL, UH...
THANKS FOR ALL YOUR HARD WORK.
HUH?

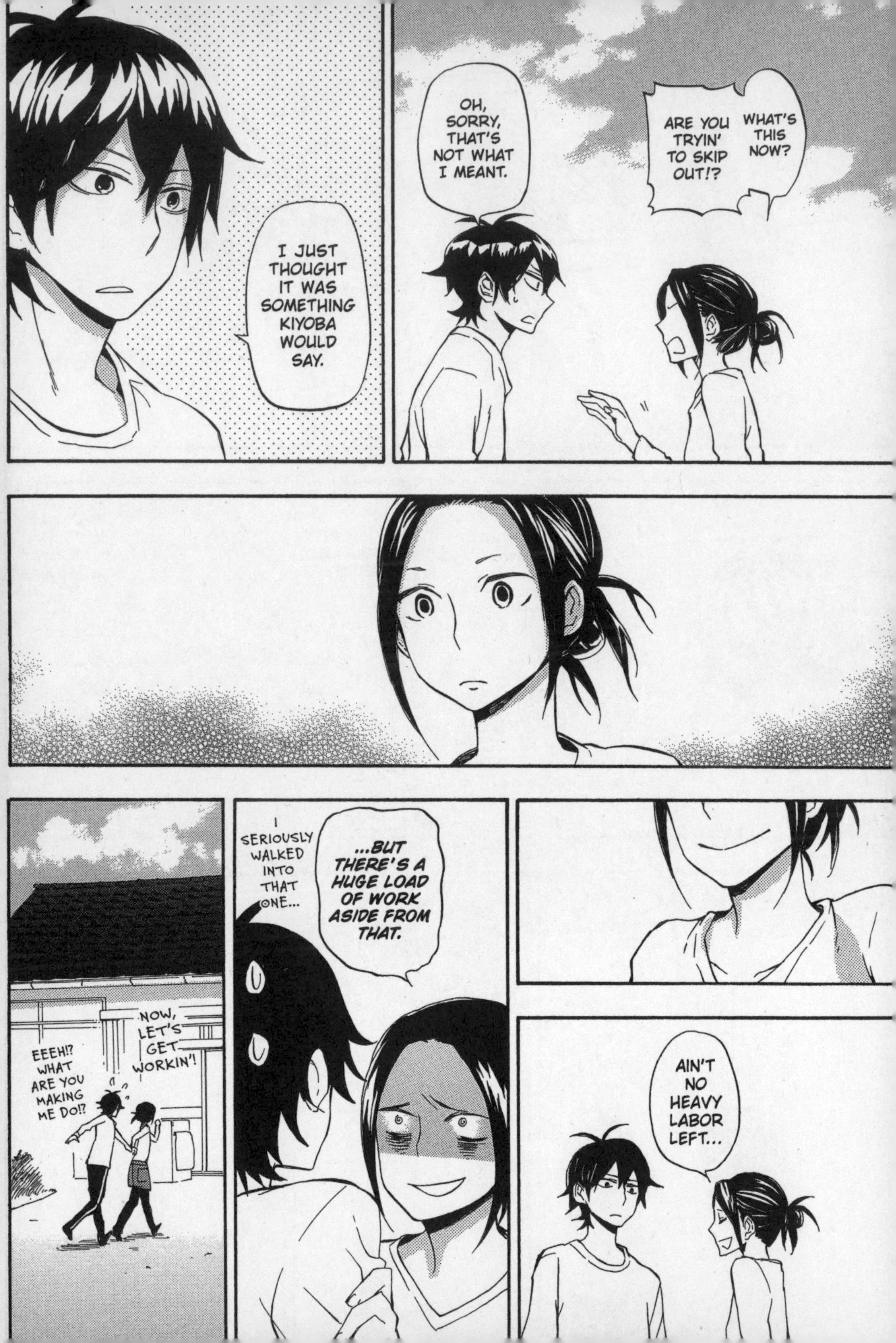
WHAT'S THIS NOW?
ARE YOU TRYIN' TO SKIP OUT!?
OH, SORRY, THAT'S NOT WHAT I MEANT.
I JUST THOUGHT IT WAS SOMETHING KIYOBA WOULD SAY.
AIN'T NO HEAVY LABOR LEFT...
...BUT THERE'S A HUGE LOAD OF WORK ASIDE FROM THAT.
I SERIOUSLY WALKED INTO THAT ONE...
NOW, LET'S GET WORKIN'!
EEEH!? WHAT ARE YOU MAKING ME DO!?

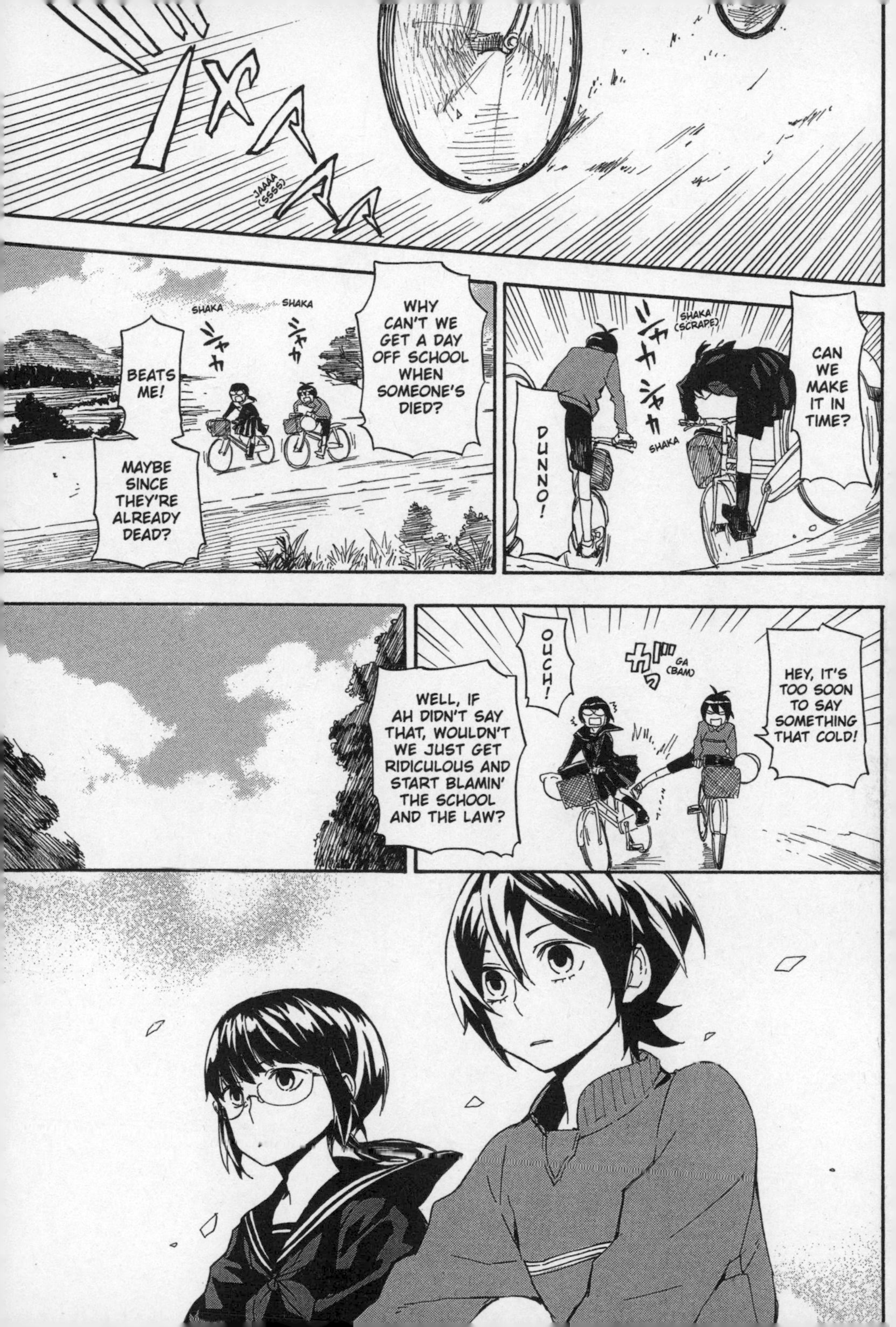

JAAAA (SSSS)
CAN WE MAKE IT IN TIME?
SHAKA (SCRAPE)
DUNNO!
SHAKA
WHY CAN'T WE GET A DAY OFF SCHOOL WHEN SOMEONE'S DIED?
SHAKA
SHAKA
BEATS ME!
MAYBE SINCE THEY'RE ALREADY DEAD?
HEY, IT'S TOO SOON TO SAY SOMETHING THAT COLD!
GA (BAM)
OUCH!
WELL, IF AH DIDN'T SAY THAT, WOULDN'T WE JUST GET RIDICULOUS AND START BLAMIN' THE SCHOOL AND THE LAW?

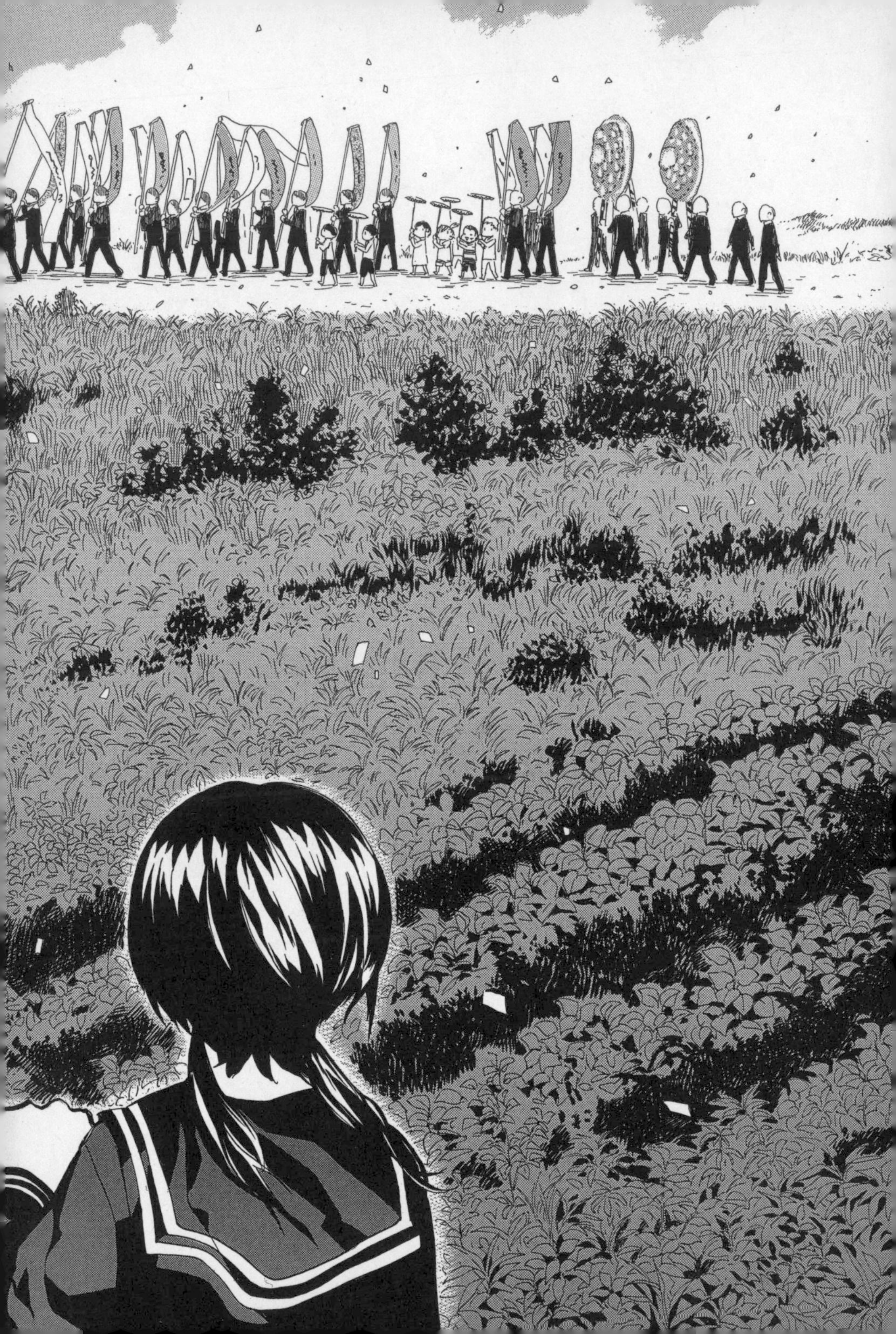

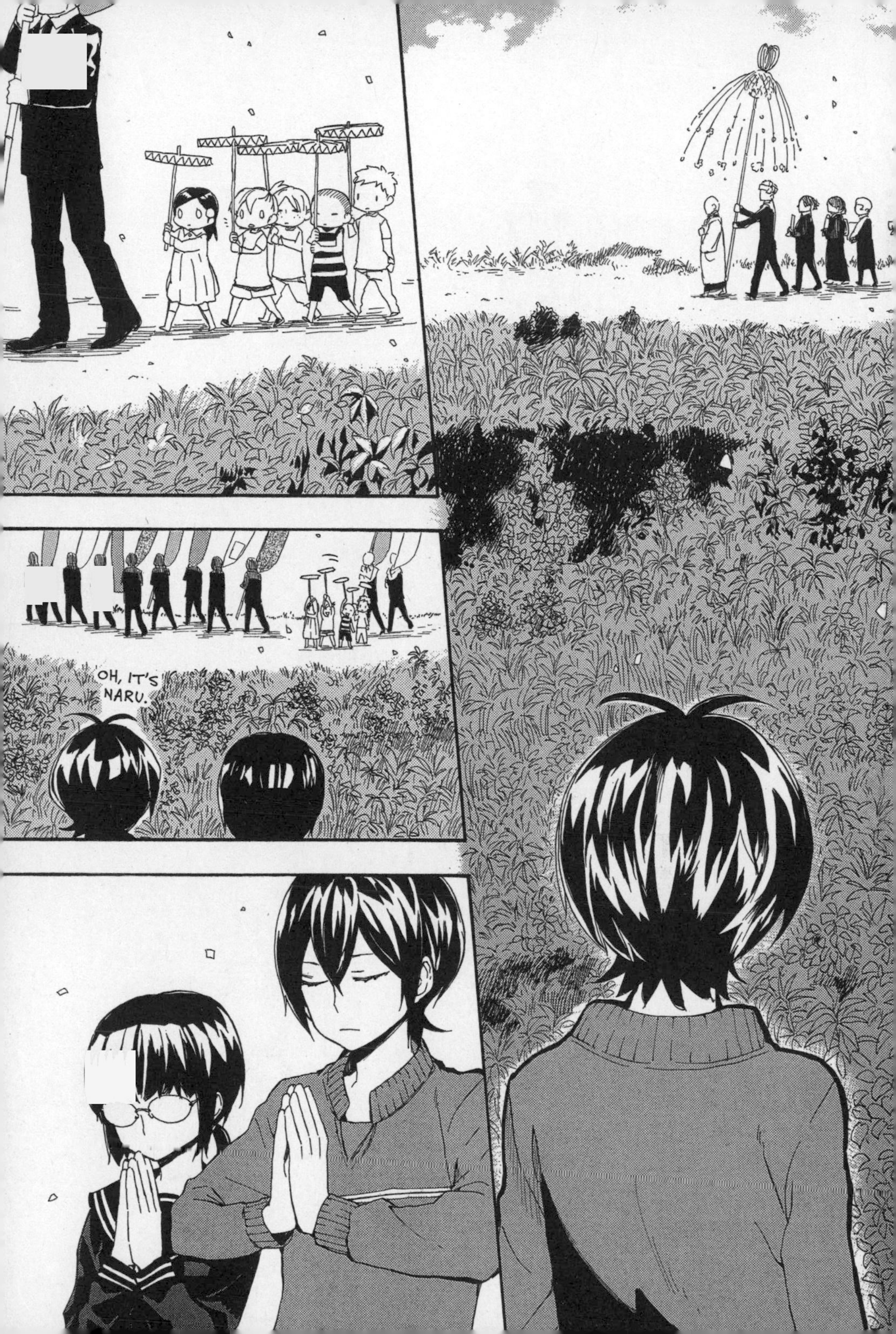
OH, IT'S NARU.

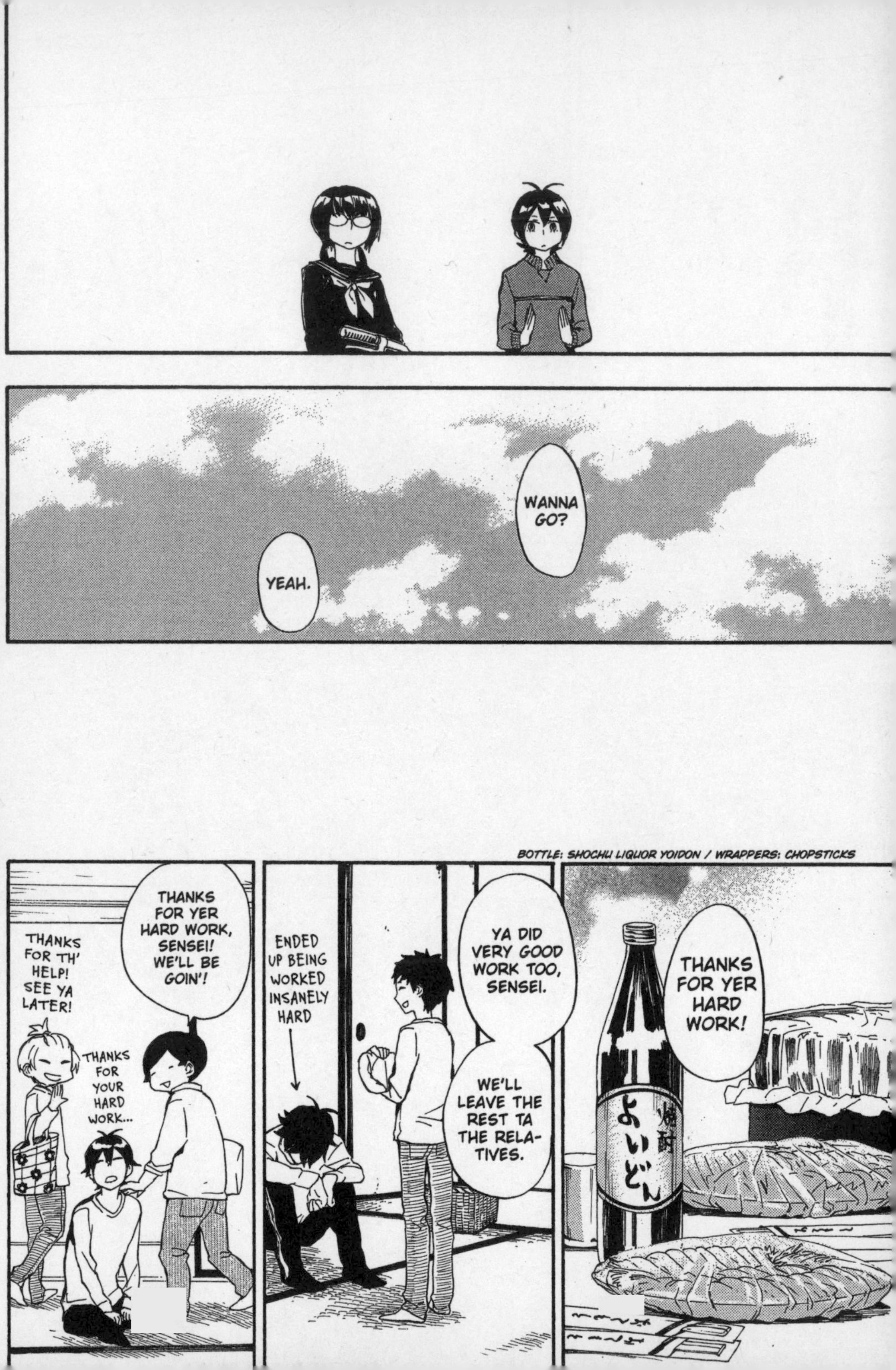
WANNA GO?
YEAH.
BOTTLE: SHOCHU LIQUOR YOIDON / WRAPPERS: CHOPSTICKS
THANKS FOR YER HARD WORK!
YA DID VERY GOOD WORK TOO, SENSEI.
WE'LL LEAVE THE REST TA THE RELATIVES.
ENDED UP BEING WORKED INSANELY HARD
THANKS FOR YER HARD WORK, SENSEI! WE'LL BE GOIN'!
THANKS FOR TH' HELP! SEE YA LATER!
THANKS FOR YOUR HARD WORK...

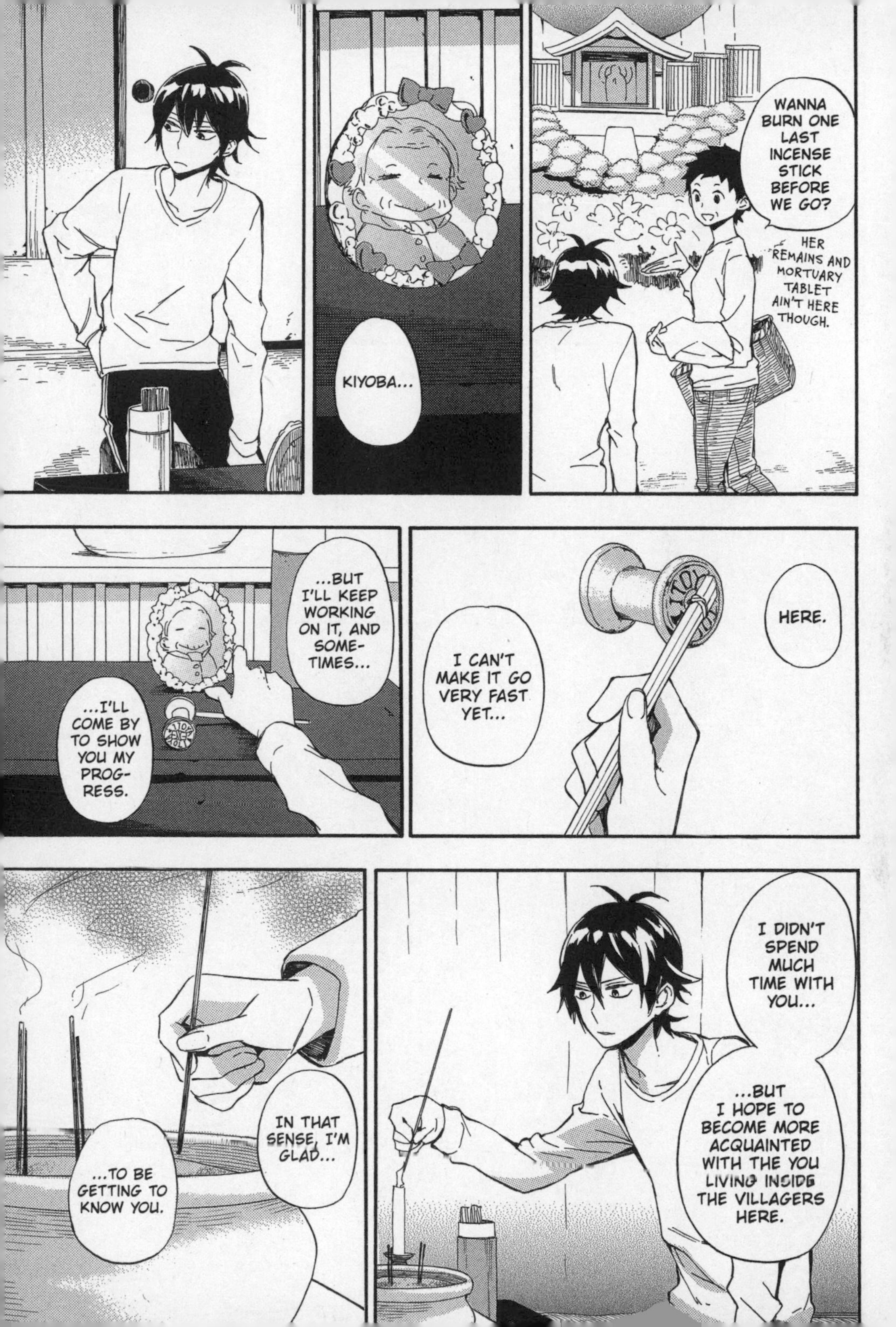
WANNA BURN ONE LAST INCENSE STICK BEFORE WE GO?
HER REMAINS AND MORTUARY TABLET AIN'T HERE THOUGH.
KIYOBA...
HERE.
I CAN'T MAKE IT GO VERY FAST YET...
...BUT I'LL KEEP WORKING ON IT, AND SOME-TIMES...
...I'LL COME BY TO SHOW YOU MY PROG-RESS.
I DIDN'T SPEND MUCH TIME WITH YOU...
...BUT I HOPE TO BECOME MORE ACQUAINTED WITH THE YOU LIVING INSIDE THE VILLAGERS HERE.
IN THAT SENSE, I'M GLAD...
...TO BE GETTING TO KNOW YOU.

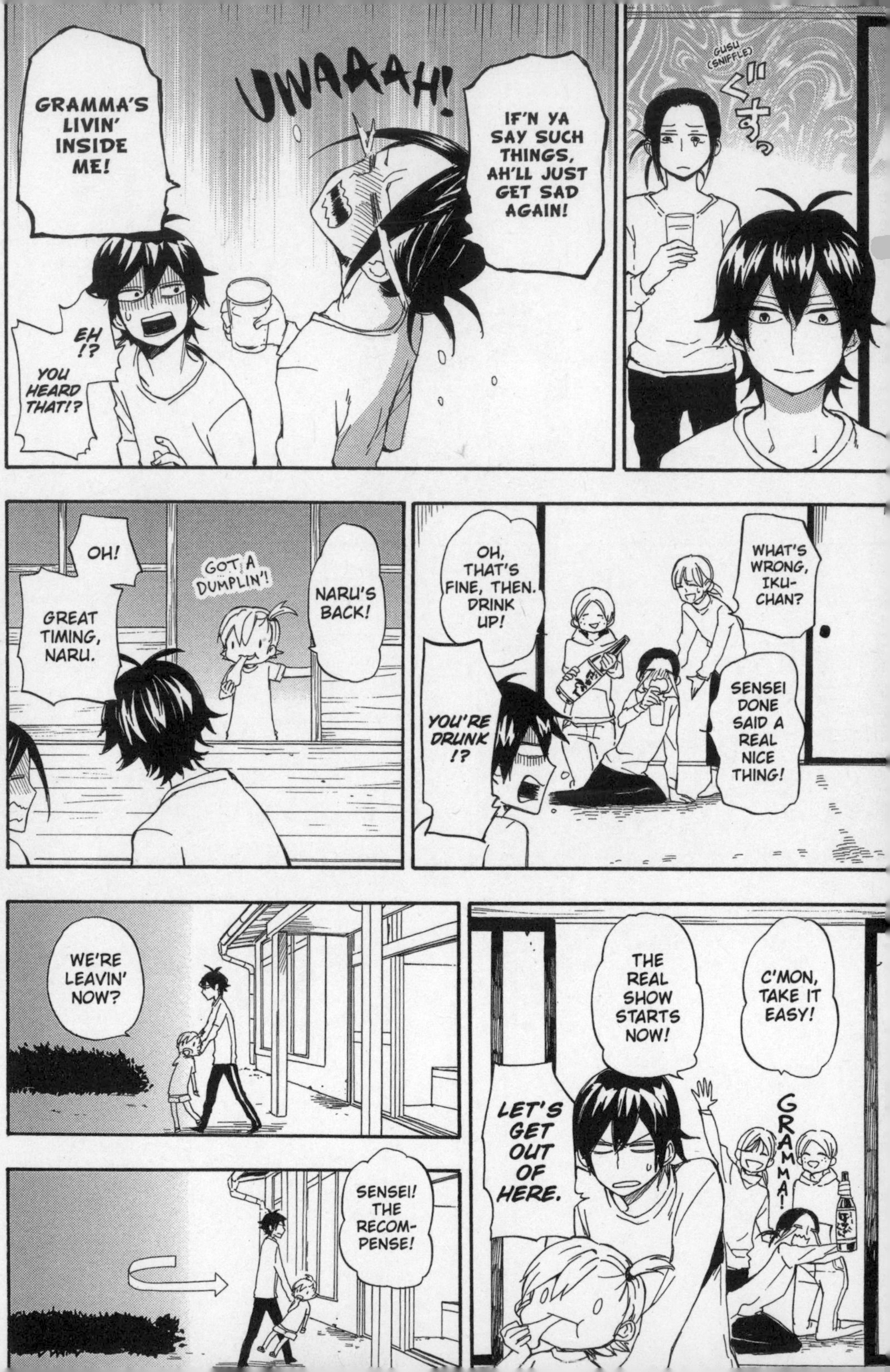
GUSU (SNIFFLE)
ぐすっ
UWAAAH!
IF'N YA SAY SUCH THINGS, AH'LL JUST GET SAD AGAIN!
GRAMMA'S LIVIN' INSIDE ME!
EH!? YOU HEARD THAT!?
WHAT'S WRONG, IKU-CHAN?
SENSEI DONE SAID A REAL NICE THING!
OH, THAT'S FINE, THEN. DRINK UP!
YOU'RE DRUNK!?
NARU'S BACK!
GOT A DUMPLIN'!
OH!
GREAT TIMING, NARU.
C'MON, TAKE IT EASY!
THE REAL SHOW STARTS NOW!
GRAMMA!
LET'S GET OUT OF HERE.
WE'RE LEAVIN' NOW?
SENSEI! THE RECOMPENSE!

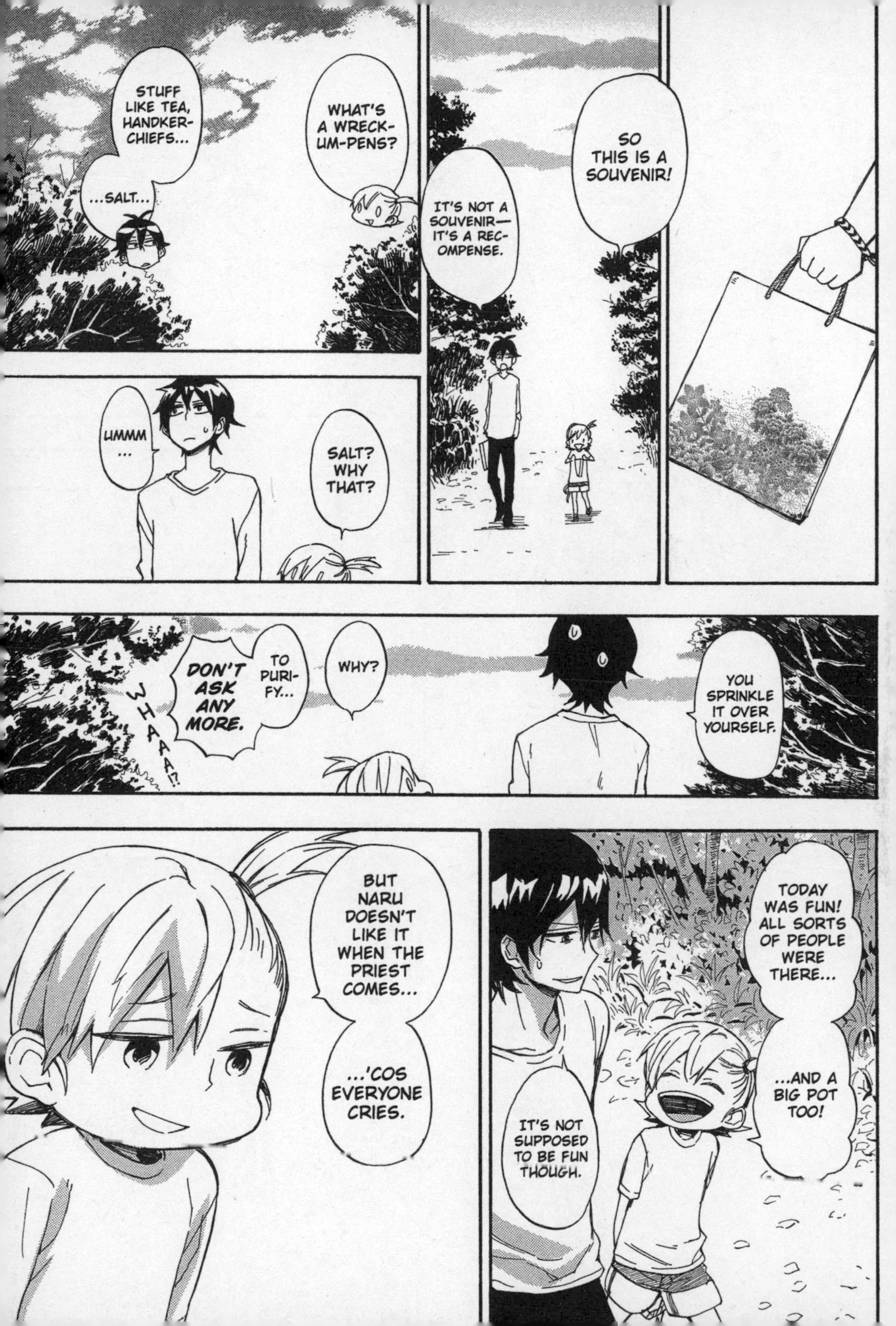
SO THIS IS A SOUVENIR!
IT'S NOT A SOUVENIR—IT'S A RECOMPENSE.
WHAT'S A WRECK-UM-PENS?
STUFF LIKE TEA, HANDKER-CHIEFS...
...SALT...
SALT? WHY THAT?
UMMM ...
YOU SPRINKLE IT OVER YOURSELF.
WHY?
TO PURI-FY...
DON'T ASK ANY MORE.
WHAAAA!?
TODAY WAS FUN! ALL SORTS OF PEOPLE WERE THERE...
...AND A BIG POT TOO!
IT'S NOT SUPPOSED TO BE FUN THOUGH.
BUT NARU DOESN'T LIKE IT WHEN THE PRIEST COMES...
...'COS EVERYONE CRIES.

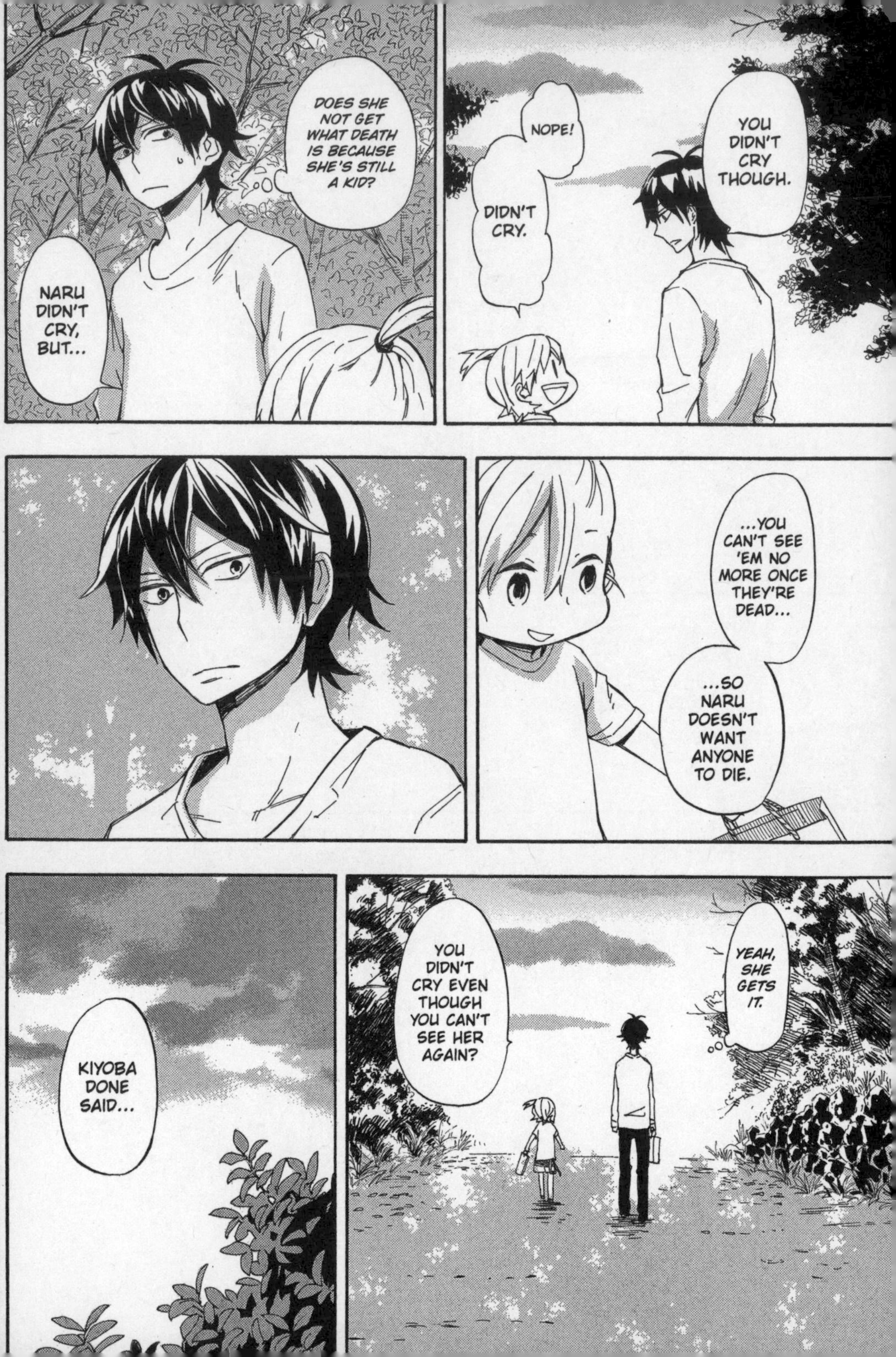
YOU DIDN'T CRY THOUGH.
NOPE!
DIDN'T CRY.
DOES SHE NOT GET WHAT DEATH IS BECAUSE SHE'S STILL A KID?
NARU DIDN'T CRY, BUT...
...YOU CAN'T SEE 'EM NO MORE ONCE THEY'RE DEAD...
...SO NARU DOESN'T WANT ANYONE TO DIE.
YEAH, SHE GETS IT.
YOU DIDN'T CRY EVEN THOUGH YOU CAN'T SEE HER AGAIN?
KIYOBA DONE SAID...

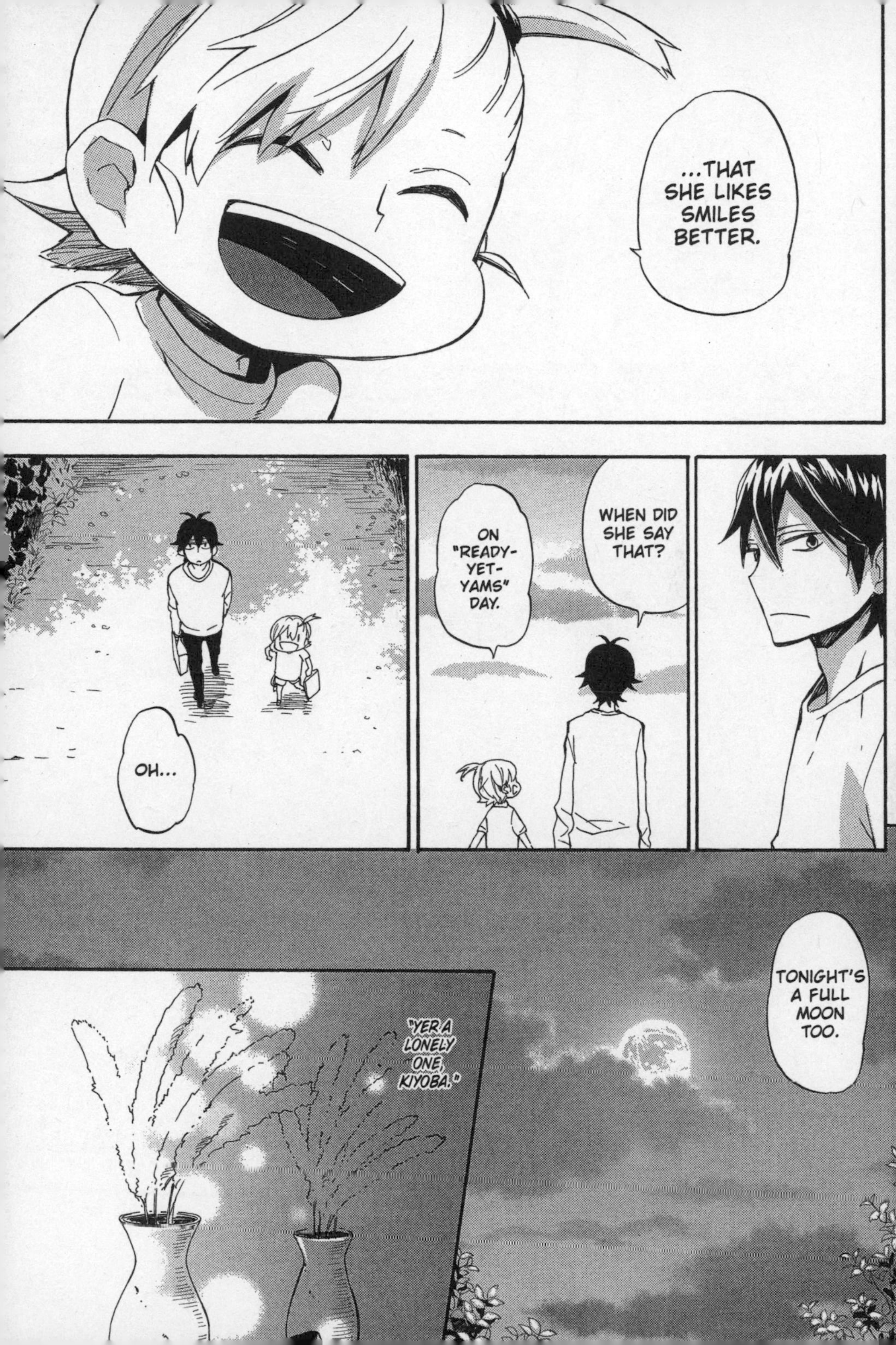
...THAT SHE LIKES SMILES BETTER.
WHEN DID SHE SAY THAT?
ON "READY-YET-YAMS" DAY.
OH...
TONIGHT'S A FULL MOON TOO.
"YER A LONELY ONE, KIYOBA."

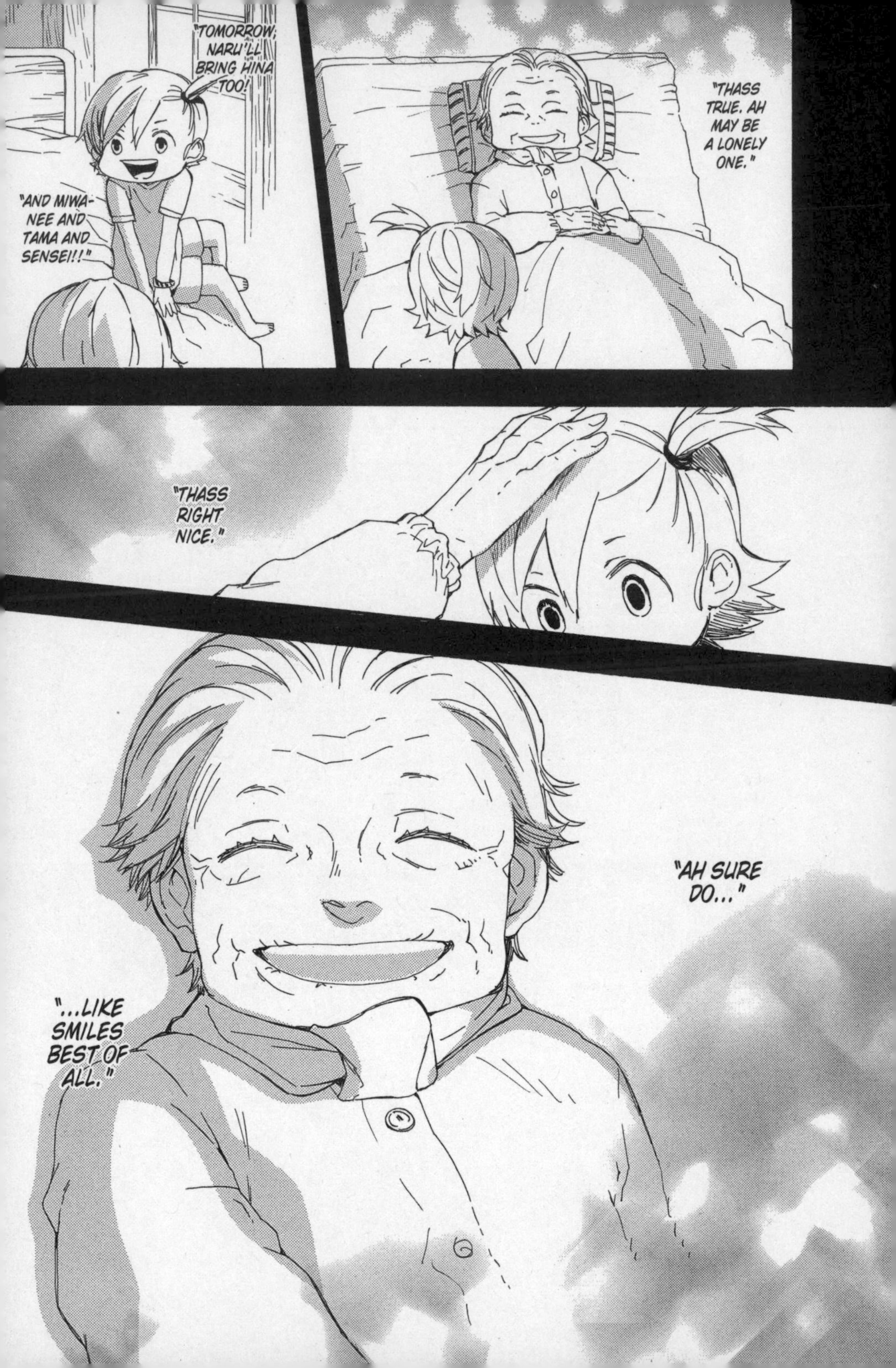
"THASS TRUE. AH MAY BE A LONELY ONE."
"TOMORROW, NARU'LL BRING HINA TOO!
"AND MIWA-NEE AND TAMA AND SENSEI!!"
"THASS RIGHT NICE."
"AH SURE DO..."
"...LIKE SMILES BEST OF ALL."

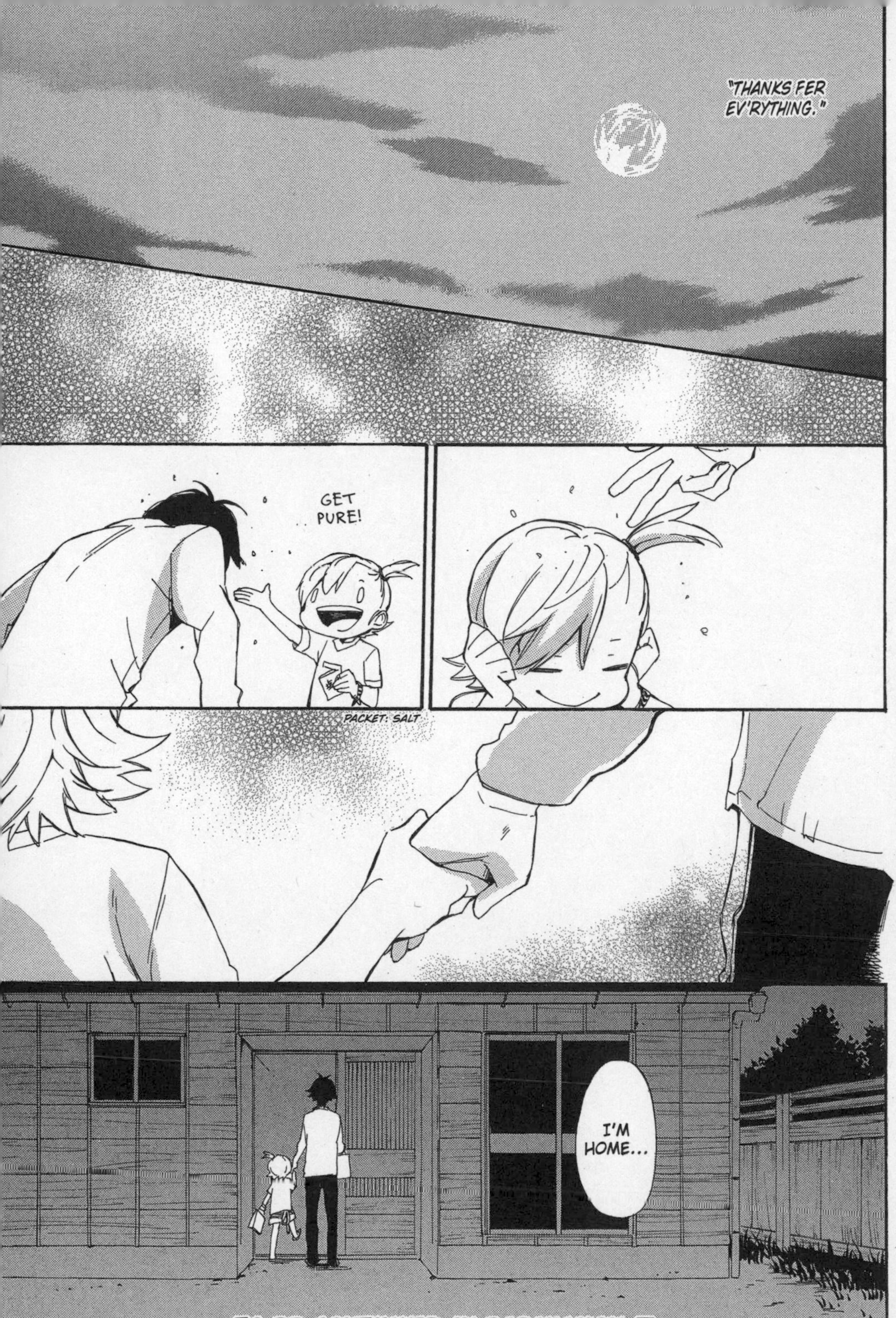
"THANKS FER EV'RYTHING."
GET PURE!
PACKET: SALT
I'M HOME...

TO BE CONTINUED IN BARAKAMON 9

BARAKAMON

BONUS: DANPO THE 8TH

(Translation: Pond)

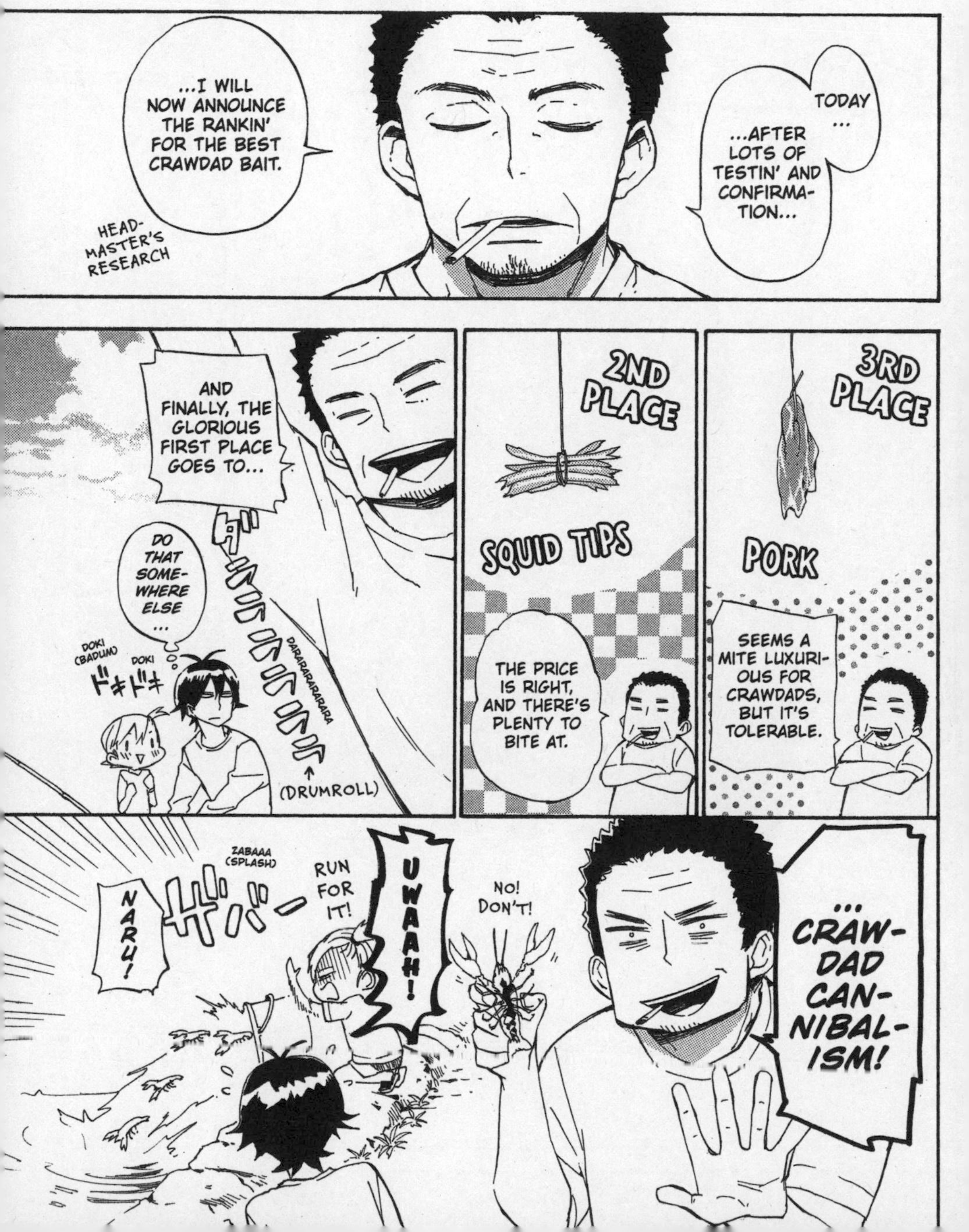
TODAY ...
...AFTER LOTS OF TESTIN' AND CONFIRMA-TION...
...I WILL NOW ANNOUNCE THE RANKIN' FOR THE BEST CRAWDAD BAIT.
HEAD-MASTER'S RESEARCH
3RD PLACE
PORK
SEEMS A MITE LUXURI-OUS FOR CRAWDADS, BUT IT'S TOLERABLE.
2ND PLACE
SQUID TIPS
THE PRICE IS RIGHT, AND THERE'S PLENTY TO BITE AT.
AND FINALLY, THE GLORIOUS FIRST PLACE GOES TO...
DARARARARARA
(DRUMROLL)
DO THAT SOME-WHERE ELSE ...
DOKI (BADUM) DOKI
ドキドキ
...CRAW-DAD CAN-NIBAL-ISM!
NO! DON'T!
UWAAH!
RUN FOR IT!
ZABAAA (SPLASH)
NARU!

Anime Version Set!!!

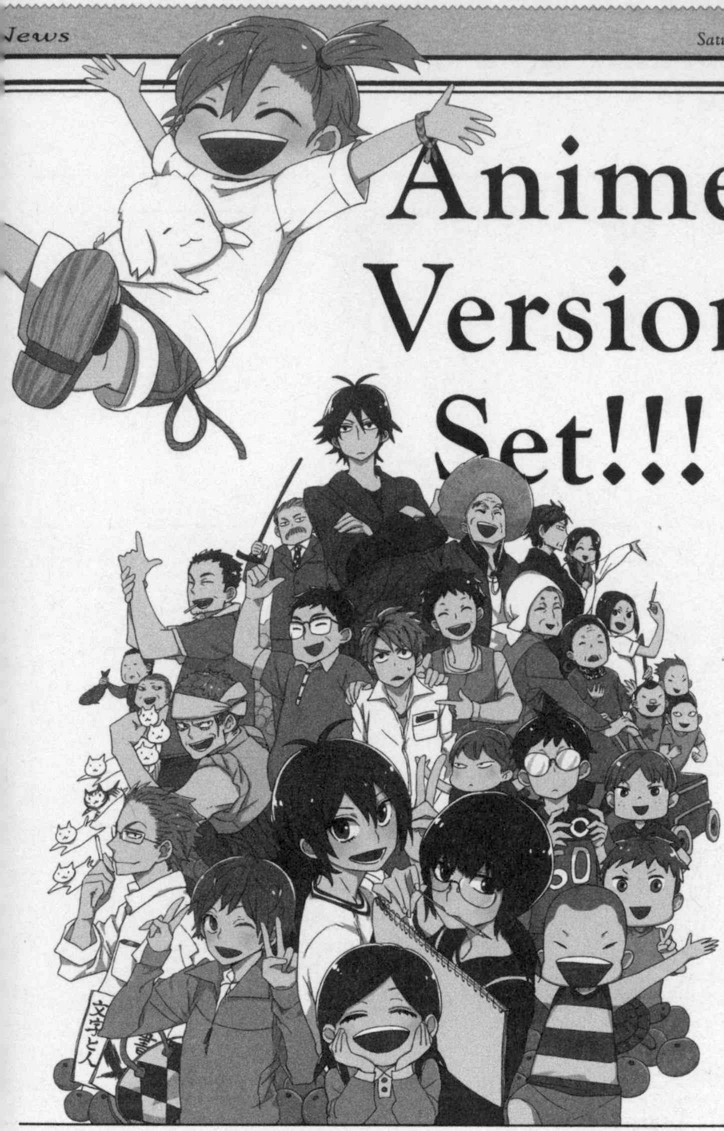

BARAKAMON NEWS

Vol.510

Everyone, thank you very much for buying Volume 8 of *BARAKAMON*! Thanks to your warm support, they've decided to make *BARAKAMON* into an anime. Thank you so very much! Follow-up information will be updated on *Gangan ONLINE* when available, so check there occasionally while looking forward to the start of the broadcast!

This time, I thought I'd introduce a little of the content from our *BARAKAMON* public Twitter account. It features Yoshino-sensei's special drawings and current status and is updated with the latest news on *BARAKAMON* when available, so please be sure to check it out!

Hooray! We're Getting an Anime!

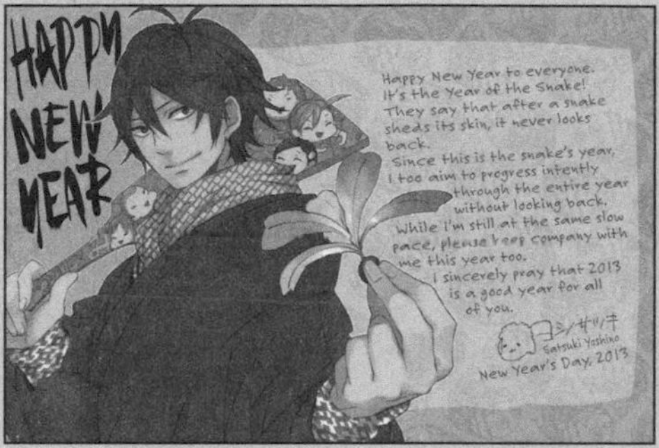
HAPPY NEW YEAR
Happy New Year to everyone. It's the Year of the Snake! They say that after a snake sheds its skin, it never looks back. Since this is the snake's year, I too aim to progress intently through the entire year without looking back. While I'm still at the same slow pace, please keep company with me this year too. I sincerely pray that 2013 is a good year for all of you.
Satsuki Yoshino
New Year's Day, 2013

⬆ There are Yoshino-sensei's specially-drawn messages that you can only see on Twitter...

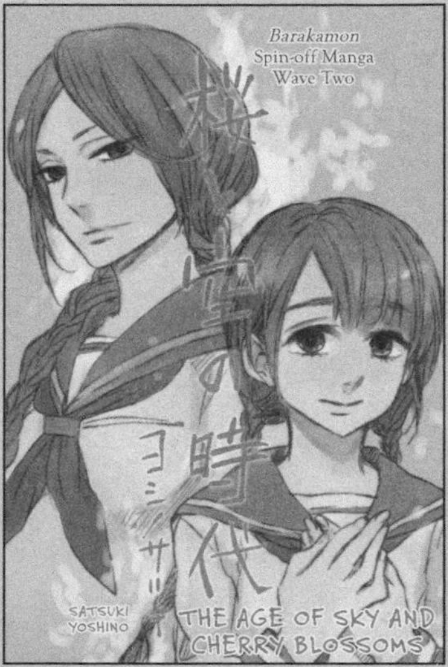
Barakamon
Spin-off Manga
Wave Two
SATSUKI YOSHINO
THE AGE OF SKY AND CHERRY BLOSSOMS

⬆ We also made this fake manga announcement for April Fools' Day! Can you tell who these two girls are?

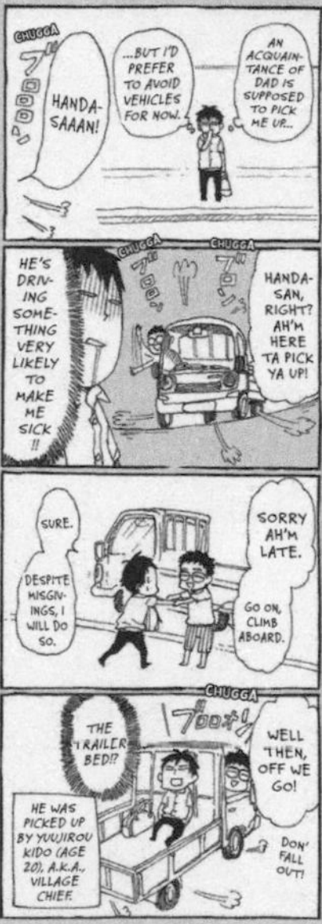
AN ACQUAINTANCE OF DAD IS SUPPOSED TO PICK ME UP...
...BUT I'D PREFER TO AVOID VEHICLES FOR NOW.
CHUGGA
HANDA-SAAAN!
HANDA-SAN, RIGHT? AH'M HERE TA PICK YA UP!
CHUGGA
CHUGGA
HE'S DRIVING SOMETHING VERY LIKELY TO MAKE ME SICK!!
SORRY AH'M LATE.
SURE.
GO ON, CLIMB ABOARD.
DESPITE MISGIVINGS, I WILL DO SO.
CHUGGA
WELL THEN, OFF WE GO!
THE TRAILER BED!?
DON' FALL OUT!
HE WAS PICKED UP BY YUUJIROU KIDO (AGE 20), A.K.A. VILLAGE CHIEF.

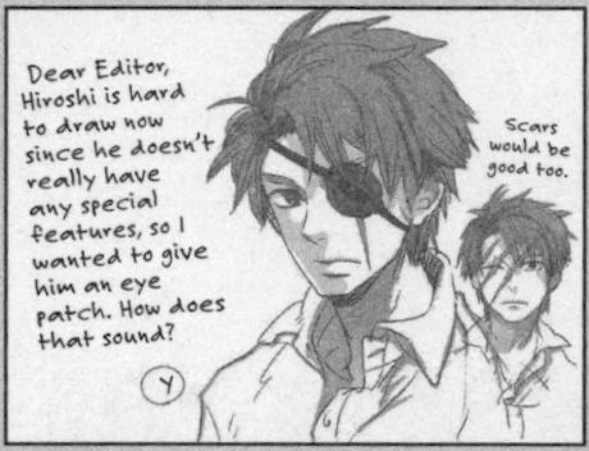
Dear Editor, Hiroshi is hard to draw now since he doesn't really have any special features, so I wanted to give him an eye patch. How does that sound?
Y
Scars would be good too.

⬆ You can also catch a glimpse of surprising meeting content (lol).

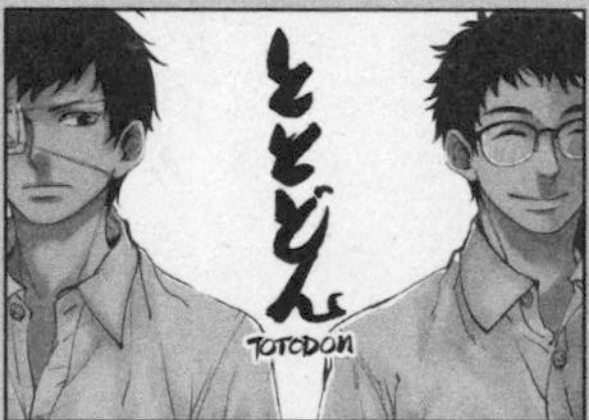
とどどん
TOTODON

⬅⬆ The highly-popular spin-off 4-panel comic about Handa-sensei's father and Village Chief, *TOTODON*. I look forward to seeing more of it.

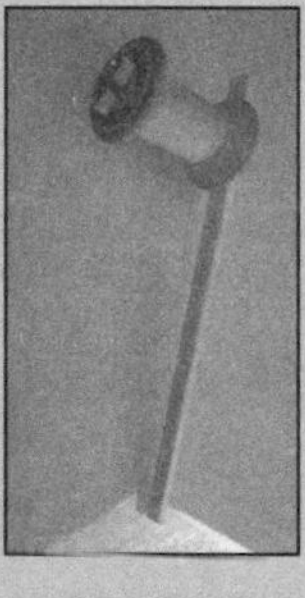

⬅ This spool tank that showed up during cleaning led to the rushed beginning of Yoshino-sensei's "How To Make Spool Tanks" series. It was pretty impressive, with videos even!

Of course, merchandise info and the latest information are also posted here as available!

https://twitter.com/go_barakamon

There's a big surprise for those who can't wait for the collected volume...!! Please turn to the next page!!

With this and that, we're feeling somewhat festive about the anime—but we're determined not to get carried away in the main story line and to continue the usual easygoing pace and mellow mood, so please be so kind as to continue with your unchanging support.

Well then, I sincerely hope to see you all again in Volume 9!!

The next volume, *BARAKAMON 9*, is scheduled for sale in

February 2016!!

New Series Announcement

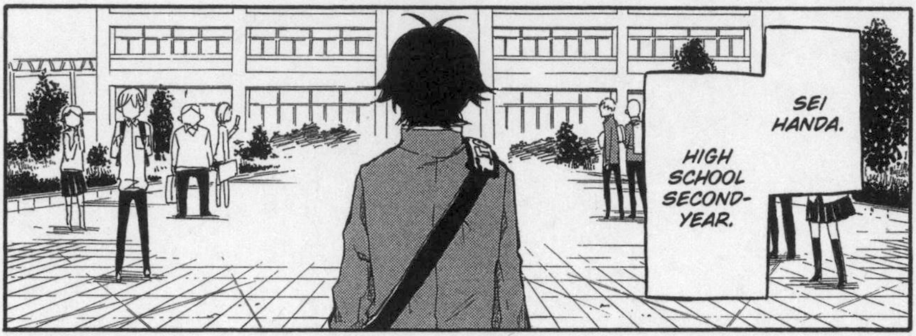
SEI HANDA.
HIGH SCHOOL SECOND-YEAR.

SIX YEARS BEFORE BARAKAMON...

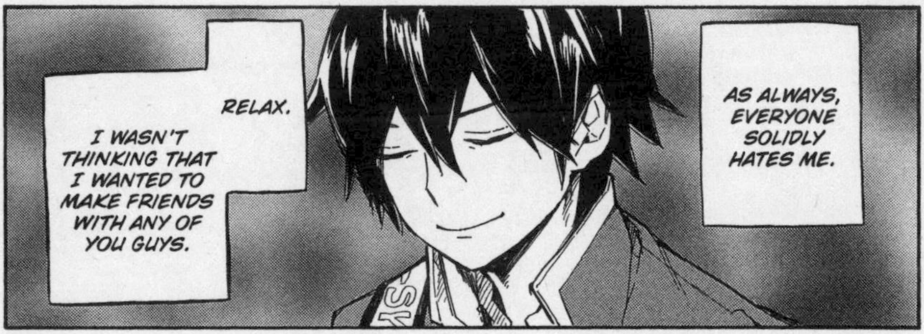
AS ALWAYS, EVERYONE SOLIDLY HATES ME.
RELAX.
I WASN'T THINKING THAT I WANTED TO MAKE FRIENDS WITH ANY OF YOU GUYS.

...THE "BOY" WAS IN THE MIDST OF DOUBT AND SOLITUDE.

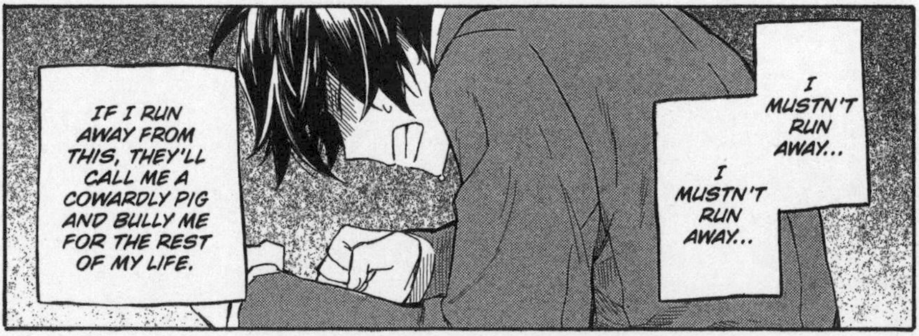
I MUSTN'T RUN AWAY...
I MUSTN'T RUN AWAY...
IF I RUN AWAY FROM THIS, THEY'LL CALL ME A COWARDLY PIG AND BULLY ME FOR THE REST OF MY LIFE.

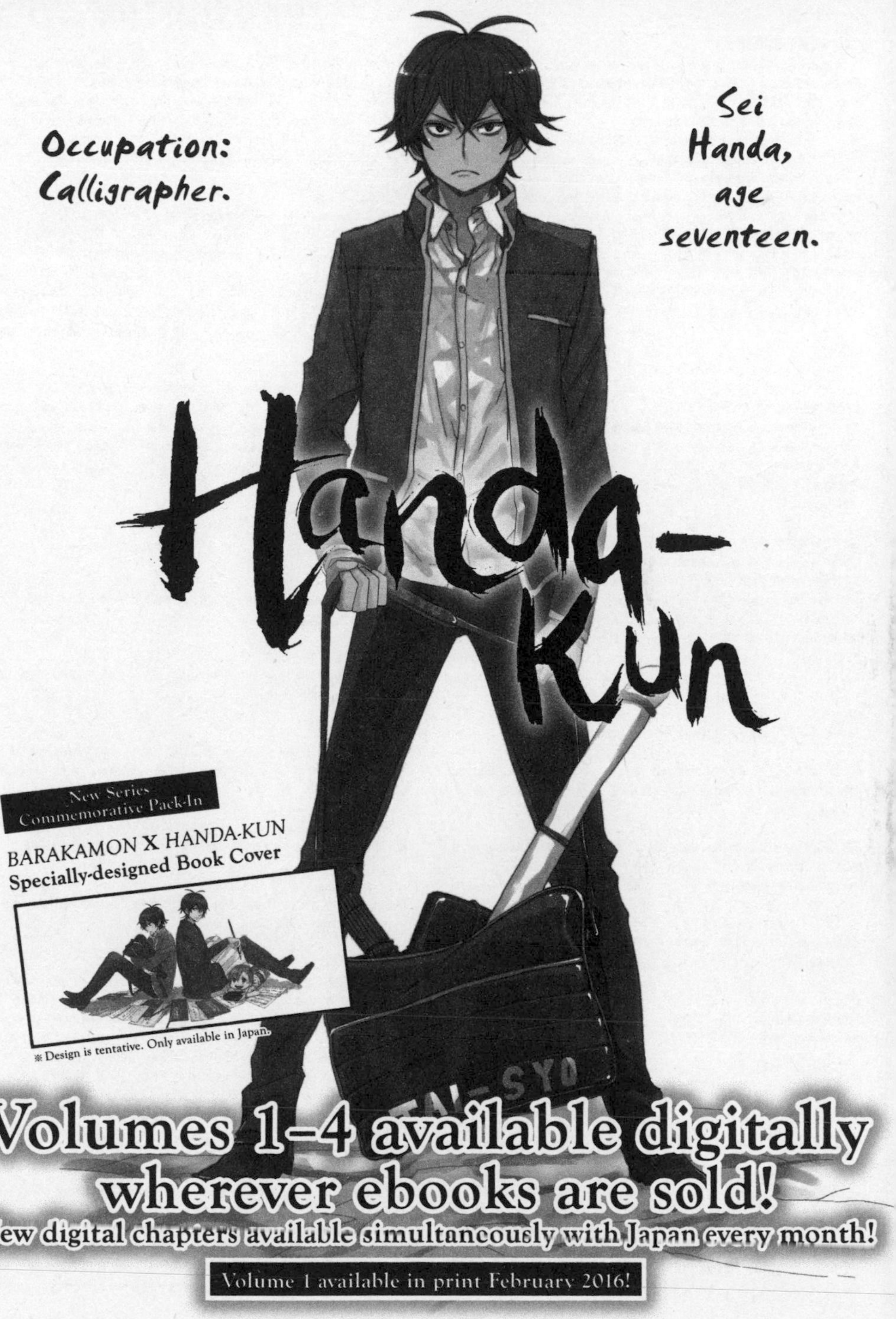
Occupation: Calligrapher.
Sei Handa, age seventeen.
Handa-Kun
New Series Commemorative Pack-In
BARAKAMON X HANDA-KUN
Specially-designed Book Cover
※ Design is tentative. Only available in Japan.
TAI-SYO
Volumes 1–4 available digitally wherever ebooks are sold!
New digital chapters available simultaneously with Japan every month!
Volume 1 available in print February 2016!

COMMON HONORIFICS

no honorific: Indicates familiarity or closeness; if used without permission or reason, addressing someone in this manner would constitute an insult.

-san: The Japanese equivalent of Mr./Mrs./Miss. If a situation calls for politeness, this is the fail-safe honorific.

-sama: Conveys great respect; may also indicate that the social status of the speaker is lower than that of the addressee.

-kun: Used most often when referring to boys, this indicates affection or familiarity. Occasionally used by older men among their peers, but it may also be used by anyone referring to a person of lower standing.

-chan: An affectionate honorific indicating familiarity used mostly in reference to girls; also used in reference to cute persons or animals of either gender.

-sensei: A Japanese term of respect commonly used for teachers, but can also refer to doctors, writers, and artists. Hence, Village Chief is not implying that Handa is a teacher when he calls him "sensei."

Calligraphy: Japanese calligraphy has a long history and tradition, with roots stemming from ancient China. One of the traditions carried over was the Chinese expression of the "Four Treasures," which refers to the brush, ink, paper, and inkstone used in calligraphy. Traditionally, an inkstick—solidified ink—is ground against an inkstone filled with water in order to produce ink with which to write. This time-consuming process helped to teach patience, which is important in the art of calligraphy. However, modern advances have developed a bottled liquid ink, commonly used by beginners and within the Japanese school system.

Gotou Dialect: Many of the villagers, especially the elderly ones, are actually speaking the local Gotou dialect in the original Japanese. This dialect is reflected in the English translation with some of the grammar elements of older Southern American English to give it a more rustic, rural coastal feel without making it too hard to read (it's not meant to replicate any particular American accent exactly). This approach is similar to how dialect is made accessible in Japanese media, including *Barakamon*, because a complete dialect with all of its different vocabulary would be practically incomprehensible to most Tokyo residents.

PAGE 5

"Fork-Mark": The actual brand name is Cup-Mark.

Fresh Cream: Cream that needs to be whipped; much of the "cream" sold in Japan would count as "heavy cream" in the U.S., since "whipping cream" has less butterfat.

Missing Ingredient?: The reason baking soda or powder is missing from the recipe is because they're making a sponge cake, which relies on air whipped into the batter for leavening purposes. Note that this involves whipping a lot of air into the eggs and sugar at high power to make it extremely frothy, then quickly but carefully mixing the flour into the foam, followed by putting the cake pan straight into the oven to avoid losing the whipped-in air before it's finished baking.

PAGE 7

"childish thinking": The original was a pun based on the dual meanings of the adjective *amai*—"sweet" and "naive."

PAGE 20

cash limit: Students on class trips are limited in how much cash they're allowed to bring with them.

PAGE 35

CBs: Tama's manga-centered shopping list mostly consists of screentone sheets, which are usually dots or grids in various sizes and densities, although there are a wide variety of other patterns available. For example, CB-601 contains bloodstains—which makes it no surprise that it's at the top of Tama's list!

dip pens: Relatively popular pens with illustrators and cartoonists since they allow you to have more control over the amount of ink applied and type of ink used.

PAGE 37

Sazae-san: Based on the manga series by Machiko Hasegawa that ran from 1946 to 1974, *Sazae-san* is a very popular family anime comedy series that's been running in the same Sunday evening TV time slot since 1969 and, in fact, holds the *Guinness Book* record for the longest running animated television series. It was also the last anime TV series to use traditional cell animation until it switched to digital production in 2013.

PAGE 43

Hina Nightingale: The original actually blends the two words together, since Japanese phonetics has "Nightingale" start with "na," to get "Hinaichingeeru."

PAGE 61

"Namu...": The first part of the phrase "*Namu Amida Butsu*," an expression of faith in the Buddha, which comes from Pure Land Buddhism. The full phrase is similar in feel to "thy will be done," while *namu* by itself is not unlike "amen."

PAGE 67

"This ain't a date!": In Japanese, Hiroshi said it wasn't a *miai*, which is a formal first meeting for a couple who has been matched up by their parents or others for possible marriage. If you think about it, job interviewing can have some similarities to dating or matchmaking, and "What are your hobbies?" is not an uncommon interview question in the U.S.

PAGE 68

SP: Short for "security police"; essentially bodyguards.

PAGE 71

"string moths": In the original, Naru misunderstands *chousho* (strength)" as "*chouchou* (butterfly)" and goes on to say that her *chouchou* is "*monshiro-chou* (white cabbage butterflies)."

PAGE 72

"weak knees": In Japanese, Naru makes the pun on "*tansho* (weak point)" and "*tansoku* (short legs)."

PAGE 74

castella cakes: A type of sponge cake that was originally introduced to Japan by the Portuguese in the sixteenth century. As you've probably guessed, this is a specialty of Nagasaki City.

PAGE 77

Beta: The stage of manga production when solid black areas are filled in.

PAGE 91

Kinokuniya: A Japanese bookstore chain, also with branches internationally (including several in the U.S.).

PAGE 98 So Many Souvenirs!

Ryouma: Ryouma Sakamoto was an important figure in the process of Japan opening to the world and changing its system of government in the mid 1800s. He was originally from Tosa, now "Kouchi," on the southern part of the island of Shikoku. However, at one point in his many activities, he fled to Kagoshima, where he helped broker peace between the local Satsuma clan and their rivals, the Choshu clan, which was instrumental to the success of the Meiji Restoration. This is how Kagoshima is able to claim him as part of their history (and as a souvenir subject). The "*zeyo*" on the towel is an old Tosa dialect version of "*desu ka* (is that?)," which has become a trademark phrase for Ryouma, as arguably the most famous person from Tosa.

Fantastic Fan: The Japanese has the pun "*Sensu no ii Sensu* (Folding Fan with Good Style)."

Poppen: This is both the name of the toy and the sound it makes; other names are "*popin*" or "*biidoru*." It's made of glass, which is very thin on the bottom of the round end and flexes in and out with a popping sound as you blow air in and out of the end of the long, thin stem.

PAGE 105

That Person: The image is a reference to Sadako from the movie *Ringu (The Ring)*.

PAGE 127

Tasty Green Tea: The design of "Oishii O-Cha" refers to the real brand O~i! O-Cha.

PAGE 132

crunchy plum: *Kari-kari ume* are unripe plums that have been treated with calcium to prevent them from growing soft before further pickling and seasoning.

PAGE 139

ear cleaning: In Japan, ear cleaning is considered a close bonding experience between parents and children, or in other intimate relationships.

PAGE 144

Wake: In Japan, the term refers to a prayer vigil over the deceased's body at their home on the night before burial. Family members stay the whole night, and friends and acquaintances may visit to offer consolation to the family, say prayers, and burn incense for the deceased.

PAGE 145

Nobunaga Oda: A famous general of the Warring States period who attempted to unify Japan by force until his assassination. Apparently, when his father Nobuhide died, the young Nobunaga showed up for the funeral in inappropriate clothing and threw incense at the mortuary tablet during the ceremony. This disrespectful behavior kept him from being approved as leader of the clan for several years. Village Chief's joke is that they're already dressed inappropriately and so will also throw incense at the funeral too.

PAGE 150

"Kansai dialect?": From living for a long time in Osaka and Kyoto, Kiyoba's son and eldest daughter have adopted the dialect of the Kansai region, which has grammar and vocabulary just as different from standard Japanese as the Kyuushuu dialect but not in the same way. For more fun, the two cities have some additional unique features to their speech beyond the standard Kansai dialect.

French!?: The French line that Kiyoba's other daughter says means, "I feel a little sad today."

PAGE 151

bamboo dragonflies: *Taketonbo* is a toy made from a propeller-shaped piece of wood attached to the top of a rod that floats and flies in the air after you get it to spin fast by sliding your hands against each other with the rod between them.

PAGE 170

"Feller": The original Japanese note was that the dialect word "*ontsan*" means the same as the standard word "*ojisan* (uncle, middle-aged man)."

PAGE 172

stewed vegetables: Because participants must refrain from eating meat or fish until the funeral is over, the villagers are preparing *nishime*, cut vegetables stewed in soy sauce and water until nearly dried.

PAGE 175

flowers: Iku and Aiko are placing white chrysanthemum flowers, or "*shiragiku*," inside Kiyoba's casket. This is the most common flower variety for funerals in Japan.

PAGE 188

interment: *Nobeokuri* literally means "field send-off" and refers to the process of taking the bones of the deceased that remain after cremation to the family grave site.

Daimyo Procession: The villagers are including a procession on foot to the grave site, modeled on the old procession of major feudal lords (*daimyo*) and their retainers when traveling between their home domain and alternate residence in Edo City (now Tokyo).

PAGE 190

paper blizzard: The actual English term would be "confetti shower."

PAGE 193

"that box": Contains Kiyoba's bones that remained after her cremation. The other item that will be left at the grave site is her mortuary tablet (*ihai*), which you can see her son holding in the procession starting on page 194. Per tradition, the tablet would have her posthumous name written in Sanskrit.

PAGE 197

post-funeral repast: *Shoujin-age* refers to a more normal meal served after the funeral has ended and the participants are no longer required to refrain from meat and fish.

PAGE 198

"Are you tryin' to skip out!?": The line Handa said to commend Iku on her hard work, "*Otsukare-sama deshita*," is something people usually say to each other at the end of a workday or after shared group work, so she's thrown off by him saying it to her early. Everyone says it to one another on page 202, when the work really is done for the day.

PAGE 204

recompense: Basically, "*henreihin*" means "thank-you gift," but it's a word that Naru would not easily recognize.

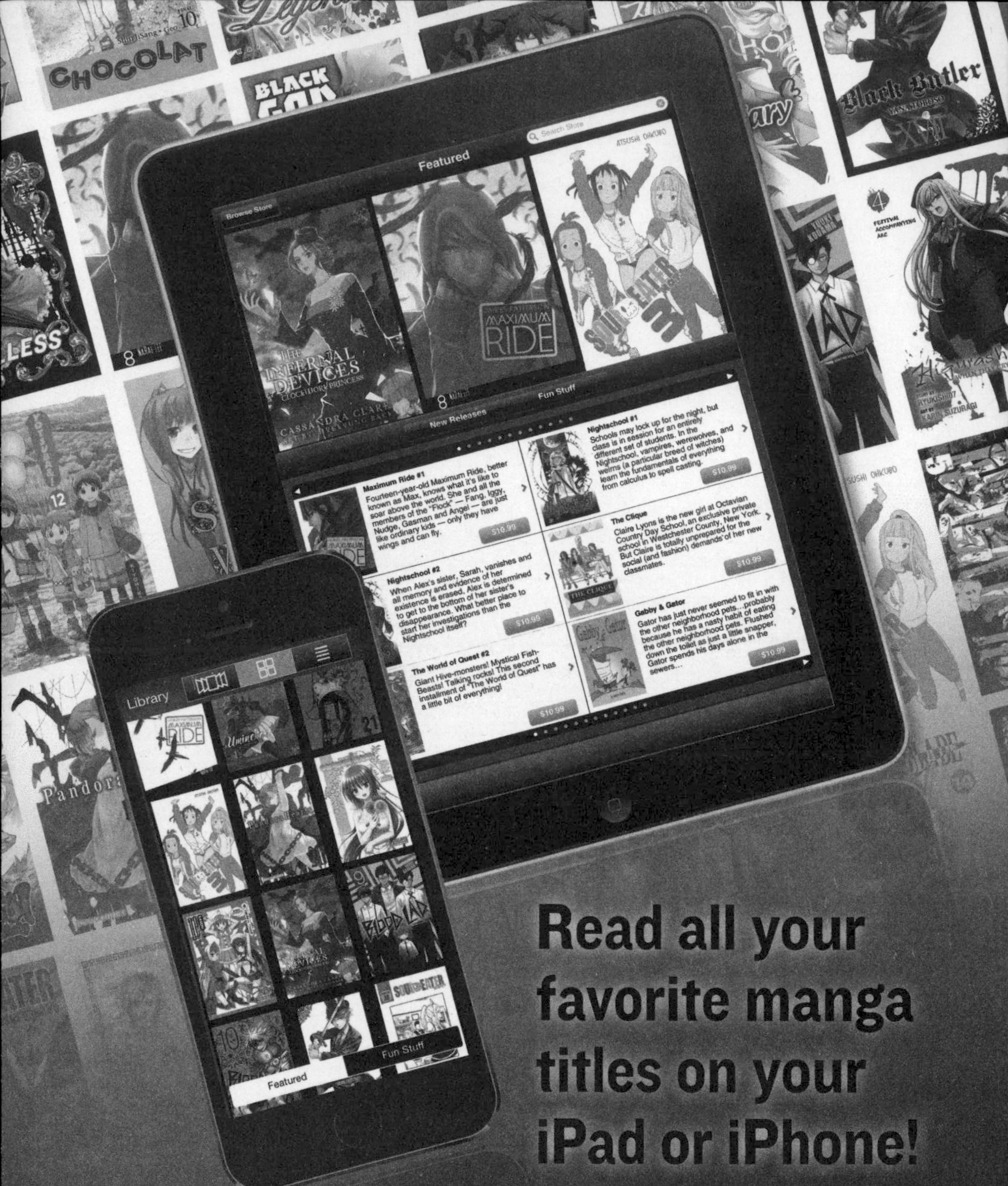
Featured
Browse Store
Fun Stuff
New Releases
Library
Featured
Fun Stuff

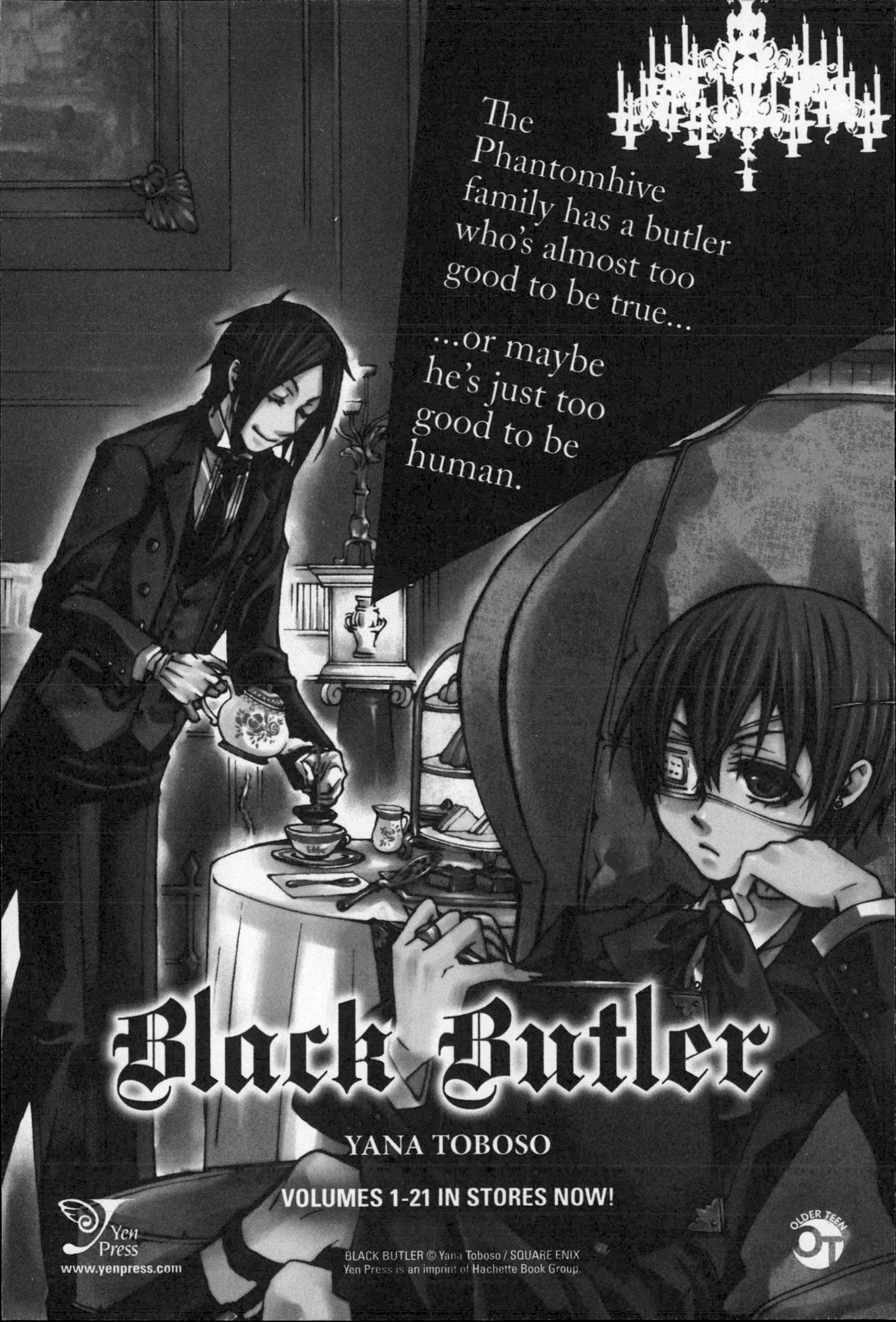
The Phantomhive family has a butler who's almost too good to be true...
...or maybe he's just too good to be human.
Black Butler
YANA TOBOSO
VOLUMES 1-21 IN STORES NOW!
Yen Press
www.yenpress.com
BLACK BUTLER © Yana Toboso / SQUARE ENIX
Yen Press is an imprint of Hachette Book Group.
OLDER TEEN
OT

WELCOME TO IKEBUKURO, WHERE TOKYO'S WILDEST CHARACTERS GATHER!!

AS THEIR PATHS CROSS, THIS ECCENTRIC CAST WEAVES A TWISTED, CRACKED LOVE STORY...

AVAILABLE NOW!!

© 2009 Ryohgo Narita
© 2009 Akiyo Satorigi / SQUARE ENIX CO., LTD.
Licensed by KADOKAWA CORPORATION ASCII MEDIA WORKS

Hello! This is YOTSUBA!

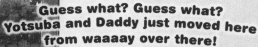

Guess what? Guess what?
Yotsuba and Daddy just moved here
from waaaay over there!

And Yotsuba met these
nice people next door and made
new friends to play with!

The pretty one took
Yotsuba on a bike ride!
(Whoooa! There was a big hill!)

And Ena's a good drawer!
(Almost as good as Yotsuba!)

And their mom always
gives Yotsuba ice cream!
(Yummy!)

And...
     And...
          OHHHH!

ENJOY EVERYTHING.

YOU SHOULD COME PLAY WITH YOTSUBA TOO!

Join Yotsuba as she delights in the
things many of us take for granted
in this Eisner-nominated series.

VOLUMES 1-12
AVAILABLE NOW!

Visit our website at www.yenpress.com.

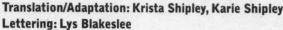

MON 8

SATSUKI YOSHINO

WiTHDRAWN

Translation/Adaptation: Krista Shipley, Karie Shipley
Lettering: Lys Blakeslee

This book is a work of fiction. Names, characters, places, and incidents are the product of the author's imagination or are used fictitiously. Any resemblance to actual events, locales, or persons, living or dead, is coincidental.

Barakamon vol. 8 © 2013 Satsuki Yoshino / SQUARE ENIX CO., LTD. First published in Japan in 2013 by SQUARE ENIX CO., LTD. English translation rights arranged with SQUARE ENIX CO., LTD. and Hachette Book Group through Tuttle-Mori Agency, Inc.

Translation © 2015 by SQUARE ENIX CO., LTD.

Yen Press
Hachette Book Group
1290 Avenue of the Americas
New York, NY 10104

www.HachetteBookGroup.com
www.YenPress.com

Yen Press is an imprint of Hachette Book Group, Inc. The Yen Press name and logo are trademarks of Hachette Book Group, Inc.

The publisher is not responsible for websites (or their content) that are not owned by the publisher.

First Yen Press Edition: December 2015

ISBN: 978-0-316-34037-3

10 9 8 7 6 5 4 3 2 1

BVG

Printed in the United States of America